The Struggle for Democratic Politics in the Dominican Republic

The Struggle for

Democratic Politics

in the Dominican Republic

Jonathan Hartlyn

The University of North Carolina Press

Chapel Hill and London

Designed by Heidi Perov
Set in Electra
by Keystone Typesetting, Inc.
Manufactured in the United States of America

The paper in this book meets the guidelines for permanence
and durability of the Committee on Production Guidelines for
Book Longevity of the Council on Library Resources.

This book was published with the assistance of the H. Eugene
and Lillian Youngs Lehman Fund of the University of North Carolina
Press. A complete list of books published with the assistance of the
Lehman Fund appears at the end of the book.

Library of Congress Cataloging-in-Publication Data
Hartlyn, Jonathan.
The struggle for democratic politics in the Dominican Republic /
Jonathan Hartlyn.
p.   cm.
Includes bibliographical references and index.
ISBN 0-8078-2406-2 (cloth: alk. paper)
ISBN 0-8078-4707-0 (pbk.: alk. paper)
1. Dominican Republic—Politics and government—1961–
2. Democracy—Dominican Republic—History.   I. Title.
F1938.55.H37   1998   97-36873
320.97293′09′045—dc21   CIP

02 01 00 99 98 5 4 3 2 1

To

Liza,

Zach,

Debbie,

Michael,

and Eric

Contents

Preface *xiii*

Abbreviations *xvii*

1. **Introduction** 3

2. **Historical Pathways**
   Neopatrimonial Authoritarianism and
   International Vulnerability 23

3. **Democratic Struggles and Failures, 1961–1966** 60

4. **Authoritarian Balaguer and Democratic Transition,
   1966–1978** 98

5. **The Struggle for Democratic Politics, 1978–1996**
   Social Evolution and Political Rules 134

6. **The PRD in Power, 1978–1986**
   A Missed Opportunity 160

7. **Balaguer Returns, 1986–1996**
   The Tensions of Neopatrimonial Democracy 189

8. **Parties, State Institutions, and Elections, 1978–1994** 219

9. **A New Transition**
   Prospects and Conclusions 258

   Appendix A. Election Results by Level of
   Urbanization, 1962–1994 281

   Appendix B. Socioeconomic and Public-Sector Data 285

   Notes 293

   References 337

   Index 357

Tables and Figure

Tables

2.1. Growth of the Armed Forces under Trujillo 47

2.2. Paths toward Neopatrimonialism 57

3.1. Transitions from Authoritarianism in Vulnerable States: Critical Factors Favoring Transition 66

3.2. Selected Economic Indicators, 1950–1961 72

3.3. Government and Security Expenditures, 1955–1964 81

3.4. The Transition of 1961–1962 86

3.5. The Transition of 1965–1966 95

4.1. Public Investments in Construction and the Office of the Presidency, 1969–1977 102

4.2. Ministries and Minister-Rank Appointments by Administration, 1930–1982 103

4.3. Comparing Three Transitions, 1961–1962, 1965–1966, and 1978 130

5.1. Levels of Poverty in the Dominican Republic and Latin America 144

5.2. Senate Reelection Rates by Party, 1970–1998 153

5.3. Chamber Reelection Rates for the Same Province by Party, 1970–1998 154

7.1. Public-Sector Expenditures, 1986–1995 195

8.1. Official Results for Presidential Elections, 1978–1994 231

8.2. Factors Favoring Crisis-Ridden Elections 244

8.3. Crisis-Ridden Elections, 1982–1994 256

9.1. Official Results for the 1996 Presidential Elections 265

9.2. Comparing Transitions, 1978 and 1994–1996 269

A.1. Election Results at the Municipal Level by Party and Level of Urbanization, 1962–1994 281

B.1. Comparative Socioeconomic Data 285

B.2. Selected Economic Indicators, 1976–1986 287

B.3. Selected Economic Indicators, 1986–1993 289

B.4. Selected Public-Sector Indicators, 1976–1986 290

B.5. The Public Sector under Balaguer, 1986–1994 291

Figure

B.1. Dominican Peso–U.S. Dollar Exchange Rate, 1982–1995 292

Illustrations

Map of the Dominican Republic 2

Rafael Trujillo and Joaquín Balaguer, 1961 71

President Juan Bosch, 1963 83

President Joaquín Balaguer, 1966 110

Women sewing baseballs at an export processing firm 141

President S. Antonio Guzmán, 1978 170

Arrests during violent protest, 1984 179

President Salvador Jorge Blanco and José Francisco Peña Gómez, 1986 184

Jacobo Majluta and José Francisco Peña Gómez in the PRD campaign, 1986 234

Dominicans waiting to vote, 1990 236

PRD senator Milagros Ortiz Bosch, 1995 242

Entrance to the Junta Central Electoral, 1990 250

Banner appealing for domestic electoral observers, 1996 263

Joaquín Balaguer, Juan Bosch, and Leonel Fernández, 1996 266

Photograph of banner appealing for electoral observers by the author; all other photographs courtesy of Diario El Caribe.

Preface

"My father's been elected a senator!" My first introduction to Dominican politics took place in 1978 when Gerardo Canto, a fellow graduate student in New Haven, explained to me that the opposition Partido Revolucionario Dominicano (PRD) had just won the recent Dominican elections in a landmark victory, though his father and the PRD were being harassed by the military. This memory must have been in the back of my mind when several years later at a conference in Bogotá, Colombia, Abraham F. Lowenthal told me that "interesting things" were occurring in the Dominican Republic that merited examination. Abe's advice and support were critical, especially as I began my work in the Dominican Republic.

I began my scholarly fascination with the Dominican Republic with a long stay over the 1985–86 academic year, funded by a Tinker Postdoctoral Fellowship and with additional assistance from Vanderbilt University. In that year, I carried out over one hundred interviews and multiple additional, more informal conversations. The interviews were of three major types. After an extensive review of press accounts of the 1977–78 period, I interviewed many of the key actors involved in the 1978 electoral process. Based on a positional methodology, I also interviewed leaders of the country's major political parties; business, civic, and labor organizations; and past and current policymakers. I supplemented these efforts with additional interviews with diplomats, professionals, and activists. Over 1985–86, I also witnessed the growing disintegration of the PRD and the electoral comeback of Joaquín Balaguer. In frequent return visits, as I expanded the scope of my project beyond the 1978 transition and the PRD period, I reinterviewed many of the same people and interviewed others. And, as a member of several international election observer missions to the country, I was also privileged to witness many historic moments in the country's political evolution. In nearly all cases, I was met with graciousness and interest. Although nearly all my interviews were carried out with the understanding that they were not for attribution, I would like to extend a collective thank you to all those individuals here.

Over the years, many people opened doors for me, but there are two who were among the first and the most important. One was Alfonso Canto (whose political career I had learned about years earlier from his son), who was extraordinarily generous with his time. The other was Frank Moya Pons, director of the Fondo para el Avance de las Ciencias Sociales (unfortunately, no longer functioning), which he graciously allowed me to make my research home over 1985–86.

During that period and in my many subsequent visits, I learned a tremendous amount from Dominican historians and social scientists, much more than can be conveyed simply by footnotes in the text that follows. Some have combined scholarly pursuits with other endeavors or have left academic work. Overall, they form a community forced to work under often difficult conditions, and, far beyond their scholarship and their teaching, many have made significant contributions to advancing Dominican democracy. Some I know primarily through their writings and others from more personal contact. An incomplete list would include, in addition to Frank Moya Pons, whose crucial help was noted above, Ramonina Brea, Julio Brea Franco, Pedro Catrain, Miguel Ceara, José del Castillo, Eduardo Latorre, Wilfredo Lozano, José Oviedo, Mu-Kien Sang, Adriano Miguel Tejada, Bernardo Vega, and Rafael Emilio Yunén.

The scholarship of and conversations with Dominican scholars and *dominicanistas* in the United States have also been very important to me, especially with Rosario Espinal, as well as with Pope Atkins, Emelio Betances, Jacqueline Jiménez Polanco, Chris Mitchell, and Martin Murphy. Although I criticize aspects of the interpretations of Howard Wiarda, I have also benefited from his knowledge and scholarship.

Many others have also been helpful. Dominican journalists have taught me much about Dominican reality. From different perspectives and in disparate ways, two of these have been Juan Bolívar Díaz and Leo Hernández. Leo arranged for me to be one of the "boys on the bus" on numerous campaign excursions by presidential candidates traversing the country in the 1986 campaign (we were all men) and helped with similar arrangements subsequently. Over 1985–86, while residing at the hospitable *pensión* of Don Rafael and Doña María (de Llaneza), I also learned a tremendous amount around the dinner table from the experiences and frustrations shared by international development workers that came to the country from all over the world. The research assistance of Milagros del Carpio and of Mercedes Blandino was also important. I treasure the friendship extended to me by the entire Blandino family over the years. I must extend a very special thank you to Tomás Pastoriza, who over the years has kept me in touch with Dominican reality by inundating me with newspaper clippings and other information; I also appreciate his invaluable assistance in the acquiring of the photographs from the archive of the *Diario El Caribe*, which appear in this book courtesy of Germán Ornes, whom I also thank. Everyone at UNC Press has been extremely helpful, including David Perry, Ron Maner, and my thorough copyeditor, Will Moore.

Generous funding from a variety of sources helped support the research that is presented in these pages. In addition to the Tinker Foundation and Vanderbilt University over 1985–86, these include subsequent support from many different parts of the University of North Carolina at Chapel Hill, including its Research Council, the Institute for Research in the Social Sciences, the Department of Political Science, the Institute of Latin American Studies, and the Institute for the Arts and Humanities—the latter a very special place. A library carrel and the excellent collection and helpful staff at UNC's Davis Library were also critical to the completion of this book. In 1990, 1994, and twice in 1996, I was a member of international delegations to observe elections in the Dominican Republic; these were sponsored at different times by the Carter Center, the Council of Freely Elected Heads of Government, and the National Democratic Institute. I lived unforgettable moments with Santiago Cantón and Mark Fieirstein in 1990, and significant ones as a member of these delegations subsequently as well.

At the University of North Carolina, I would also like to acknowledge the research assistance by Maggie Commins, Eduardo Feldman, Young-ja Bae, Kirk Bowman, Pamela Graham, A. Liesl Haas, and Mary Alice McCarthy; I urge my readers also to examine Pamela Graham's excellent dissertation on Dominican migration.

Two colleagues at UNC, Evelyne Huber and Lars Schoultz, went beyond the call of duty to read the entire manuscript and give important comments. I must also thank Emelio Betances and Rosario Espinal, who also read all the chapters and gave me many valuable criticisms; Bernardo Vega for his critical reading of several chapters; Fabrice Lehoucq and Thomas Melia for critiques of an earlier version of chapter 8; and the readers for the Press for their comments. I did not always follow everyone's valuable advice, so the usual disclaimer that this book is my responsibility applies.

Parts of articles previously published elsewhere appear in the pages that follow. Sections of chapters 2 and 3 appeared in "The Trujillo Regime in the Dominican Republic, 1930–61," in *Sultanistic Regimes*, edited by Houchang E. Chehabi and Juan J. Linz. (Baltimore: Johns Hopkins University Press, 1998). Some paragraphs of chapter 4 were previously published in "The Dominican Republic: The Legacy of Intermittent Engagement," in *Exporting Democracy: The United States and Latin America*, edited by Abraham F. Lowenthal (Baltimore: Johns Hopkins University Press, 1991). And, in a shorter and somewhat different version focused more on the 1994 elections, chapter 8 appeared as "Crisis-ridden Elections (Again) in the Dominican Republic: Neopatrimonialism, Presidentialism and Weak Electoral Oversight" in the *Journal of Interamerican Studies and World Affairs* 36:4 (winter 1994), 91–144.

This book is dedicated to five special people in my life. More years ago than I care to remember, I told two young children, Liza and Zachary, that this book would be dedicated to them. As they have grown, I have not forgotten that promise, which I am now pleased to fulfill. This book is also dedicated to my wife, Debra Levin, who has been extraordinarily supportive of my work, and to Michael and Eric, who have sometimes been curious and at other times indifferent about it. All of them have taught me about many things unrelated to Dominican politics, while being understanding about my frequent travels to and my enthusiasm about the Dominican Republic. Fortunately, they have also sometimes successfully pulled me away from working on this manuscript.

Abbreviations

1J4
Agrupación Política 14 de Junio
Political Group 14th of June

AD (Venezuelan political party)
Acción Democrática
Democratic Action

ADI
Acción Dominicana Independiente
Independent Dominican Action

AIRD
Asociación de Industriales de la República Dominicana
Association of Industrialists of the Dominican Republic

AMD
Aviación Militar Dominicana
Dominican Military Aviation

APRA (Peruvian political party)
Alianza Popular Revolucionaria Americana
American Popular Revolutionary Alliance

CAE
Comisión de Asesores Electorales
Commission of Electoral Advisers

CASC
Confederación Autónoma de Sindicatos Clasistas
Autonomous Confederation of Class-based Unions

CBI
Caribbean Basin Initiative

CCE (Mexico)
Consejo Coordinador Empresarial
Business Coordinating Council

CDE
Companía Dominicana de Electricidad
Dominican Electric Company

CEA
Consejo Estatal del Azúcar
State Sugar Council

CIDES
Centro Internacional de Estudios Económicos y Sociales
International Center of Economic and Social Studies

CND
Comisión Nacional de Desarrollo
National Development Council

CNHE (changed name to CONEP in November 1995)
Consejo Nacional de Hombres de Empresa
National Council of Businessmen

CNOP
Conferencia Nacional de Organizaciones Populares
National Conference of Popular Organizations

CONEP
Consejo Nacional de la Empresa Privada
National Council of Private Enterprise

COP
Colectivo de Organizaciones Populares
Collective of Popular Organizations

CORDE
Corporación Dominicana de Empresas Estatales
Dominican Corporation of State Enterprises

CTM
Central de Trabajadores Mayoritaria
Majoritarian Center of Workers

DDI
Directorio de Desarrollo Industrial
Directorate of Industrial Development

EPZ (also referred to as FTZ)
Export-processing zone

FENHERCA
Federación Nacional de Hermandades Campesinas
National Federation of Peasant Brotherhoods

FNP (political party)
Fuerza Nacional Progresista
National Progressive Force

FTZ (also referred to as EPZ)
Free-trade zone

GAD
Grupo de Acción por la Democracia
Action Group for Democracy

GDP
Gross Domestic Product

GSP
Generalized System of Preferences

IDB
Inter-American Development Bank

IEPD
Instituto de Estudios de Población y Desarrollo
Institute for the Study of Population and Development

IFES
International Foundation for Electoral Systems

IMF
International Monetary Fund

INESPRE
Instituto de Estabilización de Precios
Institute for Price Stabilization

ITBI (later ITBIS)
Impuesto a las transferencias de bienes industrializados (y servicios)
Tax on the value added of industrial goods (and services)

JCE
Junta Central Electoral
Central Electoral Board

LE (political party)
La Estructura
The Structure

MIUCA
Movimiento Independiente de Unidad y Cambio
Independent Movement for Unity and Change

MNJ
Movimiento Nacional de la Juventud
National Youth Movement

MNR (Bolivian political party)
Movimiento Nacionalista Revolucionario
Nationalist Revolutionary Movement

MODERNO
Movimiento de Renovación
Movement for Renovation

MPD
Movimiento Popular Dominicano
Dominican People's Movement

MR-1J4
Movimiento Revolucionario 14 de Junio
Revolutionary Movement 14th of June

NAFTA
North American Free Trade Agreement

NDI
National Democratic Institute

NGO
Nongovernmental organization

NSC
National Security Council

OAS
Organization of American States

PD
Partido Dominicano
Dominican Party

PLD
Partido de la Liberación Dominicana
Party of Dominican Liberation

PQD
 Partido Quisqueyano Demócrata
 Democratic Quisqueyan Party

PR
 Partido Reformista
 Reformist Party

PRD
 Partido Revolucionario Dominicano
 Dominican Revolution Party

PRI
 Partido Revolucionario Independiente
 Independent Revolutionary Party

PRSC (disappeared into the new PRSC)
 Partido Revolucionario Social Cristiano
 Revolutionary Social Christian Party

PR(SC) (formed from the PR and minor parties for the 1986 elections)
 Partido Reformista Social Cristiano
 Reformist Social Christian Party

SIM
 Servicio de Inteligencia Militar
 Military Intelligence Service

UCN
 Unión Cívica Nacional
 National Civic Union

UD
 Unidad Democrática
 Democratic Unity

UNE
 Unión Nacional de Empresarios
 National Union of Entrepreneurs

USAID
 U.S. Agency for International Development

USTR
 (Office of the) United States Trade Representative

The Struggle for Democratic Politics in the Dominican Republic

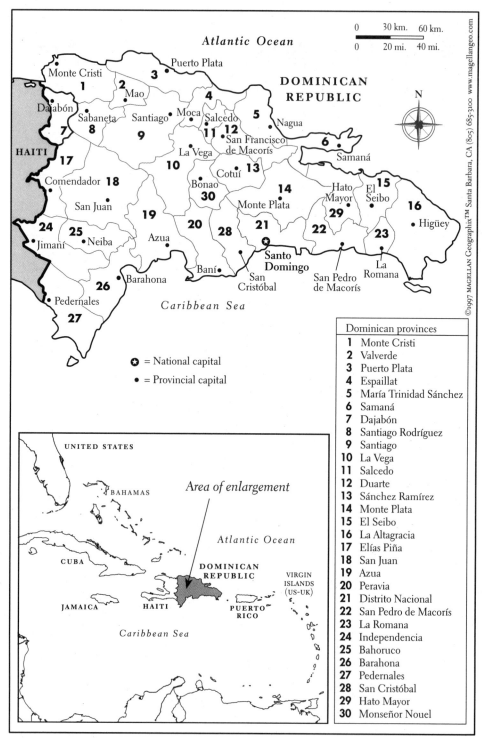

Atlantic Ocean

0   30 km.   60 km.
0   20 mi.   40 mi.

Puerto Plata

Monte Cristi
1
2
Mao
3
4

DOMINICAN
REPUBLIC

N

Dajabón

Sabaneta
Santiago
Moca
Salcedo
5
Nagua

7
8
9
11
12
San Francisco
de Macorís
6

HAITI
17
La Vega
10
Cotuí
13
Samaná

Comendador **18**
Bonao
30
14
Monte Plata
Hato
Mayor
El
Seibo
15

San Juan
19
29
16
Higüey

24
25
Neiba
Azua
20
28
21
22
23

Jimaní
Baní
Santo
Domingo
San Pedro
de Macorís
La
Romana

26
Barahona
San
Cristóbal

Pedernales
Caribbean Sea

27

✪ = National capital
● = Provincial capital

UNITED STATES

BAHAMAS

Area of enlargement

Atlantic Ocean

CUBA

DOMINICAN
REPUBLIC

VIRGIN
ISLANDS
(US-UK)

JAMAICA
HAITI
PUERTO
RICO

Caribbean Sea

Dominican provinces	
1	Monte Cristi
2	Valverde
3	Puerto Plata
4	Espaillat
5	María Trinidad Sánchez
6	Samaná
7	Dajabón
8	Santiago Rodríguez
9	Santiago
10	La Vega
11	Salcedo
12	Duarte
13	Sánchez Ramírez
14	Monte Plata
15	El Seibo
16	La Altagracia
17	Elías Piña
18	San Juan
19	Azua
20	Peravia
21	Distrito Nacional
22	San Pedro de Macorís
23	La Romana
24	Independencia
25	Bahoruco
26	Barahona
27	Pedernales
28	San Cristóbal
29	Hato Mayor
30	Monseñor Nouel

The Dominican Republic

1 Introduction

This is a book about the struggle for democratic politics and about neo-patrimonialism in the Dominican Republic. Most readers have some sense of what political democracy is; probably fewer are familiar with the term "neo-patrimonialism." Both will be discussed in more detail below, but for now consider a neopatrimonial ruler as one who governs a country as if it were an extension of his household.

In the Dominican Republic, neopatrimonial rule has been common, and political democracy has been scarce. The country's tragic history of foreign occupation, economic ruin, and civil wars during the nineteenth century helps explain why neopatrimonial rulers emerged in the Dominican Republic. The most notorious of these was Rafael Trujillo. He ruled the country from 1930 to 1961, taking many of the best agricultural lands and most productive industries as his own. Trujillo also made the *Guinness Book of World Records*: at the time of his overthrow by assassination in 1961, he had more statues of himself in public places than any other world leader. Free elections in 1962 were won by Juan Bosch. However, the democratic regime that he led survived only seven months before it was overthrown. In 1966, following the U.S. intervention of 1965, a former collaborator of Trujillo, Joaquín Balaguer, was ushered into the presidency. He too ruled the country in a neopatrimonial, albeit less brutal, fashion. Initial hopes that the end of the Trujillo era in 1961 would lead to political democracy were disappointed.

Then, in what may be viewed as a democratic transition, elections in 1978 led to Balaguer's defeat and to the first peaceful transfer of power from one political party to another in the country's history. With the inauguration of the new president, several generals were purged, and the political role of the military in the country receded. However, Balaguer was able to reassume the presidency through elections in 1986. He remained there until 1996, when— sightless and in ill health, but mentally acute—the eighty-eight-year-old Balaguer stepped down from power. Under Balaguer, over half of the government's budget flowed directly through the office of the presidency, where contracts would often be handed out at his discretion and with no effective oversight by congressional or other authorities. The struggle for democratic politics during the period from 1978 to 1996 evidenced many frustrations; this period illustrates the challenges of seeking to transform neopatrimonial political patterns and provides evidence of the difficult relationship between democracy and neopatrimonialism.

Dramatic changes have taken place in the country since the death of Trujillo. In 1961, the Dominican Republic was a predominantly rural country whose economy depended largely on the export of sugar and other agricultural crops. Under Trujillo's repressive control, few Dominicans were able to travel abroad (unless they were fleeing into exile), and thus the country's population remained largely isolated. Thirty-five years later, the country was predominantly urban, and its economy and its culture were far more linked to the outside world. The inauguration of the country's new president, forty-two-year-old Leonel Fernández, in August 1996, signaled many of these changes. Fernández had spent part of his youth as a migrant in New York, where perhaps one in fourteen Dominicans now live. The new president could talk comfortably, in either Spanish or English, about the implications of economic globalization for his country or about the records of the dozens of Dominican baseball players in the major leagues in the United States, whose games are transmitted live by cable television to the country. He assumed executive office in a country whose economy had shifted from exporting sugar to welcoming tourists, to employing workers in apparel and other industries in export-processing zones, and to relying on remittances from overseas migrants.

Yet, this was also a country that had experienced dramatic political stagnation in spite of these socioeconomic transformations. It was a country hoping that 1996 would finally represent a clearer political transition both toward democracy and away from neopatrimonialism—unlike what had ultimately occurred following 1978. The 1996 election was the first since 1962 in which neither Balaguer nor Bosch were candidates. It was itself the result of a "deal" agreed to by Balaguer due to domestic and international protest over apparent fraud in the 1994 elections; the agreement shortened his term to two years and prevented him from seeking reelection. Fernández's victory, in turn, was assured by an electoral pact between his party and that of Balaguer.

The pages to follow seek to provide an explanation for this evolution of Dominican politics. Since the 1970s, unlike several other Spanish-speaking countries of Central America and the Caribbean with a similar history of authoritarianism and foreign intervention, the Dominican Republic has largely escaped polarized politics and civil war. At the same time, its political

trajectory over this time period illustrates the difficulties of instituting democratic politics in internationally vulnerable countries where cultural, structural, and political-institutional factors remain problematic.

This book can be read at two levels. At one level, it is a political history of
the Dominican Republic, focused on the nature of the country's struggles for
political democracy, particularly at the "middle-level" of political institutions,
parties, policymaking, and elections in the contemporary period. As such, it
rejects two approaches to the study of Dominican politics that were once
common. In one, the often unsuccessful struggle for democratic politics has
been viewed essentially as the result of powerful forces such as authoritarian
traditions, imperialist powers or international economic constraints (e.g.,
Wiarda 1979; Kryzanek 1979; Cassá 1984); in another, it has been viewed
primarily as the story of forceful individuals and powerful caudillos (e.g., in
biographies of Trujillo, such as Crassweller 1966). Instead, this book argues
that it is the interaction of forces and individuals, mediated by "institutions,"
and the failure or limited success in establishing new institutions and patterns
of behaviors at critical junctures that have marked either the reinforcement of
authoritarian and neopatrimonial patterns or the limited successes of democracy in the country.

The book's emphasis is on the country's political history from 1961 to 1996.
It seeks to answer two basic questions: Why did democratic transition first fail
and then ultimately succeed in the period from 1961 to 1978? Why did democracy remain nonconsolidated over the period from 1978 to 1996, undertaking
what may be viewed as another transition in 1996? Though incomplete in
themselves, international factors and structural ones relating to the nature of
continuities and changes in state-society relations are both important parts of
the answers to these questions and will be considered below.

A central argument of the book is that it is crucial to consider political-
institutional factors. These include the domestic and international linkages of
the preexisting authoritarian regime, constraints and incentives generated by
presidentialism and certain electoral laws, and the nature of political leadership and practices under these conditions, which have often reflected and
reinforced neopatrimonialism. Thus, key elements of the country's often
tragic historical-institutional continuities and evolutions captured by the concept of "neopatrimonialism" remain a critical backdrop to understanding the
country's varying democratic transitions and its troubled experiences with
political democracy since 1961.

Thus, at another level, this book can be read as a study of the struggle for
democratic politics in a Latin American and Caribbean country (but relevant
as well to other less-developed regions) that takes into account the indepen-

dent impact of political factors in determining the success or failure of a transition to democracy and in constraining its consolidation (see Rustow 1970; O'Donnell, Schmitter, and Whitehead 1986; Linz and Valenzuela 1994; and Collier and Collier 1991). In studying possibilities for democratic transition, this book focuses attention beyond excessively broad "cultural," "economic," or "frustrated-by-foreign-intervention" arguments that tend to see political phenomena and institutional factors as epiphenomenal. These three perspectives, in particular, would suggest that the Dominican Republic is a "least likely case" for democratic rule—due to its authoritarian heritage (Wiarda 1979), dependent status, and history of occupation by foreign forces (Gleijeses 1978). Examination of three attempted democratic transitions in the country over the 1961–78 period impugns the explanatory value of these overly broad approaches to the study of democracy, while providing evidence for the value of approaches that also explicitly incorporate political factors.

Analysis of the mixed evolution of Dominican democracy over the period from 1961 to 1996 highlights the need to consider why political practices captured by the concept of neopatrimonialism were not overcome. As a concept, neopatrimonialism refers to a type of political regime with important within-type variations, which can crosscut authoritarianism and democracy (while constraining the latter). As an explanatory factor, it helps reveal why transitions to democracy from certain regimes are more difficult than from others, and it highlights how some kinds of political patterns can continue, and even be reinforced over time, in the absence of particular kinds of sustained social change or of concerted effort by political leaders from above. At the same time, this book also considers other explanatory factors to be important. These include the evolution and impact of international economic and political changes and of domestic societal changes. Similarly, chapters below address how certain specific, political-institutional structures and incentives enhanced the likelihood of neopatrimonial politics.

Thus, the book does not seek to embrace a unicausal, reductionist explanation focused exclusively on the evolution of neopatrimonialism for something as complex as the nature and evolution of political regimes and the possibilities for democratic politics in a country like the Dominican Republic. However, to the extent that the importance of political-institutional factors as independent obstacles to democratic consolidation has sometimes been underestimated in the Dominican Republic, this book highlights their importance. These cannot simply be viewed as the ineluctable consequence of past cultural traditions, which might eventually be solved only with socioeconomic modernization and in the absence of economic crisis. At the same time, they are not the only obstacle nor are they always the most important one to democratic consolidation.

Although focused on one country, this study is cast in a comparative framework. It also seeks to examine the validity of a number of arguments about democratic transitions and possibilities for consolidation by making use of within-case comparisons; therefore it is more clearly wedded to the case-oriented social science tradition than the variable-oriented one.[1] It begins with the assumption that processes of democratization are in fact examples of "multiple, conjunctural causation": they are not the result of a single cause; major causes that play a role do not operate in isolation from each other, but in interaction with each other; a specific cause may have very different, even opposite consequences, depending upon the context; and thus, there are not inevitably necessary or sufficient conditions that can be specified beyond certain very general, if still valuable, statements (Ragin 1987, 27). This is not to say that everything is important; based on comparative analysis, the rest of the book examines the ability of limited sets of variables to explain the emergence of neopatrimonialism and, in conjunction with neopatrimonialism, to explain the success or failure of democratic transitions in the country and to delineate major features of the country's political, economic, and electoral evolution since 1978.

The following chapters present an alternative both to more purely structuralist (dependency) and to culturalist views on major constraints on democracy (e.g., in the Dominican case, Cassá 1984, contrasted with Harrison 1985). This book argues that structural and cultural factors have interacted with each other within the context of neopatrimonial political institutions, with all three often mutually reinforcing each other amidst complex international constraints and occasional opportunities. A transformation away from neopatrimonialism may be facilitated by certain kinds of societal changes and by political leadership, especially in moments of transition. Thus, this book also explores the tension between human agency and structural constraints.[2] The difficult methodological issue of the agent-structure problem has been addressed here by taking a path-dependent approach to the country's historical evolution. This approach is predicated on an effort to understand the structural and cultural constraints on democratic evolution without reducing the story of the country to a destined outcome or pathway resulting from colonial or other "traditions." The discussion of more recent historical events takes a two-step approach, privileging agency. First, it seeks to understand the constraints imposed upon actors as well as the opportunities presented to them; then it examines whether their behavior and other possible behaviors fit into a range that might have been expected, given an understanding of these constraints and opportunities.[3]

Structural and cultural explanations for the failure of democracy in the Dominican Republic have often been accentuated by analysts, if for no other reason than that authoritarianism has prevailed over democracy throughout the country's history. Typically, these explanations have focused on an authoritarian political culture, imperialist and interventionist foreign powers, and distorted capitalism and its resulting class structure. There are, of course, intense disputes about which of these factors should be emphasized, disputes that will be considered at the appropriate time.

When Dominican history has not been viewed as a clash of abstract forces, it has often been portrayed as the playing field for powerful personalities. The villains (or, in some cases and for some analysts, the heroes) include such individuals as Rafael Trujillo, Joaquín Balaguer, Juan Bosch, Salvador Jorge Blanco, and various Dominican military officers and U.S. ambassadors—and much is made of these individuals' psychological makeup and daily actions.

Perspectives focused on abstract forces and on personalities are both relevant, and the "middle-range" concept of neopatrimonialism best explains why. Both forces and individuals are examined, though the book intends to demonstrate the weaknesses of excessively global arguments, while also avoiding the temptation to ascribe outcomes essentially to the conspiratorial machinations of the powerful. The book focuses primarily on domestic Dominican political processes, examining international actors and processes in terms of how they constrained, interacted with, or provided opportunities to different domestic actors. Thus, the tremendous power imbalances between the Dominican Republic and the United States are viewed as significant, but also as somewhat variable over time, as responsive to multiple causes, and as mediated by domestic actors and processes.

In developing this theoretical and comparative perspective, the book relies on a combination of primary and secondary research. It is based upon hundreds of interviews carried out with many of the key actors in Dominican political events over the recent past as well as upon direct observation of each of the country's electoral processes since 1986. It also relies on, and seeks to contribute to, recent work produced by a dynamic community of Dominican social scientists regarding how to analyze domestic political processes while placing the role of international influences in its proper context, how to transcend excessively rigid or broad structuralist or culturalist interpretations of Dominican political reality, and how to understand the importance of the country's political institutions.[4]

In its understanding of history, this book adopts an analytical perspective—

historical institutionalism—in which central attention is paid to the development of and the independent impact of institutions, which are to be understood both as formal organizations (such as political parties) and as the informal rules and procedures that structure political practices (such as neopatrimonialism) (Thelen and Steinmo 1992, 2). Since formal organizations and regularized patterns of behavior within and across them have been weak in the Dominican Republic, it is important to focus on the fact that "institutions" may also be informal rules and that mediations by powerful individuals may be the operative institution in a society, rather than participation channeled through more formal party and rational-legal governmental organizations. At the same time, constitutional rules and party norms have also structured the behavior of political actors in significant ways, especially in the contemporary period.

The central story told in the chapters that follow is the development and evolution of political patterns of behaviors and institutions. At this middle-level of analysis, the struggle unfolding in the Dominican Republic may be examined as one between a neopatrimonial mode of politics—understood both in terms of personal, centralized concentration of state power and in the blurring of public purpose and private gain by rulers—and a mode of politics that is both more regularized (channeled through appropriate organizations) and more accountable. What has marked Dominican politics has been the neopatrimonial nature of its different authoritarian regimes as well as of its democratic regime.

Change is understood to have occurred in a "path-dependent" fashion in the Dominican Republic: past patterns of interaction and institutional configurations weigh heavily on the present without determining it. Occasionally, long periods of more or less stable institutional configurations can be abruptly and dramatically changed in a process Krasner (1988) has termed "punctuated equilibrium" or in periods other scholars have termed "critical junctures" (e.g., Collier and Collier 1991), though more piecemeal institutional evolution may also occur (Thelen and Steinmo 1992, esp. 15–17). Whatever the terminology, the assumption is that "history binds." Events at one point constrain possible future outcomes. Changes in regime cannot be explained without attention to the long-term effects of past events. At the same time, key turning points or critical junctures are moments that provide potential opportunities to break with past patterns and establish new ones as well as moments that continue or establish new structural constraints.

In this respect, the Dominican Republic is not unique. Rather, this case is informed by and can shed important understanding on other neopatrimonial regimes and their evolution. The theoretical purpose of the book is not to generate yet another global or unicausal argument or central factor, but to employ middle-level arguments about transitions, regime types, and their typical institutional configurations to provide explanations for some major outcomes in the political trajectory of the Dominican Republic—while showing the relevance of these types of explanations to other country cases, placing the Dominican case in a comparative perspective.

While the book's focus is upon *democratic politics*, it also addresses broader issues of economic growth and social reform in the country by examining features of the country's economic policymaking. It builds upon two assumptions. One is that political democracy is a "good" in and of itself for a country that has known years of some of the harshest authoritarianism in the hemisphere. Another is that for political democracy to be constructed and eventually consolidated requires democratic politicians, political parties, and institutions, which is why the relative presence, absence, and impact of these kinds of actors and organizations and the actual performance of state leaders receives special attention here. Inevitably, a whole range of other issues relevant to Dominican development, to its democracy, and to its democratization more broadly are examined only briefly or not at all.

Democracy and Authoritarianism

Political democracy is a difficult concept for several reasons. These include the facts that it is multidimensional and that there is a tremendous variation in political regimes that may be considered democracies.[5] We are usually interested in knowing not only whether a country is democratic, but also whether it is a stable or consolidated democracy and how that democracy might be further democratized; factors may affect stability and democratization differently. Furthermore, "democracy" is also a term employed in everyday language; because it is widely viewed in a positive way, it is a term that political leaders and policymakers employ and manipulate for their political ends.

"Democracy" or "political democracy" can be defined by reference to three critical dimensions: public contestation, inclusiveness, and the rule of law.[6] In a democracy, the central positions of state authority are filled by leaders selected in regularly scheduled elections. Thus, *contestation* implies the extension of civil and political rights to individuals and groups and the right of political leaders to seek the support of the citizenry, whether in opposition to or in favor of governmental policies and ruling authorities. Regimes are stronger on this dimension to the extent that citizens are able to formulate and indicate their preferences and have these weighed equally. By *inclusiveness*, we refer to the extension of such rights throughout the population. As democracies have evolved, the constitutional definition of citizenship has expanded to include larger proportions of the adult population, without regard to property, literacy, gender, or other restrictions based on race or ethnicity. Although the precise nature of these rights and the means necessary to extend them have varied across time, there is now a widely understood procedural minimum: a secret ballot, universal adult suffrage, regular elections, party competition, executive accountability, and the presence of interest groups seeking access to policymaking circles.

The third dimension of democracy is the *rule of law* embodied both in constitutional and other legal documents and in practice. This presupposes a viable, functioning state as well as one that is democratically controlled. Thus, contemporary democracies are constitutional democracies, having institutions, rules, and procedures that limit the hegemony of passing electoral majorities or their representatives in order to protect the rights and preferences of individuals and minorities, the options of future majorities, and the institutions of democracy itself. These institutions, rules, and procedures should also provide for at least partial insulation of the country's judicial and electoral systems from elected leadership, as well as for qualified majorities and complex ratification procedures in order to modify the country's constitution or basic laws. The country's security forces should also be partially insulated from elected leadership, in that way being neither fully autonomous from their control nor totally beholden to their (perhaps illegal or unconstitutional) wishes.

It is important to underscore two elements of this definition. First, these rules and procedures can almost always be improved upon, even in countries long considered to be democratic. As Przeworski (1990) has discussed in a different context, there are three tensions in all democracies, and, though they may be more or less resolved, they are not ever perfectly resolvable: (1) there is no perfect way to limit the undue influence that the more economically powerful may have over government relative to others in the population; (2) direct democracy is not viable in nation-states, yet no way has been devised to aggregate and transmit citizen preferences to governments that is not problematic in some fashion; (3) and effective democratic control over the state and its security apparatus is not perfectly achievable.[7] Typologies or subtypes of democracy are occasionally built based on the extent to which these tensions appear to be more rather than less resolved, and certain minimum thresholds are obviously necessary in order to speak of democracy.[8]

Second, by focusing on rules and procedures, this definition does not require democracy to provide any particular substantive outcome. There is no guarantee that following democratic procedures will lead to certain substantive goals that may be desirable, such as eliminating absolute poverty, equalizing income distribution, or enhancing the population's health, education, or shelter. Indeed, in certain cases, a transition to political democracy may well inhibit, rather than facilitate, changes in existing social and economic arrangements. What political democracy should do more than other political arrangements—although even here it may be grossly deficient—is limit abuses by governmental authorities, inhibit sharp policy shifts opposed by vast elements of the population, and protect basic human rights while permitting citizens a voice in choosing their political leaders. Thus, political democracy refers to a political regime within a state functioning under the rule of law, not to a society, and is identified by the adherence to procedural criteria, not by the promotion of particular policies or substantive outcomes.[9]

An issue related to the question of whether or not a country's political regime is democratic is whether that political regime is stable or consolidated, whether it is likely to endure and thus strengthen its legitimacy. This is another thorny conceptual issue. How should consolidation be defined? Linz and Stepan (1996, 5–6), borrowing a term from Guiseppe di Palma, have argued that a political situation may be considered a consolidated democracy when it has become "the only game in town." They then provide behavioral, constitutional (or institutional), and attitudinal benchmarks for consolidation that partially overlap: no significant political group seriously seeks to overthrow the democratic regime; incumbent leaders do not have to confront democratic breakdown as a dominant problem; all major political and social actors become habituated to resolving conflict through existing channels and legal norms; and the overwhelming majority of the population favors democracy, even in a context of severe political and economic crisis.

The three dimensions of Linz and Stepan's analysis address a variety of concerns. The behavioral dimension points predominantly to issues of military intervention and military coups and to the absence of support for such actions by social and political actors; the attitudinal dimension points to broader societal support for democracy, even in the face of severe problems. The constitutional or institutional dimension focuses on the predominance of regularized, democratic "rules of the game," though it also incorporates behavioral and attitudinal commitments by key actors to play by these rules. As we shall see, in the contemporary Dominican Republic this latter set of concerns is especially important. The central challenge to democracy comes less from the potential for military coups or a popular rejection of democratic procedures than from the weakness of effective political intermediation and of the rule of law.

What factors help the process of consolidation? Democratic consolidation must presuppose a viable, functioning, accepted, and coherent state, including a functioning bureaucracy. Thus, three other factors are important in a mutually reinforcing manner and, at some minimum level, are also definitional requisites of democracy: a vigorous and active civil society; constitutionalism and the rule of law; and a set of political organizations, parties, and actors that are institutionalized and interact with both the state and civil society, but that are relatively autonomous from either. A fourth widely recognized factor is a viable economy (cf. Linz and Stepan 1996, 7–15).

Countries that are not "democratic" are typically referred to as either "authoritarian" or "totalitarian," or as some subtype or derivation of these two. Following Linz, this book considers "authoritarian" those regimes that have limited, but not responsible pluralism; that have no elaborate or guiding ideologies, but rather distinctive mentalities; that have neither intensive nor extensive mobilization; and that have a political leadership which exercises power within formally ill-defined, but actually quite predictable norms (Linz 1970, 1974).

One implication that follows from this discussion is that problematic democracies which fall somewhere between consolidated democracy and outright authoritarianism may exist, potentially for many years. In these cases, the formalities of democracy exist—such as elections and freedom of expression and of organization—but the practice of democracy is distorted: elections are not the only process by which governments may be formed; electoral discrimination is present; effective institutional oversight control or popular participation between elections is limited; or the armed forces or some other group exercises a tutelary power, or reserves certain areas of policymaking for itself, through veiled or not so veiled threats of violence or of a return to authoritarian rule (Valenzuela 1992, 14; O'Donnell 1994; Schmitter 1994). If one or more of these latter distortions is sufficiently marked, then it would be more accurate to characterize the regime as authoritarian, even if it is not directly ruled by the military.

There is a growing recognition of the need to denote the existence of "in-between" regimes, which may endure for some time. Conaghan and Espinal (1990, 555, 575), comparing the Dominican Republic and Ecuador, have discussed reasons for the emergence of "crisis-prone" and "hybrid 'democratic-authoritarian'" regime types that could be long lasting. Schmitter (1994, 59) has proposed distinguishing two subtypes, a "hybrid regime that combines elements of autocracy and democracy" and a "persistent but unconsolidated democracy."[10] However, due to inherent tensions and contradictions, hybridization appears to be more a short-term, unstable "improvisation" than a long-term regime type.

Nonconsolidated regimes, in turn, may persist and satisfy minimum procedural criteria, though democratic "rules of the game" never crystallize into regularized, institutionalized practices. Because they may last for quite some time, they do have "institutions" understood as informal rules and procedures that structure conduct. The characteristics of these nonconsolidated regimes, as Schmitter notes, are very similar to those of O'Donnell's "delegative democracies," where executive authority is electorally delegated the right to do whatever it desires, with little oversight control by the other branches of government and with little participation by the country's citizens in the period between elections. This conceptualization, in turn, overlaps with what I have termed neopatrimonial democracy.[11]

This discussion does not exhaust the possibilities, but it serves our purposes for this book. Movement across and within the four broad possibilities of outright authoritarianism, hybridization, nonconsolidation, and consolidated democracy is possible, and across these regime types certain other regime-level features or legacies may remain.[12] In the case of the Dominican Republic, as well as in a number of other countries around the globe, neopatrimonialism is one such central feature.[13]

Neopatrimonialism

For Weber, patrimonialism was a type of government based on traditional authority that was organized more or less as a direct extension of the royal household; officials were personal dependents of the ruler (Bendix 1962, 100n). He wrote: "*Patrimonialism* and, in the extreme case, *sultanism* tend to arise whenever traditional domination develops an administration and a military force which are purely personal instruments of the master" (Roth and Wittich 1968, 231). In the contemporary world, because legitimacy of authority is no longer based on traditional appeals, the best way to indicate the combination of attributional similarities and typological differences in domination is to refer to such rule as *neo*patrimonialism.

Neopatrimonialism possesses two key characteristics: the centralization of power in the hands of the ruler who seeks to reduce the autonomy of his followers by generating ties of loyalty and dependence, commonly through complex patron-client linkages; and, in the process, the blurring of public and private interests and purposes within the administration. At the level of ideal-types, neopatrimonial regimes can be distinguished most clearly from regimes that are based on rational-legal authority and impersonal law, as well as from regimes that legitimize themselves through ideological means.[14]

Neopatrimonialism can coexist with a variety of authoritarian or democratic regimes. If the concept is to have any theoretical relevance, though, it should be possible to draw out certain implications from the fact that it defines an alternative to a regime with more regularized and more ideologized patterns of interaction. Although neopatrimonialism refers to a kind of *political regime*, which crosscuts the earlier distinction between authoritarian and democratic regimes, there are mutually reinforcing linkages between this kind of regime type and low levels of political and social organization in formal associations and high inequalities in social structures. Issues of international dependence and vulnerability are also often very important, though not always in a unidirectional fashion.[15]

Neopatrimonialism also marks political practices and the nature of political conflict in several major ways. From one study of neopatrimonial African regimes, four practices can be identified, which we shall see are also relevant to the Dominican Republic (Bratton and van de Walle 1994). One is that in neopatrimonial regimes, political conflict is not easily identified along ideological or programmatic issues. Rather, conflict is often better characterized as simply between "ins" versus "outs" over spoils and patronage. Thus, parties tend to be deeply personalized, with an emphasis on clientelism and brokerage. A second is that presidentialism can easily slip into a pattern of clear presidential dominance, conveniently reinforcing patrimonial regime attributes. At the same time, this second feature often helps reinforce a third one: political oppositions often focus on behavior that is legal and governed by clear rules in an effort to gain power; however, once in power, these forces often fracture over the extent to which behavior should really shift from patronage toward ideology or the rule of law. A fourth is that because of its nature, neopatrimonialism inhibits the effective exercise of the rule of law, not only with regard to the functioning of state bureaucracies, but more broadly with regard to access to justice and protection of the rights of the accused.[16]

Neopatrimonialism and democracy coexist uneasily, leading to nonconsolidated or hybrid regimes. Neopatrimonial regimes vary regarding the extent to which they respect the three key elements of democracy: contestation, inclusiveness, and the rule of law. They may be viewed as more or less democratic to the extent that they respect the rights of groups to organize and to express their views without overt repression, they allow opposition forces to compete in elections in which the ballots are fairly counted, and they do not weaken or manipulate the judiciary or abuse the rule of law in their country. Yet, ultimately, this kind of democracy often appears to rely primarily on the goodwill of the leader at the top, constrained by fears of political instability or domestic and international pressure, rather than on agreement regarding a set of democratic "rules of the game." Enhancement in all three of the key elements of democracy would require a decline in neopatrimonialism. Until then, political democracy remains fragile because of the attitudes and behaviors of key political actors and because of the weakness of both effective political intermediation and the rule of law.

Neopatrimonialism inhibits the quality of democracy and democracy's ability to consolidate. It does so by its impact on the nature of a country's civil society, on the state and its bureaucracy, on respect for constitutionalism and the rule of law, and on the nature of political institutions and parties, and sometimes it does so by its consequences for the country's economy. Other consequences or mutually reinforcing linkages cut across the state and society. Formal organizations other than political parties also tend to be weak. They are generally weak both in civil society, such as producer associations and labor unions, and in the state, such as corporate, professional military, or state bureaucratic structures. Because of the low levels of formal organization by these political, societal, and state actors, the realization of binding agreements or "pacts" is often difficult. In the context of regime transitions, this inability complicates arrangements—especially with those that are longer term—with the military and the outgoing regime, among opposition parties for power-sharing, and between all these and socioeconomic actors. High levels of social inequality also reinforce clientelist political structures and inhibit the development of more independent popular organizations.

In real-world terms, determining the extent to which these consequences or linkages occur is complicated by several factors. One is that specific regimes are likely to vary to an extent from the pure ideal-type of neopatrimonialism, relying instead on some mix of patronage, law, and ideology. Another, already implied above, is that there are important variations within neopatrimonialism regarding issues such as the role of repression, the extent of the reach of the individual leader into different social sectors, the nature of his control over the military and the state, and the country's relations to foreign powers. Indeed, given the importance of the central ruler in neopatrimonialism, even more than in most other authoritarian or democratic regimes, personal factors associated with his leadership style may be relevant.[17] And, as the central ruler's grip declines in a neopatrimonial regime, one may find more decentralized forms of clientelism, brokerage, and plunder of state resources, rather than a turn to rule based more on rational-legal means or ideology.

One of the most notorious kinds of authoritarianism, unfortunately well known in the Dominican Republic, is a kind of discretional neopatrimonialism, sultanism, or neosultanism. Weber noted that all patrimonial rule incurs some element of arbitrariness; however, "where [patrimonial authority] indeed operates primarily on the basis of discretion, it will be called *sultanism*. The transition is definitely continuous" (Roth and Wittich 1968, 232). Linz has further developed the concept of sultanism as a particular form of distorted authoritarian rule based on personal rulership, with loyalty based on a mixture of fear and rewards (see Linz 1974; and Chehabi and Linz 1998).[18] The "sultan" exercises power without restraint, at his own discretion, unencumbered by ideology or bureaucratic norms. Typically there is large-scale corruption, arbitrary and capricious decisions combined with scrupulous attention to legal forms, and ruthless violence. Such a regime also differs from more classic authoritarianism by the absence of even "semi-oppositions," though sporadically "pseudo-oppositions" are permitted. Repression may also be more informal and privatized, including the establishment of private armies. Sultanism differs from the ideal-type of totalitarianism in the absence of a clearly defined ideology, in the fact that the despot fuses his private and public roles and has no clear commitment to any impersonal purposes, and in the fact that areas of the country may largely not be penetrated by the regime. Contemporary forms of these regimes can be referred to as discretional-authoritarian, neopatrimonial regimes: "neo" because they no longer base whatever claim to legitimacy they make exclusively or even primarily on "traditional" grounds; and "discretional-authoritarian," to indicate the incredible autonomy of action that the individual ruler possesses. Nevertheless, for shorthand purposes, we shall refer to them as neosultanistic.[19]

There are other kinds of authoritarian, as well as democratic, neopatrimonial regimes. Certain analytical consequences in addition to those already noted may be derived from this point. One is that the difference between kinds of authoritarian (discretional and nondiscretional) or hybrid neopatrimonial regimes may have considerable impact in an area of particular interest to us: the nature and the possibilities for democratic transition. Transitions to democracy from authoritarian, nonsultanistic regimes are more feasible than from neosultanistic ones for a variety of reasons.[20] Another is that if an authoritarian regime has strong neopatrimonial elements—strong personalized centralization of authority and a blurring of public and private roles—these tendencies will most likely carry over into the subsequent regime unless there is effective, discontinuous institutional change, representing an effort to break with this pattern. In both of these ways, nepatrimonialism is crucial to understanding the evolution of Dominican politics since 1961.

A Look Ahead

The book explores three periods in the Dominican Republic's political life in successively more detail. The first period is addressed in chapter 2, which reviews the period from colonial rule to the death of Trujillo in 1961. The second period, from 1961 to the democratic transition of 1978, is discussed in chapters 3 and 4. The third period is addressed in chapters 5–8, which analyze aspects of the struggle for democratic politics over the period from 1978 to 1996.

Chapter 2 examines the emergence of neopatrimonialism in the country and its subsequent evolution through the notorious neosultanistic regime of Rafael Trujillo. It also explains how the historical evolution of the country from the colonial period through 1961, spanning several major transition periods, was antagonistic to the emergence of democracy. In doing so, chapter 2 distances itself both from cultural accounts centered on the Spanish colonial era and on structural accounts based on imperialist domination. As explained in the first half of the chapter, from its period of colonial rule, the Dominican Republic was marked by foreign invasions and intervention, economic dependency, extensive civil war, sharp disparities of wealth, and strongman rule. In its second half, the chapter focuses on the period of Rafael Trujillo (1930–61). Trujillo's reign is analyzed as a neosultanistic regime, one of whose legacies would be a series of attributes that made a successful transition to democracy very difficult. Trujillo's rule finally integrated the nation politically and established the state as a bureaucratic entity and important economic actor, while also further breeding cynicism and profound skepticism about public institutions and activities.

By addressing the institutional causes and consequences of neopatrimonial-authoritarian rule in the Dominican Republic, the second chapter critically assesses the cultural analysis of scholars who view the country's pathos as emerging fundamentally from its Spanish colonial experience (e.g., Wiarda 1979; 1989). Similarly, this chapter questions reductionist versions of Dominican politics as epiphenomenal reflections of imperialism or class conflict resulting from distorted capitalism (e.g., Cassá 1979). Rather than seeing Dominican history as a seamless web, continually reinforcing authoritarianism, this chapter seeks to demonstrate how and why authoritarian forms of politics were reinforced throughout the country's history. Several "missed opportunities" for a turn to more liberal politics appear to have been a consequence of such factors as the nature of the country's international vulnerability, warfare and economic devastation, domestic structural factors, and leadership qualities, rather than an ineluctable consequence of cultural legacies or foreign intervention.

Chapter 3 presents a general framework for the analysis of democratic transitions, one of whose critical elements rests on the legacies of the preexisting neopatrimonial regime. It then examines the two transitions of the 1960s and the preceding tumultuous period and succeeding authoritarian interlude. Chapter 4 follows with an analysis of the Balaguer regime (1966–78) and the 1978 democratic transition. Three factors are compared across these three transitions: the nature of the preceding authoritarian regime and its relations to domestic societal forces, political opposition, and the military; international geopolitical and economic forces; and the nature of the transition process itself, including new institutional modifications, "pacts," and the resulting opportunities for democratization. There are certain important similarities across the three transitions derived from the neopatrimonial elements of the preceding authoritarian regime; but there are also critical differences that result from regime variations, as well as from the role of the other factors. Although some analysts have stressed the similarities between Trujillo's rule and that of Balaguer (e.g., Wiarda and Kryzanek 1977), key differences in the management of economic, military, and political power under the two rulers heavily influenced the democratization process, as did other international factors and the evolution of the transition process itself. The analysis of chapters 3 and 4 also permits more careful consideration of arguments related to the impact of U.S. intervention on democratic rule in Latin America.

Chapter 4 underscores the important differences between Balaguer's neopatrimonial regime and those that preceded the failed transitions of the 1960s; it also assesses the more favorable international geopolitical context of that time and the nature of the "transition from above" that took place. While structural changes generated during the Balaguer years and the role of the United States are both important, the central argument is that "political learning," attitudinal and strategic changes within the opposition party and within elements of the business sector and the military were crucial to the success of the transition from one kind of regime to another. For example, without changes in the opposition Partido Revolucionario Dominicano (PRD, Dominican Revolution Party) in the years prior to the 1978 elections, it would have been difficult to conceive of a PRD electoral victory and a successful democratic transition. These changes included not only organizational work and a "deradicalization" in a programmatic sense, but also a conscious effort to reach out to the business community and to renew and strengthen international ties out of the conviction that an electoral victory, alone, might not be sufficient to attain power. These shifts within the PRD, paralleled by others within business and military circles, cannot be readily explained by cultural or economic-dependency perspectives.

Chapters 5 through 8 examine Dominican politics from 1978 to 1996. Chapter 5 provides an overview. Chapter 6 analyzes political dynamics and patterns of economic policymaking under the PRD governments of S. Antonio Guzmán (1978–82) and of Salvador Jorge Blanco (1982–86); chapter 7 does the same for the subsequent governments of Balaguer (1986–96). Chapter 8 addresses the question of why elections in general were crisis ridden during this period and why they became increasingly so.

These four chapters highlight how the significant element of continuity apparent in political patterns over this period was due especially to neopatrimonial, political-institutional patterns and incentives, whose genesis and evolution are explained in previous chapters. At the same time, chapters 5–8 also underscore how new combinations of international, societal, and political-institutional factors interacted with previously established patterns and incentives to constrain effective economic policymaking and outcomes and to provoke crises around the most basic element of democratic politics—elections. Thus, certain features of the country's party system and electoral laws enhanced factional strife within the PRD, but not within Balaguer's party; in turn, the effects of these patterns and incentives were felt more because of the impact of dramatic international economic changes and the responses of powerful domestic societal groups following the transition.

These chapters also argue that transformations of neopatrimonial patterns are likely to result either from certain kinds of societal change or from above, by new patterns of political leadership. Chapters 5 through 7 explore why these transformations did not happen over the 1978–96 time period. Chapter 5 briefly examines key aspects of the country's dramatic economic and structural evolution over this eighteen-year period, to conclude that in spite of these significant changes, continuities in terms of high levels of poverty and low levels of formal organization continued to provide the structural bases for a political leadership committed to neopatrimonial relations. It explores reasons for the decline in the politicization of the country's armed forces, examining changes in their autonomy and declines in their professionalization. It concludes with an examination of the major formal institutional rules, informal norms, and political-institutional incentives that help explain the failure to establish new forms of political leadership under the PRD governments and the ability of Balaguer to reimpose a more clearly neopatrimonial rule.

Chapters 6 and 7 examine political patterns and styles of rule through the broad evolution and results of economic policymaking over the 1978–96 period. As chapter 6 explains, a crucial opportunity to change the country's neopatrimonial style of doing politics was lost over the 1978–86 PRD period, especially during Jorge Blanco's presidency. The chapter considers the serious

structural-economic problems the PRD governments inherited from the earlier Balaguer period and the growing economic constraints and domestic
opposition from powerful, newly organized business groups. However, it also
emphasizes how factional strife surrounding issues of presidential leadership
and succession degenerated into bitter conflicts over spoils and power, which
ultimately divided the party; this strife is explained in part by the nature of
certain political-institutional incentives. The chapter concludes that neither
Jorge Blanco nor the PRD should bear the brunt of the blame for the country's
limited economic options or economic decline, given the country's international circumstances and private-sector pressures. Yet, at the same time, they
cannot escape blame for not transforming the style of politics in the country.

Chapter 7 examines the stark reemergence of neopatrimonial rule and the
erosion of democratic government under Balaguer over the period from 1986
to 1996. Balaguer was a master at using constitutional and extraconstitutional
powers and state resources to concentrate what power he had, to divide his
opposition, and to prolong conflicts and delay decision making to his advantage. He, too, faced dramatic international constraints and societal and political opposition, but he maintained greater political autonomy through neopatrimonial rule than had the PRD governments. Balaguer was eventually
forced to accommodate dramatic changes in the Dominican economy, which
had been imposed by changing international circumstances that he had
sought initially to ignore (at least partially) and subsequently to profit from
politically as much as possible—but not before submerging the country into
its worst economic crisis of the century. The cost of his mix of policies was
increasing disorder and a loss of capacity within the state. As he handed power
over in 1996, positive macroeconomic indicators in terms of growth and inflation were combined with high levels of inequality, low levels of expenditures
in health and education, and continued high unemployment.

Chapter 8 links the country's neopatrimonial attribute to the increasingly
crisis-ridden nature of subsequent elections. Four factors to explain this trend
are identified: the vast formal and informal powers of the presidency, fears
of presidential continuity being associated with fraud, the fact that party-
leadership continuity could more easily be sustained in the face of defeat
by fraud allegations, and the dramatic weaknesses of the electoral oversight
agency that permitted parties both to allege fraud and in some cases to carry it
out. After reviewing the evolution of the electoral campaigns, the chapter
shows how presidential reelection efforts and narrow vote margins were associated with the most conflictive electoral processes, ending with the 1994 postelectoral crisis and resolution.

The concluding chapter summarizes the central theoretical goals of the book: to establish the value of a mode of analysis centered on historical-institutionalism and path-dependency, on the independent (but not exclusive) impact that political and institutional factors have on political outcomes, and on the analytical utility of the concept of neopatrimonialism in the Dominican and similar contexts. It shows how variations in several key factors discussed in chapter 8 help explain why the 1996 elections were not crisis ridden, in contrast to the preceding ones. It compares what can be considered a new transition in 1996 to the transition of 1978, using the scheme of analysis first presented in chapter 3, and it explores the regime's short-term prospects. The final section provides a brief review and summary.

2 Historical Pathways
Neopatrimonial Authoritarianism and International Vulnerability

This selective history of the Dominican Republic examines the initial emergence of neopatrimonialism in the Dominican Republic and the advent and evolution of the neosultanistic regime of Rafael Trujillo. It argues that the emergence of Trujillo's neosultanism can be understood primarily as a consequence of three factors: the condition of overall initial poverty and weak economic elites; the impact of major wars and economic devastation; and U.S. occupation, which helped to establish a strong military institution in the absence of other organized actors in the society or polity. Less important are inherited patrimonial attributes from the Spanish colonial era, especially given the fact that the Dominican Republic was a colonial backwater for much of the period leading up to its independence. This chapter emphasizes, first, how international vulnerability and authoritarian politics served to reinforce each other over the nineteenth and twentieth centuries and, second, how potential "turning points" toward a more liberal politics failed. Thus, it views the past as weighing heavily on the present—but in an occasionally disjunctive process of continuity and change, in which structural changes, institutional evolution or transformation, international forces, and elite strategies and choices all play a role.

The country's historical evolution, including particularly the consequences of several major transitional periods, has proved particularly inimical to democratic development. The optimum sequence for democracy has been highlighted in slightly different terms by a number of different scholars. Dahl (1971) has noted that sequences in which successful experiences with limited liberalization are followed gradually by greater inclusiveness appear to favor democracy. Nordlinger (1971) has argued that the nature and sequence of key crises in a country's political evolution regarding national identity, authority,

and participation are essential: the pattern most promising for the development of democracy is one in which first national identity emerges, then
legitimate and authoritative state structures are institutionalized, and finally
mass parties and a mass electorate emerge with the extension of citizenship
rights to nonelite elements (see also Valenzuela 1989, 178–82; and Diamond
and Linz 1989, 9). Rustow's (1970) "genetic" model of democracy is similar,
which has national unity as a background condition and proceeds through
subsequent phases of inconclusive struggle, compromise on democratic rules
to resolve conflict, and then habituation to these rules.

As the pages below will illustrate, the pattern followed by the Dominican
Republic has been very different. National integration was truncated first by a
Haitian invasion and then by the attempts of some Dominican elites to trade
nascent Dominican sovereignty for security by having foreign powers annex
the country (while enriching themselves further in the process). State building also suffered under the dual impact of international vulnerability and
unstable, neopatrimonial-authoritarian politics. Both integration and state
building were also impaired by bitter regional struggles based on different
economic interests and various desires for power, which accentuated the
caudillo politics of the country. In this context, there were early efforts to
extend liberal guarantees and citizenship rights to vast sectors of the population. The failure of these reform efforts served to reinforce past patterns of
behavior, though such efforts continually reemerged.

Indeed, a Dominican state arguably did not emerge until the late nineteenth century or even until the Trujillo era (1930–61); Trujillo's emergence,
in turn, was unquestionably facilitated by changes wrought by the eight-year
U.S. occupation of the island republic at the beginning of this century. Trujillo's pattern of rule closely approximated the ideal-type of neosultanism,
presented in the previous chapter, and it could not have been more inimical
to democratic rule. Nevertheless, Trujillo's remarkable centralization of
power, his monopolization of the economy, his destruction or co-optation of
enemies, and his astonishing constitutional hypocrisy were combined with
the forging of national integration, the establishment of state institutions, and
the beginnings of industrialization, however distorted. The examination of
Dominican history and of the nature of Trujillo's rule in this chapter sets the
stage for subsequent explanations of why a successful democratic transition
following the collapse of the Trujillo dictatorship was unlikely and why the
reemergence of a kind of neo-Trujilloism under Balaguer was not a surprising
outcome.

Another goal of this chapter is to provide evidence that determinist arguments about Dominican authoritarianism, resulting either from a "tradition"

created by Spanish colonial experience or from being imposed by an imperialist power, must be heavily qualified. Although the negative implications of "organic-statist" ideology for democracy are real, as are the negative consequences for democracy of many of the actions of foreign powers, too much explanatory weight is often attached to these factors.

What has marked Dominican history has been the recurrence of different kinds of neopatrimonial regimes. As discussed in chapter 1, these regimes have based their ability to rule on the extension of personal patronage networks, centralizing authority directly in the hands of the leader and blurring the distinction between the state and the private affairs of the ruler. The lack of democracy in the Dominican Republic should be traced less to its colonial heritage or to imposition by imperial powers (though these played a role) and more to the consequences of its protracted, violent, and often unsuccessful efforts to consolidate formal sovereignty, construct a viable state, achieve national integration, and impose a central authority among its inhabitants. These efforts led to cycles of "failed liberalism," leading authoritarian leaders to turn to the cultural repertoire of neopatrimonialism, preserved by a social structure favorable to such a regime's emergence. This pattern fostered a pernicious constitutional hypocrisy that has deeply marked Dominican history; in turn, the pattern itself has been deeply affected and often reinforced by the country's economic marginality and regionalism, by marked inequalities combined with weakly organized socioeconomic or other national-level actors (such as the church or the military), and by the consequences of the country's international vulnerability.

These arguments will be advanced below in six sections and a conclusion. The first three examine aspects of international vulnerability and neopatrimonial rule from the colonial era through 1916. The narrative then addresses the U.S. occupation (1916–24), which was critical in helping to usher in the Trujillo era. The evolution and characteristics of Trujillo's regime are described and analyzed in the subsequent two sections.

The Struggle for Formal Sovereignty

What was to become the Dominican Republic provides another tragic example of the effects of brutal Spanish rule. When the Spanish landed on the island of Hispaniola in 1492, an estimated 400,000 Indians on the island were soon enslaved to work in gold mines. As a consequence of mistreatment, forced labor, hunger, disease, and mass killings, it is estimated that by 1508 that number had been reduced to around 60,000. By 1535 only a few dozen were still alive. As the gold mines became exhausted and the Indians were eliminated, the Spanish moved on to form other colonies. In the 1530s, black slaves were imported by the remaining landowners, who had begun to cultivate sugar. However, livestock and, increasingly, contraband trade became major sources of livelihood for the island dwellers. Spain, unhappy that Santo Domingo was facilitating trade between its other colonies and other European powers, attacked vast parts of the colony's northern and western regions in the early seventeenth century.[1] This helped pave the way for the French to settle the newly depopulated western areas of the island, where they established a plantation society based on the exploitation of slave labor. Today's Haiti became the wealthiest colony of the seventeenth century. In contrast, the Spanish colony remained poor and unprotected (Moya Pons 1986, 15–19 and 29–32).

The nineteenth-century struggle for independence was an incredibly difficult process for the Dominican Republic, conditioned by the evolution of its neighbor. In 1791, inspired by the French Revolution, a rebellion emerged in the adjacent French colony. At that time, the prosperous Saint-Domingue (what was to become Haiti) consisted of around 520,000 people, of which some 87 percent were slaves; Santo Domingo, in turn, had only 125,000 people, of which some 15,000 were slaves (Knight 1990, 366–67). The Spanish colony was ceded first to France in 1795 as part of the Treaty of Basle between the defeated Spanish and the French, then it was invaded by the English in 1796. Five years later, black slaves in rebellion invaded from Saint-Domingue. The devastated Spanish-speaking colony was then occupied by the French in 1802, in spite of the dramatic defeat of Napoleon's forces at the hands of the former French slaves who proclaimed the independent Republic of Haiti in 1804. Santo Domingo was invaded again by Haitians in 1805 and then yet again by the English in 1809. The Spanish reclaimed it later that year, but found the colony in economic ruins and demographic decline. The main activity was subsistence agriculture, and exports consisted of small amounts of tobacco, cattle hides, caoba wood, molasses, and rum; by this time, the population consisted of less than 75,000 people, a 30 percent decline from only fifteen years before (Moya Pons 1985, 248).[2]

In the years 1820–21, two parallel but separate movements sought independence from Spain, both of which were to be short-lived. One of these efforts desired annexation by the neighboring independent republic and was encouraged by Haitian leaders who feared that a French invasion (and a return to enslavement) could begin through a weak Santo Domingo. In December 1821, Dominicans rose up in rebellion against the Spaniards, declaring themselves the Independent State of Spanish Haiti, only to hand over authority to the Haitian ruler Jean-Pierre Boyer in February of the next year. In another effort for autonomy, Dominican leaders—recognizing their vulnerability both to Spanish and to Haitian attack and also seeking to maintain their slaves as property—sent a special mission to Caracas, hoping to convince Simón Bolívar to let them join Gran Colombia, which he was in the process of forming; however, in Bolívar's temporary absence, the mission failed (Moya Pons 1985, 255; 1986, 15–18).

The twenty-two-year Haitian occupation that followed is recalled by Dominicans as a period of brutal military rule, though the reality is more complex. It led to large-scale land expropriations (particularly against the church and absentee landlords) and failed efforts to force production of export crops, impose obligatory military services, restrict use of the Spanish language, and eliminate traditional customs such as cockfighting. It reinforced Dominican's perceptions of themselves as different from Haitians in "language, race, religion and domestic customs" (Moya Pons 1985, 266).[3] Yet, this was also a period that definitively ended slavery as an institution in the eastern part of the island.[4]

A potential turning point in 1844 was soon lost. A successful revolt against the Haitian dictator Boyer in 1843 paved the way for what became a successful independence (or secession) effort in 1844; it did not lead, however, to effective state construction or constitutionalism. Foreshadowing future conflicts, there were two major conspiracies working for Dominican independence: one, led by the liberal merchant Juan Pablo Duarte and his La Trinitaria society and supported by the Santanas and other eastern cattle ranchers, sought full independence; another, dominated more by occupants of administrative posts under Haitian rule, sought separation from Haiti under French protection (Moya Pons 1985, 265–67).[5] Trying to construct republican, constitutional rule in the context of a devastated economy, an impoverished and regionally divided population, and a polity without functioning institutions would have been difficult under any circumstances. An additional factor mediating against constitutional rule was that national security concerns remained paramount, enhancing the role and the value of militarism. Over the next several decades, unscrupulous leaders negotiated away Dominican sovereignty out of a belief that defense from Haiti required it and for their own personal gain.

Ambivalent Sovereignty, Political Instability, and Financial Dependence, 1844–1916

The seven decades from 1844 to 1916 were characterized by bewilderingly complex interactions among Dominican governing groups, opposition movements, Haitian authorities, and representatives of France, Britain, Spain, and the United States. Duarte and the liberal merchants who had led the initial independence effort were soon swept out of office and into exile, and the independent tobacco growers and merchants of the northern Cibao valley, who tended to favor national independence, were unable to consolidate control of the center. Government revolved largely around a small number of caudillo strongmen, particularly Pedro Santana and Buenaventura Báez (initially allies who became rivals), and their intrigues involving foreign powers.[6]

Support from foreign powers was pursued in defense against Haiti, eventually leading to the Spanish reannexation. In the 1850s, the Dominican Republic actively pursued the possibility of a treaty of friendship with the United States, which would have included ceding or leasing Samaná Bay to the United States.[7] This was met by opposition from Britain and France and by outright alarm in Haiti, which feared the consequences of a proslavery power on Dominican soil; this soon led to a renewed Haitian invasion attempt. Even as Santana and Báez occasionally battled each other, fear of Haiti and a desire to strengthen his own domestic position eventually led Santana, who had originally sought to ally with the United States, to negotiate reannexation to Spain in March 1861. However, Spanish domination was soon contested within the country, with aid from Haiti. Protracted war against Spain ended with renewed Dominican independence in July 1865.

Shortly after independence was gained from Spain, another episode in the long and often tragic history between the Dominican Republic and the United States took place. President Andrew Johnson desired naval stations in the Caribbean, even as Báez and other conservative Dominican groups, working through U.S. citizens with financial interests in the Dominican Republic, sought the annexation of the country to the United States. Dominican nationalists rebelled and found a strong ally in the chairman of the Senate Foreign Relations Committee of the time, Charles Sumner, who on this issue gave President Ulysses S. Grant his first major legislative defeat; the 1869 treaty was ultimately rejected by the U.S. Senate. President Grant continued to seek territory in the Dominican Republic until 1873 (see Nelson 1990, 101; Martínez-Fernández 1993, 592–93). This would be one of the first of many subsequent episodes in which Dominican political struggles would be battled out by Dominicans as much in Washington as in their own country.

As a result of the effort to regain independence in 1865, the country was again devastated by war, with vast sectors of the population armed and politically and regionally fragmented. Once the Spanish were vanquished, the numerous military and guerrilla leaders began to fight among themselves. Gradually, pro-Báez forces (Baecistas) revolved around what came to be known as the Partido Rojo, and the anti-Báez forces, more fragmented and mostly of northern interests, formed the Partido Azul. Although Báez managed to serve as president briefly in 1865–66 and for longer periods in 1868–74 and 1878–79, in the period from 1865 to 1879 there were twenty-one different governments and at least fifty military uprisings (Moya Pons 1985, 274).[8]

The country was in almost continual civil war until the end of the 1870s. Gradually the key national political struggle following the founding of the second republic in 1865 came to revolve around the "Rojos" and the "Azules," a division which approximated that between conservatives and liberals elsewhere in the region. The struggle combined economic, regional, and personalistic motivations (cf. Sang 1996a, 70–71). The Rojos were a centralized movement, concentrating the more conservative powerholders of the northwest, south, and east, who tended to identify with Buenaventura Báez. The basis of their wealth was predominantly large livestock haciendas and the export of precious woods, such as caoba. In turn, the Azules coalesced primarily from the more liberal, smaller tobacco growers and merchants of the northern Cibao, with some of Santana's former supporters from the east. Although the Azules were more imbued with liberal predilections, they also often came to power through conspiracy and rebellion—and were overthrown in the same fashion. The general that was to impose the most successful and brutal dictatorship on the country in the period, Ulises Heureaux, emerged from the Azules. To a considerable extent, the various regions of the country were better connected to their respective external markets than they were to each other, as internal transportation and communication networks were extremely poor. Regionalism based in part on the structurally different societies of the east and the north was superimposed over personalistic rivalries for power (Moya Pons 1986, 178–80; Cross Beras 1984, 111–41). The central state was incapable of defeating the regional uprisings. Thus, a clear national identity and authoritative state structures were still lacking.

The century ended with the increasingly neosultanistic seventeen-year reign of Ulises Heureaux (1882–99, indirectly from 1884 to 1887), who was an able military leader and a shrewd, despotic political leader and who ably reached out to the country's emerging sugar interests.[9] Foreshadowing the "sultanistic" features of Trujillo's rule in the next century, Heureaux had extensive private investments, such that "the separation between the president's private means and state finances was vague, fluid and often nonexistent" (Hoetink 1982, 80).[10] Ironically, the dark-skinned Heureaux, who grew up in poverty, oversaw changes in society that would make the emergence of another figure of his background more difficult, except under the circumstances generated by U.S. intervention.

During Heureaux's rule and in the subsequent decades, aided by rising international demand, the country's economic structure began undergoing more substantial change. With favorable state policies, modern sugar estates began to replace cattle-ranching estates, even as exports of coffee and cacao expanded; domestic financing of the state shifted from the more "liberal" tobacco merchants of the north to the producers of the south. A Dominican bourgeoisie began to emerge, involving both the enrichment of old families and new immigrants.[11] The first railroads were completed and other basic infrastructure built. Initial attempts at professionalizing the army and bureaucratizing the state were made, even as educational reforms were introduced. However, as the regions became more connected, social stratification on the basis of race also became clearer and more stable: "More than before, unequivocally negroid features became an obstacle for individual mobility; the new national elite used the pretext of descent as a criterion of selection with greater consistency than had been possible in a time when humble soldiers of fortune, fighting in whatever revolution offered them chances, might become powerful over night, and when fortunes could still be made or lost in a few days of political turmoil" (Hoetink 1984, 296).

Two other legacies of Heureaux were debt and instability. Heureaux took out loans for 1.67 million British pounds on very onerous terms in an attempt to pay off an earlier loan, gain greater room to maneuver in the face of domestic creditors, enrich himself, grease his political machine, and also carry out the public works and other projects for which the foreign loans were ostensibly sought. The European bondholding company went bankrupt, in part because its representative in the Dominican Republic was paying more attention to his own business dealings in collaboration with Heureaux; the Dominican claims were transferred in 1892 to the San Domingo Improvement Company of New York. At the same time, the collapse of world sugar prices and markets in 1883–90 was also profoundly affecting the country. This financial crisis led Heureaux in 1891 to sign a trade agreement with the United States in which he promised to sharply reduce or to eliminate Dominican tariffs on U.S. imports in return for U.S. tariff concessions on sugar and a few other Dominican products. The agreement soon led to bitter disputes with the country's European creditors and trading partners and helped to solidify U.S. dominance over the country (Welles 1966, 478–96; Murphy 1991, 12–18). The Dominican Republic came to exemplify the growing intromission of the United States in the affairs of its Caribbean neighbors.[12]

Following Heureaux's assassination in 1899—in a plot by former associates he had spurned—the country again largely experienced political chaos, ending in U.S. military occupation in 1916. There were four revolts and five presidents over the subsequent six years. Weak protoparties and clientelistic politics built around caudillo figures and regional uprisings furthered economic chaos and political instability. National politics revolved primarily around the conflict between the followers of Juan Isidro Jimenes (Jimenistas) and Horacio Vásquez (Horacistas), both of whom had been involved in plots against Heureaux. The only long-term presidency of this period was that of Ramón Cáceres (1905–11), a cousin of Vásquez and a conspirator in Heureaux's assassination. Cáceres's assassination led to another period of political turmoil, promoting the economic disorganization that facilitated the U.S. intervention.

Gradually, control of Dominican affairs by its northern neighbor grew. Pressures by European creditors on the Dominican Republic (as well as the Anglo-German blockade of Venezuela in 1902–3), led to President Theodore Roosevelt's "corollary" to the Monroe Doctrine. Anxious to preclude European intervention in the Caribbean because of debt problems, Roosevelt unilaterally declared that the United States would assume the police powers necessary to insure adequate repayment. By 1905, Dominican customs was headed by a U.S. appointee, a relationship that became formalized in a 1907 treaty, which also paid off all previous loans with a new one that converted private U.S. bankers into the country's only foreign creditors. The United States took these steps not only to block European actions and insure bond payments, but also because it viewed customs revenue as the main booty in Dominican politics and hoped that U.S. control would promote greater political stability in the country. U.S. investments in sugar lands and sugar mills also gradually expanded, becoming dominant during the period of U.S. military occupation (Calder 1984, 4; Lowenthal 1972, 21; for the text of the 1907 treaty, Welles 1966, 1005–11; Murphy 1991, 19–22). U.S. interest in the Dominican Republic (and in neighboring Haiti) expanded both for commercial reasons and for strategic reasons, including fear of Germany's establishing a foothold in the region (see Knight 1990, 223). In 1914 extensive U.S. pressure on local Dominican leaders, with threats of direct intervention, ultimately led to the naming of a provisional president and the holding in October of the second more-or-less free (indirect) elections for president, elections won by Juan Isidro Jimenes, ostensibly for a six-year term. President Jimenes soon confronted a rebellion by the head of the armed forces, General Desiderio Arias, and requested arms from the United States to help him put it down.[13] Instead, U.S. troops were landed to "protect the life and interests" of the American legation and other foreigners, and the president resigned (Moya Pons 1983, 468–70). Dominican politicians, in turn "continued their fratricidal struggles for power, particularly over control of the now vacant presidency" (Calder 1984, 10). Dominicans expected a brief U.S. military presence that would depart following elections, and even U.S. officials had not planned for a lengthy occupation, though it ultimately lasted until 1924.

Weak Formal Institutions and Constitutional Hypocrisy

In 1916, the ultimate consequences of international vulnerability—occupation by a foreign power—occurred yet again for the fragile republic. Before turning to an examination of the U.S. military occupation of the island republic and its relationship to the emergence of Trujillo, however, let us briefly review the evolution of domestic social and political forces during the pre-Trujillo period and the massive gap between constitutional doctrine and practice. Although Heureaux's dictatorship and the processes of economic growth helped generate more coherent social groups and a more coherent state toward the end of the century, Lowenthal's broad generalization about the country on the eve of the intervention remains valid: "From the time of independence until the U.S. occupation of 1916 ended the period of *caudillo* politics . . . the Dominican Republic was not characterized by a powerful triad of oligarchy, church and military, but rather by exactly the reverse: an insecure grouping of elite families, a weak and dependent church, and no national military institution" (Lowenthal 1969b, 53). This combination of weak social forces and national institutions proved strongly congruent with patrimonial-style politics.[14]

The church was dramatically weakened by the Haitian occupation of 1822–44, though it probably remained the country's only national institution. During that period, church lands were expropriated, and the church was repressed. Many church leaders supported the 1844 effort for independence, but they subsequently failed in their attempts to have the new Dominican governments return their lands to them. Throughout this period, the church suffered a severe shortage of priests, while it also resisted with only partial success the efforts to introduce secular reforms in education. Church authorities often played an important role in the conspiratorial politics of the period—at first more united in favor of annexation with Spain, and subsequently more divided. Two church leaders even served as presidents: Fernando Arturo de Meriño in 1880–82 before being named archbishop of Santo Domingo, and the subsequent archbishop, Adolfo A. Nouel, for four months in 1913. However, the church remained essentially poor and was hardly a strong, autonomous force. It was only under Trujillo that the church began to rebuild its wealth due to its close association with the dictator, and a concordat between the Dominican Republic and the Vatican was signed in 1954, trans-

forming the Catholic Church into the country's official religion and extending other rights and privileges to the church (Moya Pons 1986, 62–66;
Martínez-Fernández 1995).

Elite families had comparatively shallow historical roots, making the construction of national projects or the forging of lasting compromises even more
difficult. The country's colonial oligarchy did not survive the first struggle for
independence. The Dominican colony that first gained its fleeting independence in 1821 was already an impoverished and largely unpopulated state.
Between 1795 and 1822, more than two-thirds of the Dominican population of
Spanish origin was forced to emigrate from the island; those who remained
saw their main wealth—livestock—largely decimated (Moya Pons 1985). Under the Haitian occupation, a new landowning oligarchy emerged. However,
in the second half of the nineteenth century, it remained fluid, fragmented,
and insecure as politics and control of the state generated the rise and fall of
new groups—although some were able to sustain themselves, and certain
migrant groups, such as the Cubans, rapidly established themselves within
the elite. As a consequence of the Haitian occupation, nonwhite family
groups had joined the elite, a phenomenon that accelerated in the second half
of the nineteenth century because change in social status became closely tied
to military and political activities, "regardless of the skin color or social origin
of the persons concerned" (Moya Pons 1986, 200). Only in 1880 did the
beginnings of agricultural modernization and commercialization and of
greater ties to the outside world shake the Dominican Republic out of its
isolation as Cuban and U.S. investors began pouring money into sugar plantations and railroads began to be built to facilitate trade in tobacco, cocoa, and
other products. However, nascent Dominican exporters were increasingly
pushed aside by U.S. sugar companies, and local merchants suffered a setback
when Dominican finances fell under direct U.S. supervision. In addition to a
relatively small and fragmented wealthy elite, there were small groups of
intellectuals, some imbued with liberal thought. However, there was little
effective mobilization of the population through ideology, except in the context of confronting perceived military threats or through clientelistic ties (Betances 1995b; Cross Beras 1984).

The absence of stable government or a central state also meant that the
country essentially lacked a national military institution that did not depend
upon individual leaders or loyalties. The response to threats of renewed invasion after 1844 came from local militias controlled by caudillos, enhancing
their prominence in the national arena. As regional caudillos rose and fell
from power, the presumably "national" military force was also often radically

reorganized to reflect the change. Under these conditions, no military institution could form that was part of the state, but had a corporate identity separate from the individual leader at the top. Even Heureaux confronted severe financial and organizational difficulties that severely limited his ability to form a military, and little progress toward professionalization was made under his rule (Sang 1996b, 92–104).

In this context, liberal ideas did not penetrate deeply into the country. Constitutions and formal-legal institutions were often ignored or were ex post facto rationalizations, keeping liberal doctrines alive but at the cost of hypocrisy and cynicism. The Dominican Republic appears to fit the general pattern in Latin America by which the number of constitutions correlates inversely with a country's democratic experience (cf. Hartlyn and Valenzuela 1994, 111)—with practically no democratic history until well into the second half of the twentieth century, the country has experienced a substantial number of new constitutions and other modifications. In the Dominican Republic, as in other authoritarian cases, the adoption of a new constitution, especially in the late nineteenth century, often reflected an authoritarian leader's effort to legitimize or extend his rule; this was a pattern that was to continue well into the twentieth century. However, at times in the Dominican Republic, as elsewhere on the continent, new constitutions were also generated during democratic "turning points," although both these texts and the more open regimes that produced them tended to be short-lived. Thus, for nearly all of Dominican history, unconstitutional regimes have utilized constitutionalism to augment their claims to legitimacy, rather than to employ them to establish general "rules of the game" to which they or other major power-holders in the society would commit themselves. At the same time, reformers and democratic leaders sought to generate liberal constitutional texts and to live by them.

The country's first constitution in 1844 was a remarkably liberal document. It was influenced directly by the Haitian constitution of 1843 and indirectly by the U.S. constitution of 1787, by the liberal 1812 Cadiz Constitution of Spain, and by the French constitutions of 1799 and 1804 (see Brea Franco 1983, 1:85–87). Because of this inspiration, it called for presidentialism, a separation of powers, and extensive "checks and balances." But, its liberal nature was to be short-lived. General Pedro Santana, claiming that the legislative restrictions on the executive were excessive in a period of war, forced the constitutional assembly to add an article granting the president extraordinary powers. Also, although the constitution did not permit immediate presidential reelection, the assembly proceeded to elect Santana to two consecutive terms. This initiated a pattern in the country of executive predominance imposing constitutional hypocrisy, in which a careful attention to form was matched by substantial violations of democratic process and rights.

However, genuine efforts to impose more liberal constitutions restricting centralized, authoritarian power continued. Thus, an even more liberal constitution was prepared in 1854. However, it was also almost immediately modified to place all control over the armed forces directly in the hands of the president, which vitiated it as an effective legislative check on executive authority. Then, an essentially authoritarian "constitutional text" was enacted later in 1854, because Santana, eager to insure himself even more "constitutional" authority successfully pressured the congress for the change. The congress was reduced from two chambers to a single seven-member senate that was to meet only three months a year; and the power to suspend civil and political rights was given to the president for use as he deemed necessary. However, the country soon descended into a lengthy civil war in which figures from the Cibao region emerged victorious. In 1858 in Moca, an even more liberal and democratic constitutional text was enacted; yet, as in 1854, this one was never implemented. For the first time in the country's history, though, the constitution called for direct elections for major elected posts; it also prohibited presidential reelection, decentralized authority, and prohibited the death penalty for political crimes (Campillo Pérez 1982; Espinal 1987a, 32–38; Moya Pons 1986, 174–84).

From the enactment of a Dominican constitution in 1865, following the forced departure of the Spanish, to the U.S. military intervention in 1916, there were an additional sixteen constitutional changes. Most of these were associated with a change in leadership or with an effort by a leader to provide a legal fig leaf to cover an extension of his term of office. Yet, these changes also represented a struggle between the two different authoritarian and liberal constitutional traditions represented by the constitutions of 1854 and 1858—a struggle in which, for a considerable time, the liberal version emerged triumphant only on paper. Thus, when Báez and the Rojos took power in 1865, they forced the congress to enact a more authoritarian text, in imitation of that of 1854; but when Báez was overthrown a year later, a more liberal text was decreed. In turn, when Báez reassumed the presidency in 1868, there was another constitutional shift. With the revolts and change in government that followed, the constitution changed in each year from 1874 to 1879. The pattern continued in the next decade, when the leader of the Azules, Gregorio Luperón, called for a national convention to enact a new liberal constitution, which it did in 1880. This text, in turn, was reformed three more times before the end of the century (in 1881, 1887, and 1897). And, in 1907 and 1908, political changes were once again associated with constitutional modifications. By 1880, though, one can at least assert that the liberal constitutional *doctrine*, though of course not the practice, emerged triumphant in the country (Moya Pons 1986, 182–83).

A few facts will highlight how far doctrine strayed from practice. From 1844 to 1899, over a dozen leaders elected in some fashion to office were forced to resign due to the pressures of armed revolts. By one count, after the Spanish departure of 1865 until 1899, the country experienced fifty uprisings, which helped lead to twenty-one new governments. The first individual who was not a general to reach the presidency, although not by truly open elections, was Ulises Francisco Espaillat in 1876; his promising civilian, liberal government, however, lasted less than six months. The first somewhat free elections in the history of the country were realized in May 1878, following a formal pact between two of the major candidates, pledging to support the rule of law and the result of free elections; however, the agreement was broken only two months into the one-year term of President Ignacio María González when Gregorio Luperón, the losing candidate and other major signatory of the preelectoral pact, successfully carried out a revolt that forced González's resignation and exile (Campillo Pérez 1982, 89–93). The first president to complete a constitutional term in office was the Monsignor Meriño from 1880 to 1882, who did so even while suspending constitutional rights and in spite of armed opposition (see Cross Beras 1984).

Weak sovereignty, unstable political rule, fragmented and fearful economic elites, and international financial dependence helped to reinforce the weakness of liberal political ideas and government. In the context of a powerful foreign power willing and able to intervene, these conditions were to lead to yet another dramatic episode in the country's tragic history.

United States Occupation and the Emergence of Trujillo, 1916–1930

The U.S. occupation of the Dominican Republic was a critical turning point in Dominican history, though not for the reasons intended by the occupying force. Before turning to the intentions of the United States and the consequences of its actions, let us explore why the United States intervened.

In the face of Dominican refusal to accept all the financial and military conditions requested following the landing of the U.S. troops, State Department and Navy Department officials implemented a plan for a U.S. military government in the country in November 1916, following its approval by President Wilson. The legal and diplomatic justification for the intervention built on presumed increases in Dominican debt in violation of the 1907 treaty. The actual mix of motives that lay behind the occupation is still a matter of scholarly debate, though few would argue with Knight's overarching characterization of the United States as a "reluctant imperialist [that] wanted hegemonic power in a dependent hemisphere" (1990, 224). Some focus on the protection of U.S. economic interests. An economic argument in the narrow sense is difficult to sustain given the minimal U.S. investments in the country, even compared to Cuba or Mexico, and given the fact that Dominican leaders had in fact generally favored foreign economic interests. Understood in a broad sense (sometimes blurring with strategic concerns) of seeking not only guaranteed access to the Dominican market, but control of the sea lanes close to the Panama Canal and to markets throughout the continent, this could be considered a background motive. Others note U.S. strategic or geopolitical concerns, especially with a potential German presence in the Caribbean since General Arias and other Dominican politicians were openly pro-German. There is no question that top U.S. policymakers were concerned about German designs on the hemisphere. Thus, this too was certainly a background factor; whether it was also an immediate or precipitating factor is unclear as there is little reference to Germany in papers of U.S. diplomatic and military personnel in the Dominican Republic until after the occupation. Finally, a third background motive that almost certainly played a role is the Wilson administration's liberal interventionist zeal: a combination of self-righteousness, a sense of superiority, and a desire to bring "good government" to Latin American peoples.[15]

The goals of the U.S. occupation forces were surprisingly vague and only gradually began to take shape. Their immediate actions were intended to establish control over the country quickly and ostensibly to insure peace and stability. Military officers were named to major posts in the executive branch, while press censorship was imposed and steps were taken to disarm the population; the legislature, in turn, was "suspended." Eventually, the military moved to implement what could be characterized as "technocratic Progressive" reforms, under the assumption that certain socioeconomic, financial, and administrative changes would generate the conditions for political and constitutional stability. Programs were enacted in education, health, sanitation, agriculture, and communications; highways were built and other public works carried out. In addition, both a census and a cadastral survey were taken, the latter allowing land titles to be regularized and U.S. sugar companies to expand their holdings dramatically.[16]

Ultimately, the most significant measure was the establishment of a new Dominican constabulary force. In the Dominican Republic, as elsewhere in Central America and the Caribbean, U.S. officials hoped that the establishment of new constabulary forces initially under U.S. tutelage would permanently depoliticize the armed forces in these countries, serving to bolster stable, constitutional government. In the Dominican case, the newly formed Guardia Nacional Dominicana suffered from a lack of resources, from difficulties in attracting good recruits, and from unclear objectives, as its duties and size made it fall somewhere between a police force and a military force. Only after the mid-1921 announcement of a plan for withdrawal did the U.S. military government focus its attention and resources on creating a force (Fuller and Cosmas 1974, 45–52; Calder 1984, 54–60; Moya Pons 1983, 477–78).

The extrication of U.S. troops was conditional on there being elections (as was to be the case four decades later); to this end, the U.S. military sponsored important reforms. The United States helped oversee the naming of a provisional president and the enactment of new electoral laws, including the establishment of a separate electoral oversight agency, the Junta Central Electoral (JCE, Central Electoral Board), and provisions for proportional representation to insure a degree of minority representation in the legislature. The electoral law of 1923 also prohibited the country's police and military from voting. Under U.S. oversight, the old caudillo figure Horacio Vásquez won the March 1924 elections; in words that still resonate today (see chapter 8), the losing candidate, Francisco J. Peynado, alleged that "the complex web [*la tupida malla*] of irregularities prevented a large number of my sympathizers from exercising their right to vote," but significantly he ultimately accepted the legitimacy of his defeat. After the inauguration of Vásquez and the naming of a coalition cabinet in July 1924, all U.S. marines withdrew (Campillo Pérez 1982, 170, 316–29; on the role of Sumner Welles, and his frustrations, in creating the JCE, see Hanson 1994, 323–27).

Perhaps this could have been a turning point. But President Vásquez was not the figure to seek to break with old patterns of political power, especially as the state was now an even greater prize than in the past. Vásquez governed ineffectively and corruptly, dramatically expanding public employment and ultimately seeking unconstitutionally to prolong his term—he now did so in a country in which the United States had helped establish a relatively effective national military institution where one had previously not existed and in which traditional powerholders were weak. Then, in the 1920s, the United States began to move from military occupation, the most complete involvement possible in the affairs of another country short of formal colonization or annexation, to an opposite extreme of noninterventionism. This approach emerged in reaction to the growing Latin American and international opposition to U.S. occupations in the Caribbean and Central America and was facilitated by the absence of any perceived threat to continued U.S. influence in the area from an outside power; this approach gradually transformed into President Roosevelt's "Good Neighbor" Policy. Largely unintentional, but nevertheless predictable consequences of the occupation combined with continuing patterns of Dominican domestic politics and the U.S. shift toward noninterventionism to provide an opportunity for the head of the country's newly established military force not only to take power, but then to consolidate his grip on it.

Rafael Leónidas Trujillo Molina was born in 1891 and raised in San Cristóbal, a small town near the capital, in a family of modest means of mixed Spanish, Creole, and Haitian background. He began his meteoric rise within the newly established Guardia Nacional Dominicana in 1919. In late 1921 he entered the Haina Military Academy as a second lieutenant, and by 1924 he was a captain of the then-renamed Policía Nacional Dominicana responsible for the city of Santiago. Impressed by his hard work and organizational skills, President Vásquez promoted him quickly to major and then to lieutenant colonel and chief of staff. In June 1925, Trujillo became a colonel and the head of the country's police force. Two years later he was named brigadier general, a promotion linked to the transformation of the police force into a national army, which took place in May 1928. In less than ten years, Trujillo emerged from being an obscure minor officer in a newly formed constabulary force to being the head of the country's army. As was to be discovered, he harbored strong sentiments of social rejection and of animosity against the country's elite families, the so-called *gente de primera*, whom he was to force to work for him and often humiliate, and whose homage and admiration he actively pursued (Crassweller 1966, 39–51, 104).

At the same time, the country's neopatrimonial political patterns continued based on personalistic and clientelistic rule, questionable constitutional maneuverings, intrigue, and occasional rebellion—all of which predated the U.S. occupation. President Vásquez, elected for a four-year term in 1924, modified the constitution four times, arranging for his term in office to be extended an additional two years. At the age of seventy, he changed the country's electoral law to make it difficult for the opposition to win and sought reelection in part upon the urging of political associates. Ultimately, this led to an uprising against the president some three months before the scheduled elections, with considerable popular acceptance. Through complex negotiations that preserved the form of constitutionalism, the presumed leader of that rebellion, Rafael Estrella Ureña, became provisional president pending the elections; Trujillo had played a critical, secretive role in insuring the success of the rebellion against Vásquez.

An elaborate, occasionally bloody charade then ensued. Two political groups emerged for the elections, one with Trujillo and Estrella Ureña as presidential and vice presidential candidates respectively. The army was employed almost as a private instrument of repression by Trujillo, leading the JCE to resign some nine days before the elections and the other party to withdraw the day before. Official results gave Trujillo the victory by a 99 percent margin and admitted to a 45 percent abstention rate.[17] Following the election, Trujillo sought to reassure the U.S. legation that he would seek its guidance and counsel.

Although the political events that eventually brought Trujillo to power were consistent with the past political patterns in the country, several consequences of the U.S. military occupation and the "lessons" Trujillo may have learned greatly strengthened his capabilities as head of the newly formed military force. The U.S. military occupation had changed the Dominican Republic. The major regions of the country were now even more firmly linked to Santo Domingo, the capital city, by highways and improved communications. The population was largely disarmed, limiting further the possibilities of armed uprisings as in the country's past history. In addition, the U.S. military had demonstrated efficacy in confronting a guerrilla challenge during the occupation period and in controlling the population through a variety of repressive measures. Difficult to determine are the lessons this provided, particularly to the newly formed and newly trained centralized police force that was one of the legacies of the intervention.

The intention had been that a depoliticized police force would insure stable, constitutional support. Yet, there remained two alternative outcomes. One was that the new armed force would fractionalize, provoking civil war (as would happen years later in April 1965). The other was that the head of this new force, in part because of the changes instituted during the occupation, could more effectively control the country in a dictatorial fashion, as in fact occurred under Trujillo.[18]

Finally, the policy of nonintervention espoused by the State Department was to assist Trujillo. Trujillo apparently surmised (correctly, as it turned out) that the United States might accept a government he headed if it appeared to come to power through elections, even questionable ones, although an outright coup d'état would be unacceptable; this is a possible explanation for Trujillo's support for the complex Santiago plot to overthrow Vásquez. The United States had accepted the questionable extension of Vásquez's term in office from four to six years, as it had been accomplished respecting constitutional formalities. And in 1930, the U.S. minister in the country, Charles Curtis, had reluctantly accepted Estrella Ureña's provisional presidency, in part because it had complied with constitutional requirements. During that period of complex negotiations between President Vásquez and Estrella Ureña, negotiations which took place in part in the U.S. legation, Curtis indicated that the legation would not under any circumstances recommend U.S. recognition of a Trujillo administration. Trujillo had hoped that he, rather than Estrella Ureña, could become the provisional president (Crassweller 1966, 62–67). Curtis's views notwithstanding, the State Department did not want to be open to the charge of intervention in the Dominican elections, especially in the absence of any serious threat to U.S. lives and property.

At the same time, it also appears that in U.S. military circles, Trujillo's takeover of power was viewed favorably. In subsequent years, Trujillo would continue to sidestep U.S. diplomats in Santo Domingo when necessary, assiduously cultivating his U.S. military contacts, even as he provided attention and lavish gifts to U.S. congressional representatives and the hired lobbyists he thought could gain him influence in Washington. Thus, in Trujillo's first visit ever outside of the Dominican Republic, to the United States in 1939, he was accompanied by a U.S. marine officer who had stayed on as an adviser after the occupation period. Trujillo's warmest receptions were among the military; for example, Major General James C. Breckinridge, who had been Trujillo's commanding officer in the Guardia Nacional in 1924, received him with honors as the head of the marine barracks at Quantico Military Base.[19]

In sum, Trujillo's rise to power and initial consolidation were due to a constellation of factors. They built upon historical neopatrimonial patterns and their associated structural features in the country. These patterns included caudillo rule marked by struggles of "ins" versus "outs," weak formal organizations in society as well as in the polity, ineffective rule of law, and presidential dominance within the country. In turn, these patterns were products of a fragile economic and social structure with weak and fragmented elite sectors, with little industry, and thus with almost no middle-sector or working-class groups. But, Trujillo's emergence and consolidation of power also depended upon two other factors: (1) institutional and structural changes as a result of U.S. occupation, including the establishment of more professional armed forces and improved transportation and communication services in the country and (2) the U.S. shift to a policy of noninterventionism, which facilitated the success of his plotting. A stronger military and improved communications and infrastructure in a country that was still relatively poor, unintegrated, and isolated meant that Trujillo had the means to put down potential regional rebellions without necessarily having to incorporate and control the entire country's population.

The role in Trujillo's emergence and consolidation of the country's prolonged self-doubts about and actual constraints on sovereignty is complex. The country's insecurity and the politics it had helped to generate, in which some leaders assiduously cultivated foreign incorporation, certainly weakened national integration and state building and facilitated foreign intervention. In turn, the ruinous debt accumulated by the country's first neosultanistic leader, Heureaux—carried out in part to help him gain independence from domestic creditors—ultimately helped set the stage for subsequent U.S. intervention. Although U.S. occupation helped strengthen national integration by the construction of infrastructure and other measures, it further weakened the country's major social and political actors, led to the formation of the Guardia Nacional, and opened the way for Trujillo's emergence. In this context, in a pattern that began deep in the nineteenth century and continues to this day, domestic Dominican actors based their actions in part upon their calculations about U.S. actions. In 1930, expectations of U.S. involvement and a potential veto against Trujillo entered (incorrectly, as it turned out) into the calculations of a number of key Dominican actors. Subsequently, Trujillo was able to articulate a vision of regaining national sovereignty as an ideological underpinning for many of his actions.

Trujillo in Power: Evolution

Trujillo's regime quickly moved beyond the traditional Dominican caudillo regimes of the nineteenth century, so that by the end of his first term (if not sooner) its neosultanistic tendencies were clear. By the end of his second term, it was evident that this regime's despotic and totalitarian features went beyond those of Heureaux, his historical predecessor. There would be occasional partial liberalizations in response to international pressures, particularly following the Haitian massacre of 1937 and in the immediate post–World War II era. But Trujillo's accumulation of wealth and power would continue, reaching a peak in 1955. The regime's deterioration began shortly thereafter, however, accelerating in 1958. Of all the cases considered in a recent comparative volume, the Trujillo regime is probably the closest approximation to the ideal-type of neosultanism developed by Chehabi and Linz (1998).[20]

Before turning to a consideration of how various factors initially sustained and then, in some cases, undermined Trujillo's rule, it will be useful to have a brief chronological overview of these years, from 1930 to 1961. Upon assuming office in 1930, Trujillo quickly began a strategy of concentration of personal power, state building, and national consolidation, while gradually enunciating a discourse of nationalism, work, order, and progress. During his first year in office he dealt with three uprisings against his government (including one led by his vice president), the deterioration of the country's financial situation, and, just eighteen days after he assumed office, a devastating cyclone that swept through the capital city. In response to the cyclone, Trujillo was granted sweeping emergency powers, which he utilized to consolidate his grip on power; the disaster also put Trujillo back in contact with a number of U.S. military figures, who were to become his crucial allies, even as various U.S. officials were impressed by his apparent administrative efficiency.[21] During the remainder of his first four-year term in office, Trujillo discovered and brutally repressed several other conspiracies. In 1931, he also took the critical step of creating Partido Dominicano (PD, Dominican Party), funded by a 10 percent deduction from its members' paychecks and concentrating all decision-making powers directly in his hands; for example, he held undated letters of resignation from officeholders in all three branches of government. Other parties were forced to disband.

Trujillo's megalomania and his desire to accumulate wealth also became evident in this first term in office. Pico Duarte, the highest mountain in the Antilles, was renamed Pico Trujillo; and, Santo Domingo, the capital city, was renamed Ciudad Trujillo.[22] By 1934, Trujillo had imposed a series of monopolies on salt, meat, and rice and had taken other steps that made him the country's richest man, foreshadowing the incredible concentration of wealth that he would build over the next three decades.[23]

Carefully orchestrated elections ensued. With all other parties abolished, Trujillo easily gained reelection in 1934. Officially, his party received 100 percent of all votes cast. However, in apparent response to the international outcry following the brutal, large-scale massacre of Haitians along the border in October 1937, Trujillo stepped aside in 1938 and allowed his vice president, Jacinto Peynado, to be elected president. Once again, only one party presented candidates, and it received 100 percent of the votes cast. And, when Peynado died in 1940, his term was completed by the vice president, Manuel de Jesús Troncoso de la Concha.

In the 1940s, Trujillo considerably expanded his economic holdings while retaining political power. In the midst of World War II and with Trujillo actively cooperating with its war effort, the United States did not object to his holding power directly; thus, Trujillo was elected to a third (five-year) term in 1942 as two parties went to the polls with exactly the same lists, the PD and the

Trujillista party. Short-lived but real pressure for democratization followed the end of World War II. Accordingly, Trujillo briefly liberalized, allowing communist exiles to return, and the regime experienced its first labor strikes. But, Trujillo cracked down again as international pressures for democratization eased in the context of the emerging Cold War, and he was reelected in 1947. In that year, two regime-sponsored opposition parties were allowed to run, and each officially received a similar vote of just under 4 percent of the total, which was carefully distributed so that each could win exactly one deputy seat. The 1940s also witnessed frustrated exile invasions against the regime, even as the country's military apparatus continued to expand considerably.

Trujillo's initial schemes to enrich himself, as noted above, revolved around the creation of state or commercial monopolies. He then gradually moved into industry, forcing owners to allow him to buy up shares, while also enjoying healthy commissions on all public-works contracts. After World War II, Trujillo expanded into the industrial production of such products as cement, chocolate, cardboard, flour, paint, and alcoholic beverages, often in collaboration with local investors or with Spanish or Syrian-Lebanese entrepreneurs who had settled in the country. From 1938 to 1960, manufacturing establishments doubled and the number of employees increased almost two and a half times (Moya Pons 1990a, 514). Trujillo also nationalized the electric company, and in 1941 he bought up the U.S.-owned National City Bank, which he renamed the Banco de Reservas.

Trujillo's largest investments were in sugar, however. As late as 1948, with the exception of a few properties owned by the Vicini family, the country's sugar industry was foreign owned. Trujillo entered the sugar industry both because of the additional power he would wield and in order to enrich himself. He began modestly with a small mill in 1949, then began construction of a massive (and economically irrational) mill while gradually pressuring foreign companies to sell by using the press, promoting labor disturbances, and citing the companies for health and labor violations. By 1956, twelve of the sixteen mills in the country belonged to the Trujillo family, all except the country's largest one at Central Romana (which was being negotiated when he was killed) and three owned by the Vicinis. As he expanded his economic holdings, "[t]he organized and systematic use of every State power in furtherance of Trujillo's private ends was conspicuous" (Crassweller 1966, 257). This ranged from privileged access to energy and water, to free use of military labor, to the use of the state banking system for Trujillo's benefit. The planning and implementation of the entire sugar operation were so poor that except for the numerous subsidies it would have lost money (Murphy 1991, 24–26).[24]

While retaining direct control over the military, in 1952 and again in 1957,

Trujillo had his pliant brother, Héctor B. Trujillo, elected president. The voting "results" again demonstrated near or total unanimity for the single candidate.[25] The regime appeared to be at its apogee in 1955, when the country sponsored a massive world fair to celebrate the twenty-five years of the Trujillo era. At that point, Trujillo's domination of the island appeared absolute, even as support from the United States for its staunch anticommunist ally was also high. Yet, the fair represented a massive drain on the country's budget, as did Trujillo's cash purchases of several sugar mills and the country's electric company, even as the country entered a period of much slower growth; and the willingness of Dominicans to resist the regime more openly within the country gradually grew in the face of the megalomania of Trujillo's political and economic actions and the intensification of operations by exiles against him. In 1956, the kidnapping of Galíndez marked a turn toward a more erratic and brutal use of repression, as Trujillo's rhetoric focused less and less on the national goals he had initially articulated and more on the "communist" threat.[26] The crisis deepened after Fidel Castro's triumph in Cuba on January 1, 1959; it ended—for Rafael Trujillo—in a blaze of bullets in May 1961.

Trujillo in Power: Explanations and Characteristics

How was Trujillo able to maintain nearly total control over a country for so long? Five sets of factors are important. First are the background historical factors of geographical isolation, weak traditional powerholders or other potential challengers, and a more effective repressive apparatus. Second, and related to these, is Trujillo's success in building upon and enhancing state structures, especially those related to repression. Yet, his prolonged rule did not rely on repression alone. He also employed ideological arguments, initially revolving around economic nationalism, anti-Haitianism, and Catholicism, to project himself domestically and to justify his vast financial empire. Fourth, Trujillo used various economic and political means to mesh strategies of repression, co-optation, and corruption, while enhancing his own personal wealth and power. Finally, international factors played a central role, especially given the country's dependence on the United States. Trujillo pursued an active policy toward the United States, and he was helped initially by his strong contacts with the U.S. military and by the U.S. "Good Neighbor" policy of nonintervention and then by the U.S. focus on anticommunism. Indeed, a dramatic shift in U.S. attitude toward Trujillo was crucial in the denouement of his regime.

Important historical and structural factors in Trujillo's ascendancy were

discussed in the previous section. They include the country's relative socioeconomic backwardness, weak and divided social forces and political actors, improved communications and transportation, and better trained police
and armed forces—all in combination with the initial U.S. policy of nonintervention.

Trujillo built on these, enhancing the state's repressive features. He used all
means at his disposal to reinforce the natural isolation that was a consequence
of his subjects' living on an island. By his second term, he had begun to
employ more sophisticated technological measures of control over the population, beginning with interception of correspondence. Over time, reflecting
some of the more totalitarian features of the regime, his methods expanded to
telephone tapping, surveillance of foreign diplomats and journalists, and targeted assassinations, both at home and abroad (see Vega 1986b). Foreign radio
programs were often jammed, foreign press reports kept out, the mails cen-
sored; few Dominicans were given permission to travel abroad.

Central to Trujillo's domination of the country was control over an expanding armed forces and police, which were clearly his personal instrument
rather than a national institution.[27] Trujillo remained as commander in chief
of the armed forces even when he was not formally president (in 1958, in the
face of U.S. pressure, Trujillo claimed to have stepped down as commander in
chief, but this ostensible move was never publicized within the country). As
table 2.1 illustrates, Trujillo expanded the size of the armed forces and police
dramatically while he controlled the country. When he assumed power, the
country's security forces numbered just slightly over 2,000. This number grew
steadily over the 1930s and 1940s and then increased dramatically so that by
1955 the security forces numbered around 20,000, nearly ten times what they
had been twenty-five years earlier. Five years later, as Trujillo clung desperately to power, the number had grown to around 31,000. Not surprisingly, this
growth was also reflected in government expenditures. In spite of a sharp drop
in the government's overall budget in the 1930s due to the effects of the
depression, the military budget grew: in 1929, it was US$1.5 million, 9.4 per-
cent of the government budget; in 1938, it was US$1.84 million and 16 percent
of the budget. In subsequent decades, as the economy improved, the military
portion expanded even more dramatically.[28] By the mid-1950s, the best-
trained troops and the best military weapons—not only planes, but tanks and
other military hardware—had been transferred to the Dominican equivalent
of the air force, known as the Aviación Militar Dominicana (AMD, Dominican Military Aviation), controlled by Trujillo's eldest son Ramfis. In March
1959, Trujillo announced the formation of an "anticommunist foreign legion";

Table 2.1. Growth of the Armed Forces under Trujillo

Year	Army	Air Force	Navy	Police	Total	Increase (%)[1]
1924	—	—	—	—	1,243	
1929	—	—	—	—	2,128	71
1932	—	—	—	—	2,179	2
1935	—	—	—	—	2,770	27
1938	3,081	31	100	627	3,839	38
1944	5,269	76	135	900[2]	6,380	66
1948	6,298	171	1,042	1,622	9,133	43
1955	13,500	2,000	3,000	1,500	20,000	119
1958	11,400	2,214	2,900	1,500	18,014	−10
1960	17,500	10,000[3]	3,500	(See air force.[3])	31,000	72

Source: Vega (1992, 225, 445).
[1]Percentage increase from previous total reported.
[2]Figure for police taken from 1942 figures.
[3]Total for air force, police, and newly created legion forces.

over time, the legion forces became largely Dominican and comprised other private armies linked to the regime as well (Vega 1992, 417, 420, 430).

Trujillo still confronted challenges within the armed forces. The role of Ramfis highlighted the fact that the morale, autonomy, and abilities of the armed forces were affected by nepotism, rotation of officers, and manipulated promotions. Ramfis was made a full colonel in the army at the age of four and a brigadier general by the age of nine; he resigned that rank when he was fourteen, but by the time he was twenty-three he was again a brigadier general, as well as the chief of staff of the air force. On at least two occasions, Trujillo simply promoted trusted civilians to high positions in the army (Anselmo Paulino Alvarez in 1949 and Johnny Abbes in 1958). Several of Trujillo's brothers entered the army after the U.S. marines had left and, through their family connections, eventually became generals; other relatives also held high posts in the military or the government. Trujillo's brothers in the military were permitted to engage in small-scale corruption, protection rackets, and contraband; generally, though, the bureaucracy operated in a reasonably honest fashion out of fear of Trujillo (Bernardo Vega, letter to author, September 1994). After consolidating his grip on power in the 1930s, which included dismantling a plot emanating from the military in 1931, Trujillo confronted renewed military plots against him, which he also dismantled successfully, in 1939 and 1946. Trujillo's network of domestic and international spies took on an additional dimension in 1957 with the creation of the dreaded Servicio de Inteligencia Militar (SIM, Military Intelligence Service), headed by Johnny Abbes.[29]

One of the most brutal uses of repressive forces by Trujillo was the large-scale massacre of Haitians in October 1937, resulting in an estimated 5,000 to 12,000 deaths.[30] What combination of factors ultimately led Trujillo to order this action remains unclear. After an extensive review, Vega (1988c, 390–95) asserts that although a desire to "whiten" the country probably played a central role, numerous other factors contributed, including an aspiration to control critical border areas more effectively in the face of growing illegal Haitian migration, the ineffectiveness of deportations, and the actions of some Dominican military more involved in profiting from illegal migration than in controlling it (see also Murphy 1991, 129–34). By this massacre, Trujillo sought to assert centralized control over all Dominican territory and to prevent any potential threat to his regime that could emanate from Haiti, as so many conspiracies had in the country's past. Before the massacre, Trujillo had also sought to influence Haitian politics and to bribe key officials (in fact, a bribe helped lower the compensation he paid to Haiti after the massacre). In the 1940s, towns and military outposts were founded in the border regions, the church was encouraged to extend its missionary work into the region, new roads were constructed, and greater commercial links were established.

Yet, Trujillo's regime was not based purely on repression, though over time it increasingly used such means of control. Trujillo articulated certain ideological positions with the collaboration of several leading intellectuals that resonated across different social sectors of the population. His was the first prolonged period in the country's history when the country was not directly intervened by Spain, the United States, or Haiti. Trujillo built upon the country's antipathy to Haiti to help articulate a nationalist ideology appealing to traditional Hispanic and Catholic values.[31] Especially in the 1930s, he also asserted a vision of discipline, work, peace, order, and progress. As these ideas became embodied in a number of large-scale public works and construction projects, particularly as the economy began moving out of the depression in the late 1930s, they almost certainly gained him respect—if not support—among some elements of the population; indeed, he presented himself in a messianic form. By the 1950s, and particularly after signing a concordat with the Vatican in 1954, Trujillo would often attack "international communism" as a threat to the country's traditional values, which he claimed he was seeking to uphold.[32] Yet, Trujillo never articulated a fully formulated ideology;

indeed, even his espousal of anticommunism changed dramatically in his final, desperate days.

Trujillo also waved the ideological banner of economic nationalism, although it sometimes cloaked his personal accumulation of wealth. This was facilitated by the country's abject dependency on the United States and by its tragic history. In fact, many of his economic measures were inferior to those taken by other Latin American states in the same period. Yet, in seeking to legitimize his rule, Trujillo could argue that he ended U.S. administration of Dominican customs, retired the Dominican debt, and introduced a national currency to replace the dollar. The 1924 convention that paved the way for the withdrawal of U.S. troops had maintained an extensive role for the United States in Dominican internal economic affairs and in the customs house in order to ensure the prompt repayment of the country's outstanding debt and to prevent accumulation of new debt without U.S. approval; in the words of one U.S. diplomat, the country remained a "tutelary state."[33] After extensive negotiations, Trujillo signed an agreement with Cordell Hull in 1940 (ratified in 1941) ending the U.S. administration of Dominican customs. Finally, in July 1947, employing reserves built up during the war years, Trujillo completely paid off the country's foreign debt. Shortly afterward, the country established a central bank and a national currency (the peso) to replace the U.S. dollar, which had been employed until then in lieu of a local currency; although initially respectful of the central bank's autonomy, toward the end of his rule, Trujillo openly violated it.[34]

Thus, ideologically Trujillo portrayed himself with some success as a forger of the Dominican nation, builder of the state, and defender of its economic interests. As he amassed a sizable fortune, Trujillo also built up the Dominican state, reduced direct control by foreigners over the economy, and stimulated incipient industrialization. He and his propagandists, though, exaggerated both the efficacy of the measures he took and the role of his regime in restoring the country's financial independence and sovereignty, while downplaying the tremendous costs his economic measures ultimately represented for the nation.

Economically, Trujillo eventually became the single dominant force in the country by combining abuse of state power, threats, and co-optation. Although certain of the country's economic elite maintained some individual autonomy, there was no possibility for independent organization. Trujillo enjoyed humiliating those who had previously enjoyed both social prestige and economic wealth; they intensely disliked him, but were forced to conform. Only in Trujillo's last two years did any concerted opposition emerge from within the economic elite (Wiarda 1975, 370–74). Indeed, Trujillo's economic holdings at the time of his death were incredibly extensive, further concentrating control of the country in his hands. He controlled almost 80 percent of the country's industrial production. About 60 percent of the country's labor force depended directly or indirectly on him, 45 percent being employed in his firms and another 15 percent working for the state (Moya Pons 1990a, 515). Thus, Trujillo's domination of the island was increasingly economic, as well as military and political.

The only organization that retained any degree of autonomy within the country was the Catholic Church; yet, until the very end of his rule, it remained abjectly loyal to him. This was a church that had been decimated by the Haitian occupation of the nineteenth century, and by 1930 its existence was still relatively precarious. Trujillo favored the church tremendously, subsidizing the construction of church buildings, enhancing religious education, providing stipends for clergy, and ultimately providing other prerogatives to the church through a concordat with the Vatican in 1954; the number of priests was also increasing dramatically. Ricardo Pittini, the archbishop of Santo Domingo and leader of the church from 1933 until 1960, was an open admirer of Trujillo and provided unequivocal support for his regime. An open break between Trujillo and the church came only in early 1960.[35]

Politically, Trujillo combined guile, cynicism, ruthlessness, and co-optation. There was careful manipulation of constitutional norms and legal requirements that were ostensibly being followed faithfully,[36] a single-party apparatus totally dominated by Trujillo, and incredible manipulation of individuals, who found themselves moved and removed from public office in complex and disconcerting fashion, even as personal rivalries were promoted and tested. At its apogee, the PD had branches throughout the country, helping to keep Trujillo appraised of local realities, needs, and potential threats to his rule. The party's charitable activities, homages to Trujillo, and campaign efforts were financed largely by a percentage taken from the salaries of public employees. Although the PD played no role in either political recruitment or policy formulation, in certain periods of the Trujillo era it did help to legitimize his rule. Trujillo made voting mandatory, and not having one's identification card stamped to show one had voted could be risky. Universal male suffrage had legally existed in the Dominican Republic since 1865, with some exceptions regarding property (but never literacy) under some of the constitutions in force during the nineteenth century; Trujillo then expanded suffrage to women in 1942, after permitting them a symbolic vote in two elections in the 1930s (Campillo Pérez 1982, 316–29).

Trujillo's political style fueled distrust and conspiracy. He was known to be generous with money as well as willing to go to elaborate lengths to plot revenge or assassination. His ruthless political abilities were particularly evident in his response to democratic pressures from the United States after World War II in the face of greater labor activism within the country. He convinced Dominican communists in Cuban exile to return and function openly and legally, which they did in 1946 with the misplaced belief they would be able to act effectively. In that year, only the second major strike under Trujillo's reign took place (the first was in 1942). However, repression increased in 1947, and one month after his May 1947 reelection, Trujillo had the Communist Party declared illegal. A wave of repression effectively destroyed both the communists as well as the nascent independent labor movement; meanwhile, Trujillo took advantage of the growing U.S. anticommunist attitude in the Cold War.[37]

Various domestic factors were thus critical in sustaining Trujillo's grip on power, but international ones were critical as well. Trujillo's complex web of conspiracy, intrigue, and violence extended well beyond Dominican borders, as he provided support for various regional dictators and plotted against perceived foreign enemies, some of whom provided support for exile groups plotting against him. The governments most hostile to Trujillo in the 1940s were those of Ramón Grau San Martín in Cuba, Rómulo Betancourt in Venezuela, and Juan José Arévalo in Guatemala; Trujillo was involved in plots against the governments of the first two, as well as against other governments. As early as January 1945, Juan Bosch in exile in Cuba was actively seeking weapons and funds for a possible invasion and overthrow of Trujillo.

Given the Dominican Republic's past history and continuing dependency, its complex relations with the United States was also of central importance. Early in his rule, Trujillo found strong backing among military contacts he had forged during the U.S. occupation, which counterbalanced an often hostile State Department. Trujillo employed public relations firms and assiduously cultivated contacts with the military and individual politicians in the United States to enhance his reputation and sustain U.S. support. He went to elaborate lengths to demonstrate domestically that he retained support from the United States, and U.S. diplomats often expressed their frustration at being manipulated by Trujillo, even as U.S. military personnel openly praised his rule. Until the final crisis years (1959–61), the most critical period for Trujillo was in the immediate post–World War II era when hostile U.S. diplomats were able to block his efforts to purchase arms and promoted a more active policy in support of democracy. However, as the Cold War emerged, this policy receded. Thus, an effort by Dominican exiles to launch an invasion against Trujillo's regime from Cayo Confites off Cuba in 1947 was largely stopped by the Cuban government with U.S. pressure playing a contributory role (and another invasion effort in 1949 also failed). By 1955, U.S. civilian diplomats were joining with their military counterparts in praising Trujillo for his anticommunism, though this warm embrace only lasted until 1958 (Hartlyn 1991; Vega 1992, esp. 463–67). And, by 1959, as the ideological, economic, political, and international bases of the regime continued to erode, more and more domestic and international actors were asking about how Trujillo was to be removed from office and who would replace him.

Ultimately, then, the basis of Trujillo's power rested on a firm control of the state's repressive apparatus, on an ability to dismantle plots or prevent them through fear or cunning, and on U.S. forbearance. Shifts in the last two ultimately led to his undoing, as will be discussed in the next chapter.

Conclusion

The historical evolution, socioeconomic development, and political-institutional patterning of the Dominican Republic were all inimical to democratic development and favorable to the emergence of neopatrimonial, and ultimately neosultanistic, rule. Warfare, economic destitution, and insecurity were bred by the country's relationship with Haiti and other foreign powers; the consequences of its international vulnerability and the actions of foreign powers were enhanced by the activities of unscrupulous leaders. Unifying, integrative institutions such as the church, the military, or political parties were fragile, and the country's social structure and dominant economic sectors were also weak and fragmented. In an interactive fashion, these factors all were affected by and reinforced a pattern of unstable, militarized politics built around caudillo politics. In addition, there was a consistent failure of liberal ideas at potential turning points, which fed a growing pattern of constitutional hypocrisy. In combination with the establishment of a strong national military institution during the U.S. occupation, this helped set the stage for the coming to power of what became the neosultanistic Trujillo regime.

This chapter argues that the links between the colonial era and the failures of Dominican democracy were not inevitable, but were complex and mediated by other factors. There are numerous historical and methodological criticisms of reductionist interpretive efforts to link the failure of democracy in the region to an authoritarian legacy of Spanish colonial rule (for one careful and devastating critique that may be missed, see Waisman 1987, 104–6; see also Hartlyn and Valenzuela 1994; Diamond and Linz 1989; Rueschemeyer, Huber Stephens and Stephens 1992). Historically, these types of political culture arguments underplay the extent to which the cultural heritage from Spain was mixed; instead, they often base themselves on impressionistic evidence or on the unproven notion that certain doctrines reflect widely shared values in the population. Methodologically, to the extent that culturalist explanations are based on a neoplatonic conception of values, they are problematic. As Waisman (1987, 104) notes, in this view, values or "traditions" are "reified abstractions" that "are assumed to be separate from the empirical social world and yet connected with it through the process of institutionalization (in fact, a process of reflection, in which social structures are treated as the manifestation of underlying values)." (For writings on the Dominican Republic in this political culture tradition, see Wiarda 1989; Wiarda and Kryzanek 1982; and Kryzanek 1977.) The fact that Latin culture and liberal democracy have coexisted for many decades in such countries as Chile, Costa Rica, Italy, Venezuela, and, more recently, Portugal and Spain, would also appear to be problematic for culturalist arguments of this type. Yet, in their defense, it might be argued that they are still valid for the Dominican Republic. Indeed, part of the problem with these kinds of political culture arguments is that, as generalizations about the region as a whole, they tend to gloss over both significant differences regarding the degree to which certain traits have been evident, as well as differences in political evolutions across the continent. The question remains: how useful are these kind of culturalist arguments in explaining Dominican political patterns?

One of the strongest proponents of a political-culture approach for Latin America, emphasizing the impact of the Spanish colonial heritage, is Howard Wiarda, also a noted scholar on the Dominican Republic. He has argued that the Spanish colonial system, a "rigid, top-down, hierarchical, and authoritarian system," was imposed on the island of Hispaniola in the sixteenth century, and lasted "through three centuries of Spanish colonial rule, on into the independence rule of the nineteenth century, and even to the present. For even now, the sixteenth-century Spanish model of a bureaucratic-authoritarian state serves as an alternative to the liberal one, a top-down system that has by no means disappeared from the Dominican consciousness" (Wiarda 1989, 426, 427). This view suggests an excessively "destined" pathway—culturally rather than structurally based—from the past to the authoritarian present.

One problem with this view is that it does not explain how the cultural tradition was effectively transmitted, given that colonial institutions and most elements of the original colonial settlers nearly disappeared. Another problem is that differing arguments about the consequences of being a colonial backwater have been made. Wiarda notes (and historians concur) that by the mid-sixteenth century Hispaniola had become an unimportant and largely ignored part of the Spanish colonial empire, and that traditional institutions of Spanish colonialism, particularly a landed oligarchy based on the hacienda system and the church, were notoriously weak by the early nineteenth century and, in fact, remained so over the century; indeed, one can concur with his judgment that the country lacked "any institutions at all" (viewing institutions as formal organizations) on which to base a viable sociopolitical order. However, this means that what was to become the Dominican Republic had little of the reality of effective Spanish colonial political and social governance present elsewhere on the continent. If the Spanish colonial system was most notorious in the Dominican Republic for its weakness, it is difficult to see how that "tradition" could be the principal causal factor explaining subsequent authoritarianism. Furthermore, this kind of approach also cannot explain why the country was incapable of developing institutions (formal organizations) subsequently.[38]

The other major problem is that others have argued that being a backwater of Spanish colonialism—which the Dominican Republic clearly was—*favored* subsequent democratic evolution, such as in the cases of Costa Rica or Chile (e.g., Booth 1989; Rosenberg 1991, 17–19, 336–38). Valenzuela (1989, 172–73) disputes this view for the case of Chile. He has noted that Chile had a conservative, Catholic, royalist ethos and a large, traditional landowning class; thus, the purported "benefits" of being relatively ignored by colonial authorities were not present. For him, the critical factor is that in the Chilean case, following the disruptive wars of independence, there was very little institutional continuity from the colonial order to the constitutional precepts that began to be applied early in Chilean development.[39] If we accept that the Chilean case may have been marked both by more traditional colonial domination and by institutional discontinuity, then it is more clearly the Costa Rican example that complicates arguments that authoritarianism in the Dominican Republic stems essentially from a legacy or a tradition established during Spanish colonial rule. That is particularly true because there are impressive similarities between the two countries in terms of their colonial eras: both were colonial backwaters that experienced "the leveling effect of . . . poverty and isolation" (Booth 1989, 388)—albeit in somewhat different ways and perhaps in a more exaggerated fashion on Hispaniola—and neither economy was centered on large-scale export agriculture based on forced labor or slavery. Yet, this did not favor democracy in the Dominican Republic as it did in Costa Rica.

The way out of this puzzle is to analyze how the link to the colonial era was mediated by other critical factors. The role of ideas in political action needs to be understood within their social setting and in terms of the institutions and social groups that promote and sustain them (Downing 1992, 8; Waisman

1987); the failure of "liberal ideas" in the Dominican Republic was rooted also in the failure of the social and political forces that sustained them to become politically hegemonic. Authoritarian rulers, eager to justify their rule in a structural setting favorable for neopatrimonialism, employed a "cultural solution" that was available to them from the repertoire of ideas present in the country's past history. Rather than view Dominican evolution as a "destined pathway" from an era of Spanish colonial rule into a brutal experience of postindependence, one must examine the links between the colonial era and subsequent critical moments in Dominican development in a path-dependent fashion.[40] In doing so, it is also important to examine the confluence of domestic structural factors and international geopolitical ones. Indeed, one obvious critical difference between Costa Rica and the Dominican Republic is the absence of war and economic devastation in the former. Costa Rica was not marked by the same kind of geographic vulnerability; thus a modest economic prosperity built upon its relatively greater social and economic equality was able to emerge. And, unlike its northern Central American neighbors, which were wreaked by bitter civil conflict between liberals and conservatives emerging out of the colonial era, in Costa Rica (also in contrast to Chile) there was a greater degree of institutional continuity, dominated by aristocratic, civilian conservatives who avoided militarization.

The story of economic destitution, vulnerability, and war in the Dominican Republic was very different from Costa Rica's comparatively placid evolution (land inequalities and presidential usurpation of power and revolt, however, remained important in Costa Rica almost until 1949; see Lehoucq 1996). In the Dominican case, warfare helped generate a pattern of civil war, economic destitution, and regionalism, and it sponsored the lack of both effective national integration and an effective central state until a military caudillo could accumulate sufficient military and administrative power to impose a brutal order. Indeed, much more analogous is the experience of Venezuela. Venezuela was also an unimportant area during the colonial era, with weak traditional institutions such as the church; however, many wars were fought on what was to become Venezuelan soil, and military prowess and leadership became highly prized.[41]

In the Dominican case, there are additional geographic and ethnic factors whose relative importance are difficult to gauge. Concerns about national security and a willingness to trade sovereignty for protection were generated by the fact that the small country shared an island with Haiti—concerns which were heightened by racial, linguistic, and cultural issues. The territorial division of a small island and the manipulation of racial and ethnic fears intensified distrust and militarization.

If not an ineluctable consequence of its colonial history, then perhaps Dominican authoritarianism was an imposition by imperialist powers?[42] International vulnerability has different meanings, but the most significant loss is unquestionably that of national sovereignty. Of the Spanish colonies that gained their independence in the early to mid nineteenth century, the Dominican Republic is certainly at the extreme in the extent of its loss of sovereignty and its perceived vulnerability throughout the late eighteenth and nineteenth centuries.[43] In no way does it represent a defense of the actions of foreign powers or unscrupulous foreign speculators to emphasize that it is critical to understand the domestic consequences of this vulnerability. The historical narrative in chapter 2 has indicated that this vulnerability helped lead to an emphasis on leadership based on military might, to a willingness to seek out foreign protectors, and to the reality of renewed loss of national independence. At the turn of the century, the United States did seek dominance of the Caribbean and Central America due to a complex number of economically and security-oriented motives, dominance which it largely achieved and which unquestionably had a number of often negative and unforeseen consequences for these countries (for one brief but synthetic analysis, see Coatsworth 1994, 4–11). Thus, there is an intimate link between international vulnerability and the country's authoritarian history; however, this does not constitute an automatic relation. It is not possible to blame occupation by foreign forces, alone, for the lack of subsequent Dominican democracy: neither U.S. intervention in the country's economic affairs, its 1916–24 military occupation, nor the nineteenth-century Haitian or Spanish occupations truncated what would otherwise have been a democratic evolution.[44]

In this context, perhaps the most important turning point for the country came over the period of 1916–30. As in Nicaragua and neighboring Haiti, the consequences of the U.S. military occupation were the creation and strengthening of a national military institution and the enhancing of the value of the state, where other sources of power and wealth were still few. With the shift in U.S. foreign policy toward nonintervention, these outcomes facilitated the rise to power of Trujillo, who had a profound effect on Dominican institutions and psyches. Under Trujillo, a central state was built and national integration was achieved, but under a perverted discretional neopatrimonial rule that inhibited the development of independent political or social organizations or institutions.

This discussion regarding relevant factors leading toward neopatrimonialism or neosultanism in a number of different Latin American countries is summarized in table 2.2. Although some of the categorizations necessarily include an element of arbitrariness, the overall trends are clear. The strongest,

Table 2.2. Paths toward Neopatrimonialism

Country Cases	Cuba	Dominican Republic	Haiti	Nica-ragua	Costa Rica	Chile	Colom-bia	Vene-zuela
Factor								
A. Spanish colonial backwater: weak "patrimonial culture"	no	yes	yes	yes	yes	int.	no	int.
B. Overall initial poverty and weak economic elites	no	yes	yes	yes	yes	no	no	yes
C. Major wars and economic devastation	yes	yes	yes	yes	no	no	yes	yes
D. U.S. occupation, helping to establish strong military institution in absence of other organized actors in society or polity	int.	yes	yes	yes	no	no	no	no
E. Political outcome through mid-twentieth century: strongly neopatrimonial or neosultanistic?	int.	yes	yes	yes	no	no	no	yes

Note: int. = intermediate.

clearest path to neosultanism in Latin America has been a combination of three factors, (B), (C), and (D) in the table: initial poverty and weak, fragmented economic elites; exacerbated by major wars and economic devastation that exalt the role of military strongmen; and crystallized by a U.S. occupation that helps establish a strong military institution in the absence of other organized actors in society or the polity. No clear link can be drawn from a strong Spanish colonial tradition to this kind of rule. Costa Rica was quite similar to the Dominican Republic (and several other cases) in this respect, but with a contrasting outcome in the twentieth century because of important differences on the other essential variables. Another route to neopatrimonial rule has been simply the first two factors, (B) and (C), without the role of the United States in helping to centralize military authority, as witnessed by the cases of Gómez in Venezuela or, in the late nineteenth century, of Heureaux in the Dominican Republic.[45]

The Trujillo regime is a very close approximation to the ideal-type of neo-sultanism presented in chapter 1. It was based on personal rulership, with loyalty based on a mixture of fear and rewards. Trujillo exercised power without restraint within his small, island republic, at his own discretion, unencumbered by ideology or bureaucratic norms. During his reign, as Trujillo accumulated fabulous wealth and power, the country experienced large-scale, but centralized and controlled corruption; arbitrary and capricious decisions, combined with scrupulous attention to legal forms; and ruthless violence.

Similar to what Chehabi and Linz (1998) indicate in their discussion of the ideal-type, the Trujillo regime also differed from more classic authoritarianism by the absence of even "semi-oppositions," though sporadically "pseudo-oppositions" were permitted.[46] Only toward the end, though, did repression become more informal and privatized, including the establishment of private armies. And, over the three decades of Trujillo's rule, the regime became substantially more bureaucratized and institutionalized. Compared to other Latin American regimes that approximated neosultanism (such as the Duvaliers in Haiti, the Somozas in Nicaragua, or Noriega in Panama), Trujillo's rule may have been the one with the most totalitarian tendencies in terms of its use of technology to seek to control all aspects of the lives of Dominicans, including their private lives, and in terms of control over communications, transportation, education, and intellectual and cultural life. Except for the church, which was abjectly supportive of the regime (in what appeared to be a mutually beneficial arrangement) until almost the very end, there were no independent organizations or associations in the country. Although the regime did not have as clearly defined an ideology as the ideal-type of totalitarianism, Trujillo's regime did employ ideological elements built around anti-Haitianism and economic nationalism to legitimize itself and to fashion certain policies. It more clearly differed from the ideal-type of totalitarianism in that Trujillo fused his private and public roles, having no clear commitment to any impersonal purposes, and in that not all rural areas of the country were penetrated by the regime.

In some respects, the Trujillo regime was a culmination of past historical patterns, upon which it built. Yet, it also made its profound mark on the Dominican Republic. In spite of Trujillo's brutality, venality, and perversion of civic and democratic values, his apparent commitment to order, "strong" government, state building, national integration, and economic nationalism helped to generate a degree of public acceptance among the most vulnerable elements of the population that lived under him. Indeed, in an opinion poll taken in the early 1980s, a surprising 25 percent of those surveyed said they believed that the thirty-one-year Trujillo regime had been a "good government," though this favorable opinion tended to be concentrated among older, less educated, and more rural strata of the population (Vega 1990a, 157–58). However, regimes such as that of Trujillo are incapable of legitimizing and institutionalizing themselves for the long term due to their very nature.

In the next chapter we turn to an analysis of why transitions to democracy from neosultanistic regimes such as those of Trujillo are extraordinarily difficult. The chapter examines the assassination of Trujillo, the immediate aftermath of the end of his regime, and considerations of the lingering effects of his rule.

3 Democratic Struggles and Failures, 1961–1966

Trujillo's assassination in 1961 initiated an important period of struggle for democratic politics in the Dominican Republic. However, transitions to democracy from neosultanistic regimes are especially problematic, as the comparative literature on democratic transitions argues and an examination of the events following Trujillo's death confirms. At the same time, democracy in the Dominican Republic advanced further at this time than might have been expected, in part due to the initially supportive but ultimately counterproductive role of the United States. By one count, there were fourteen different governments in the country from 1961 to 1966, though six of them lasted sixteen days or less and two of them overlapped for four months under foreign military intervention in 1965 (Ventura 1985). In that sense, this period was analogous to the one that followed Heureaux's assassination in 1899.[1] The early 1960s were marked by intensive U.S. involvement in the Dominican Republic's internal affairs and by a surprisingly free and fair democratic election in 1962. However, seven months after his inauguration, the winner of those elections, Juan Bosch, was overthrown by a military coup. A civil-military conspiracy attempting to bring him back to power in April 1965 led to a military intervention by the United States out of an exaggerated fear of a "second Cuba." This eventually led to elections in 1966, which ushered in a period of relative stability, though not of democracy. It would not be until 1978 that one could speak of a democratic transition that lasted for more than a few months.

This chapter is organized in three sections. In the first, a framework of analysis built around three clusters of factors is presented. As already indicated, there are reasons to believe that the nature of the preexisting authoritarian regime is important in explaining the likelihood and the nature of a transition. Similarly, especially in small, vulnerable countries, international factors are likely to play an important role in explaining the transition process. Finally, the importance of the mode of transition and the overall transition process is considered. The next two sections then examine the "failed transitions" of 1961–62 and of 1965–66, ending with tables that summarize the discussion in terms of these key factors. The transitions of 1978 and 1996 are analyzed in chapters 4 and 9, respectively, in terms of these same three clusters of factors.[2]

Framework for Analysis

Based on the comparative literature on democratic transitions, the likelihood of success or failure of transitions to democratic rule can be examined as a consequence of three interrelated clusters of factors. These are the nature of the preexisting authoritarian regime and its relations to key actors; the international geopolitical and economic context; and the transition process, which includes the interaction of the mode of transition with the continuing influence of the previous two sets of factors.

Preexisting Authoritarian Regime, Society, and Political Opposition

There are many reasons to believe that the nature of the authoritarian regime prior to a transition process will profoundly affect the character and outcome of the process.[3] Thus, transitions to democracy from extreme kinds of neopatrimonial regimes—neosultanistic regimes—are more fraught with difficulty than transitions from other kinds of authoritarian regimes. This is not only because these regimes are commonly found in countries with an absence or weakness of past democratic experiences, but more specifically because of the nature itself of this kind of rule.

The risks of transition from neosultanistic regimes arise from the regime's respective relationships to the military, societal forces, and the political opposition. First, in neosultanistic regimes, because of the tyrant's absolute control and terror, it is difficult for forces within the military to gain autonomy and for regime moderates to emerge and to act openly; the military in these regimes is often viewed as the personal instrument of the particular ruler, rather than as a national institution, and thus its fate may be perceived as inextricably linked to his. A military institution that is somewhat more autonomous may well facilitate a transition, as it can break with a tyrant unwilling to carry out a transition.

Second, independent organizations within civil society are typically not countenanced by neosultanistic regimes. One possible source of tension that can facilitate a transition from such a regime revolves around the extent of monopolization of the economy by the tyrant and his cronies and the extent of rivalry with other economic actors. However, the weaker societal organizations are, the more difficult it is for political oppositions to find allies in society and to build viable alternatives. It also means that constructing democracy following the transition is even more complex, for new associations and organizations emerge, organize, and interact with little prior experience with democratic politics.

Finally, neosultanistic regimes attempt to repress all political opposition—moderate as well as revolutionary. Not even semi-oppositions are countenanced, though pseudo-oppositions may be permitted for tactical reasons such as international image. A critical factor is obviously the nature and relative strength of both moderate and revolutionary oppositions and the ability of democratic oppositions to represent and channel popular demands, while also forging necessary compromises. In general, the likelihood of democratic transitions should be enhanced when moderate oppositions committed to political democracy are stronger and revolutionary oppositions seeking more radical socioeconomic change are weaker.

This overall description of relations between neosultanistic rulers and the military, societal forces, and political oppositions does not imply there cannot be variations within neosultanistic regimes over time or across such regimes regarding the extent of their domestic control. As already noted for Trujillo in chapter 2, a neosultanistic leader's ties to these groups can change over time, with important implications for the possibilities of regime continuity, its revolutionary overthrow, its shift to an authoritarian if not neosultanistic regime, and its democratic transition or instability.

Assuming a nonrevolutionary transfer of power, three critical issues emerging from the previous authoritarian period are (1) the extent to which a significant sector of private economic power, independent of the previous ruler, exists and whether conflict or cooperation between these economic actors and those more closely linked to the previous ruler emerges; (2) whether any preexisting political parties are capable of reemerging, or whether these were effectively destroyed by the despot, requiring the emergence of a totally new set of parties and political actors; and (3) the ability of new state leaders to purge the military or otherwise gain control of it.

International Geopolitical and Economic Context

Especially in Central America and the Caribbean, the United States has played a hegemonic role since the turn of the century. This does not mean that it has been able to determine all political outcomes in the region, or that its goals and interests have been consistently the same. These have tended to vary, depending upon the interplay of perceived national security interests, private commercial influence, and the "democratic" impulse of a given administration and upon the willingness and desire of the United States to intervene at all. As a consequence, the extent and nature of U.S. involvement in the internal affairs of the countries in this area have varied significantly; nowhere is this more evident, in fact, than in the fluctuating attitude of the United States toward neosultanistic leaders. Thus, two key issues emerge—not only the extent to which the United States intervenes in the internal affairs of the other country, but the nature of that intervention based on whether there are other goals that may be more important to the United States and perhaps potentially in conflict with the goal of fostering democracy.

At the same time, these are small, vulnerable, open economies, and trends in international prices, openness of major export markets, and the impact of investment or financial decisions by transnational corporations or international financial institutions may be considerable. By themselves, these may not fully determine the failure or success of a democratic outcome, but they certainly can play an important contributory role.

The Mode of Transition and the Transition Process

One central argument that has emerged in the extensive literature on democratic transitions is that nonrevolutionary, elite-led "transitions from above" have tended to be more successful in generating stable political democracies than have "transitions from below," in which mass actors played a more central defining role (such as in Guatemala in 1946, Bolivia in 1952, Cuba in 1959, and Nicaragua in 1979) (see O'Donnell and Schmitter 1986; Stepan 1986; Karl 1990; Karl and Schmitter 1991; for additional citations, a review, and an analysis, see Hartlyn, 1998a). Transitions away from authoritarianism from below, with extensive, unorganized mass mobilization or considerable political violence, have either led in Latin America to authoritarian revolutionary regimes or to authoritarian reversals of radical democratic regimes. At the same time, in this book, transitions from above are also understood to have a crucial role for the popular sectors, through actual or potential independent mobilization, and through strong, visible mass support for moderate opposition leaders, which raises the costs of repression for authoritarian leaders, encouraging them to negotiate.[4]

Two distinct types of transitions from above may be identified (O'Donnell and Schmitter 1986). One is characterized by extensive negotiations and "pacts" between elements of the outgoing regime and the incoming democratic opposition (often supplemented by pacts within the democratic opposition and sometimes with agreements on socioeconomic policy); another is characterized by a more dramatic collapse of the outgoing authoritarian regime. Because of the extensive web of guarantees it confers upon powerful actors, the former kind may well encourage stability, but inhibit further democratization, particularly in the social and economic realms. The latter, on the other hand, may increase the short-term risk of authoritarian reversal, but enhance the probability of more extensive democratization. In both cases, however, one typically has a clear transfer of power from the authoritarian dictator to a democratically elected leader.

Yet, transitions from neosultanistic regimes may have elements of either transition from above "by collapse" or from below, while typically having a somewhat different dynamic that results from the need to have a provisional government (see Linz and Stepan 1996, esp. 44–45, 51–65; O'Donnell 1989, 73–74). Given the nature of these despotic regimes, if the dictator does not die of natural causes, he is typically removed by assassination or conspiracy within the armed forces (which could lead to a transition "by collapse"), by violent protest from civil society or revolutionary struggle (originating a transition from below), or by some combination of these. Depending upon how the dictator is removed, it may be possible for family members or other close associates to retain power, in which case a transition is unlikely. In the case of an armed revolt or revolution, it is likely that those who eliminated or overthrew the dictator will assume power themselves in a nondemocratic fashion, often in the form of an interim or provisional government. An immediate transition from neosultanism to a democratically elected government is almost impossible because the leader would never countenance democratic elections during his rule and because of the absence of other moderate, somewhat autonomous forces within the regime willing to negotiate such a move, combined with the absence of independent societal organizations and political institutions and parties within the country. These latter forces can only emerge following the fall of the dictator, usually in the context of a provisional government of some sort. However, even if a provisional government is formed that promises democratic elections, ultimately these may be postponed or manipulated. Another complicating issue is commonly a legacy from the previous dictatorial period of conspiratorial, manipulative politics and an absence of trust.

As this discussion indicates, there are inextricable links between the nature of the previous regime and the mode of transition. For this and other reasons, there is a potential risk of placing an undue importance on mode of transition as the single most important factor explaining subsequent democratization. The importance of the mode of transition may be exaggerated, reifying it as a critical juncture in a country's history when in fact it may not be.[5] The institutional rigidities and constraints that are the true legacy of transition periods may be miscast; a misplaced emphasis may result in overlooking the nature of "missed opportunities" that a transition represented, or in missing critical elements with lasting consequences engendered by the transition.

The transition process needs to be conceptually disentangled into three elements, which are present in an unequal mix in different cases. These are (1) the nature of the authoritarian regime, existing social and political forces, the international context and other structural, institutional, and cultural factors that helped determine the transition mode itself, some of which (themselves in a process of change) continue to have an influence on subsequent outcomes; (2) new institutional arrangements generated by the transition itself; and (3) opportunities or potentials opened up by the transition.[6] Much of the literature on transitions has collapsed the first two into one category—downplaying the continuing posttransition impact of many of the factors included in the first and highlighting the second as the "mode" or, for many Latin American cases, the constraining political, military and socioeconomic pacts —while ignoring the third. Yet, the continuing effects of factors from the first set of elements listed in the paragraph above may mean that the ultimate outcome of a transition process depends as much or more on them than on the mode of transition.[7] Various social, political, and international factors that have a distinct impact on the institutional forms of the transition may continue to have an important evolving posttransition impact. Continuing factors of change (e.g., an economic crisis or long-term foreign intervention) may have a profound effect on the possibilities for constructing legitimate government and may overwhelm choices regarding a set of institutions or policy choices made during a transition period that might have otherwise survived. However, just as important as economic legacies and continuing economic problems, if not more so, may be the evolving nature of the parties and the party system, if any has been inherited from the country's past, shaped by the most recent authoritarian experience.

While transitions are moments of institutional and sometimes constitutional change, institutional patterns are not necessarily fixed by the transition mode, both because they may be overwhelmed by inherited or new problems and because some kinds of transitions, particularly nonpacted ones, are open-ended in some of their political and institutional implications. Transitions, even pacted ones, embody not only constraints but also potential opportunities to generate long-lasting new patterns of democratic behavior; depending

Table 3.1. Transitions from Authoritarianism in
Vulnerable States: Critical Factors Favoring Transition

Preexisting authoritarian regime, society, and political opposition

- Greater autonomy from ruler by military, societal forces, and political opposition

- Tense economic relations between ruler and his cronies and other powerful economic actors, leading latter to favor moderate opposition

- Stronger democratic parties and political opposition not viewed as "threatening" by economic elites and weaker revolutionary opposition

International geopolitical and economic context

- High involvement of foreign power in the short term may be potentially beneficial for the promotion of democracy but over the long term may leave negative legacies of enmeshment in domestic affairs

- Democracy ranking highest in the hierarchy of policy goals of the foreign power (e.g., for the United States, such goals have included stability, anticommunism, protection of U.S. investments, and promotion of democracy)

- The effects of international economic constraints or opportunities, in trade, investment, finance, and aid (over the long term economic growth may undermine authoritarian rule, whereas over the short term, economic crisis does)

The transition process

- The nature of the mode of transition: assuming a nonrevolutionary transition, "from above" through pacts rather than through regime collapse; with mass violence playing a smaller rather than a larger role; if a provisional government, it represents a clear break with the previous regime and elections are neither manipulated nor excessively delayed

- New institutional realities, sometimes embodied in new constitutional texts, generated by the transition mode itself and influenced by the first two general sets of factors (which in a process of change continue to influence and to constrain subsequent outcomes): not continuously in question while fostering respect for democratic "rules of the game"

- Opportunities or potentials opened up by the transition to break with past patterns of antidemocratic behavior, taken advantage of especially by top party and government leaders upon the nature of political leadership and its interaction with other political and socioeconomic variables, these may or may not be realized.

Thus, it is risky to assume that pacts or decisions made at the time of transition will endure and be the predominant influence on subsequent democratic evolution; of equal potential significance is the continuing legacy of institutional and party forms and the impact of changing domestic and international socioeconomic forces, particularly in periods of dramatic crisis such as the current one. The central aspects of transitions requiring scrutiny are the constitutional and institutional modifications that may have been introduced and the extent to which key actors respect and seek to change them. At the same time, one must remain alert to "missed opportunities" that moments of transition may have presented. Old patterns of doing politics may reassert themselves in particularly inimical ways in periods of crisis following the transition— which, the next chapter argues, occurred in the Dominican Republic.

A summary of the three-part framework that emerges from the discussion in this section is provided in table 3.1. With it in mind we can now turn to the transition from the Trujillo regime. It illustrates well the severe constraints imposed on the possibilities of successful democratic transition by the nature of his regime and other historical legacies, as well as the contradictory elements of U.S. intervention and the limits of its efficacy, especially in the immediate post–Cuban Revolution, Cold War atmosphere.

Failed Transition, I: From Assassination to Coup, 1961–1963

It is not difficult to discern why a transition to democracy from the Trujillo dictatorship was highly problematic. Trujillo's domination of the island republic was extensive: the military were his personal instrument, no independent societal organizations existed, and no political opposition was countenanced. Ultimately, economic deterioration, exile activism, and the dramatic shift in the U.S. attitude toward Trujillo emboldened domestic opposition and conspirators.

A transition to democracy from neosultanistic or other neopatrimonial dictatorships would appear most likely when the armed forces were somewhat autonomous from the despot, eventually being purged or otherwise controlled by the new democratic leaders, and when there was a strong moderate (but weak revolutionary) opposition, based both on independent societal economic actors and preexisting democratic parties. Given the weakness of all domestic actors in the Dominican Republic and the extent of Trujillo's control over the military, none of these conditions were present, except for the absence of a strong revolutionary opposition. Some requisites began to emerge toward the end of the Trujillo era; however, following Trujillo's assassination, only the overwhelming presence of the United States helped insure an end to the Trujillo era, permitting the armed forces to break with the Trujillo family and oppositions to emerge openly. Considerable instability and uncertainty followed Trujillo's assassination in May 1961, as various family members and close regime associates sought to retain power. With considerable pressure from the United States, it took some eight months following Trujillo's assassination to establish a provisional government that represented a clear "collapse" of the Trujillo regime.[8] That government, dominated by anti-Trujillista, but conservative and economically wealthy forces, called for elections that they expected to win easily. To their surprise, those elections were won by Juan Bosch, recently returned from exile. He campaigned successfully on the basis that the cleavage in the country was not between Trujillistas and anti-Trujillistas, but between rich and poor.

Structural conditions as well as short-term socioeconomic factors were also inimical for a democratic evolution. The country remained relatively poor, rural, and isolated. Under Trujillo's rule, alongside economic growth and limited modernization, there had also been a pattern of concentration of land and of income. The period surrounding his assassination was also one of serious economic stagnation. Yet, because Trujillo's massive holdings were turned over to the Dominican state, there was an opportunity for redistribution of land and other assets.

Given the weakness of revolutionary opposition, class-based political violence did not preordain the failure of democracy at this time. The mode of transition "from above," albeit by collapse, was relatively controlled and peaceful, with important elements of mass mobilization. The overwhelming U.S. presence and the conviction of the members of the anti-Trujillo provisional government that they would easily win, led them to schedule and eventually to hold elections. However, there was considerable class-based anxiety among dominant economic interests, which ultimately grew as it combined with church fears and military opposition, mobilized in the context of heightened ideological misgivings generated by the Cuban Revolution and fed directly by the presence of Cuban exiles on the island.

Although it did not last, democracy advanced further in the country at this time due to the role of international factors than one would have expected based on the country's past history and the legacies of the Trujillo era. The risks of Trujillo *continuismo* or of a provisional government "hijacking" democracy were both avoided, as truly democratic elections were held. However, from the perspective of powerful socioeconomic actors, elements of the military, the church, and the U.S. government, the "wrong" candidate won the elections and by a wide margin; Bosch was an intransigent reformist and a noncommunist. Perhaps if Bosch had been a pragmatic anticommunist, these conservative forces would have tolerated him. What is clear is that this democratic transition failed; a military coup overthrew the Bosch government only seven months after it took office. Domestic political and social forces coalesced against Bosch, and ambivalent U.S. actions were increasingly motivated more by Cold War fears than by a concern for fostering democracy.

Tracing the shifts in loyalty of prominent individuals, though, indicates that for many of the political and political-military actors, a central issue was more one of power, of "ins" versus "outs," than of ideology. The Trujillo era enhanced this tendency in Dominican politics because it tremendously increased the stakes at the center with regard to control of the state, without producing institutions that could help to mediate conflicts and facilitate compromise. Under Trujillo, the country achieved greater integration as a nation-state, as well as more effective centralized control and policymaking. When Trujillo's property was expropriated, control of the central state apparatus became even more important for politicians, for new industrialists dependent on continued state subsidies of different sorts, and for others seeking state contracts, spoils, or jobs.

The Death of the Despot and International Geopolitics

A negotiated exit from Trujillo was impossible because of his intransigence, leading to the multiplication of efforts to be rid of him through other means. By the late 1950s, Trujillo was facing challenges from all sides: growing domestic opposition, exile activism, and international pressure from Latin American governments—particularly from Venezuela with the return to power of Rómulo Betancourt. The country's economy was suffering, and an aging Trujillo's own mental acuity was declining. Trujillo came to rely increasingly on a set of advisers that were strongly anti-American and were more willing to use violence, including his son Ramfis, who was especially bitter after the U.S. military flunked him out of the Army War College at Fort Leavenworth. The advisers took steps—such as the killing by means of a staged auto accident of the anti-Trujillista middle-class Mirabal sisters in November 1960—that further alienated upper- and middle-class elements (see the remarkable historical novel, Alvarez 1994). Fearing invasions by exile armies and domestic unrest, Trujillo dramatically expanded the size of the armed forces, sponsoring the creation of a number of paramilitary groups and private armies by close associates.[9]

However, a critical factor—if not the central one—in explaining Trujillo's fall was the shift in attitude of the United States. Just a few years could make a tremendous difference, as the contrasting fates of the Somozas and the Trujillos demonstrates. In September 1956, when the Nicaraguan president Anastasio Somoza was gunned down by an assassin, a surprised President Eisenhower instructed that a helicopter take him to a hospital in the Panama Canal Zone, where he eventually died, and the United States saw the transfer of power within the Somoza family with equanimity. In May 1961, however, when Trujillo was assassinated, the CIA was intimately involved in the plots leading up to his death, and the United States interfered extensively to insure that Trujillo's family would not retain control of power. The change in attitude of the United States can be explained principally by one fact: the Cuban Revolution.[10]

The Cuban Revolution led the United States to shift to a far more interventionist policy in the region. In the Dominican Republic from 1959 to 1961, the "United States engaged in its most massive intervention in the internal affairs of a Latin American state since the inauguration of the Good Neighbor Policy" (Slater 1970, 7). This extensive involvement continued even following the death of Trujillo, culminating with the 1965 intervention and its aftermath. A summary of U.S. policy intentions during this period is provided in President John Kennedy's dictum that, in descending order of preferences, the United States would prefer a democratic regime, a continuation of a Trujillo regime, or a Castro regime, and that the United States should aim for the first, but not renounce the second until it was sure the third could be avoided.

Domestic opposition, exile activities, and international pressure all expanded together. The country's political crisis gradually sharpened after June 1959, when a failed invasion attempt from Cuba took place. A major underground movement emerged soon thereafter that was brutally crushed in January 1960; children of the wealthy were among the victims of this repression, pushing more of the economic elite into the active opposition. For the first time, the Catholic Church expressed its disapproval. International pressure built inexorably. In June 1960, the OAS's Inter-American Peace Committee condemned the Dominican Republic for human rights violations, which constituted the first time the OAS had attacked the internal policies of a noncommunist American state. That same month, Trujillo was linked to a failed assassination attempt on Venezuelan president Betancourt, leading to the imposition of sanctions against his regime by the OAS in August.[11] Trujillo attempted again (as in the 1945–47 period) a controlled "liberalization" for external consumption, but the United States and other international actors were now openly skeptical. Prior to the OAS meeting, Trujillo resigned as

Rafael Trujillo (left) and Joaquín Balaguer toasting together on January 2, 1961.
Trujillo was assassinated five months later.

head of the PD, and in August his brother resigned from the presidency, to be replaced by the vice president, Joaquín Balaguer. Free elections were promised and opposition parties were asked to organize; two token pseudo-opposition parties were created in December 1960. Out of desperation, Trujillo began to turn to the Soviet bloc. The Communist Party was legalized in June 1960, but emissaries seeking help from the Soviet Union met with no success. The Eisenhower administration increased the economic pressure on Trujillo by insuring the Dominican Republic would not continue to experience a bonanza due to the cancellation of Cuba's sugar quota in July 1960: the value of Dominican sugar exports to the United States went from US$12.2 million in 1959 to US$41.4 million in 1960, and then down to US$31.5 million in 1961 before jumping to US$88.7 million in 1962 (Oficina Nacional de Planificación 1968, 207). Toward the end of the year, under the urging of both the United States and Venezuela, OAS economic sanctions were extended to include prohibitions on members' exports of petroleum, trucks, and spare parts to Trujillo's regime.[12]

The country's growing political crisis, international isolation, and Trujillo's response all helped induce a major economic crisis. As table 3.2 indicates, the country's economy declined dramatically over 1959–61, compared to the 1950–58 period: GDP stagnated, both public and private investment under-

Table 3.2. Selected Economic Indicators, 1950–1961

Indicator	1950–58	1959–61
Change in GDP (%)	6.5	0.3
Change in public investment (%)	10.7	−18.7
Change in private investment (%)	14.0	−32.0
Change in exports (%)	5.4	3.8
Change in imports (%)	9.8	−15.5

Source: Oficina Nacional de Planificación (1968, 17).
Note: Percentages were calculated from economic series based on 1962 constant prices.

went a sharp retrenchment, and imports declined sharply. Public investment declined in order to expand current spending, especially on the military, while balancing the budget; private investment, heavily concentrated, took its lead from the government. Massive capital flight by Trujillo and his close allies was financed by restricting imports, paralyzing investment, and drawing down international reserves. Trujillo's orthodox financial insistence on balancing the budget and sustaining a positive balance of trade are quite remarkable, although understandable in light of how government profligacy had fed past foreign interventions in the country. Unemployment almost certainly increased as public investment dried up and as merchants were restricted in the goods they could import for sale (see Oficina Nacional de Planificación 1968, 23–24).

In this context of political and economic crisis, conspirators who had largely been former supporters of the regime—at first vigorously and then ambivalently encouraged by the United States—assassinated Trujillo on May 30, 1961. This fact did not yet mark the end of the Trujillo era, for their plot was discovered before they could move against other major members of the Trujillo clan, and the one general who had collaborated with them faltered in his will.[13] Thus, it was not clear what kind of regime would replace Trujillo. Members of the Trujillo family sought to retain power; President Balaguer fought for an independent power base; multiple underground movements began to function more openly; and exile groups, including Juan Bosch's PRD, soon returned to the island. In the days after Trujillo's assassination, a U.S. Navy task force patrolled offshore, prepared to implement previously approved plans for armed intervention. Its purpose was to block any possible Cuban involvement and to prevent the success of any procommunist movement in the country (Lowenthal 1972, 11, 26).

Transition by Regime Collapse and Provisional Government

The break with the Trujillos came only months later, and the mechanism of a provisional government was required. Ultimately, given international pressure and domestic mobilization, this was a form of transition through regime collapse with some elements of popular mobilization. The complex details sketched below highlight three key issues: the inability of nonrevolutionary anti-Trujillo forces to "pact" or to compromise with each other (a failure explained by the lack of institutions and exacerbated by a legacy of conspiracy and intrigue, by a fragmented military whose support was assiduously sought by various political actors, and by a polarized atmosphere generated by the Cuban Revolution and the defense of economic privilege); the weakness of the revolutionary left, which in spite of its efforts and its own inflated sense of importance (which fed into U.S. paranoia) made few organizational inroads into the country;[14] and the ambivalent impact of the United States as it focused increasingly on preventing the emergence of a new "Castro regime."

Following Trujillo's assassination in May 1961, Balaguer clung to power in the face of international skepticism and growing internal opposition. OAS sanctions were retained on the grounds that the extent of change represented by the new Balaguer regime was uncertain. The United States added pressure by keeping its informal boycott of Dominican sugar, but other actions were ambivalent. Both President Balaguer and Trujillo's son Ramfis, commander of the armed forces, began to implement "democratization" measures, exiling some of the most visible symbols of repression and promising free elections for May 1962.[15] Yet, because it feared the breakdown of order could favor communist groups, the United States opted to work with Balaguer and the army while putting pressure on them to move the country toward liberalization. This controlled liberalization confronted growing domestic opposition, fueled by the return of political exiles, as well as opposition from Venezuela.

Gradually, the Balaguer government faced serious domestic opposition from three primary sources. One was the PRD returned from exile. Another, more immediately, was the Unión Cívica Nacional (UCN, National Civic Union), which was formed in July 1961 by prominent Dominican businessmen, most of whom had benefited under Trujillo, and which was to become a conservative, but anti-Trujillista movement. The UCN was led by Viriato Fiallo, an anti-Trujillista who had once been imprisoned by the regime. The third was the Agrupación Politica 14 de Junio (1J4, Political Group 14th of June), which took its name from the failed invasion from Cuba of June 14, 1959, and from the underground Movimiento Revolucionario 14 de Junio (MR1J4, Revolutionary Movement 14th of June) destroyed by Trujillo in January 1960. The 1J4 would become a leftist, Fidelista party. In spite of differences, all three were united in their desire to rid the country completely of the Trujillos. Rumblings from within the armed forces were also heard; in July 1961, for example, an air force uprising against Ramfis Trujillo was put down (Gleijeses 1978, 38–40; Wiarda 1975, 1:291).

Events gradually drove the United States to adopt a more forceful policy. As part of the liberalization strategy, Balaguer was encouraged to incorporate the opposition groups into a coalition government, but they continued to resist Balaguer's overtures. Nevertheless, following the exit of Trujillo's hated brothers, the "Wicked Uncles," in late October, the United States called for a partial lifting of OAS sanctions against the country. Then Trujillo's son, Ramfis, still head of the armed forces, suddenly decided the pressures of office were too much and opted for a gilded exile.[16] At the same time, Ramfis urged his uncles, Trujillo's brothers, to return to the island, which they did on November 15, but the United States was determined not to allow them to return to power, fearing that the violence and instability that would be provoked would favor communism (which the United States perceived it had done in Cuba, and which Cuba was now prepared to help). Balaguer, opting to break with the Trujillos and side with the United States, dramatically refused to step aside. In the face of a threatened U.S. military intervention if they tried to reimpose themselves and of serious opposition from Balaguer and within the Dominican armed forces, Héctor and José Arismendi Trujillo and a number of their close collaborators fled into exile four days after they returned.

Thus, in mid-November the Trujillo period finally came to an end as the regime collapsed. The country celebrated, ripping down statues, destroying busts, and attacking other symbols of the dictatorship. Trujillo's political apparatus also disintegrated. The two token opposition parties Trujillo had organized in December 1960 officially disappeared in August 1961; and, on December 28, 1961, the PD was formally dissolved with the party property reverting to the state. Opposition groups argued that all of Trujillo's wealth should pass to the state (Lowenthal 1972, 11; Gleijeses 1978, 46–47; Slater 1967, 198–200; Wiarda 1975, 1016).

Opposition to Balaguer, Trujillo's presidential designee, continued to grow. In late November, the UCN organized an eleven-day general strike against the government (the first in the history of the country). With U.S. pressure on both sides, a compromise was forced, and for the first sixteen days of January Balaguer presided over an uneasy, coalition council of state, which constituted the provisional government. However, the putting down after two days of an attempted coup led by an emerging military strongman—air force general Pedro Rodríguez Echavarría, who had been a key figure in the break with the "Wicked Uncles" in mid-November—also forced Balaguer's exile. On January 18, 1962, a second council of state was formed by members of the UCN; this was the provisional government that organized the democratic elections held at the end of the year.

The Provisional Government and Democratic Elections

A number of risks to democratic transitions are presented by provisional governments. They may opt to postpone elections for an indefinite period, or they may hold elections (often quickly) that basically permit followers of the former dictator to win because they are the only organized force in the country. Neither of these occurred in the Dominican Republic, as the weak council of state depended heavily on U.S. support and expected to win the elections easily with Balaguer in exile and their self-image as anti-Trujillistas secure.

The extensive involvement of the United States and its commitment to the holding of elections was critical. In his remarkable memoir, the U.S. ambassador at the time explains in detail all the United States did to further the key "policy objectives" that were "to keep the provisional government in office, help it hold elections, and help get the winner into the Palace alive" (Martin 1966, 30).[17] From his perspective, the five major threats were as follows: coup plotting, particularly by some of the members of the council of state; the possible return of Balaguer from exile; "Castro/Communist agitation"; conflicts among the parties; and problems associated with the JCE and managing the administration of the elections (Martin 1966, 246). The U.S. government remained extensively involved in each of these areas.

The council of state was composed largely of individuals who represented business and professional interests who had chafed under Trujillo's dictatorial rule and his mocking of the traditional wealthy of the country. Two of them, Antonio Imbert Barrera and Luis Amiama Tió, the sole survivors of the conspirators who had killed Trujillo, now devoted much of their time to further conspiracy in an effort to seize power directly. Thus, although the members of the council of state had been uneasy collaborators of Trujillo, they certainly did not want to bring back the old regime. However, they also did not want to pursue radical reforms; essentially, they wanted to protect their wealth and status.[18] At the same time, because of the brave anti-Trujillo position many of the UCN had taken during the difficult May to November period, when the outcome of Trujillo's assassination was still unclear, they were convinced the UCN would win democratic elections for which the United States was pressuring (see Wiarda 1975, 382–85).

Initially, the UCN and the 1J4 worked together closely. They both perceived themselves as civic action movements opposed to the Trujillo dictatorship, though the latter was comprised more of students (though often of wealthy families) with vaguely radical and nationalist ideas. Over 1961, however, the 1J4 became more radical, attacking the U.S. presence and charging the UCN and the council of state with being reactionary forces. A hard core within the party was convinced a Cuban-style revolution was possible in the country, although it failed in its efforts to organize the infrastructure to carry out an armed revolt prior to the elections; increasingly marked by defections by those opposed to the radical line, the party ended up boycotting the December 1962 elections (Gleijeses 1978, 73–74).[19] At the same time, in part due to U.S. pressure, the UCN began purging its ranks, and those of associated labor and civic organizations, of radical leaders (Kurzman 1965, 66–67).

However, there was another political organization which rapidly emerged, eventually to eclipse the UCN. Founded as a party in opposition to Trujillo in Cuba in 1939 by Juan Bosch and other exile leaders, the PRD was to win the election because of its organization and its message. Bosch returned from exile in October, after having first sent a three-person delegation in July to investigate conditions in the country. His party soon recognized that the country remained overwhelmingly rural and that the party capturing the rural vote had the best chance of winning. The PRD initiated extensive organizational efforts throughout the country, and by March 1962 it could claim 300,000 registered members. It made a conscious effort to organize a peasant organization, the Federación Nacional de Hermandades Campesinas (FENHERCA, National Federation of Peasant Brotherhoods), which although ostensibly nonpartisan had close ties to the PRD.[20]

The PRD message was also far more effective than that of the UCN, and Bosch was a more effective speaker than Viriato Fiallo, the presidential candidate of the UCN. The PRD shifted the terms of debate from one about the struggle against Trujilloism—which favored the UCN—to one about the poor. Bosch was able to speak plainly to the rural population, promising to be attentive to their needs, to issues of jobs, food, and land. Bosch spoke of the UCN as the party of white people and of *tutumpotes*, the aristocratic wealthy (see Bosch 1965, 85–87, for a discussion of the term and how he employed it in the campaign).

There were a multitude of other parties and movements, as would be expected following the lifting of a ban on political activity.[21] Of these, the most important was the Partido Revolucionario Social Cristiano (PRSC, Revolutionary Social Christian Party), centered at the time on a surprisingly radical Christian ideology, although it suffered a split prior to the elections. Other small parties were led by figures who broke from the PRD and the UCN. In the province of San Juan, a local caudillo retained support. At one time, twenty-nine "parties" were participating in the campaign, and ultimately six candidates presented themselves for the presidency.

The campaign was disorganized and fraught with tension and widespread allegations of fraud. The council was governing on the basis of Trujillo's last constitution, as amended to establish the council in December 1961. It mandated elections for delegates to a constitutional convention on August 15 and presidential and congressional elections on December 20. Two months prior to the proposed August elections, however, preparations had not yet begun; after complicated machinations up to the last minute, the August elections were canceled and it was decided that the congress elected along with the president in December would also rewrite the constitution.[22]

Conspiracy and distrust marked the campaign and the election. Rumors of coup plots and of intended frauds abounded (for one list of coup plots and a useful analysis of some of the counterproductive consequences of efforts—largely shaped by the U.S. government—to enlarge the police force and re-orient the Dominican military, see Wiarda 1975, 298–310, esp. 308–9). In mid-October, as part of an effort to dismantle another potential coup by Imbert and Amiama, Ambassador Martin arranged for Bosch and Fiallo to meet and agree to a political pact to respect the results of the elections, offer assurances and cabinet seats to the losing party, and be a constructive "loyal opposition."[23] Bosch later wrote he agreed to the meeting and the pact because Betancourt urged him to do so (Bosch 1965, 104). Under the watchful eyes of the U.S. and Venezuelan ambassadors, the two candidates emended the text prepared by U.S. diplomats and agreed to it. Ultimately, it would have an impact, but a limited one. Following the election, Fiallo told Martin "bitterly" that Bosch had won due to fraud, yet he did ultimately acknowledge Bosch's victory publicly (Martin 1966, 225–29, 300).[24]

Even as attacks against Bosch mounted, especially false accusations that he was a communist, Bosch's own often-noted ambivalence toward power and his sense of fatalism were apparent in this campaign, as they were to be during his presidency and in subsequent campaigns. Twice he threatened to withdraw from the campaign. Once was over the question of whether the ballots would be printed on colored paper or not (which he sought, and achieved, since many of his supporters were not literate). The second time was with regard to accusations made by different elements of the church that he was a communist. Just three days before the elections, at the conclusion of a nationwide television debate with Father Lautico García, the key figure behind the charges, Bosch was asked if he intended to run, and he answered: "I do not wish to be a candidate because I know the PRD will win the elections, and if it does, the government I head will not be able to rule. It will be overthrown in a short time on the pretext that it is communist" (cited in Wells 1966a, 280). He ultimately did run, election day was relatively peaceful, and the election results provided him with a convincing victory.

From the perspective of democratic rule, the results were too one-sided, although democratic consolidation was probably unlikely in any event, particularly given Bosch's fatalism. Both the PRD and the UCN drew their support fairly evenly across rural and urban municipalities, as appendix A highlights. Bosch's organizational efforts and campaign themes in rural areas won the PRD significant support in the absence of a candidate from the Trujillo era. Bosch won a clear majority of 58.7 percent of the votes in the 1962 presidential election, with Fiallo receiving 30.1 percent (Wiarda 1975, 1050). At the congressional level, the PRD won in all but five provinces, gaining twenty-two of the twenty-seven senators and forty-nine of the seventy-four deputies (chosen by closed list proportional representation); the UCN won in only four provinces, thus electing four senators, and twenty deputies. A small caudillo-based party swept San Juan province, electing a senator and four deputies.[25] Nevertheless, the Dominican Republic had carried out a democratic election and a democratic transition was underway.

Bosch's Overthrow and the Breakdown of Democracy

The issue of who was "more to blame" for Bosch's overthrow in September 1963, only seven months after being inaugurated, is still heavily disputed. What is unquestionable is that an important historical opportunity was lost.

Democracy was almost starting from scratch in the country. There was no experience with democratic politics, either by interest groups or political parties, both of which were inchoate. Indeed, most actors were accustomed to a struggle for power through conspiracy and the threat and ultimately the use of violence, and many continued in that guise, though they also employed the new freedoms of expression to seek to polarize opinions. As the above narrative underscores, in the context of key domestic factors highlighted in table 3.1 relating to the preexisting authoritarian regime and the mode of transition, successful democratic elections were, if anything, unlikely (or structurally under-determined) in 1962.

The country had attained democratic elections to a large extent due to the extensive involvement of the United States. However, it is far more difficult for a foreign power to sustain democracy in another country than to insure that elections are held. The U.S. government anxiously wanted a democratically elected government in the country to succeed, especially in the context of the recently launched Alliance for Progress, but its deep fear of a second Cuba meant that other goals were subordinated to that of insuring that "Castro-Communist" subversion would not succeed. Complex plots revolving around efforts by Haitian exiles to oust Duvalier in neighboring Haiti and U.S. fears that Castro-Communism could emerge victorious on that part of the island further complicated the picture. The ability of domestic groups opposed to Bosch to exploit U.S. fear of communism was clear; indeed, some elements of business, the church, and eventually the military possessed a genuine paranoia that could be cultivated and expanded upon (polarization that was fed in part by an influx of Cuban refugees). The United States could have done more to sustain Bosch—and in some ways may have undermined him—but the United States did not actively promote his overthrow in 1963.

A focus on societal forces, political opposition, and the military and on the regime's relations to them is useful in distinguishing this experience from subsequent ones. The country inherited certain economic, political, and military patterns from the Trujillo era, all of them inimical to democracy. Ultimately, what lay behind Bosch's overthrow was the lack of democratic commitment and the tremendous insecurity of the country's economic elites and their political leaders in the UCN following their defeat at the polls. Their fears were exacerbated by the heightened importance of controlling the central state apparatus, as a consequence of changes in the economy realized under Trujillo and of the expropriations of a number of his holdings. This was particularly the case of many of the newly emergent industrialists and merchants, who had collaborated economically with him, centered in Santo Domingo; a clear line between Trujillo's "expropriable" investments and their private investments could not always be drawn, and thus their economic bases were not fully secure (see Moya Pons 1991). Furthermore, the notion that, after humiliation at the hands of a Trujillo, they might have to confront democratic power sharing and redistributionist reforms, however modest, was probably difficult for many to countenance. Domestic opposition to Bosch only intensified following the elections, especially among the business groups that dominated the UCN and among extremist elements of the church. Bosch was initially conciliatory, but then increasingly intransigent. The opposition of church and business elements deepened following enactment of the new constitution, with its more secular tone and more expansive view of civil rights and state expropriation of private property. In fact, though, many had begun working for Bosch's overthrow from the moment he was inaugurated.

Exacerbating this issue was the absence of any effective tradition of political opposition. It is important to underscore that regardless of the results of the elections, democratic consolidation would have been extraordinarily difficult. The fact that the electoral outcome gave Bosch and the PRD an outright majority determined only the particular nature of the conflicts that were generated. If Juan Bosch and the PRD had not attained an absolute majority, immobilism and deadlock between the presidency and the congress and charges of unconstitutional behavior as the president sought to circumvent the legislature, combined with accusations of communism, might well have been the means to mobilize opinion for a coup within society and the military. Instead, the opposition forces arrayed against Bosch were able to mobilize opposition on the basis of fears of the consequences of his overwhelming victory.[26] At the same time, Bosch's relations with his own party cadres and other party leaders became increasingly strained as he sought to limit the influx of party sympathizers into government jobs and to maintain his own influence; indeed, by the time of his overthrow, his party was itself divided and considerably weaker than it had been at the time of the election. Although the Dominican radical left was small and divided, parts of it, inspired by the Cuban example, were committed to armed guerrilla struggle, further helping to polarize the existing situation in the country (for a useful analysis of the different radical movements, actual size, internal divisions, intended and actual policies, and relations with Cuba, see Gleijeses 1978, 99–103).

The military's commitment to democratization was also problematic. Bosch did not control the military and treated them carefully. He maintained their budget even as he increased budget outlays for the police, with active U.S. support (see table 3.3). Although in the December elections the armed forces largely supported Bosch over Fiallo, because of the latter's anti-Trujillismo, the military was both factionalized and filled with officers who had their own political ambitions—their model officer, after all, had been Trujillo. Following Trujillo's demise, it was more accurate to see politics in the country "as a constant struggle among changing alliances of civilian and military cliques, not in terms of confrontation between civilian authority and the military establishment" (Lowenthal 1969b, 40).

Finally, there is the issue of political leadership and the figure of Juan Bosch himself. Bosch governed honestly and democratically, but he did not act pragmatically in the face of the hostile opposition he confronted; his mass following also experienced the predictable *desencanto* that follows any democratic transition and the subsequent inability to carry out reforms promised during the campaign. For several observers, Bosch could have done far more to attempt to prevent his overthrow by addressing some of the fears of his opponents (e.g., see Martin 1966 and Lowenthal 1972).

Table 3.3. Government and Security Expenditures, 1955–1964

Year	Total Expenditures	Total Security	Police and Justice	Armed Forces
Trujillo and Balaguer				
1955	$129.0	$29.2	4.3%	18.3%
1958	$164.9	$48.2	8.3%	20.9%
1959	$155.7	$56.0	9.6%	26.4%
1960	$143.7	$44.1	7.4%	23.3%
1961	$137.2	$40.6	6.6%	23.0%
Council of State				
1962	$210.0	$46.3	5.6%	16.5%
Bosch				
1963	$215.9	$56.3	9.6%	16.5%
Triumvirate				
1964	$243.0	$66.2	10.7%	16.5%

Source: Oficina Nacional de Planificación (1968, 445, 459, 480).
Note: Expenditures in current DR$ millions. Total expenditures include central government, municipalities, and social security institute. Total security expenditures include police and justice and armed forces. Percentages reported for police and justice and for armed forces are based on total government expenditures.

Polarizing conflicts emerged even before Bosch was inaugurated. A major one revolved around the proposed draft of the constitution, which led to heightened tensions particularly with elements of the business sector and the church. Most importantly, industrialists who had prospered under Trujillo formed the Asociación de Industriales de la República Dominicana (AIRD, Association of Industrialists of the Dominican Republic) in February 1962 to seek to further their interests and preserve state protection for industrial production. The association was one of the harshest critics of Bosch's constitution. In conjunction with three other business associations, it took out large newspaper ads warning of the "gravity of the danger if the proposed text were adopted" (Wiarda 1975, 399; see also Moya Pons 1991). They charged that the constitution limited the traditional rights of the church, opened the door for potential expropriations, and threatened foreign investment, all of which it did in a much more timid fashion than their extremist rhetoric suggested. The new constitution, in fact, was promulgated in May with only minor modifications. In many ways, it was a model democratic constitution.

In addition to the constitutional text, other issues frightened the insecure industrial and landowning elites. A proposed law that permitted confiscation of enterprises gained by poorly defined "illicit enrichment" was perceived as allowing the administration to expropriate almost any enterprise it desired, given the realities of past collaborations with Trujillo. The law was also viewed as restraining the ability of landowners to fight to regain state lands that Trujillo had originally taken from them, lands that Bosch wished to redistribute to peasant families (Wiarda 1975, 405–6). In other historical periods, Bosch's measures and rhetoric may not have inflamed fears to the extent they did; but in this immediate post-Trujillo and post-Castro era, industrial and landowning elites were sensing both opportunities to recoup or consolidate gains and increased risks of revolution.

Not all members of the upper class agitated against the Bosch government. Indeed, a large number of Dominican professionals, many of whom had been linked to the UCN in the campaign, publicly stated their opposition to a coup (Lowenthal 1972, 35). Other figures from socially prominent families—many of which were located in Santiago and were, in fact, less wealthy than some of the emerging new rich—also did not actively oppose Bosch, though they did not participate in his government either. Their very real influence, however, was based "not [on] economic or political power but social prestige" (Lowenthal 1969b, 38), in contrast to the emerging Santo Domingo economic elites who did assiduously seek Bosch's overthrow.

The pro-coup coalition in society began to develop a more conscious strategy. Right-wing industrialists flocked to a political group, the Acción Dominicana Independiente (ADI, Independent Dominican Action), and to the newly created, umbrella Consejo Nacional de Hombres de Empresa (CNHE, National Council of Businessmen).[27] They also collaborated with dissident church elements upset by the secular tone of Bosch's government and constitutional text, and beginning in August they helped to mobilize peasant "rallies of Christian reaffirmation." The UCN soon helped create a coalition with five other parties in open opposition to Bosch, and in close cooperation with the ADI.[28]

Ultimately, however, such an overthrow required participation from elements of the armed forces. Relations between Bosch and the military became tense over certain issues specifically related to the military. Bosch attempted to limit corruption and graft within the military. There were also confusing issues regarding relations with Haiti; in April 1963, Bosch reacted to the oc-

President Juan Bosch giving a speech in September 1963, shortly before being overthrown and forced into exile.

cupation of the Dominican consulate in Port-au-Prince by threatening war and sending the Dominican military to the border, an action they viewed as unnecessarily risking their lives and institution.[29]

Moreover, Bosch's civilian opponents also assiduously sought military support. The charges that Bosch was potentially or actually a communist, made by the Dominican opposition and cleverly magnified abroad, had a major impact on the Dominican military, keenly aware of the fate of Batista's army in neighboring Cuba. In this context, Bosch refused to impose limits on communists, limits urged on him by the U.S. ambassador and by exile friends of his such as Figueres of Costa Rica, Betancourt of Venezuela, and Prío Socarrás of Cuba (Guerrero 1993, 79–80; Wiarda 1975, 319; Martin 1966). Radically anticommunist and anti-Bosch priests "educated" the Dominican military on the dangers of communism. At a minimum, U.S. military attachés expressed their anticommunist and anti-Bosch attitudes.[30] In July 1963 a major crisis was averted when two high-ranking military officers who had called for Bosch's overthrow were forced to resign, but new conspiracies continued.

Even as the strength of the coup coalition grew, the support for Bosch weakened within his party and the peasantry. Bosch (like Trujillo before him and Balaguer subsequently) was imbued with a basic fiscal conservatism born from his reading of the consequences of past fiscal profligacy for the country. The Dominican state sector had expanded dramatically under the council of state, which had hired 20,000 new people; and Bosch did create almost 28,000 additional jobs in the state sugar sector (Moya Pons 1991, 53–58). However, patronage demands remained intense, and conflicts between Bosch and his party intensified in part because he refused what he perceived to be excessive patronage demands of party leaders, although personality conflicts and other feuds also emerged (Guerrero 1993, 208–9). The peasant federation that had been so important to his election fell into quiescence, although its existence raised fears of peasant activism against landowners and even of a peasant militia opposed to the military (Wiarda 1975).

Actions by the coup coalition finally crystallized in September 1963. A general strike led by business and industry, ostensibly against communism and not the government, was held on Friday, September 20. The following Monday, an exchange of gunfire on the Haitian border, which Bosch interpreted as an attack against Dominican territory, led Bosch to order the military to prepare to bomb Port-au-Prince; they, in turn, sought greater information regarding the events on the border, which apparently involved fighting by Haitian troops against rebel forces in the border area (details remain murky, see Guerrero 1993, 143–60). The next day, top military officers met with the intention of demanding Bosch energetically to condemn communism and remove suspected communists from his government. Bosch sought the resignation of air force colonel Elías Wessin y Wessin, author of a strongly anticommunist article in the May–June issue of the magazine of the armed forces. When he met resistance from the top military hierarchy, he wrote out a letter of resignation. With firm pressure from the head of the air force, in the early morning hours of September 25, Bosch was finally deposed by the Dominican military. He and a good part of his cabinet were kept under house arrest, and Bosch was finally sent into exile on September 29 (for a detailed chronology, see Guerrero 1993, 77–78, 163–80, 257–74). The AIRD had not openly joined the strike, but shortly after the coup its president and other business leaders also traveled to Puerto Rico to justify it.

Although the array of forces against Bosch were impressive, it is also true that he did not actively oppose his overthrow, nor did forces favorable to him within his party or within society mobilize at the time in his support. Bosch told a small sector within the military, led by Colonel Rafael Tomás Fernández Domínguez, to desist from coming to his aid because, he explained later, they were hopelessly outnumbered. He also insisted the PRD not mobilize a resistance campaign because that could lead to a bloodbath (Gleijeses 1978, 103–6; Guerrero 1993, 183–98, esp. 195). For Bosch to have blocked this coup plot—and subsequent others that would inevitably have followed—would almost certainly have required a different political strategy and perhaps even a different political personality. His own analyses impressed upon him the difficulty of building democracy in the country's social context.[31]

The U.S. reaction to Bosch's overthrow in September illustrates the fact that the promotion of democracy and of Bosch's government was subordinate to a strategy to prevent a second Cuba. When the coup threat finally came and Ambassador Martin requested an aircraft carrier to block it in a fashion similar to the events of November 1961, he was informed by the State Department that unless there was a threat of a communist takeover, which there did not appear to be, there would be no military intervention or show of force (Lowenthal 1972, 28–29; Martin 1966, 570).[32] The United States strongly condemned the coup and withheld recognition and aid until December, but a determination was made early on that the United States did not want Bosch back because, in Martin's words, "he isn't a President" (Martin 1966, 601).

Table 3.4 summarizes the evolution of this transition in light of the three clusters of factors that were presented at the beginning of chapter 3. In terms of the first cluster, the preexisting neosultanistic Trujillo regime was clearly inimical to a successful democratic transition. In spite of the regime's approximation of the neosultanistic ideal-type, of the country's institutional near vacuum upon Trujillo's demise, and of weak societal and political actors, a

Table 3.4. The Transition of 1961–1962

I. Preexisting authoritarian regime: neosultanistic

Military:	Viewed as personal instrument of tyrant
Societal organizations:	Practically nonexistent
Political opposition:	No organized opposition until after assassination
Economic allies:	Not autonomous, dominated by tyrant and insecure

II. International geopolitical and economic context

Hierarchy of U.S. policy goals:	Perceived communist threat viewed as real, ultimately subsumed democracy goal
Extent of U.S. involvement:	Extremely high, employing all means short of direct military intervention

III. The transition process

Mode of transition:	Trujillo regime "collapse"; provisional government, internationally imposed free elections; former ruler's allies not participating; no pacts
Institutional changes and continuities:	Opposition "left" party wins absolute majority, heightens fears in atmosphere of international polarization and military continuity

clear "break" with the Trujillos was achieved as the old regime "collapsed," and a provisional government was formed in 1962. In terms of the third cluster, this mode of transition is more fraught with risks than other kinds. But, the potential risks—of a provisional government subverting democratic elections either because it represents the old regime or a new radical leadership—were averted and democratic elections were successfully organized. However, here the second cluster of factors becomes primary. These elections were facilitated by the extraordinary degree of U.S. involvement, which was able to meld its anticommunist and democratic promotion objectives together in the absence of any serious revolutionary threat; yet, the elections were not undergirded by a broad compromise on the rules of the game across major political and economic actors, even as support for Bosch from the U.S. government weakened. Thus, conservative socioeconomic forces soon coalesced with political, military, and church figures to overthrow the elected president. In a situation in which the PRD possessed an absolute majority, the institutional changes that Bosch, his new constitution, and his proposed reforms represented were perceived as too threatening, even though middle-sector and popular-sector groups remained relatively weak and unorganized. The coup highlighted the domestic and international factors that explain why democracy failed at this time: political leaders remained unable to create a broad coalition or an effective political pact in support of democratic rules of the game, in an increasingly polarized country in which the defense of economic privilege could be imbued with anticommunism, even as the fear of a second Cuba increasingly outweighed other considerations for U.S. policymakers.

Failed Transition, II: From Coup to U.S. Intervention to Extrication Elections, 1963–1966

If Bosch's regime was overthrown in 1963 ostensibly because of its alleged communist nature, what is evident is that weak radical leftist elements were in fact strengthened by the coup and that the country experienced further polarization over the next several years. The three-year period that ensued—from the coup to civil war and U.S. intervention to the "extrication elections" that brought Joaquín Balaguer to power in 1966—has been extensively analyzed by other scholars, especially from perspectives of international relations and revolutionary movements (see Gleijeses 1978, 427–50, for one bibliographical essay). The focus in these pages will be primarily on analyzing the issue of the "extrication elections" of 1966 as a second failed transition to democracy, rather than on reviewing the tragic events of the Dominican civil war and U.S. intervention. This examination of Dominican events in the light of the factors presented in the introduction to this chapter highlights the extraordinary difficulties that democratic processes confronted.

Seeking Controlled Elections from Above and Coup Plotting from Outside

The military that overthrew Bosch immediately declared communist, Marxist-Leninist, and Castroite doctrines and parties illegal and the controversial 1963 constitution "nonexistent"; they also announced their willingness to turn power over to civilian forces (Guerrero 1993, text of communiqué on 241). After indecision and some squabbling, a governing triumvirate was named, and the UCN and five other small parties that had coalesced in opposition to Bosch divided up cabinet seats. By December, the triumvirate was dominated by the conservative businessman Donald Reid Cabral; and after June 1964, when it became a two-person executive, the government turned out to be a weak and increasingly isolated authoritarian regime that sought to prolong and to legitimize itself unsuccessfully.[33]

The government had low levels of legitimacy because of its origin, and the country continued to suffer deep economic problems that heightened existing political tensions. A massive surge in imports helped generate serious balance-of-payment problems. These imports were fed in part by extensive contraband trading by an increasingly factionalized and corrupt military. Economic difficulties and concerted pressure from merchants and industrialists finally forced the government to close the military *cantinas* that served as the contraband outlets in July 1964.[34] A few months earlier the government had begun to impose a stabilization plan and had turned to the IMF for a standby credit loan. Strikes and protests in May 1964 left an untold number dead, scores wounded, and hundreds arrested (Wiarda 1975, 1475–76).

In these circumstances, Reid's key domestic allies became increasingly disgruntled. Reid began to lose the support of industrial and especially commercial interests and of the military. He also began to lose the favor of his third key base of support, the U.S. government (cf. Lowenthal 1972, 42). He sought to prolong his stay in office by scheduling elections for September 1965 that would exclude the participation of his two potentially most significant opponents who remained in exile, Bosch and Balaguer, even as many of the politicians who had initially supported the coup now attacked the government. Opinions within the U.S. government were increasingly divided over how strongly the United States should support the Reid administration, especially as policymakers realized the extent of his government's unpopularity and the possible destabilizing implications of a controlled election; at the same time, unfavorable views of Bosch remained high.[35] Thus, the U.S. government continued to support Reid, even if ambivalently, and the growing Dominican opposition was unconvinced that the United States would apply effective pressure to insure free and fair elections. Without such international pressure, Reid's Dominican opponents were convinced he would simply seek to extend his stay in office.

In turn, both Bosch and Balaguer, who had formally created his Partido Reformista (PR, Reformist Party) in July 1963, conspired with military and civilian groups. Bosch became convinced that only through military action could he "return to constitutional power without elections" (the slogan of his effort); not all figures within his party agreed, and many were marginalized from the coup plotting. As a result of the efforts of Bosch and Balaguer, though, a number of civil-military conspiracies emerged. In January and February 1965, a number of military personnel were sent abroad, weakening the activities of one set of officers favorable to Balaguer, whose stated intentions were to form a military junta that would then hold elections.

Failed Transition from Below, U.S. Intervention, and Extrication Elections

In April 1965, a "constitutionalist" civil-military conspiracy to bring Bosch and the PRD back to power became a popular uprising, which the United States feared would result in a communist takeover. Reid's unsuccessful efforts to dismantle the conspiracy on April 24 led to U.S. intervention four days later (see Gleijeses 1978). The intervention was catalyzed by the failure of the "loyalist" Dominican military faction headed by General Elías Wessin y Wessin, which the United States had been backing, to control what had evolved into a civil-military rebellion led by "constitutionalist" forces. These remained in control of Santo Domingo's downtown area, but were surrounded by U.S. troops.

Most analysts concur that the U.S. intervention, in which as many as 23,000 troops were ultimately involved, was the result of an exaggerated fear regarding a potential second Cuba (see Draper 1968; Gleijeses 1978; Lowenthal 1972; Slater 1967; Wiarda 1975). As such, not only was the intervention itself unrelated to democracy promotion, but it inhibited potential democratic progress in the country. On May 6, an effort was made to legitimate the intervention by adding a Latin American military presence through an OAS-established Inter-American Peace Force (the last necessary vote in the OAS came from Reid Cabral's representative, despite questions about whether it was the legitimate Dominican government at the time). As it became clear that the costs of a purely military solution to the continuing presence of constitutionalist forces in downtown Santo Domingo were too high, the United States sought political solutions. Initially, it considered "constitutionalism without Bosch" as a possible solution, with PRD leader S. Antonio Guzmán to be named president. But negotiations broke down in late May between Guzmán and U.S. government leaders, who feared he was too close to Bosch. The United States increasingly came to prefer the establishment of a provisional government followed by elections—as specified by an OAS resolution—as the best extrication strategy.

As part of this strategy, Héctor García Godoy was named provisional president in September 1965, launching yet another U.S. effort "to keep the provisional government in office, help it hold elections, and help get the winner into the Palace alive" (to repeat Martin's words about the Bosch election of

1962). García Godoy was a member of a prominent Dominican family, the manager of a large tobacco company, and briefly the minister of foreign relations for Bosch. Ultimately, negotiations to arrange a peaceful surrender of the constitutionalist forces in downtown Santo Domingo, to prevent a new outbreak of hostilities, and to provide for elections were successful. In the face of sharp economic decline and fiscal collapse, the United States and the OAS provided emergency assistance.[36] General Wessin y Wessin was forced into exile, but following his departure, a disproportionate number of "constitutionalist" officers followed him abroad, compared to "loyalist" ones (Gleijeses 1978, 277–81).

Balaguer, who had returned to the country on June 28, and Bosch emerged as the two main presidential candidates for the June 1966 elections. Bosch, understandably, felt betrayed by the United States, which had blocked his possible return to power and turned on his militant supporters. Although he returned to the Dominican Republic in September 1965, he ventured out to campaign for the elections only three times.[37] Balaguer, in turn, ran a skillful and energetic campaign, promising peace and stability. He was able to re-group Trujillo's old Partido Dominicano, at least partially. As the election results in appendix A illustrate, Balaguer's support in 1966 was overwhelm-ingly from rural municipalities; Bosch and the PRD drew most of their sup-port from the cities.[38] It was also clear that Balaguer was the candidate favored by most conservative business interests and by the officer corps that retained control of the armed forces and now felt hatred toward Bosch, the PRD, and elements of the left. Furthermore, many Dominicans were convinced that Balaguer was also the candidate strongly favored by the United States. At the same time, U.S. policymakers did not view a victory by Bosch as a serious security threat to the United States.[39]

Consequences of the Intervention and Alternative Scenarios

Given the circumstances under which the 1966 elections were held and the subsequent absence of civil and political rights, it is not possible to consider these elections as a democratic transition, in contrast to 1962.[40] In comparison to cases of outright military rule, blatant foreign imposition, or outright fraud, though, the Dominican case in 1966 is ambiguous. In part this is due to the fact that Balaguer ran a skillful campaign and possessed a degree of real popular support, even while he was deemed trustworthy by other powerful Dominican actors. In the end, he won a convincing victory and his party received comfort-able majorities in congress with twenty-two of twenty-seven senators and forty-eight of the seventy-four seats in the chamber. If the electoral consequences had been to generate a government respectful of democratic rights and able and willing to control repression by the armed forces, these elections might have led to a democratic transition in the short term; but that did not turn out to be the case. Balaguer did name two PRD leaders to his cabinet, but, reflecting the country's continuing polarization, they were forced to resign from their party, which protested their participation. Balaguer gained greater control over the military than either Bosch or Reid had achieved; and he moved rapidly to reform the constitution in a more presidentialist and less democratic direction and to institute neopatrimonial-authoritarian, but not neosultanistic, rule with extensive U.S. support (see chapter 4).

The 1966 elections were in part "demonstration elections" for international opinion and for domestic U.S. consumption, providing legitimation for the U.S. intervention and the basis for the withdrawal of U.S. forces; but they also had extensive consequences within the Dominican Republic.[41] Technically, the elections were probably free; many Dominicans, though, would argue they were not fair in terms of Bosch's ability to campaign. The United States sought to make the elections free, and the numerous international observers who attended—including a UN mission; the Inter-American Commission on Human Rights; an OAS electoral assistance mission; a forty-two person OAS electoral observation mission; and some seventy, generally pro-Bosch U.S. liberals headed by Norman Thomas and Bayard Rustin—reported that they were (Slater 1970, 171–82; Gleijeses 1978, 281).[42] Yet, for most Dominicans, unaccustomed in any event to free and fair elections, the situation was hardly propitious. In 1965, the United States had not helped rid the country of the family of a hated dictator as it had in 1961. Rather, it had prevented a constitutionally elected president who had been deposed from returning to power and, by its continuing military presence in the country, had cast a cloud over his candidacy. Although the civil war had been contained largely to urban areas, it left some three thousand dead and a country even more polarized and committed to conspiratorial politics. Many in the country viewed Balaguer's electoral victory as tainted and his administration as lacking in moral legitimacy.

Ultimately, the events of this period must be viewed as representing a failure of U.S. policy, particularly as related to the ambivalent U.S. commitment to the promotion of democracy. Although the United States helped prevent a direct continuation of Trujillismo by its actions in 1961–62, and although it played a key role in the democratic 1962 elections, its extensive involvement in Dominican affairs did not translate into successful democracy; from multiple internal causes, Bosch was overthrown a few months after his inauguration. Bosch's overthrow and the civil-military conspiracies it eventually spawned, combined with the U.S. fear of a second Cuba, set the stage for the 1965 U.S. military intervention. At the time of the intervention, some argued that it was a success: the lives of foreign citizens were protected, violence was halted, a communist takeover was prevented, and constitutional processes were restored.[43] Yet, critics charged, the cost remained high, regardless of how favorable a situation this was for the United States to exercise its power. In addition to its cost in human lives, it once again drew the United States into Dominican politics as a central actor, reinforcing conspiratorial and cynical attitudes toward politics that have been so inimical to Dominican democracy. Indeed, one probable cost was that the intervention encouraged right-wing forces both in the Dominican Republic and around Latin America in the belief that they did not need to accommodate the demands of nationalist reform movements, even as it drove previously committed democrats, such as Juan Bosch, to reject democratic procedures (though he subsequently moved back to them) (see Lowenthal 1969a, 134, 148).

More recently, as the Dominican Republic has evolved into a political democracy, the argument has been made that "it appears that the United States may have helped effect a structural transformation in the Dominican Republic which could not have happened without something like the 1965 intervention occurring" (Nash 1985, 10). This latter argument rests on two main points. The first is that in the late 1960s the United States provided generous economic assistance to the island republic, at levels that would not have been forthcoming in the absence of the intervention. The second is that this economic aid assisted in the country's structural transformation that helped move Dominican democracy forward.

There are at least three problems with this view. One is that the structural transformation that took place in the country was an unintentional by-product of the initial U.S. decision to intervene; the intervention itself was not related to seeking either democracy or economic development in the Dominican Republic, but to perceived U.S. security concerns. In the same way that one cannot directly "blame" the U.S. military occupation for Trujillo's rise, one cannot "praise" the intervention for the subsequent economic changes, though they resulted in part from the generous economic aid the United States provided the country to help support the Balaguer regime. A second problem is that there are many possible paths to democratization, and it is not at all clear that the structural transformation that did take place was the only one potentially supportive of democratization. One might well imagine other transformations, generating stronger and better organized popular sectors and political actors, potentially even more favorable to Dominican democratization, and realized without a U.S. intervention. Finally, the mix of motives and actions by the United States during this period reinforced the reality of its overwhelming presence and the critical role that it often played in the internal affairs of the Dominican Republic. Historically, in the Dominican Republic and throughout the Caribbean and Central American region, that reality has frequently worked directly against democratic forces. Yet, even when it may occasionally promote democratization, as it did at different moments in the Dominican Republic, it inhibits its consolidation.

At the same time, one cannot be too sanguine about what a return of Juan Bosch to power would have meant for the prospects of democratic consolidation in the country in the 1960s, although in no way does this justify the U.S. intervention. One can imagine three scenarios based on Bosch's return at different points—scenarios that initially assume something that obviously was not present in the late 1960s: a U.S. government not fearful of potential communist threats. If the constitutionalist coup had succeeded on April 25, as it almost did, then Bosch would have returned to power without extensive mass mobilization, ostensibly in order to complete his term (which was due to end in February 1967). It is conceivable that he could have done so and that democratic elections would have been held in 1967. Whether Balaguer would have been permitted to return from exile to compete in these elections is not clear, but the possibility of continuing a gradual process of strengthening civil society, building political institutions,and establishing a pattern of competition for power through elections may have stood a chance. However, for Bosch to have been able to govern effectively would have required far more effective effort at *mutual* accommodation than had been evidenced in his initial term in office. Returning to power at the head of a civil-military conspiracy would almost certainly have led his opponents to seek to do the same to him (again). Bosch's return to power would have been derived from military action by armed forces he did not control; these armed forces would almost certainly have remained politicized and keenly aware of their centrality. Powerful societal forces embodied in the partisans of different military and civilian figures would have sought military support for intervention against Bosch. This democratic scenario would obviously have been enhanced by the elimination of the military, which was not really an option at the time for many reasons, including perceived threats from Haiti and the Cold War atmosphere. However, an initial significant purging and then careful oversight of the remaining officer corps along with other requirements specified above— however difficult—could have meant a more favorable outcome for Dominican democracy.

In Latin America, successful democratic consolidation has required both the protection of core elite interests and the elite's perception that it does. In a second scenario, if Bosch had returned to power following the extensive mass mobilization of April 25–28, his government would almost certainly have been more radical, supported by more politicized military officers and popular-sector groups. Such a Bosch government might have brought about more far-reaching modifications within the armed forces and implemented other reforms that could ultimately have led to a more egalitarian social structure and to more far-reaching social and political democratization. Yet, to what extent Bosch or other civilian political figures could have controlled the newly emboldened military actors remains an open question; and comparative evidence suggests that such a transition "from below" was even more likely to engender efforts to undo it by powerful societal interests conspiring with military factions against their suddenly reformist brethren (for another view on these scenarios and others, see Gleijeses 1978, 287–99).

In a final scenario, we can speculate on what might have transpired if Bosch had in fact won the 1966 elections. Given the U.S. presence in the country, he would have been able to assume power; but structural and societal conditions, combined with his own fatalistic analysis of the situation, could conceivably have led very quickly to renewed coup plotting by the dominant military factions, which he did not control, with the active support of the distrustful societal groups that helped engineer his overthrow in 1963. The country remained deeply polarized and fearful in 1966, in an atmosphere dominated by the Cold War and the Cuban Revolution and in which the United States had demonstrated how dramatically it would overreact to even the remotest possibility of another Cuba.

Table 3.5, which summarizes the evolution of this failed transition in light of the three clusters of factors discussed earlier in this chapter, also helps to underscore the difficulties of achieving success in the counterfactual scenarios. Given the short-lived nature of governments following Bosch's overthrow in 1963, one cannot speak of a distinctive, preexisting authoritarian regime, unlike 1961; but these fleeting authoritarian regimes highlighted the serious institutional vacuum of power and the fragmentation of the military, which no one fully controlled. Reid Cabral, unlike Trujillo, was never well ensconced in power, and even more ephemeral governments asserted power until the U.S. intervention. The struggles over April 25–28 and the U.S. intervention helped to polarize political groups and passions in the country. Technically, the country had two alternative governments for the four or so months until García Godoy was named provisional president on September 3, 1965. The Dominican military had divided into warring groups, becoming the power base of alternative civilian bands. Economic elites remained relatively

Table 3.5. The Transition of 1965–1966

I. Preexisting authoritarian regime: inchoate and/or provisional	
Military:	Autonomous, factionalized, and bitterly divided after civil war
Societal organizations:	Weak, fragmented
Political opposition:	Opposition parties barely tolerated; political actors polarized after civil war
Economic allies:	Insecure and weak
II. International geopolitical and economic context	
Hierarchy of U.S. policy goals:	Perceived communist threat dominant, but gradually receding; "extrication" elections to facilitate removal of U.S. troops
Extent of U.S. involvement:	Military intervention, and all other means
III. The transition process	
Mode of transition:	Potential transition from below thwarted by U.S. intervention; provisional government, internationally imposed negotiated surrender of rebel forces and elections; no pacts
Institutional changes and continuities:	Political actors polarized by civil war and intervention; limited, failed efforts at power sharing; imposed constitutional framework of presidential dominance; military politically active and semiautonomous

weak and insecure. As was true following the demise of Trujillo, there was nearly an institutional vacuum, although now in a situation that was more violent and polarized.

Turning to the second cluster of factors, the role of the United States was obviously paramount in determining the process of 1965–66, especially coming as it did on top of a long history of deep U.S. enmeshment in Dominican affairs, most recently in the 1959–62 period. Following the 1965 intervention and with a continued overwhelming display of force, the United States negotiated the handing over of power to a provisional government and the holding of elections. The anticommunist objective was dominant, but it was also important for the U.S. government that the elections be perceived as competitive and fair. The provisional government of García Godoy sought to portray a neutral image, and the president left office with a degree of good will. However, his government was totally dependent upon the United States for economic and military support. Balaguer was widely perceived to be the candidate favored by the country's major industrial and commercial interests, the victorious group within the armed forces, and the U.S. government.

As earlier in the decade, the mode of transition was again from a provisional government. What began as a PRD-backed military conspiracy to bring Bosch back to power transformed itself into more of a "transition from below" with important elements of mass mobilization. This helped spark the military counterreaction, whose failure set the stage for the United States to intervene. Subsequently, the United States imposed a provisional government, selecting a skillful individual who sought to portray an image of neutrality, and also oversaw the entire electoral process. Thus, there was never a risk of the provisional government either postponing or hijacking the elections. However, eerily anticipating the reemergence of (ex)communist leaders in the formerly socialist countries in the 1990s, circumstances were propitious for a figure emanating from the Trujillo regime to emerge victorious.

Conclusion

In November 1961, some six months after the despised dictator Trujillo was assassinated, Dominicans celebrated wildly as it became clear that his neo-sultanistic rule would not be retained by members of his family. Almost five years later, in July 1966, Trujillo's puppet president in 1961, Joaquín Balaguer, assumed the presidential office, which he was then to occupy for twenty-two of the subsequent thirty years. During the tumultuous period following Trujillo's death, two elections were held and two potential democratic transitions ultimately failed as the United States remained deeply enmeshed in Dominican affairs and intervened militarily in April 1965.

Legacies from Trujillo's neosultanistic regime combined with factors associated with the mode of transition to complicate the likelihood of democratic transition in this period. In contrast, the role of international factors, especially those concerning the U.S. government, was complex and variable. It is highly unlikely that democratic elections would have been held in the country in 1962 without an extensive U.S. role; yet, the United States ultimately did not prevent the coup that ousted Bosch shortly after he assumed power. Bosch's overthrow generated multiple military conspiracies. Given the historical legacies and the nature of the mode of transition, it is questionable whether efforts to bring him back to power would ultimately have succeeded in ushering in a longer-term democratic period if the United States had not intervened in 1965. Regardless, I concur with those who condemn the intervention and argue that at that point a Dominican road should have been allowed to develop, even though I am not optimistic about the chances of democratic success. Just a few years after aiding in the removal of the Trujillos and in fostering a democratic election, U.S. intervention truncated a popular rebellion and helped polarize the country politically, flaming disbelief in democratic procedures and ultimately ushering to power a close collaborator of Trujillo. The elections of 1966, which helped extricate foreign troops from the country, led to President Balaguer's authoritarian, neopatrimonial regime from which twelve years later a weak, unstable political democracy was to emerge. Chapter 4 analyzes this twelve-year period and democratic transition.

4 Authoritarian Balaguer and Democratic Transition, 1966–1978

In the previous chapter, we discussed the failure of democratic transitions over the 1961–66 period. The 1966 elections ushered in an elected, but authoritarian regime, as evidenced by the nature and outcome of the 1970 and 1974 electoral processes. Subsequently, however, elections held in 1978 led to the first peaceful transfer of political power from one group to another in the country's history, as twelve-year president Joaquín Balaguer handed power over to S. Antonio Guzmán of the PRD. The military temporarily stopped the vote count, and a coup appeared imminent in order to maintain Balaguer in power; yet both international and domestic pressure insured that the electoral results, at the presidential level, would be respected.

From various broad theoretical perspectives, the Dominican Republic was not a likely case for a democratic transition in 1978. In broad terms, economic, cultural, and "frustrated-by-foreign-intervention" arguments emerged that were pessimistic about the possibility for democratic politics in Latin America as the democratic wave of the late 1950s and early 1960s receded.[1] The first set of arguments focused particularly on economic dependency and argued that the logic of capitalist growth on the periphery limited the possibilities for political democracy in less-developed countries, particularly as they moved toward intermediate levels of industrialization (one of the most thought-provoking is Evans 1979). A second set of arguments emphasized that the continent's cultural, colonial heritage of patrimonialism and corporatism represented a distinct tradition distinguishable from a liberal, democratic one (Wiarda 1982; Veliz 1980; Dealy 1992). A third perspective argued that direct U.S. intervention has had a negative impact on the possibilities for democratic rule in Latin America. Although defeat in war and military occupation by the United States and other Allied powers led to democratization in several countries following World War II, U.S. covert and direct military actions have often had both immediate and long-term negative consequences for democra-tization in Latin America (on Guatemala, see Trudeau 1984).

Chapter 4 will not question the applicability of these arguments for all cases in all time periods. Rather, the intent is to challenge their implicit determin-ism and their reification into general theories about Latin American politics. The Dominican Republic is a particularly useful case study for this purpose because these three sets of arguments appear particularly applicable in the Dominican context.[2] In an article published one year before the PRD's elec-toral victory, one analyst wrote:

> It is obvious that the PRD . . . is headed toward a period of political de-cline and decay. The strong beliefs held by many PRD leaders that the fu-ture of Dominican politics lie[s] in the introduction of fair elections, an independent legislature, guaranteed freedoms and the rule of law have been destroyed by the entrenched governing traditions of authoritarian-ism, paternalism and reactionary politics (Kryzanek 1977, 141).
>
> . . . Political party opposition cannot effectively check or challenge or change Dominican government. . . . Balaguer's use of public relations, military repression, paternalism and co-optation of enemies ensures that his regime can weather any opposition challenge (Kryzanek 1977, 142).

Subsequently, a number of analyses by Dominican and U.S. scholars of the 1978 transition have sought an explanation primarily in the interventionistic role of the United States in the electoral process (e.g., from very different perspectives, see Cassá 1984, 216–20; Cassá 1986, 372–74; and Kryzanek 1979).

In contrast, this chapter will present evidence in support of the view that the framework developed in the previous chapter (see table 3.1) provides a more satisfactory explanation of the outcome. That framework points to factors (1) related to the nature of the authoritarian regime and its relations to domestic societal forces, political opposition, and the military; (2) to the international geopolitical context; and (3) to the transition process. Under Balaguer, impor-tant structural changes also occurred within and across social groups that had an impact on these factors, making accommodation within an open political regime more likely. The nature of Balaguer's relationships to economic groups and to the military ultimately weakened his administration, even as "political learning" by the major opposition party and by certain business groups also were important in facilitating a democratic transition. Although U.S. influ-ence was crucial in insuring the integrity of the Dominican electoral process, interpretations that focus primarily on this fact underestimate other key factors and do not place U.S. influence in an appropriate interactive context.[3]

The chapter is organized in three sections. The first one highlights the neopatrimonial features of the Balaguer regime (1966–78), and then explores its relationships to different social sectors, especially business groups, the military, and political parties. The second section analyzes the changes and evolution in the major opposition party, the PRD, following the departure of the radical wing with the party's founder, Juan Bosch, in 1973. The rest of the party moved toward an explicitly electoral, accommodative stance; but, reflecting a kind of political learning, it did not simply deradicalize to assuage business groups and the U.S. government. Rather, it aggressively reorganized for electoral purposes and sought international connections to buttress its goal to seek power by democratic means, recognizing that winning a majority of the votes alone was probably insufficient. The final section examines the dramatic events surrounding the 1978 elections to show how some of the military and business groups calculated their opposition to a potential coup, "learning" from the country's recent history. It also considers the importance of the U.S. role in dismantling the coup and overseeing the transition process.

Balaguer's Twelve Years, 1966–1978

Certain critical differences are apparent between Trujillo and Balaguer, expressing differences between the arbitrary, discretional power of neosultanistic regimes and the power wielded by neopatrimonial-authoritarian regimes. These differences in the treatment of economic, military, and political power —which resulted in part from changes in Dominican society and in international circumstances—played a role in facilitating a democratic transition, which the country had been unable to realize in the early 1960s. Economically, under Balaguer, neopatrimonialism was combined with the emergence of independent, private economic groups. The military were never his personal instrument, as they had been of Trujillo, and Balaguer was unmistakably a civilian. Politically, Balaguer never attempted or achieved the extent of control that Trujillo did. Rather, he assiduously practiced a policy of cooptation; semi-oppositions flourished and eventually a real opposition emerged. The fact that Balaguer was a civilian figure who paid attention to constitutional and electoral formalities further facilitated the high levels of U.S. economic, military, and political support.[4]

Authoritarian and Neopatrimonial Rule

Balaguer, puppet president of Trujillo at the time of his assassination and briefly afterward, was the dominant figure in the Dominican Republic in the period from 1966 to 1978. Given the authoritarian and neopatrimonial style of his twelve years in office and his direct link to the Trujillo period, there were obviously some elements of continuity. However, Balaguer's treatment of economic, military, and political issues varied in significant ways from that of Trujillo, and the dynamics of electoral cycles and the consequences of some of the country's socioeconomic changes in this period were quite significant for eventual democratization in 1978.

As discussed in chapter 2, Trujillo came to dominate completely the country's political, economic, and military power over the 1930–61 period. He expanded capitalist development in the country, though often in an economically irrational and megalomaniacal style, while buying out many foreign investors. Upon his death, Trujillo's substantial holdings were nationalized, leading to a massive state sector—though one that was not rational from a planning perspective. In his wake, Trujillo left a vacuum of institutions and organizations. At the same time, his manipulative and repressive tactics left a legacy of conspiratorial, distrustful, and cynical politics. The country was further polarized and in crisis as a consequence of the 1965 civil war and U.S. intervention.

The man who became president was a complex figure, with an astounding drive for power. Balaguer was an astute politician, physically unimposing but a master orator, patient, and with a keen sense of timing. He was above all a political pragmatist—willing to be ruthless if necessary, but not eager to employ repression and violence unnecessarily. His rhetoric focused on the values of order and stability, and he continued to link Dominican nationalism to what he viewed as its Hispanic, Catholic essence and to anti-Haitian themes. He was both a realist about power politics and a conservative nationalist, recognizing the overwhelming reality of the U.S. presence, but retaining a certain disdain of that country and its leaders. Willing to take U.S. aid, his conservative instincts and nationalist interpretation of Dominican history led him to be a fiscal conservative, like Trujillo and unlike neopatrimonial leaders in other countries (cf. Bratton and van de Walle 1997, 67–68). Public expenditures were focused inordinately on public works and construction, while investments in health and education languished (for a valuable, extended discussion of the personal, ideological features of Balaguer's rule, see Cassá 1986, 375–510).

Balaguer ruled in an authoritarian fashion. Human rights violations by state security agents were unacknowledged and unpunished, and civil and political liberties were curtailed. In both 1970 and 1974, in the face of open military harassment, most opposition forces opted to abstain from participation in elections; but political liberalization beginning in 1976 set the stage for Balaguer's electoral defeat two years later.

*Table 4.1. Public Investments in Construction
and the Office of the Presidency, 1969–1977*

	1969	1970	1971	1972	1973	1974	1975	1976	1977
Total (DR$ millions)	$80	$89	$116	$138	$158	$168	$251	$231	$265
Construction as percentage of total public capital expenditures	40	44	42	42	42	28	30	29	37
Central government (DR$ millions)	$41	$53	$71	$91	$108	$105	$153	$153	$146
Presidency's percentage of central government expenditures on construction	81	90	97	94	95	94	96	95	98

Source: Alemán et al. (1976, 178–83); Alemán et al. (1978, 240–55).
Note: Total includes expenditures by central government and decentralized institutes. Based on actual expenditures, which typically varied significantly from initially budgeted expenditures, especially regarding the role of the presidency (e.g., in 1975 only 10 percent was initially budgeted for the presidency, and in 1976 only 0.8 percent).

Balaguer also governed in a neopatrimonial fashion. Neopatrimonial regimes are marked by a concentration of power and resources in the executive and by a blurring of public and private purposes, features present over the 1966–78 period. One of the first steps Balaguer took was to have the congress modify Bosch's 1963 constitution. The new constitution promulgated in November 1966 enhanced presidential powers and permitted unlimited presidential reelection, while removing material from the earlier constitution objectionable to the church and to business interests (Brea Franco 1983).

For many years, Balaguer also exercised direct personal control over state resources to an extraordinary degree. One key mechanism was the public-works budget. State funds earmarked for roads and urban construction came predominantly from the central government, and most of these flowed directly out of the president's office, rather than from the public-works, health, or other appropriate ministry. In turn, dams and irrigation projects were handled for the president primarily through other public-sector agencies, (ironically) termed autonomous institutions (see table 4.1 and Alemán et al. 1978, 257–59). Contracts were handed out without any competitive bidding process. They were also heavily concentrated; a 1975 survey by the International Labor Organization found that six firms accounted for 95 percent of the value of civil-works contracts at that time (reported in World Bank 1978, 69). Although Balaguer

Table 4.2. *Ministries and Minister-Rank*
Appointments by Administration, 1930–1982

Administration	Ministries	Other	Appointments Ministerial	Other	Total
Trujillo era (1930–61)					
R. Trujillo (1930–34)	10	—	34	0	34
R. Trujillo (1934–38)	11	—	45	0	45
Peynado (1938–40)	8	—	14	0	14
Troncoso (1940–42)	10	—	22	0	22
R. Trujillo (May–August 1942)	10	—	12	0	12
R. Trujillo (1942–47)	12	1	40	1	41
R. Trujillo (1947–52)	14	1	62	7	69
H. Trujillo (1952–60)	19	1	121	12	133
Juan Bosch					
J. Bosch (1963)	13	1	16	1	17
Joaquín Balaguer					
J. Balaguer (1966–70)	12	13	46	18	64
J. Balaguer (1970–74)	13	19	37	58	95
J. Balaguer (1974–78)	14	32	38	77	115
PRD					
S. A. Guzmán (1978–82)	13	1	36	6	42

Source: Calculated from Ventura (1985).
Note: Ministries without portfolio (*sin cartera*) listed under "other." Balaguer gave ministerial rank to numerous other public employees; for example, over 1974–78, he did so to some of the governors, the director general of the Modern Art Gallery, and a director of a hospital.

insisted that corruption stopped "at the door to his office," he openly acknowledged the legitimacy of what were politely termed "commissions," paid by private contractors to other public officials, and which he claimed he was unable to control in any event; his family members were showered with ostensible donations and gifts by favored contractors. In sum, associates enriched themselves on the basis of public-works contracts as well as by supplying the state's numerous entities with inputs, supplies, and spare parts.

Balaguer also centralized power by shifting potential competitors in and out of office frequently and by ignoring official lines of command. Ministerial rotation was high, and by granting ministerial rank to large numbers of individuals Balaguer ridiculed any notion of the cabinet as a functioning executive body; the contrast with PRD governments is substantial (see table 4.2). Alongside the formal bureaucratic structure of the state were the informal cliques of Balaguer's true confidantes, all ultimately dependent upon him. Similarly, he controlled party nominations to congressional lists, which he manipulated to insure rotation. In spite of the fact that his party gained overwhelming majorities in congress in 1970 and 1974, congressional incumbency rates for those years were very low (see tables 5.2 and 5.3 in the next chapter).

In his relations with the business sector, Balaguer also operated in a neopatrimonial fashion, with a semicorporatist veneer. Balaguer inherited the massive state apparatus that had been built upon Trujillo's nationalized holdings. Although he did not actively shrink the size of the state, he pursued a policy of what might be termed "passive privatization" by stimulating private-sector growth alongside a continued important state role, especially in sugar and construction. Import-substituting industrialization surged under Balaguer, as a system of individualized exemptions initiated under Trujillo was expanded and systematized. Industry expanded due to protection realized by means of exonerations of duties and taxes on imported goods and raw materials as well as other fiscal incentives. Although there was a bureaucratic approval process, which incorporated an important role for established industrial interests, each request for tax favors also required the signature of the president.[5]

Economic Record and Relations with Major Social Groups

Balaguer's economic record was strong in general, macroeconomic terms. From 1966 to 1978 the country experienced high economic growth, averaging 7.6 percent increase in real GDP over the whole period and 11 percent in the years from 1968 to 1974, among the highest worldwide in that period (Dauhajre hijo 1984, 16, 37). Growth was based upon increased export earnings, import-substitution in consumer goods, and public investment projects (especially roads, dams, and urban construction projects), and it was facilitated by the U.S. sugar quota and generous U.S. economic assistance.

Balaguer's innate conservatism was evident in his management of the public sector: his policies were dramatically different from those of populist authoritarians on the South American continent. A very tight check was kept on public-sector employment levels and wages: the number of government employees grew from around 98,000 in 1966 to only around 119,000 in 1976, while real wages in the public sector fell by 35 percent from 1969 to 1977. In addition, expenditures in education and in health were also extremely modest.[6] This permitted many of the state's capital projects to be funded from ordinary revenues, without access to borrowed funds. State revenues came inordinately from taxes on trade.[7] Not surprisingly, this mix of policies complicated Balaguer's ability to garner increased popular support in urban sectors. On the one hand, public-works projects were concentrated in urban areas, especially Santo Domingo; on the other hand, these projects tended to be capital intensive, favoring particularly the contractors and public officials involved in the transactions. At the same time, sharp austerity policies, limited social expenditures, overall repressed wage levels, and legal and practical restrictions on labor organizing hurt the urban popular sector. As elsewhere, import-substituting industrialization gradually involved less and less job creation as well (see World Bank 1978, 53–57).

In spite of its initial successes, Balaguer's industrial policy ultimately had two other negative consequences. Gradually, it undermined the president's position by promoting the development of new business groups, some of which became increasingly independent from the state and resentful of Balaguer's patrimonial style and perceived favoritism toward the large Santo Domingo industrialists. Most significantly for subsequent administrations, Balaguer's policy had a corrosive effect on state finances, as the extent of tax exonerations granted to industry expanded over time.[8]

Even as elsewhere in Latin America doubts about the wisdom of import-substituting industrialization were growing, Balaguer proceeded vigorously with his policies. It did not take long for criticisms of the strategy to emerge. These focused on issues such as the fiscal burdens for the state, excessive reliance on foreign technology and inputs, industrial concentration in the capital city, small impact on the country's massive unemployment problem, and high costs and profits at the expense of quality. Yet, Balaguer probably ignored these critical reports, because the Santo Domingo industrialists most favored by his policies (some of whom had initiated their careers under Trujillo) were key coalitional partners. Furthermore, Balaguer may well have believed that, in conjunction with his public-works projects, supporting these industrialists would help him establish a political base in the capital city, where most of the fighting in 1965 had taken place and where his electoral support was disproportionately weak (see especially Moya Pons 1990, chap. 6).

Balaguer managed relations with the business sector in an ostensibly corporatist, but essentially patrimonial fashion through institutions such as the state Comisión Nacional de Desarrollo (CND, National Development Council), which served as a forum for the elaboration of overall government plans and policies; the Directorio de Desarrollo Industrial (DDI, Directorate of Industrial Development), which was responsible for approving incentives under the industrial-development law; and the monetary board that officially set monetary policy. The overwhelming number of private-sector representatives to these entities were appointed individually by Balaguer. The CND was established in 1967 as a national planning board with a mix of around fifty governmental and private-sector figures; initially even the U.S. ambassador attended its meetings. Through time, because of the prestige of the CND as a kind of co-governing assembly, pressures grew to expand its membership; the president gradually acceded, until the CND became totally unmanageable in size. It also began to languish following 1972, when landowning groups entered into conflict with Balaguer over his agrarian reform policies. Although other state agencies nominally had business representation determined independently by private-sector organizations, even here it was evident that personalistic criteria also weighed heavily. During these Balaguer years, industrial development favored Santo Domingo at the expense of Santiago and, especially, other regions of the country. The movement of a few highly visible firms from Santiago to Santo Domingo was interpreted as a massive industrial flight to the capital, and some Santiago businessmen resented what they felt was a personalistic, discriminatory decision-making process dominated by the Santo Domingo industrial group. At the same time, with industrial growth came the resentment of medium-size industrialists of the prerogatives of the large industrialists with differential access to Balaguer's inner circle (on Balaguer-business relations, including the CND, the DDI, the monetary board, and Santiago resentment, see Espinal 1985, esp. 94–123; other sources include Moya Pons 1986; del Castillo 1981; and the author's interviews in 1986 with industrialists).

As a result of the incentive policies and strong economic growth, the wealth of large private entrepreneurs increased and new groups of businessmen developed around middle-sized firms, which were heavily dependent upon protectionist state policies. As the state was in direct control of a large share of the country's major agricultural export crop and had considerable autonomy—an autonomy concentrated to a remarkable degree in one individual—there was little chance of sectoral conflict and thus of any need for a "populist alliance" of industrialists and workers "against" large landowners, as occurred in other Latin American countries in their populist periods (e.g., Argentina or Brazil). Organized labor remained extremely weak and fragmented due to a combination of repression, co-optation, and restrictive labor legislation. Labor unions were also weakened by fostering the creation of rival unions, by replacing union leaders who lacked legal protection, and sometimes by outright repression. Real wages suffered as the minimum wage was increased nationwide only once during this twelve-year period (author's interviews in 1986 with labor leaders from the major labor confederations; Espinal 1985, 123–43).

Relations with the rural sector were also complex. Market forces and government policies both tended to hurt the rural poor. There was increased land concentration over this period. Government exchange-rate and price policies discriminated against the rural sector in favor of both industry and, to a lesser extent, broader urban interests. Yet, Balaguer retained significant popular support in rural areas through his ideological appeals, which he combined with clientelism and selected public works. In 1972, a new agrarian reform law spurred a short-lived increase in the numbers of beneficiaries, while also causing Balaguer to lose the support of some landowning groups.

Unequal land distribution and pro-urban policies spurred massive rural-to-urban migration, but the presence of Haitian migrant labor mitigated Balaguer's harsh treatment of Dominican rural labor and peasantry. The country's two major landowners were the Consejo Estatal del Azúcar (CEA, State Sugar Council) and the Central Romana, owned during the Balaguer years by Gulf and Western.[9] Under Balaguer, there was both ostensibly legal, temporary, contractual migration and clandestine, occasionally permanent migration from Haiti. The legally questionable contracts between the CEA and the Duvalier government in Haiti were treated as secret documents, even as the treatment of Haitian workers in the Dominican Republic was brutally worse than what they were promised when hired. Anti-Haitian prejudice, magnified by the government, further complicated efforts for collective action on sugar plantations to unite Dominican and Haitian workers. Haitian workers were never permitted to organize, and the Dominican sugar unions, which operated under conditions of sometimes severe repression during the Balaguer years, rarely sought them out (Murphy 1991, 80–97, 153–55).[10]

Guerrilla challenges did emerge, but they were sporadic and unsuccessful. Given the polarizing experience of the 1965 civil war and U.S. intervention, some readers may be surprised they met with such little success. Yet, in a comparative context, this is less surprising. In the conclusion to his comparative analysis of Latin American revolutionary movements, Wickham-Crowley (1992, 320) argues that revolutionaries came to power in the region from 1956 to 1990 (a) when guerrilla movements based in rural areas developed strong peasant support and military strength, (b) when furthermore these movements, in the face of neosultanistic regimes (which he terms patrimonial-praetorian regimes or "mafiacracy"), successfully developed cross-class alliances against the hated dictator, (c) who eventually fell in the face of national resistance and the loss of U.S. support. The only two successful cases he examines, Cuba in 1959 and Nicaragua in 1979, involved the overthrow of neopatrimonial regimes (with Somoza's regime in Nicaragua having more neosultanistic characteristics, like that of Trujillo, than Batista's in Cuba). Why no revolution took place against Trujillo has been analyzed indirectly in chapter 2. While he was in power, support for violent options in the rural sector was complicated by Dominican-Haitian tensions, and throughout the country there were practically no independent organizations of any kind, in contrast to Batista's Cuba. In the months before and after Trujillo's assassination, the turn to a far more interventionist policy by the United States toward the Dominican Republic (following Batista's fall) and the emergence of a moderate opposition in the form of the PRD became additional factors in explaining why the Trujillo regime did not suffer the same fate as Batista in Cuba in 1959. Twenty years later, Somoza in Nicaragua was also overthrown by a revolutionary, armed insurgency at the head of a broad cross-class alliance. The contrast between Somoza's Nicaragua and Balaguer's Dominican Republic is even greater than that between Batista and Trujillo, with regard both to potential guerrilla strength and rural support and to the nature of the two regimes. In the Dominican Republic, the peasantry was largely not available for guerrilla overtures, due in part to the hyperexploitation of Haitian labor, to the co-optating features of the 1972 land reform, and to significant migration. The 1965 civil war was brief and almost exclusively an urban phenomenon, leaving the rural areas untouched. Some potential revolutionary leaders radicalized by the 1965 civil war migrated or were exiled; others, appraising the lack of rural support, focused on civil-military conspiracies and urban terrorist acts. Balaguer did receive extensive U.S. military and intelligence assistance; yet, in addition to his regime's evident ability to dismantle potential revolutionary threats, it is also important to underscore Balaguer's own cross-class and especially upper-class support.

Over time, though, urbanization, industrialization, and economic growth generated larger numbers of professional and middle-sector groups, which increasingly chafed under Balaguer's *continuismo* and were potentially open to the appeals of an opposition group such as the PRD. And, even as Balaguer's efforts to gain urban support met with little success, his rural support gradually eroded (compare the elections results for the 1966 and 1978 elections at the municipal level in appendix A).

In sum, Balaguer's relations with different social groups in the Dominican Republic were predominantly neopatrimonial in nature. With the partial exception of business, most social sectors retained low levels of organization. At the same time, he did not govern in a neosultanistic fashion. The governing coalition was between Balaguer qua state, owner of a substantial part of the country's leading export product and a major industrialist in its own right, and established and emerging industrialists; at the same time, Balaguer maintained a significant popular base in rural areas. Growing dissent was to be found in urban areas, especially among middle-sector and professional groups.

Balaguer and the Military

One of Balaguer's most difficult challenges was the military, which never became his personal instrument. Given the country's history and most immediately the fates of both Bosch and Reid, Balaguer had reason to fear threats from the armed forces. In fact, several times he did confront direct challenges to his rule from military conspirators, even as relations between business and Balaguer became strained by the growing incursions of high-ranking military officers into business and into politics. But Balaguer gained the respect and, to a certain extent, the obedience of the Dominican military as a result of his ties to the Trujillo period, his anticommunism, his statesman-like caudillo figure, and his acceptance of military repressive acts and large-scale corruption.

Balaguer viewed major potential challenges as emanating *both* from "constitutionalist" military sympathizers and from followers of the leading "loyalist" general, Elías Wessin y Wessin. Thus, he purged almost all of the former and many Wessinistas from the armed forces. The military leader of the constitutionalists, Francisco Caamaño, had been sent abroad in January 1966 and then mysteriously disappeared in October 1967, to Cuba as became public knowledge years later. Wessin y Wessin was forcefully retired from the army and sent abroad by García Godoy the day after he became provisional president in September 1965. From abroad, Wessin y Wessin created a political party and lobbied to be allowed to return to the country, which finally occurred in January 1969. He was active in both conspiratorial politics (with leftist movements and parts of the PRD and military sympathizers) and electoral politics. After a relatively poor showing in the 1970 election, Wessin y Wessin apparently continued his conspiracies with military sympathizers against Balaguer. Balaguer successfully dismantled one such coup effort with a dramatic confrontation on television in April 1971, and the general was again sent into exile until shortly after the 1978 elections (Atkins 1981, 60–67). Meanwhile, Balaguer allowed the remaining military to become top heavy and illegally wealthy while employing "divide and conquer" tactics to control them.[11] Two major military "groups" coalesced in the mid-1970s, with the one around General Neit Rafael Nivar Seijas somewhat more "political" than the one around General Enrique Pérez y Pérez. Balaguer carefully balanced their power by shifting them from one position to another over his twelve years in

Following his election in 1966, Joaquín Balaguer governed as a civilian with strong military support. However, the armed forces were not under his personalized central control in the way they had been under Trujillo.

office, even as gradually it became more complex to categorize the top generals. In 1971, he suddenly had the two switch jobs, and then continued to move them into various different positions. In 1975, one of Balaguer's balancing moves led to a major crisis. His naming of Nivar as police chief (for a second time) was bitterly protested by Pérez y Pérez and three other top military officers, who submitted their resignations and made veiled threats. Balaguer ultimately reappointed the protesting officers to other posts outside of the military while retaining the loyalty of the bulk of the armed forces. Then, in November 1977, he put Pérez y Pérez in charge of the army's key first brigade, as the election campaign intensified (Atkins 1981, 71–88; Latorre 1975, 312–21).

Even as Balaguer confronted threats from the military, his regime also faced a variety of other conspiracies and rebellions from groups on the left (some having points of contact with rightist military elements). These groups were met with harsh repression, assassinations, and "disappearances," which also often extended to journalists, labor leaders, and others. According to one estimate, there were some 650 political deaths or disappearances from 1966 to 1970, with 275 in 1970 alone. In 1969, Balaguer asserted there were unknown, "uncontrollable" elements within the military and the police, but later he argued that although they were known he lacked the evidence to prosecute them. Repression remained high in 1971 when General Pérez y Pérez was appointed as chief of police in January and openly established a paramilitary death squad, La Banda. Following international pressure generated by the efforts of Peña Gómez of the PRD, violence declined when Balaguer briefly arrested several members of La Banda and then forced Pérez y Pérez and Nivar to switch positions in October 1971; Nivar had complex links with Peña Gómez and other PRD and leftist leaders. However, political violence and assassination continued throughout the rest of Balaguer's regime, although it declined further after 1975. In 1972, one author estimated there had been two thousand political assassinations in the previous five years; another author estimated that three thousand were killed between 1966 and 1974.[12]

Through time, the private economic activities of top officers grew. As we saw in chapter 3, business-military tensions had emerged during the period of the triumvirate (1963–65), when military contraband trade led to protests by local merchants and industrialists. Under Balaguer, particularly by his third term in office, investments by the military in public works, hotels, commerce, sugar, livestock, and light manufacturing were increasingly resented by private businessmen. They perceived it as unfair competition and were sometimes pressured to sell their firms or their products against their will (interviews by author with businessmen and high government officials in 1986; see also Gómez Berges 1985). While obviously not reflecting a move toward military professionalism, this also represented a degree of military autonomy from centralized control unknown in the Trujillo era, when only Trujillo family members and direct confidantes in the military dared behave in this fashion.

Balaguer and the Political Opposition

In dealing with the political opposition, Balaguer both granted a relatively free hand to the armed forces to carry out repressive acts and assiduously practiced a policy of co-optation and limited toleration of moderate oppositions. A few PRD and other party figures were brought into his government after the 1966 elections, and following subsequent elections Balaguer also offered public office and international posts to candidates of the defeated parties. Similarly, several radical opponents were permitted to accept posts at the public university or even in certain state agencies such as the planning office. In this context, semi-oppositions, often of disgruntled former supporters, were permitted to operate openly even as the major political opposition was never totally quashed and eventually reemerged. Partially to embarrass Balaguer, the PRD and a new party created by retired General Elías Wessin y Wessin, the Partido Quisqueyano Demócrata (PQD, Democratic Quisqueyan Party), both refused to participate in the 1968 municipal elections. Only the small Partido Revolucionario Social Cristiano (PRSC, Revolutionary Social Christian Party) agreed to participate, giving a semblance of legitimacy to the process (Latorre 1975, 346).

A brief review of the 1970 and 1974 elections will suggest both the strengths and the weaknesses of Balaguer's political strategy oriented toward seeking a limited popular base for himself while constraining opposition participation. In electoral terms, Balaguer was obviously aided by the fact that the major opposition party, the PRD, ultimately refused to participate in either election. In 1970, Balaguer confronted stiff opposition from important moderate figures within and outside his party, the PR, and a combination of political shrewdness and luck helped him gain reelection. There was an important challenge within his own party. Although Balaguer had modified the constitution to permit reelection, his vice president and a key organizer of the PR had also expected to succeed Balaguer in 1970. As early as 1968, however, it was clear that Balaguer was having second thoughts. Given that he did not retain effective control of his own party and that he had largely ignored it since the 1966 elections, Balaguer encouraged the formation of a new political party, *using government funds*, which could serve him if necessary. The Movimiento Nacional de la Juventud (MNJ, National Youth Movement) soon became a viable organization; and when Balaguer threatened to leave the PR and campaign outside of it, Augusto Lora, his vice president, was effectively forced out of the party to become the leader of and ultimately the candidate of an insignificant new political party (interviews by author with a major figure behind the MNJ, journalists, and others in 1986).[13] Hector García Godoy, the 1966 provisional president, was another significant potential challenger in the absence of the PRD, which had officially declared it was abstaining. Fortuitously for Balaguer, García Godoy died on April 20 (from a heart attack), just weeks before the election. In the end, four opposition candidates presented themselves: Lora; retired general Wessin y Wessin; Alfonso Moreno Martínez, representing the increasingly moderate Christian democratic PRSC; and a replacement for García Godoy.

These forces complained that a fair campaign and elections were impossible if Balaguer remained in the presidential office. Given their ideological moderation and Balaguer's desire to retain a veneer of legality, negotiations ensued. A remarkable ad hoc solution to the opposition's lack of trust in the formal institutions and rules emerged: Balaguer agreed to step down temporarily from the presidency. Thus, one month before the election, the president of the supreme court temporarily assumed the presidency. Under these circumstances, Balaguer focused on his successful economic record and on how he could best manage the threat from the left, regarding which he ably took advantage of the kidnapping of the U.S. Air Force attaché by members of the leftist Movimiento Popular Dominicano (MPD, Dominican People's Movement) in March 1970.[14] Balaguer officially received 57 percent of the vote, and his coalition won twenty-six of twenty-seven senate seats and sixty of the seventy-four seats in the chamber. When he was inaugurated for a second term in August 1970, he incorporated several opposition figures into his cabinet, and rewarded as well his political allies (Campillo Pérez 1982, 262–64).

The 1974 elections were potentially a more serious challenge for Balaguer, as the PRD sought to participate. As the elections neared and Balaguer feared defeat, he encouraged the military to take an even more direct, repressive role in the electoral process. Beginning in early 1973, opposition parties spanning the ideological spectrum began joining together for the purpose of ousting Balaguer in the context of the elections. Bosch at the head of the PRD dominated this Bloque de Dignidad Nacional (National Dignity Bloc), which brought sixteen political groupings together. However, the coalition suffered a major setback when Bosch left the PRD in November 1973 and denounced participation in the elections. After his departure, the PRD and four other parties formed a new coalition, the Acuerdo de Santiago (Agreement of Santiago), and the National Dignity Bloc, vastly weakened by these defections, divided again. A few months before the elections, it appeared that five opposition parties or coalitions would oppose Balaguer, although it was clear that Balaguer's only serious threat came from the PRD coalition. Fearing a defeat at the polls, Balaguer encouraged the military to step up the pressure against his opponents, harassing and repressing their activists, destroying their propaganda, and intimidating the population. The smaller parties that remained in the National Dignity Bloc withdrew in the face of the blatant military partiality (interview by author with an opposition candidate in 1996).[15] Then, on the day before the election, the PRD coalition, fearing a bloodbath, decided to pull out. Luis Homero Lájara Burgos, a former chief of police under Trujillo, was the only figure who opposed Balaguer in the elections. Balaguer was reelected, officially with 85 percent of the vote. He immediately asserted his intention to install a "government of national unity," which not surprisingly did not prosper. After mounting postelectoral protests, the PRD launched a massive two-day "silent protest" in mid-July. In his August inauguration speech, Balaguer promised to introduce a number of constitutional reforms, including the prohibition of immediate presidential reelection; none of the measures were considered in the congress, which was totally dominated by his party. Although these two electoral processes highlight Balaguer's authoritarian abuse of power, they also demonstrate a space for political opposition that was never evident under Trujillo.

And, as the 1978 elections approached, economic, military, and political issues all appeared less favorable for Balaguer. Balaguer's legitimacy had rested on economic growth and on an ideology of peace and order in the face of subversion and chaos. Although the country had survived the first OPEC oil shock remarkably well as a result of a sugar boom—in spite of having to import all its oil—by 1976 export earnings began to decline and industrial growth to lag. With the country's economic slowdown came greater business disgruntlement. Paradoxically, even as economic slowdown became a short-term problem for the regime, socioeconomic changes induced by earlier economic growth under Balaguer also worked to undermine his regime. Substantial economic growth, industrialization, and urbanization expanded middle-sector and professional groups supportive of more institutionalized access to state power and, thus, of democratization. Another problematic feature was Balaguer's physical decline, particularly his failing eyesight, which became public knowledge in January 1977. Politically ambitious military personnel maneuvered for power and influence, and opposition forces were emboldened, as especially U.S. policy began to focus more on issues of democracy and human rights with the inauguration of President Jimmy Carter in January 1977. Yet, without the changes that had occurred within the PRD between 1974 and 1978, electoral victory and a successful democratic transition would not have occurred in 1978.

Evolution of the PRD toward Moderation and Pursuit of Electoral Victory

Following the bitter experience of 1965–66, the PRD went through a divisive phase of polarization, as two opposing lessons were learned. The phase ended with the startling decision of Juan Bosch—the leader of the radical faction—to leave the party in 1973; José Francisco Peña Gómez, an ambivalent supporter of both conspiratorial and electoral routes to power, ultimately sided with the moderates and elections.

From a Hardline PRD to Party Division

Once Balaguer's government was inaugurated in July 1966, the PRD moved quickly from a policy of "creative and constructive opposition" to one of "just, revolutionary and nationalist opposition" (see Espinal 1982, 58–60), as the charismatic Peña Gómez was elected secretary general of the party. Peña Gómez, increasingly the second figure in the party after Bosch, had helped precipitate the events of April 1965 by successfully calling the people into the streets from his radio program; he soon accused Balaguer of seeking to destroy the PRD by a policy of "corrupting at the top and repressing at the bottom" (*corromper arriba y golpear abajo*) (Gleijeses 1978, 160–61; phrase cited in Gautreaux Piñeyro 1994, 70). Bosch left the country shortly after the PRD's fourth convention in October 1966. Then, in mid-1967, at a congress of social-ist youth held in Sweden, he asserted that liberal democracy was impossible in the Dominican Republic given its social structure. What was needed, he said, was a unified left to struggle for a "dictatorship with popular support" (text of speech in González Canahuate 1985, 232–40; see also Bosch 1991, esp. 126, 217). As a consequence of his new objective, Bosch called for PRD electoral abstention, a policy followed in 1968 that had generated increased friction within the party.

At the same time, because of its large mass base, the PRD became a target of pressures and infiltrations by other leftist groups. The MPD, many of whose members came to occupy important posts within the PRD during this period, with the apparent support of Peña Gómez, called for a "revolutionary coup d'état," seeking coalitions with right-wing military elements (particularly those close to General Wessin y Wessin). The Dominican Communist Party, in turn, actively supported Bosch's anti-election thesis (interviews by author in 1986 with PRD activists of this period).[16] Conspiracies flourished, and ineffec-tive terrorist activities were met by repression; a repeat of 1965, with a success-ful civil-military conspiracy to overthrow Balaguer, was not to occur.

The more moderate elements of the PRD, disheartened by Bosch's rejec-tion of electoral politics, combated the party's official adoption of Bosch's thesis and abstentionism. Most were also marginalized from the conspiratorial side of PRD politics during this period. Following the abstention in the 1968 municipal elections (subsequently, these midterm elections were no longer held), conflicts continued in the party between the moderate electoral faction and the more radical abstentionist one. An initial Benidorm Agreement was reached with Bosch in Spain in November 1968, which did not completely commit the party to Bosch's position (see González Canahuate 1985, 36–37). In an even more difficult compromise between Bosch and moderate PRD leaders, the 1970 PRD convention approved the thesis of "dictatorship with popular support" in principle, rather than officially, and called for absten-tion as the only viable policy in the face of government repression and Bala-guer's efforts to seek reelection. To insure that the PRD would remain abstentionist and to retake control of the PRD and begin to implement his new political strategy, Bosch returned from his self-imposed exile just before the 1970 elections.

With Bosch's return to the country, the party underwent a new phase that ultimately ended with his departure and the party's division. Bosch began a purge of MPD and other leftist activists from the PRD and successfully urged Peña Gómez and other PRD activists associated with conspiratorial activities to go abroad.[17] He refused to conspire further with Wessin y Wessin, and thus the PRD was not involved in the 1971 plot that Balaguer uncovered. A change in party statutes permitted Bosch and a new "permanent commission" of his loyal adherents to centralize power. At the same time, Bosch began a process of education for party militants. In the meantime, Peña Gómez helped to coordinate international pressure on the Balaguer regime, both in Europe and in the United States, to stop the repressive activities of the paramilitary La Banda. Protests were carried out in both New York and Washington, in addition to demonstrations within the Dominican Republic.

Not for the first or the last time, Bosch appeared to be playing a complex game. Through him the PRD was conversing with political parties across the ideological spectrum, which were united only by their desire to remove Balaguer from power; these groups eventually coalesced to form the National Dignity Bloc. Yet, Bosch remained purposefully vague as to whether the PRD would participate in the 1974 elections. At the same time, with the MPD activists—who had conspired with elements of the military and plotted terrorist acts—out of the party, Bosch was trying to reshape the PRD organization into more of a vanguard-type party with his people in key posts, marginalizing moderates. Both the formation of the National Dignity Bloc and the plans for reshaping the PRD were temporarily suspended as a result of the quixotic invasion of the Dominican Republic by Caamaño and nine other guerrillas in February 1973.[18] Caamaño's leadership role in 1965 had radicalized him, leading him to Cuba and eventually to this failed invasion which led to his death at the hand of the Dominican military thirteen days after he landed. Bosch's statements doubting Caamaño's presence in the country were seen by some as somewhat treasonous of an old friend, whereas Peña Gómez provided cautious moral support.[19]

Growing contradictions within the party sharpened as a result of Caamaño's invasion, which led Bosch and Peña Gómez to go into hiding because of threatened government repression. Relations between the two grew even more distant at this time. Bosch's new institutional structure had left the secretary-general with few functions and much less power when he returned from his studies abroad in early 1973 (del Castillo 1981, 67–68, which also provides a valuable general analysis of the party division). Bosch's reorganization was placing people who agreed with his goal of national liberation and vanguardist strategy into key positions of authority. Differences with Bosch grew as Peña Gómez articulated the need to strengthen ties with allies in the United States that could help the PRD. In a speech on July 29, 1973, on "American Liberals and National Revolution," Peña Gómez argued that liberals in the U.S. Congress, such as Frank Church and William Fulbright, were better tactical allies of the revolutionary struggle than Fidel Castro or Mao Tse-tung, and he sustained his arguments about the usefulness of these international ties in seventeen speeches over the next month.[20] In other speeches during this period, Peña Gómez reiterated the importance of the PRD campaign in the United States regarding the curtailment of the actions of La Banda and stressed the need for the PRD to work "within the system," given the absence of conditions for any other kind of struggle.[21] Thus, from his earlier more radical posture, Peña Gómez ultimately came to side with the more moderate elements of the party. The power struggle between Bosch and more moderate figures intensified. Peña Gómez's previous radical efforts had proven ineffective, and he was being squeezed out by Bosch and his new strategy. Thus, Peña Gómez and the moderates came together; they needed his charisma and visibility, and he needed their financial and organizational capabilities.

The crisis finally came to a head in November 1973, when Bosch decided to break with the PRD. A few weeks later, Bosch officially created the Partido de la Liberación Dominicana (PLD, Party of Dominican Liberation), taking with him the group of intellectuals he had been cultivating. Under his iron grip, the PLD was a more radical party and was intended to be a smaller, better disciplined, and more tightly organized party, with the "quality" rather than "quantity" that could more effectively promote his hopes for national liberation and a dictatorship with popular support.[22] Bosch's actions stunned the country, as they came just months before the 1974 elections and as he was cooperating with a vast array of parties across the ideological spectrum in a front to oppose Balaguer. The division he provoked helped pave the way for Balaguer's successful reelection, as Bosch stepped up his attacks against the uselessness of going to elections in Balaguer's manipulated authoritarian setting, in which opposition participation would only serve to legitimize a fraudulent exercise.[23]

Yet, with Bosch's departure, the PRD decided to participate in the 1974 elections. With Peña Gómez playing a central negotiating role, the PRD became the axis of the five-party Santiago Agreement coalition, formed in December 1973. PRD leaders felt it was risky to go to elections alone, as the party division had just occurred, and talks with opposition parties regarding a joint opposition to Balaguer had been proceeding prior to Bosch's exit. The PRD chose to ally both with parties on the right, "so we could not be accused of being communist," and on the left, "so Bosch could not accuse us of being reactionary" (author's interview with a prominent PRD leader in May 1986). The Santiago Agreement was a recreation of the PRD's conspiratorial alliance of the late 1960s with the MPD on the left and General Wessin y Wessin and his PQD on the right, though now with electoral intentions.[24] After several nonpartisan figures rejected the presidential nomination of the coalition, S. Antonio Guzmán, a prominent PRD leader, finally acceded to it. General Wessin y Wessin, though still in political exile because of his foiled coup plot of 1971, became the vice presidential nominee.

As the election approached and the military repression intensified, the PRD threatened to abstain unless the government provided special guarantees. Finally, just forty-eight hours before the elections, Guzmán opted to abstain with strong encouragement from other party moderates. Along with many PRD leaders at the time, he believed that Balaguer's last-minute concessions were insufficient and, more importantly, that the military would not allow the PRD to reach the presidency even with a convincing electoral victory, and that a bloodbath could ensue; Guzmán was further concerned about trying to govern at the head of such a heterogeneous coalition. Other leaders, including Peña Gómez, argued the PRD should not withdraw. Abstentionism led to disappointment throughout the PRD militancy and supporters; yet, some PRD leaders were fearful of being accused of legitimating Balaguer's government by participating in elections, mocked by Bosch as "electoral slaughterhouses."[25]

PRD Moderation Leading Up to the 1978 Elections

The frustrations of abstention and the exit of Bosch from the PRD facilitated the development of a new conscious strategy to gain electoral victory that involved domestic programmatic and organizational components and the forging of international ties. Thus, what was involved was not only "deradicalization" in a programmatic sense (e.g. removing demands for the nationalization of Gulf and Western holdings), but also a conscious policy of renewing and strengthening the international ties that had been weakened first as a result of Bosch's ideological vision and then by the 1973 split in the party. Because of the predominant U.S. role in the country, a "counterlobby" to Balaguer's strong diplomatic and corporate ties was important. Also required was extensive organizational work, in order to pressure Balaguer to hold honest elections and then to win them and assume power. By August 1975, the

PRD had announced its intentions to participate in the 1978 elections, although whether it would seek a consensus candidate outside the party or present its own had not yet been decided.

Throughout 1975, Peña Gómez and other PRD leaders traveled abroad to strengthen international ties, though not only with U.S. liberals. They reestablished and strengthened ties to the Socialist International as the party sought an ideological mooring in democratic socialism. The PRD's efforts came at a time when the Socialist International was also more interested in expanding its programs in Latin America (author's interview with former head of Dominican office of the F. Ebert Foundation in 1986). In his speeches during the year, Peña Gómez highlighted the potential importance of the international connections for the PRD and how the party was now asking for international solidarity as it sought power in 1978 by peaceful means. The importance of these international connections were a major theme in Peña Gómez's major addresses to the PRD at the 1976 and 1977 conventions. At the same time, Peña Gómez continued to moderate his statements and his tone, emphasizing that the PRD rejected violence and foresaw the next (PRD) government as a gradualist and transitory one. Just as important, the PRD constructed a more responsive and internally democratic party structure (González Canahuate 1985, 67–79).

The vigorously contested November 1977 PRD convention resulted in Guzmán being chosen as the presidential nominee. Guzmán was an ideal PRD candidate in 1978 in many respects, for both domestic and international reasons. His PRD and anti-Trujillista credentials were intact. Yet, he was also a conservative landowner widely known to Santiago businessmen, in part as a result of his membership in a regional private development group, the Asociación para el Desarrollo, Inc. A schoolmate of Bosch's, the former PRD leader had asked him to serve as his secretary of agriculture in his 1963 government. In 1965, Guzmán was the favored candidate of a number of liberal U.S. policymakers to serve as provisional president following the U.S. invasion, though in the end top U.S. policymakers rejected him because of his perceived closeness to Bosch (Gleijeses 1978, 266–68). At the same time, as a result of those negotiations, he became known to a wide number of U.S. policymakers, including Cyrus Vance, then deputy secretary of defense, who subsequently served as President Jimmy Carter's secretary of state during the 1978 Dominican elections.[26] Guzmán was Bosch's vice presidential candidate in the 1966 elections and gained additional campaign experience and visibility within the country as a result of the 1974 campaign.

Yet, there was opposition to Guzmán's serving as the PRD candidate in the 1978 elections, out of a concern that he would not be an intellectual match to the wily Balaguer in the tough campaign that was foreseen and because of his conservative views. As secretary general of the party, Peña Gómez promoted multiple candidacies for the PRD presidential nomination, which he explained publicly at the time as a way to promote institutional vitality; the Guzmán camp believed it was primarily out of a desire to prevent their man's nomination. Peña Gómez knew that his own candidacy was out of the question, as he was distrusted in business circles.[27]

Following a stormy, contested convention, Guzmán emerged as the PRD nominee and the party remained united behind him. Of the two other leading candidates, Jacobo Majluta became the vice presidential nominee and Salvador Jorge Blanco was made president of the party. In 1978, compared to the past elections, the party platform was more moderate regarding the expropriation or nationalization of foreign holdings and the promotion of other reforms, while emphasizing "Change Without Violence" as the major campaign theme. The PRD sought to mobilize popular support, to gain the sympathy of professional and middle-sector groups frustrated by the perceived injustices of a personalistic, neopatrimonial system, and at least not to alienate major business groups. The struggle for the party nomination generated interest in the PRD, brought new people into the party, and showed a dramatic contrast in style with the manner in which Balaguer's Partido Reformista was managed. At the same time, the PRD consciously moderated its programmatic goals and its ideological style; yet, votes alone would not assure presidential succession.

Transition "from Above": The 1978 Elections

The 1978 elections—the electoral defeat of Balaguer, the thwarting of a military coup in the making, and the successful accession to power of the PRD presidential candidate, Antonio Guzmán—represent a democratic transition. Following the PRD's successful mass mobilization to win the elections convincingly, what followed was a cautious, staged transition "from above" in which Balaguer was provided certain guarantees by means of a distortion of the congressional votes to provide his party with a majority in the senate; yet, the attempt to tie Guzmán's hands completely, particularly regarding treatment of the military, was not successful. All sides were forced to compromise, though the transition and the conciliation were weighted heavily toward elitist bargaining and limited reform.

In spite of the deterioration of the Balaguer regime and the conscious efforts of the post-Bosch PRD to provide a moderate electoral alternative, a transition from Balaguer to Guzmán was far from a foregone conclusion.

Major business groups, especially in the capital, were still largely Balaguerista and distrustful of the PRD, particularly of Peña Gómez. Yet, business discontent had grown somewhat as a result of economic decline, military incursions into economic activities, and—especially in Santiago, the country's second largest city and the capital of the Cibao area—regional frustrations over the personalistic decision-making process that was perceived as weighted toward the capital city's interests. There was growing criticism of aspects of Balaguer's economic policies, particularly his disregard of the agro-export sector. At the same time, in part because of the PRD's international campaign and in part because of President Carter's administration, the pressure on Balaguer to hold honest elections was more intense. Balaguer permitted Peña Gómez and other PRD leaders to speak freely on the radio. He also legalized the Communist Party, perhaps hoping it would take votes away from the PRD.[28]

Balaguer also had considerable problems with his own deeply factionalized political party, the PR. Family members and certain military officers were playing an increasingly significant role, alienating other party activists. One of the clearest indicators of the sharp divisions among his own backers was the struggle over the vice presidential post. The vice presidency was viewed as critical, particularly by some of the military who felt the septuagenarian Balaguer, who was also losing his eyesight, would not last another four years. In an attempt to counterbalance the ambitions of the dominant military group and to strengthen his vote in Santiago and the Cibao region in general, Balaguer picked Fernando Alvarez Bogaert as his vice presidential candidate. Alvarez was an ambitious politician in his own right. As general manager of the State Sugar Council, he had also had major conflicts with General Nivar (who felt he had not been allowed to prosper as other officers had); subsequently, Alvarez had been forced to resign in a corruption scandal and had been sent abroad as an ambassador (see Atkins 1981, 100). Balaguer's surprise announcement about Alvarez came at the party convention on March 14, 1978, only two months before the elections. On April 18, several top military officers kidnapped the vice presidential nominee and demanded he resign at gunpoint. Finally, on May 5, less than two weeks before the elections, Balaguer substituted Alvarez with the more pliable incumbent vice president, Carlos Goico Morales.[29]

By the time Alvarez was replaced, Balaguer's campaign appeared to be in trouble. Many PR activists were sitting out the elections, displeased by the congressional and local-level candidacies that had been picked with the influence of the military group (Gómez Berges 1985, 55–61). But the campaign was not moribund. Demonstrations in major cities were assured large crowds by busing in hundreds from other cities (author's interview with PR politician,

1985); and in a surprising show of stamina that reemerged even in the 1994 campaign, Balaguer crisscrossed the country in the final weeks of the campaign while newspapers were filled with campaign publicity showing the public works built in each region during his period in office. Radio and TV audiences were saturated with campaign spots. And scare ads suggesting a PRD victory would mean a return to civil war and violence appeared.

In the meantime, the PRD was carrying out a far-reaching campaign with international legitimacy, financial support, and technical campaign services provided by parties of the Socialist International and particularly the AD of Venezuela. Portugal's prime minister, Mario Soares, visited the country and lent his support to the PRD. In contrast to 1974, the military harassment of the PRD was not as intense (for a summary of the major incidents, see *Nuevo Diario*, May 5, 1982; also Atkins 1981). Neither party employed polling to help determine campaign strategy, and both parties remained confident of victory. Nevertheless, Balaguer heightened fears and indirectly invited military action by stating in front of a group of veterans a few days before the elections that "what is at risk in these elections is not the destiny of a man or of a party, but the destiny of the Armed Forces and the destiny of the country" (cited in *Nuevo Diario*, May 5, 1982).[30]

Yet, there was apparent resistance within the armed forces to carrying out a coup, in spite of widely shared doubts about the PRD. Reasons for this included fear of adverse international reaction, division among the top military, and for some, doubts whether Balaguer would support such a move. Some junior officers also felt a coup would largely protect the position of senior officers, prolonging their tenure, and others feared that a coup could again provoke a civil war.

The position of the United States was followed with intense interest in the country. The sudden replacement of Robert Hurwitch by Robert Yost as U.S. ambassador just before the elections was interpreted as a U.S. tilt toward the PRD, as Hurwitch was viewed as pro-Balaguer.[31] Foreign observers, some invited by the government, and some not, flocked to the election. In response to Balaguer's invitation, the OAS sent a team of three former Latin American presidents under the leadership of the Ecuadorian Galo Plaza. The Democratic Conference, a coalition of liberal organizations with strong ties to the U.S. Democratic Party—with whom the PRD had developed solid links—also sent an official observer, Gregory Wolfe, as part of a group of Socialist International observers. Observers were also sent by the AD of Venezuela, the Socialist Party of Japan, and the Socialist Worker's Party of Spain. These observer teams, encouraged by the PRD, played a central role in mobilizing international opinion.

Foiling an Attempted Coup

In the end, some of the more politically ambitious military did try to thwart the PRD electoral victory. As electoral results came in after polls closed on May 16, it became increasingly evident that the PRD was gaining a wide margin of victory. A military contingent stopped the vote count at the JCE around 4:00 A.M. on May 17, as the military in some areas around the country harassed PRD candidates and poll watchers. An attempt to remove the summary vote tallies (*actas*) of the voting stations in Santo Domingo from the headquarters of the municipal board responsible for Santo Domingo failed; a leader of the board gave the *actas* to former president Galo Plaza, who hid them in his hotel room. Key players in the effort to subvert the elections included Chief of Police Nivar, who had been extremely active in Balaguer's campaign, and the secretary of state for the armed forces, Beauchamp.[32]

Yet, the actions were poorly coordinated, lacked critical support across the armed forces, and had only the tacit blessing of Balaguer himself, who was keeping his options open. The coup plotters were unable to get General Pérez y Pérez (commander of the army's crucial first brigade) to go along immediately with the plot, "unless ordered directly by Balaguer"; in other words, he did not say no outright, as he was calculating the extent of possible domestic and international opposition. In fact, domestic and international actors opposed to a coup effort were appraised fairly early of which military were involved and which were wavering, as Balaguer remained indecisive (author's interviews, 1986). Late in the night of May 18, after learning that the vote count would be able to proceed and in the face of extensive pressure, Balaguer broke his public silence, maintained since the election, in an ambiguous speech. He urged that the election results be respected, but did not acknowledge defeat, accused the PRD of fraud, and attacked outside intervention. In a meeting on May 19, an important group of junior officers rejected participation in a coup effort. International and domestic pressure to respect the electoral results and frustrations regarding the venality and politicization of certain top officers both played a role, even as the potential polarizing consequences of a coup were recognized by the phrase "no one wants another 1963 [coup] because no one wants another 1965 [civil war]." Finally, at a May 20 luncheon meeting, attended by thirty-six generals and several senior PR politicians, efforts by Nivar, Beauchamp, and Jorge Moreno to have a coup declared, were rejected (Atkins 1981, 108–10; author's interview with Dominican military, 1986).

Another ambiguous actor during these crisis days was Juan Bosch. Bosch and the PLD participated in the campaign, but claimed that it was impossible to displace Balaguer through elections and that a vote for the PRD was a wasted vote. In the tense days of the coup crisis, rather than calling for the election results to be respected, Bosch appealed for a provisional, coalition government. These and other indications suggest that Bosch preferred that Balaguer retain power, either because his hatred of the PRD was so intense or because he did not want his prediction about the uselessness of elections to be proven wrong.[33] In the subsequent weeks (and even years later), Bosch alleged that the whole matter was determined by the U.S. government (author's interviews, 1986).

The immediate threat of a coup was dispelled just a few days after the elections, following intense domestic and international pressure. But Balaguer then began a complex process that would provide him with guarantees that he would not be harassed. He played a masterful game of getting the military accustomed to the idea that they would hand over power, while keeping the PRD doubtful as to whether in fact he was going to step down. The period between the elections and the inauguration was extremely tense and crisis filled.

International pressure unquestionably played an important role in dismantling the coup in the making. Galo Plaza, representing the OAS, obviously played a crucial, dramatic role, both in safekeeping critical voting results and in informing Balaguer that the vote count would be able to proceed. The PRD had assiduously developed international contacts. Member parties of Socialist International and their leaders, especially President Carlos Andrés Pérez of Venezuela and Prime Minister Mario Soares of Portugal, mobilized support for the vote-counting process.

The actions of the United States were especially important. Already two weeks prior to the elections, the U.S. embassy had forecasted (internally) that the PRD was the likely winner of the elections, although not based on polling data. Especially with Antonio Guzmán as the PRD candidate, the U.S. government was comfortable with a PRD victory. Thus, prior to election day, the Dominican Republic was simply not an important agenda item in Washington, and the general policy of supporting fair and honest elections could hold as the U.S. "strategic objective" (this term was used by a former high-level U.S. diplomat in Washington in a 1986 interview with the author). Another indicator of the lack of strategic importance of the country during this period is that the Dominican Republic is not mentioned *even once* in the memoirs of either President Jimmy Carter (1982); his secretary of state, Cyrus Vance (1983); or his national security adviser, Zbigniew Brzezinski (1983). Following the intended coup, PRD friends in the U.S. Congress and elsewhere in Washington urged firm protests; part of the logic was that this was a very different kind of intervention than that of 1965, for it was simply urging

respect for the results of democratic elections. The outgoing assistant secretary of state for inter-American affairs, Terence Todman, sought to be more
cautious; but the National Security Council (NSC) adviser for Latin American affairs, Robert Pastor, and the incoming assistant secretary of state, Viron
Vaky, who at the time was still ambassador in Venezuela, felt it was appropriate for the U.S. to speak vigorously in defense of respecting an electoral result.
Carter and Vance actually strengthened the language of their diplomatic
protests that were sent to Balaguer; Vance's personal acquaintance of Guzmán was important in this respect. Also of central importance was the fact that
the U.S. military gave a strong message to the Dominican military that there
was no "dual-track" policy, that military intervention was repudiated.[34] Following a request by the NSC and the State Department, General McAuliffe,
head of the U.S. Southern Command in Panama, called General Beauchamp
to confirm U.S. opposition to any coup effort (author's interviews with high-
level U.S. policymakers in 1986 and 1990).

In sum, the role of the United States and to a lesser extent of other international actors was crucial in dismantling the coup in the making. Yet, it is an
error to assert the elections provided the United States with an "opportunity to
direct that country's internal political situation" (Kryzanek 1979, 51)—for this
misunderstands the entire logic of the pragmatic PRD strategy of developing a
counter-lobby to Balaguer in the United States, given the realities of the U.S.
role in the country, and places events such as the 1965 invasion on the same
conceptual plane of "interventionism" as pressuring a dependent "democratic" government to respect the results of its elections.

In addition, there was important domestic societal mobilization in defense
of free elections, although domestic and international repudiation efforts of
the coup attempt reinforced each other. Key intellectuals and professionals
helped mobilize domestic and international opinion behind the scenes, even
as they also placed advertisements calling for the election results to be respected. The vast majority of the business sector still supported Balaguer; and
large-scale industrialists, especially in Santo Domingo, were reluctant to express themselves publicly against him. However, Santiago businessmen, all of
whom knew Guzmán intimately, and with the strong urging of church officials, reluctantly broke the ice with an advertisement calling for the electoral
results to be fairly counted and the popular will (*la voluntad popular*) to be
respected (author's interviews with several of those who signed the advertisement and others, 1986). Subsequently, Santiago businessmen in the capital
pushed Santo Domingo businessmen into taking a similar position. Newspapers were filled with numerous advertisements from professional, educational, labor, and other organizations. Indeed, all the country's newspapers,

except *El Caribe*, and all the country's radio news shows, except two, editorialized in favor of abiding by the election results (Díaz 1980). The dangers of an increased military role, the specter of 1965, the fear of violence and bloodshed, and concerns regarding international isolation eventually overrode concerns about the personal and business risks in going against the current president. Also important were the changes in the PRD, the conservative nature of the PRD's presidential candidate, and the fact that what was at issue was urging respect for an accomplished event—an electoral result. The PRD's prudent, cautious attitude during these days was also important. It was astounding that no shots had been fired or people killed; the PRD had made a firm determination to play "by the rules."

Elite Bargaining and Tacit Pact Making

In a neopatrimonial country such as the Dominican Republic, a transition from above could occur, not only under the strong shadow of the United States, but also in ways that would reflect and perhaps ultimately reinforce the country's low levels of institutionality and respect for the rule of law—even as formal allegiance to constitutional forms would ostensibly be respected. This was evident both with regard to political and military issues. First of all, Balaguer was anxious to provide himself with some political protection. According to the Dominican constitution, power is transferred three months after the elections, on August 16. Balaguer intimated his strategy to buy himself time and negotiating room in his speech of May 18, which accused the PRD of massive electoral fraud. Employing a conservative, pugnacious lawyer, Marino Vinicio "Vincho" Castillo, Balaguer began a drawn-out legal process through the JCE, alleging that the PRD had illegally registered hundreds of thousands of Haitians and with the assistance of Venezuela computer experts had carried out massive computer fraud; at the same time "backdoor" negotiations to adjust the results were begun.[35]

Ultimately, a legal abomination known as the "historic decision" (*el fallo histórico*) allowed the transition to go through. On July 7, 1978, the JCE ruled that serious irregularities had prevented votes potentially attributable to the PR to be cast and counted; therefore, it arbitrarily adjusted the results in four provinces, enough to give Balaguer's party a majority in the senate (one seat in the chamber of deputies was also shifted). The senate is important because it names members of the JCE as well as judges, who would hear potential charges for corruption or human rights abuses.

PRD leaders have insisted that there were no negotiations, that the adjustment of results was an imposition by Balaguer. At the same time, Carlos

Andrés Pérez asserted he "supported the internal negotiations, after all, Balaguer felt he had a right to guarantees" (author's interview, 1986, in Santo Domingo). The United States does not appear to have played a central role, though it was kept informed by Balaguer of his intentions. It took the attitude that the central issue was the presidential election: in the words of one former high-level U.S. diplomat, "this was a minor blip that didn't affect the overall transition, what's a Latin election without a deal of some kind?" (author's interview, 1986). Rhetorically and legally, the PRD strenuously objected to the JCE's decision. The Dominican supreme court threw out the PRD's claim, since the JCE is constitutionally prescribed to be the final arbiter in all electoral matters. Yet, it is important to highlight what the PRD did not do: it did not encourage mass protest.

Balaguer then sought to constrain Guzmán and the PRD even further, especially with regard to military matters. The procedure and the ultimate outcome highlight why one can comfortably assert there was a democratic transition in 1978 that reflected both neopatrimonialism and the importance of the United States. In July, Balaguer's lame-duck congress quickly approved new organic laws for the armed forces and the police. One of the new measures stipulated that civilian authorities could not remove officers from a military post before two years time had elapsed. Shortly thereafter, Balaguer reshuffled top military appointments, placing Nivar, Pérez y Pérez, and other key generals in critical posts from which legally they could now not be shifted for two years. Guzmán's hands appeared to be tied, both politically and militarily.

Yet, beginning on inauguration day and continuing thereafter, Guzmán dealt forthrightly with the Dominican military, simply ignoring any legal restrictions. On inauguration day, taking advantage of the presence of a high-level U.S. delegation, Guzmán forcibly reshuffled several top military officers, weakening their control over troops and their potential to mount a coup challenge. Nivar was relieved as head of the army's first brigade, and several other top generals were also forced out. Pérez y Pérez survived in August, but was eventually ousted in November, as was the case with several other generals in the following months (for details on removals, see Atkins 1981, 137–40; also author's interviews with U.S. diplomatic and military personnel and a retired high-level Dominican military officer, 1986). Without calling into question Guzmán's courage on this issue, one can only conclude that without U.S. support these military changes in violation of Dominican law would not have been likely.

In other countries in the region over the 1980s, the continued autonomy and lack of accountability of the armed forces to the top civilian authorities called into question the extent to which one could refer to the inauguration of a civilian president as a "democratic" transition. In the Dominican case (un-like Guatemala in the 1980s) the United States had sufficient influence—and (unlike El Salvador or Guatemala during this period) no national security concerns—to apply pressure and support domestic civilian efforts. The 1990 transition in Chile provides a different type of contrast to the Dominican transition, while highlighting the practical and ethical dilemma between de-mocratization and institutionalization. Here, the two democratically elected presidents, Patricio Aylwin and Eduardo Frei, both have felt obliged to respect the antidemocratic, but entrenched constitutional and legal prerogatives of the Chilean armed forces that they have been unable to change through the legislature. This respect for institutionality has clearly constrained democracy in that country, yet in the longer term the ability to enforce more strictly the rule of law to the advantage of democracy may be enhanced. In the Domini-can case, ignoring legal niceties and relying directly on the backing of the United States, both reflected and reinforced neopatrimonial and dependent features of Dominican political reality.

Conclusion

By the time an exercise such as this is completed, there can be a sense that the particular outcome was overdetermined, that it *had* to occur. It is important to underscore that the 1978 transition in the Dominican Republic did not appear that way to the actors living the process day to day, nor even to many of them as they reflected on it in retrospect (author's interviews over 1986–90). Nor can one simply argue that the country had a democratic transition because it was now more modernized, more affluent, more urban, and with a larger middle class, or simply because of U.S. intervention. It is only by understanding the particular implications of these processes for organizational development within society and institutional ties across the regime and key state and soci-etal actors that we can make sense of them. Thus, especially compared to the earlier processes of 1961–62 and 1965–66, conditions were more favorable for a transition in 1978 in each of the three clusters of factors we have previously identified: the nature of the preexisting authoritarian regime, the interna-tional geopolitical and economic context, and the mode of transition. The three transitions are compared along these key dimensions in table 4.3.[36]

The nature of the preexisting regime—authoritarian and neopatrimonial—and its relations to major social and political groups is perhaps the most crucial factor.[37] The differences between Balaguer's and Trujillo's regimes and their ties to social and political groups mattered in terms of facilitating the transition.

Unlike neosultanistic or inchoate regimes, there was not now a near-total institutional vacuum in society and the polity. By the time Balaguer assumed power, the country was no longer as isolated, and societal and political actors were stronger than had been the case under Trujillo. If Balaguer had been even more like Trujillo, his regime might have had more sultanistic tendencies, but given the development of social and political forces and the country's international circumstances, it could never have approximated the features of the Trujillo regime. Yet, Balaguer *was* a different kind of leader, and he established new kinds of relations with economic allies and the political opposition. Societal organizations independent of the regime were able to form and articulate demands, and business groups ultimately spoke in defense of democracy and, thus, in favor of the moderate PRD opposition. A vigorous political opposition was able to form and campaign actively, although its own increasing moderation facilitated the process—especially in a context in which there was no active revolutionary threat. The Dominican military were neither completely beholden to the ruler nor totally autonomous. The nature of the regime and its relations with other actors meant there were moderates in both the regime (ultimately, Balaguer himself) and the opposition (the PRD).

The international geopolitical context was also more favorable. Under the Carter administration, the United States had an active policy toward the region that could focus more exclusively on human rights and democracy in the absence of perceived national security threats (Schoultz 1981, 4–16); in the Dominican Republic in particular, there were simply no perceived national security threats. The absence of such perceived threats was especially helpful in insuring that U.S. civilian and military policymakers provided a similar prodemocratic message, rather than the "dual-track message" historically prevalent. The U.S. support for respecting election results was aided by the strategy of the PRD to moderate its policies and to seek out international allies, cultivating allies within the United States to counteract those of Balaguer. U.S. support could be effective for reasons highlighted in a recent comparative study of U.S. efforts to promote democracy in the region, which —while not sanguine overall about such efforts—concluded that they tend to be the most successful where they are needed primarily in "highly unusual, very finely balanced circumstances" to "tip the scale" toward democratic forces that have already established themselves, or in the smaller Central American and Caribbean countries that are "most penetrated by and vulnerable to the United States" (Lowenthal 1991a, 400). In this case, the United States pressured for democratic elections and then helped to "tip the scale" by insisting that the results be respected, but it did not create or unite the opposition or manage its campaign. Yet, the almost reflexive nature of U.S. involve-

Table 4.3. Comparing Three Transitions, 1961–1962, 1965–1966, and 1978

	1961–62	1965–66	1978
I. Preexisting authoritarian regime			
	Neosultanistic	Inchoate and/or provisional	Neopatrimonial and authoritarian
Military:	Viewed as personal instrument of tyrant	Autonomous, faction-alized, and bitterly divided after civil war	Somewhat autono-mous, visible cliques
Societal or-ganizations:	Practically nonexistent	Weak, fragmented	Weak, but some present
Political op-position:	No organized opposi-tion until after assassi-nation	Opposition parties barely tolerated; political actors polarized after civil war	Opposition parties toler-ated
Economic allies:	Not autonomous, domi-nated by tyrant and insecure	Insecure and weak	Weak but increasing au-tonomy
II. International geopolitical and economic context			
Hierarchy of U.S. policy goals:	Perceived communist threat viewed as real, ultimately subsumed democracy goal	Perceived communist threat dominant, but gradually receding; "extrication" elections to facilitate removal of U.S. troops	No visible communist threat; democracy important goal
Extent of U.S. in-volvement:	Extremely high, em-ploying all means short of direct military inter-vention	Military intervention, and all other means	High-level, diplomatic, and economic means
III. The transition process			
Mode of transition:	Trujillo regime "col-lapse"; provisional gov-ernment, internation-ally imposed free elections; former ruler's allies not participating; no pacts	Potential transition from below thwarted by U.S. intervention; pro-visional government, in-ternationally imposed negotiated surrender of rebel forces and elections; no pacts	From above, negotiated with guarantees for departing ruler; tacit political pact

Table 4.3. Continued

	1961–62	1965–66	1978
Institutional changes and continuities:	Opposition "left" party wins absolute majority, heightens fears in atmosphere of international polarization and military continuity	Political actors polarized by civil war and intervention; limited, failed efforts at power sharing; imposed constitutional framework of presidential dominance; military politically active and semiautonomous	Inherited constitutional framework of presidential dominance; but some power sharing; military purged

ment and the active pursuit of that involvement by domestic Dominican actors further illustrates an entrenched legacy that has often distorted domestic politics and that ultimately is itself an obstacle to further Dominican democratization (cf. Hartlyn 1991, 206–9; Lowenthal 1991, 400–401).

The country's economic evolution and international economic circumstances also favored transition. Over the long term, economic growth may undermine authoritarian regimes as it helps to establish new social groups. As we saw, this was especially the case with business interests that chafed under Balaguer's personalistic style, though the establishment of larger numbers of professional, urban interests probably also helped the PRD. And, in the short term, economic downturn negatively affects the popularity of incumbent government leaders and almost certainly hurts authoritarian regimes, whose basis of legitimacy rests more broadly on the provision of stability and growth than does the legitimacy of democratic ones: in 1978, the Dominican Republic was continuing to confront a serious economic downturn, especially in contrast to the initial boom years under Balaguer.

The third set of factors relates to the mode of transition and to the transition process. Both the nature of Balaguer's regime and the international context facilitated a negotiated transition from above. Extensive guarantees were provided to the outgoing Balaguer and informal assurances were provided to key economic actors. Although these structural and institutional features are important in explaining shifts in behavior by key actors, the role of agency in insuring the success of the transition may be highlighted by three key things that did not happen. One is that the opposition PRD did not follow a more confrontational, mobilizational strategy, even in the face of significant provocation. It accepted the rules of the game and also feared losing international support if it was viewed as fostering violence. A second is that Balaguer apparently did not play a major, direct, and conscious role in planning a coup to preserve his power. Balaguer may have given tacit approval for a coup, and he certainly appeared willing to take advantage of the efforts to thwart the election carried out by his military henchmen, if they seemed likely to succeed in a way that might buy him time and ease domestic and especially international pressures. Yet, he also appeared to fear that an open coup could well leave him not only internationally isolated, but potentially shunted aside by ambitious military officers. Finally, the business sector did not ultimately refrain from calling for the election results to be respected, though they might have been unwilling to speak out at all, out of fear or acquiescence.

The three experiences with transitions in the Dominican Republic analyzed in chapter 3 and in this chapter present some contrasts as well as a number of important similarities to neopatrimonial African transition cases.[38] Based on their examination of those cases, Bratton and van de Walle (1994; 1997) assert that transitions from neopatrimonial regimes more commonly begin with mass protests from below. However, as we have seen, the ability to do this in neosultanistic regimes like that of Trujillo may be limited by the strength of the security forces. It may also be constrained by international actors. The pattern of mass protest Bratton and van de Walle describe was more evident in the Dominican Republic over the 1963–65 period, but the ultimate result of mass mobilization in 1965 was an intervention by the United States. As a consequence of this intervention, of the increased operating space for political opposition over the 1976–78 period, and of the PRD's desire to retain the support of the U.S. government, it is not surprising that the PRD (with their campaign slogan, "Change without Violence") sought to control and channel mass mobilization in the face of a Balaguer, whose regime did not generate the same extent of fiscal chaos and economic crisis as those in many African countries in the early 1990s. International geopolitical and economic factors, including the proximity and importance of the United States, and domestic economic management affected by historical memory, appeared to play different roles in the Dominican Republic than in the African cases, and thus Bratton and van de Walle may well conflate features particular to certain African countries in a narrow time period to all neopatrimonial regimes.

However, the evolution of the Dominican Republic in terms of these three within-case comparisons of transitions do buttress a number of other findings from Bratton and van de Walle's analysis. One has to do with the greater risks of transitions from below, which they see as offering "few opportunities for participants to nurture the democratic art of give-and-take" (Bratton and van de Walle 1997, 257). Another has to do with the importance of the preexisting regime, in which transitions from neopatrimonial regimes with some experience in respecting the rights of political opponents tend to lead to more democratic outcomes than transitions from more restrictive regimes. Thus, the "competitive one-party system" in their typology is the neopatrimonial regime with the most similarities to the Balaguer administration in the 1970s and is also the neopatrimonial regime from which they assert the prospects for political democracy are the greatest, because there can be sufficient agreement on the basic political rules of the game to permit an election that each side believes it can win (Bratton and van de Walle 1994, 483–84).

A new era appeared to be upon the country in 1978. In the Dominican case, the democratic transition was from one civilian ruler to another, and it occurred without a formal constitutional break. As elsewhere in Latin America, regime change took place with apparent constitutional continuity, and elite negotiations were fundamental in circumscribing democratization (though often not through the more visible or apparent "deals"). As we shall see below, the Dominican military and even the Balaguer-controlled senate were not to become the most important problems for Dominican democracy. Of greater significance were such factors as the international economic context, distrust by a more vigorously organized business community, and factional strife within the PRD.

5 The Struggle for Democratic Politics, 1978–1996
Social Evolution and Political Rules

No one in 1978 could have forecast the country's trajectory over the next eighteen years. The country experienced both far more dramatic socioeconomic change than had been imagined—indeed, a rapid transformation of the bases of the country's economy—as well as a surprising extent of political stasis. Reflecting a commonly held view at the time, one set of authors asserted that the subsequent 1982 elections were "the final face-off between the old presidents—an aging and deteriorating Balaguer, and a forceful, irreverent Juan Bosch" (Rodriguez and Huntington 1982, 32). Instead, the further erosion of the PRD helped lead in 1986 to the dramatic return of Balaguer to the presidency for ten additional years and to a near victory for Bosch in 1990. Then the eighty-nine-year old Balaguer set the terms for his stepping down from the presidency in 1996, handing power over to Bosch's young heir, who had formed an electoral alliance with Balaguer's party in order to win.

The history of the struggle for democratic politics in the Dominican Republic over the period 1978–96 reflects numerous disappointments. As we saw in the previous chapter, there were some reasons to be optimistic that the 1978 transition would lead to a period of political change away from neopatrimonialism and toward democratic consolidation. These reasons included societal changes, the dramatic weakening of the Dominican military, and the practices and statements of the PRD leaders. Yet, the period from 1978 to 1986, when the PRD was in the presidency must be viewed more as a "missed opportunity," which allowed some old patterns to reassert themselves, most clearly once Balaguer reassumed power.

How can we best explain this juxtaposition of socioeconomic change and political blockage? Political change away from neopatrimonialism can be induced by certain kinds of social change and facilitated by political leadership from above. In the absence of these, important elements of historical continuity and of political stasis are likely to remain. Ultimately, this is what happened in the Dominican Republic during this period, though some important political changes will also be noted in the chapters to follow.

The ensuing explanation for the overwhelming element of continuity apparent in political patterns and outcomes over the 1978–96 period rests primarily on the following factors: (1) path-dependent neopatrimonial political-institutional patterns and incentives; (2) ultimately strengthened by the timing of the transition with regard particularly to the impact of international economic issues on societal forces, the state, and regime actors; (3) reinforced as well by certain features of the country's political-party system and by electoral laws that enhanced factional strife within the PRD, but not within Balaguer's party; and (4) the responses of powerful domestic societal groups, which shaped and limited government responses, although these groups accommodated and adapted to neopatrimonial forms of politics, more than actively manipulating or sustaining it.[1]

A neopatrimonial polity rests on and reinforces a structural, societal situation of both high levels of inequality and weak levels of formal organization, especially among poorer sectors of society. One major potential element of change, then, can be found in significant societal change that affects this situation. Yet, as we shall see in the first section below, the vast societal changes induced by international forces largely did not impact the existing high inequality in the country and led to only a modest expansion in the scope and strength of civil society.

Neopatrimonial regimes also often rely on a cultural repertoire of available and acceptable behaviors, which are based on the country's history and facilitated by existing institutional arrangements. A major potential element of change, then, can be found in political agency from above. Given the PRD's democratic trajectory and its commitment to the principle of no presidential reelection, there was hope that a new style of governing could be imposed from the top. In the second section below, several constitutional rules and institutional factors that rationalize neopatrimonial behaviors for a president in the pursuit of political power and policy success will be highlighted, as will other political-institutional incentives that help explain the divisive behavior that affected the PRD. Included as well is a brief discussion of a potentially puzzling feature of the Dominican case, especially in a comparative perspective: the dramatic decline in the military "threat" to democracy.

Economic and Social-Structural Changes and Continuities

What facilitates a break with neopatrimonial patterns, toward greater institutionalization? One possibility is that international economic pressures and domestic societal changes may induce fundamental changes in the country's economy and society that reshuffle the way interactions take place within society and across societal groups, the state, and the regime, encouraging less unequal societies and stronger societal organization. These changes, in turn, may help to foster democratic evolutions in politics and institutions, but are unlikely to determine fully their success.

The country's democratic period examined here overlapped with dramatic structural changes in the country's economy, serious economic strain, and partial efforts to achieve economic stabilization and market-oriented structural reform. Economic policy reflected conflicting government goals in the context of these pressures and objectives. Over the period from 1978 to the mid-1990s, the country experienced a dramatic economic reorientation away from traditional exports, having a significant state presence, toward a reliance on services dependent upon private and foreign investment. This has meant that the Dominican Republic's economic growth has begun to rely less and less on specific state policies and actions; yet, organized interests and political struggles in society have largely continued to revolve around the state and around control of the presidency.

Democratic forces during this period were unable to establish institutions and patterns of behavior and policymaking to break with past neopatrimonial patterns. Given Balaguer's past trajectory, it is not entirely surprising that his comeback to power represented a renewal of neopatrimonial trends, though their extent and nature are remarkable in a comparative Latin American perspective. The PRD governments of Guzmán (1978–82) and of Jorge Blanco (1982–86) that preceded his return to power did attempt to establish some new patterns of behavior; however, in the end they sustained and even reinforced neopatrimonial trends, and their failures helped usher Balaguer back into power.

The Dominican Republic is a case of massive economic restructuring due less to concerted market-oriented state policy than to dynamic forces in the international and domestic arenas. Changes in international economic conditions and in the policies both of the country's major trading partner and of international financial institutions helped induce dramatic overall transformations in the structure of the Dominican economy and society. These, in turn, strengthened elements of Dominican civil society, while weakening others in an uneven process. They limited the usable power of the state over the economy as a whole, and they also increased the economic risks of disorder (whether from above in a military coup or presidential *auto-golpe* or from below), as the country became more dependent upon tourism, foreign investment in export-processing zones, and remittances and flows of short-term capital from overseas Dominicans. However, by themselves, these changes were insufficient to lead to a dramatic change away from neopatrimonialism.

Socioeconomic Transformation

When Trujillo died in 1961, the Dominican Republic was largely a rural, isolated country. In 1960, almost 70 percent of the country's 3 million people lived in rural areas and 63.7 percent of the country's labor force was in agriculture. Over the subsequent three decades, the Dominican Republic evolved from a predominantly rural society to a majority urban one, with an increasing concentration of people in Santo Domingo. By 1990, it was estimated that 60.4 percent of its 7.2 million people lived in urban areas (Inter-American Development Bank 1982, 346; 1995, 262).

A comparison of the Dominican Republic with ten neighboring Central American and Caribbean countries in 1960 highlights the country's relatively low level of GDP per capita (the second lowest of the ten countries), its high levels of illiteracy, its high proportion of agrarian labor, and its relatively small penetration of television and air travel. Examining these indicators over the next thirty years, the Dominican Republic is most similar to the poorer Central American countries of El Salvador, Guatemala, Honduras, and Nicaragua. At the same time, like the region as a whole, the country did experience dramatic changes over the 1960–90 period. The country's sharp increase in urbanization is reflected in the rapid decline in the share of the labor force in agriculture from 1960 to 1990, while the growth of television and especially of air travel reflect continued modernization, the growth of tourism, and international migration. Illiteracy levels declined only in the 1980s, reflecting the government's lack of emphasis on education prior to that. This data suggests the Dominican Republic became more urban and more internationalized over the past thirty years than Guatemala, Honduras, or Nicaragua, remaining comparable with El Salvador (see table B.1).

These comparisons, however, do not do justice to the nature of the transformation the country has undergone, especially since the mid-1980s. At the turn of the century until the late 1970s, the Dominican Republic's economy was fundamentally based on the export of selected agricultural crops, such as sugar, tobacco, coffee, and cocoa, and of minerals, such as ferronickel. However, over the 1980s, this changed dramatically as a consequence of new international constraints and opportunities and domestic problems. Most fundamentally, the country's U.S. sugar quota (which enabled much of its sugar to be sold at higher-than-world market prices) fell precipitously. This was due to such factors as the dramatic expansion of production by protected European producers of sugar beets, which led the European Common Market to shift from importing to exporting sugar; growing domestic U.S. production of sugar beets and corn syrup; and the increased replacement of sugar by corn syrup and artificial sweeteners. In addition, over the 1980s the terms of trade for other traditional Dominican export crops declined. The country was also deeply affected by the debt crisis and by the dramatic increase in world interest rates, both of which exacerbated the country's balance-of-payments problems, forcing stabilization measures in the mid-1980s. Devaluation over the mid-1980s and the inability of a weak labor movement to adjust real wages helped establish the foundation for new growth patterns and new sources of foreign exchange in the context of other demographic and international changes (see Vega 1993b; Alemán 1994).

One significant demographic change relates to the large Dominican migration to the United States. This migration was largely initiated in the early 1960s and grew even more in the aftermath of the 1965 intervention; it then increased in the context of the country's economic crisis in the 1980s. The migration process steadily came to represent a significant source of foreign exchange for the country, as complex patterns of flows and counterflows of funds, peoples, goods, and services emerged between the two countries (for excellent overviews see Graham 1996; Mitchell 1992; Grasmuck and Pessar 1991, 18–50).

Another change centers on several preferential market-access schemes, especially to U.S. markets, which also provided new opportunities for the country. The U.S. Caribbean Basin Initiative (CBI) approved in 1983, the CBI textile program of 1986, the CBI II law of 1987, and other measures enhanced the possibilities for the Dominican Republic to export certain quota-affected consumer goods (such as clothing and footwear) to the United States from free-trade or export-processing zones (FTZs or EPZs), while limiting the country's ability to generate backward linkages.[2] In 1990, with the simultaneous entry of the Dominican Republic and Haiti into Lomé IV, the country also became a beneficiary of a ten-year European preferential trade and aid agreement with former colonies around the world.

Trade figures underscore the dramatic transformation of the Dominican economy over a short period of time. Traditional exports declined sharply from the early 1980s: from a peak US$1.188 billion in 1981, they gradually declined to only US$530 million in 1993. The value of raw sugar exports fell precipitously from US$513 million in 1981 to US$112 million in 1993. During this same period, imports grew from around US$1.45 billion in 1981 to US$2.11 billion in 1993 (see tables B.2 and B.3 for total trade figures; see also Banco Central, *Boletín Mensual* 1985, 105; Banco Central, 1995, 73, for value of sugar exports; note that, following U.S. convention, 1 billion equals 1 thousand million).

How were foreign-exchange shortfalls suggested by this apparently massive negative balance of trade managed? The economy was now more and more dependent upon foreign exchange generated from three sources: expanding EPZs, from which exports are not reported in these figures; tourism; and remittances from overseas Dominicans. The EPZs also became the country's most important new source of employment over the 1980s.

The first export-processing zone in the Dominican Republic was created in La Romana in 1969. Legislation basically permitted tariff-free importation and exportation of goods from the zones, with only limited ability to sell to the domestic market; exemption from all corporate taxes for fifteen years (renewable); no restrictions on foreign investment or ownership; and no restrictions on profit repatriation (see Reyes Castro and Domínguez 1993, 9). Initially, growth was very slow. In 1980, export-free zones represented only around 16,440 jobs, reaching 25,660 in 1984. But subsequent growth was dramatic, doubling to 51,230 by 1986 and doubling again to 101,300 by 1990. By 1991, EPZs had grown from employing just under 1 percent of the country's economically active population to over 4 percent; this was just slightly less than that represented by the domestic manufacturing sector, whose employment levels had actually fallen by some 11,000 jobs over the 1980–91 time period (Reyes Castro and Domínguez 1993, 12,31).[3] Employment in the EPZs was heavily concentrated in apparel and textiles, at around 70 percent in 1992, followed by footwear, at about 9 percent in 1992 (Reyes Castro and Domínguez 1993, 31–32). The estimated net contribution to foreign exchange earnings from the EPZs grew from US$57 million in 1981 (5 percent of total traditional exports) to US$250 million in 1991 (38 percent of total traditional exports) (Reyes Castro and Domínguez 1993, 25).[4]

The dramatic expansion in EPZs was generated by a combination of factors. In addition to the significant changes in U.S. legislation and U.S. restrictions on apparel and textile imports from the Far East and apart from the political instability in Haiti, another key factor was the major devaluation of the Dominican peso over the 1983–86 period, which significantly lowered local costs for free-zone producers, especially with regard to wages. Specific government policies toward the sector had little to do with its expansion and may even have been counterproductive (see Thoumi 1988, esp. 19). In the early 1990s, the contribution of EPZs to the Dominican economy continued to grow; yet, their linkages to the rest of the Dominican economy were limited, and the country was competing for investments with its neighbors primarily based on overall costs (transportation, labor, etc.) and stability (which deeply hurt EPZs in Haiti at this time), rather than based on a skilled labor force. However, by 1996, some establishments began moving their operations to Mexico, to take advantage of even more favorable circumstances generated by provisions of the North American Free Trade Agreement (NAFTA) and by the Mexican peso devaluation of December 1994; as of mid 1997, the U.S. Congress had not approved proposed legislation providing the countries of Central America and the Caribbean with at least temporary parity with NAFTA provisions (see Vega and Despradel 1994, 266–68; and Dauhajre hijo et al. 1996, 230–31, 272–75, for a brief discussion of parity issues).

A second source of foreign exchange for the Dominican Republic, by the 1990s, was tourism. Growth began slowly, following enactment of the 1971 Tourist Development Law and then expanded over the 1980s; tourist arrivals (including visits by overseas Dominicans) expanded from a figure of less than 600,000 in 1980 to one of over 1.4 million in 1992. In mid-1995, the country reported having around 29,200 hotel rooms, the largest number in the Caribbean.[5] The growth in the contributions of tourism to the country's foreign-exchange earnings was continuous over the 1980s and into the 1990s. One source notes that overall exchange earnings from tourism grew steadily from US$206 million in 1981 (18 percent of the value of traditional exports) to US$877 million in 1991 (133 percent of the value of traditional exports) (Reyes Castro and Domínguez 1993, 25). For 1989, the Inter-American Development Bank (IDB) reports that tourism revenues were around US$910 million, with net foreign exchange earnings of around US$200 million (around 22 percent of gross earnings) (Inter-American Development Bank 1990, 97–98). Thus, by the end of the decade, because of tourism's dramatic increase and sugar's precipitous fall, net foreign-exchange earnings from tourism were equivalent to those from sugar exports. Although difficult to prove, politicians and observers alike have argued that awareness by political leaders of tourism's sensitivity to political stability almost certainly has helped to constrain protest activities, especially by leading political actors.

There has also been a dramatic increase in the participation of women in the workforce, while an already weak organized labor movement became further fragmented organizationally and was largely incapable of organizing in the free-trade zones. The percentage of women in the labor force grew from less than 10 percent in 1960 to 38 percent in 1990. Women workers are especially concentrated in the EPZs; in 1992 it was estimated that 60 percent

Women sewing baseballs in a factory in one of the country's first export processing or free trade zones established in La Romana in November 1981. An overwhelming percentage of the workers in factories located in these areas are women.

of all employment in this sector was female. In contrast, women made up around 30 percent of employment in the tourism industry and only 19 percent in agro-industry (Reyes Castro and Domínguez 1993, 33; Safa 1995, 23; also Safa 1995 and 1997, for discussion of exploitation of women and changes in gender relations). With the democratic transition in 1978, there was a slight surge of collective bargaining by organized labor. However, over the 1980s this declined again as political support and economic conditions declined. Party factionalism, labor infighting, and economic crisis led to further labor fragmentation over the 1980s and early 1990s. At the same time, EPZ companies actively discouraged the establishment of unions in the free-trade zones; from 1981 to 1990, only two trade unions were officially recognized in any of the FTZs. In 1992 the country finally replaced Trujillo's 1951 labor code with new legislation, and, with the threat of U.S. trade sanctions looming, legally recognized ninety unions over 1991–93 (fifty-five of them in the year following the code's enactment in July 1992). However, reflecting labor's continuing weakness, as of 1993 not a single collective-bargaining agreement had been signed by an EPZ company (Espinal 1987b; Reyes Castro and Domínguez 1993, 48–50; Government of the Dominican Republic 1993, 27; author's interviews in 1986 with labor leaders and in the 1990s with labor leaders and a prominent labor lawyer).[6]

The third major new source of foreign exchange for the country has been remittances from the expanding community of overseas Dominicans. Following the brief 1965 civil war into the early 1970s, the United States facilitated migration of Dominicans to the United States; many of these could be considered "political migrants" because they often came from disgruntled urban sectors. However, from the late 1970s and especially since the mid-1980s, there has been a dramatic jump in overall migration levels, motivated increasingly by economic reasons and facilitated by family ties. Migrants typically were urban, middle-sector professionals. By the early 1980s, the U.S. consulate in the Dominican Republic issued more visas than in any other country in the region except Mexico. The 1980 U.S. census counted around 120,000 Dominican-born individuals in New York City; a figure that had jumped to 225,000 in the 1990 census. Many consider that these figures undercount the true number of Dominicans in New York, with unofficial estimates ranging as high as 500,000 in the New York metropolitan area (Graham 1995, 10–11, 25); New York could well be the second largest Dominican city.[7] There are also significant Dominican communities in Puerto Rico, Venezuela, and Spain, spawned by the economic crisis years of the 1980s and then by family networks. The total estimated number of Dominican-born individuals living outside of the Dominican Republic in 1990 ranged from 500,000 to 1,000,000; given the country's total estimated population of 7,000,000, some 7 percent to 14 percent of those born in the Dominican Republic live overseas.[8]

Estimating the value of remittances from overseas Dominicans is also difficult, but this value has unquestionably grown considerably. Employing the value of private, unrequited transfers in the balance-of-payments data as an imperfect and almost certainly understated proxy, that figure jumped sharply from US$34 million in 1975 to US$123 million in 1976 and then steadily grew over the 1980s to US$329 million in 1991. Other estimates have ranged from US$427 million for 1988 to US$528 million in 1992 to figures approaching US$1 billion for 1995.[9] Thus, at the same time that out-migration was perceived as a tragic brain drain, though also an important political safety valve that removed disgruntled middle-sector individuals from the country, it was also a critical support to the country's economy. More recently, returning migrants have played significant economic, social, and political roles in the country, belying any static notion of all Dominican migration as a one-way, permanent step.

Socioeconomic Continuities

Alongside these dramatic changes, continuities in terms of high levels of poverty and of reliance on informal sector activities have persisted. Unemployment estimates over the 1980s and 1990s have ranged from 19 percent to 25 percent. Household surveys of microenterprises in 1992 and 1993 outside of agriculture found that one in five families made their livelihood in this fashion. Roughly one-third of the country's economically active population outside of agriculture worked in these microenterprises; total informal-sector activity was even higher as these surveys excluded domestic work and certain kinds of street vendors (Inter-American Development Bank 1994b). Figures in table 5.1 illustrate the high levels of poverty and extreme poverty in the country. They also show how these can change abruptly over time (as a consequence of inflation and other issues) and how in 1989 they were roughly intermediate in comparison to several other Latin American countries. As this table shows, in 1989 the Dominican Republic had a higher percentage of households in poverty than Chile, Costa Rica, Jamaica, Mexico, and Venezuela, and it had fewer under the poverty line than Brazil, Guatemala, and Panama. In 1989, the country had more urban poverty than Argentina, Colombia, Paraguay, and Uruguay, but less than Bolivia, Ecuador, El Salvador, Honduras, and Peru.[10]

What impact have these continuities and these processes of urbanization, domestic and international migration, changing gender relations, and economic restructuring had on neopatrimonial relations in the country? One conclusion is that a leadership committed to sustaining neopatrimonialism could find structural bases to continue to do so, as in fact was the case particularly with Balaguer. The country's dramatic societal transformations did not centrally affect the country's high levels of inequality nor the extent and nature of organization in society. For the most part, the changes ultimately

Table 5.1. Levels of Poverty in the Dominican Republic and Latin America

Country (Year, Survey)	Extreme Poverty (%)	Poverty (%)
Dominican Republic (1986, National)	10.5	18.3
Dominican Republic (1986, Urban)	7.1	11.7
Dominican Republic (1989, National)	13.7	24.5
Dominican Republic (1989, Urban)	12.7	23.3
Dominican Republic (1992, National)	9.0	20.6
Dominican Republic (1992, Urban)	5.0	10.9
Argentina (1989, Buenos Aires)	1.6	6.4
Bolivia (1989, Urban)	23.2	54.0
Brazil (1989)	18.7	40.9
Chile (1989)	1.5	10.0
Colombia (1989, Urban)	2.9	8.0
Costa Rica (1989)	1.1	3.4
Ecuador (1987, Urban)	4.0	24.2
El Salvador (1990, Urban)	14.9	41.5
Guatemala (1990)	39.5	67.0
Honduras (1989, Urban)	22.7	54.4
Jamaica (1989)	1.1	12.1
Mexico (1989)	7.3	22.6
Panama (1989)	13.2	31.8
Paraguay (1990, Asunción)	0.6	7.6
Peru (1990, Lima)	10.1	40.5
Uruguay (1989, Urban)	0.7	5.3
Venezuela (1989)	3.1	12.9

Source: Dauhajre hijo et al. (1994, 76, 77 [Dominican poverty and extreme poverty levels for 1986 and 1989 adjusted downward by income expansion coefficients]; 82 [citing data from Psacharopoulos et al. 1993, typographical error inverting data corrected]). The data for other countries are based on household surveys compiled by the Inter-American Development Bank.

served to remove potential dissidents from the country through migration and to fragment key parts of Dominican civil society, especially among working-class and other popular sectors. Both of these permitted continued vulnerability to neopatrimonial claims and weakened formal organizations among these groups. Domestic manufacturing stagnated, and largely union-free firms in free-trade zones boomed as informal-sector activities remained important and government employees saw their standard of living decline. Lack of sustained progress in reducing poverty and declines in the provision of basic services in education and health have also negatively affected popular sectors. And economic downturns and crises deeply affected the Guzmán and especially the Jorge Blanco administrations, and partially hurt Balaguer.

There is also evidence of sufficient attitudinal support for authoritarian and neopatrimonial practices. A 1994 national opinion survey found typically authoritarian attitudes and values across extensive elements of the population.[11] They were especially correlated with people who lived in rural areas, had low levels of education, and were in lower socioeconomic strata. The survey also found that women, on average, held more authoritarian values (except with regard to the family) and that younger and especially older groups in the sample did as well. These groups also tended to be among those that stated they participated the least in political or other organizations and were among the least interested in political matters (Duarte et al. 1996, 46–51).[12] In the context of a political leadership committed to enhancing democracy, these attitudes could be viewed as amenable to change, rather than as "obstacles that must be initially overcome" before democracy is possible (Karl 1990, 5).

Although a structural and attitudinal "space" remained for a leadership committed to neopatrimonial politics, changes in the country's political economy did place new limits on the state and on the ability of presidents to abuse and manipulate state resources. One limit had to do with the fact that economic growth became less directly dependent on specific state policies (and thus some firms were less vulnerable to state pressure) and more reliant on the maintenance of an overall macroeconomic stability, with low inflation and a competitive exchange rate. Another had to do with the impact of fiscal crisis on state institutions, enterprises, and personnel; over time, the state was forced increasingly to subsidize state enterprises, rather than remaining able to plunder them. Both of these limited the extent to which state finances and resources could be abused (though, as became evident in other countries similarly affected, they would also have constrained the possibilities for populist or welfare-oriented policies). The country's continuing economic vulnerability to the United States also left it open to pressure, not only on standard macroeconomic issues, but also on issues favored by U.S. human rights and labor organizations that gained increasing influence within U.S. foreign policy circles. As domestic firms became more diversified and the country's society expanded with economic growth, the possibilities for more independent elements within civil society to emerge was also augmented, though principally within business and middle-sector groups. Popular organizations, usually territorially based, did emerge, but were unable to sustain or to coordinate their actions over time. And, by the early 1990s, more vigorous civic, feminist, and other types of movement organizations were emerging; the role of some of these in the 1996 elections is examined in chapter 9.[13]

Political-Institutional Changes and Continuities

Another way that a break with neopatrimonial patterns may be induced is by new leadership, newly created institutions, and specific policies. Can new political leaders help generate other patterns of politics? Are new institutions emerging that induce different sets of incentives and ultimately behaviors? Are state development policies helping to generate political support for the regime? Are they strengthening civil society and its ability to interact with the state and the regime through more regularized means? Or, on the contrary, are state policies and policymaking more reflective of, and ultimately reinforcing of, neopatrimonial patterns?

As discussed in the previous chapters, neopatrimonialism refers to a kind of political regime which crosscuts the distinction between authoritarian and democratic regimes, while having a clear impact on the nature of that authoritarianism or democracy. As discussed in chapter 1, neopatrimonialism and democracy can coexist, but uneasily. There may be variations in the extent to which neopatrimonial regimes respect the key elements of democracy: contestation, inclusiveness, and the rule of law. But, strengthening each of these key elements of democracy would ultimately require weakening neopatrimonialism.

The Military

One threat that receded over this period, without totally disappearing, was that of military incursion into politics. This was achieved by establishing a model of civil-military relations that combined neopatrimonial elements, partisan balance, and financial constraints, often ignoring established legal norms, rather than seeking a model of professional, partially insulated, democratically controlled armed forces. The PRD administrations managed to weaken the military institution and to promote individuals to high posts loyal to the president. Balaguer brought back to active service officers who had been loyal to him. However, over the ten years of his presidency, the armed forces increasingly became a weak, underpaid, top-heavy, and largely unprofessional institution.

The first dramatic change to the military came on the day of Guzmán's inauguration. As discussed in chapter 4, he forced the resignation of several generals that could have proved a threat to his regime. Over the next two years, over thirty generals were either retired, demoted, or sent abroad. Guzmán followed this up with additional steps to remove the military from partisan politics, while instituting a more concerted policy of rotating officers to break up regional pockets of civilian-military alliances that had become established under Balaguer. Guzmán also earned the trust of the remaining military in a number of ways. One was by his conservative views and anticommunist policies—apparent in his foreign policy, in his attitudes toward foreign investment, and in his clashes with the more progressive vision of other PRD leaders. He also endorsed Balaguer's last-minute, generous salary increases for the military and provided additional modest budget increases (Atkins 1981, 135–47). By the end of his administration, Guzmán could number several military among his closest and most loyal associates. At the same time, Guzmán became increasingly embittered and fearful of what his successor from his own party, Jorge Blanco, might do to embarrass him or his family. Tragically, the man who had done so much to remove the military from politics earlier in his term began expressing to them his fears of Jorge Blanco's radicalism, hoping they might prevent his coming to power; the overlap of ideological differences and personal animosity between the two had become so extreme.[14]

Jorge Blanco further transformed the armed forces. In the first half of his administration, he removed many of the remaining older officers, thus giving opportunities to the younger officers he promoted. He also agreed to modest modernization of military equipment and encouraged training, professionalism, and respect for military rules and regulations. By these means, he soon established close relations with many top officers. But, in his last two years, Jorge Blanco "did not know when or how to stop" as he accelerated a pattern of massive retirements, typically after first rapidly promoting officers (Moya Pons 1995, 418). To outside observers, the logic was not always clear since some of those retired appeared to be professional, well-trained individuals. Tensions grew with the U.S. government, which complained that its military training funds were being wasted as careers were cut short. In addition to further limiting the ability of the military to participate in politics, another intended consequence was probably to constrain the room of maneuver of any incoming administration in terms of promotions. The result was a military force that was no longer a direct political threat and was institutionally weak. However, other political leaders feared Jorge Blanco was creating a military that would remain loyal only to him. As all the major political parties moderated their policy positions, though, there was declining support from any group in society for military intervention.

However, in the same way that Balaguer's maneuvers in 1978 largely did not prevent Guzmán from taking steps against certain officers, so Jorge Blanco's actions ultimately did not limit Balaguer's options in 1986. Yet, Balaguer had little interest in strengthening the military too much; by the time he returned to power in 1986, he was prepared to accept the fact that he would not be able to retain power either by overt military pressure or through a coup, given U.S. pressure and the extent of organized domestic opposition. What Balaguer did want was a military that was loyal to him. Thus, when he reassumed the presidency in 1986 and in subsequent years, he simply brought a number of officers who had been close to him back into active service. As many of these previously retired officers continued to age, ostensibly while on active duty, this strategy of Balaguer's became known as *abuelismo* (from the Spanish word for "grandfather"). Even though recalling previously retired officers was in violation of the Organic Law of the Armed Forces, as many of Guzmán's actions had been, no effective judicial challenge could be mounted given Balaguer's sway over the judiciary and possible alternative interpretations of presidential constitutional powers.

Over the 1986–96 period, the military receded further as important political, strategic, or economic players, especially in contrast to the role they had played during Balaguer's first twelve years in power. The contexts were substantially different. In 1966, Balaguer took office shortly after a civil war that had provoked serious intramilitary rifts and left a legacy of polarization and, among some, a continued commitment to violence. In 1986, by contrast, there were no active political forces committed to the use of violence or seeking to conspire with the military against the government. As in his first period, Balaguer sought to place trusted officers in key places, occasionally rotating them to keep them off balance. However, far more than in the 1960s and 1970s, he now made a mockery of any sense of military professionalism or career path, permitting the budget to decline, paying appallingly low salaries (and thus inviting corruption), allowing the armed forces to become one of the most top heavy on the continent, and making generals out of individuals like his personal chauffeur.

The decline in military professionalism continued to accelerate the longer Balaguer remained in office. Thus, by June 1995, the armed forces had seventy-seven generals, half of which had no official function or held posts usually taken by colonels; and there were some five hundred colonels (officially earning around US$200 a month), though the military institution only required one hundred. Not surprisingly, given the low salaries and lack of official functions for many officers, corruption was rampant. Among the more notorious cases described to me, one general in the presidential palace ostensibly charged a *peaje* (a toll) to facilitate appointments with the president and supplemented his salary by collecting checks to phantom employees (known as *botellas*) in government agencies.[15] Because of their presence along the Haitian border, the Dominican military played an important role in acquiring Haitian labor for state sugar mills and also in "facilitating" contraband trade between the two countries (especially during the period of the international blockade) (Rosario Adamés 1995, 8–17; author's interviews in 1995).

Balaguer's policies helped provoke unhappiness within the ranks of the military, especially among frustrated individuals in the lower ranks who perceived their chance of advancement as blocked by the individuals who had been brought back from retirement and were remaining in place. Over the 1990s, although some military might well have been willing to provide Balaguer armed support if called to do so, it appears the Dominican armed forces were becoming increasingly divided in their political loyalties. In both the 1994 and 1996 elections, the major presidential candidates and parties all possessed the support of at least some military officers. Opposition parties did not complain of centralized military harassment against them, though there was evidence of military bias at the local level. In sum, due to important changes in the domestic arena and the international context, and to the actions of the PRD and the more cautious and cynical steps subsequently taken by Balaguer, the Dominican armed forces largely ceased to be a political threat to democracy. At the same time, the armed forces (or parts of them) remained a potential neopatrimonial instrument of the president in power, not being a professional, well-organized, semiautonomous, democratically accountable state institution. In the absence of a professional, apolitical ethos, it remained possible for politically ambitious individuals within the military to rise through the ranks and represent a potential threat to civilian authority.[16]

Political-Institutional Incentives in a Context of Economic Constraints

Inherited institutions, impunity for excesses in the previous administration, and economic crisis all played a role in subverting the possibilities for change under PRD administrations. Once in power, the PRD governments discovered a statist, porous economic structure; strong demands from their party faithful for jobs, contracts, and favors; and a weak, underpaid public-sector bureaucracy, prone either to corruption or to extortion. These factors facilitated clientelist practices. They combined with suspicions about favoritism by the president or his collaborators within the party to feed distrust across factions. There were also no sustained efforts to document or to make information public regarding major past scandals or human rights abuses—much less to attempt to bring anyone to justice. The resulting sense of impunity may have encouraged an atmosphere of laxity about expected behavior. Under Guzmán, the lack of sustained investigations into the past was due to a perceived sense of government weakness and limitations and to the fact that, given Balaguer's continued control of the senate, the judiciary remained largely beholden to him.

The PRD governments were also limited in their abilities to carry out political and economic reform by international constraints and domestic social factors. Shortly after the transition to democratic rule, the country began to confront serious economic strains due to international circumstances outside of its control. Moreover, these were made worse because of a confluence between the inherited oversized, inefficient state and opposition from a fearful and more vigorously organized business community. The PRD thus faced an unfavorable, international economic (but not political) context and significant societal opposition.

Policy errors as well as decisions fed by desires for short-term political gain by PRD leaders clearly exacerbated the situation. The party yielded to internecine infighting, with its leaders ultimately succumbing to neopatrimonial patterns of behavior in both economic policy and political struggles, rather than breaking ground toward new ones. In 1982, the PRD's successful presidential candidate, Jorge Blanco, had been opposed by President Guzmán, who had favored his vice president Majluta. And, in 1986, the PRD's unsuccessful candidate, Majluta, had been opposed by President Jorge Blanco, who had supported Peña Gómez. Over the next several years, the factional strife between Peña Gómez and Majluta first weakened and finally divided the party, leading to Majluta's departure and facilitating Balaguer's reelection.

The PRD's divisive behavior can be explained in part by the country's type of constitutional structure and the PRD's party structure, as comparative analysis suggests. In "the essentially patrimonial world of Bolivian parties," the initially revolutionary Movimiento Nacionalista Revolucionario (MNR, Nationalist Revolutionary Movement) increasingly became a party in which members of congress were selected based on rewards to factional leaders. Over time, this "converted the legislative assembly into an arena from which assaults on the executive power were launched" by factional leaders demanding a greater share of patronage as they prevented the effective construction of an MNR-led state by infighting and by blocking executive initiatives in congress. Dominican parties like the PRD are similar to Bolivian parties—or to those in other countries such as Venezuela—in being hierarchical and closed, with power concentrated in the hands of a few top leaders (Gamarra and Malloy 1995, 404–6, 418, 419).

Parties matter in the Dominican Republic in ways that they do not in countries such as Brazil and Ecuador, where they never developed into a small number of strong organizations with at least initial ideological coherence. Under Trujillo, elections were fraudulent, but voting was both universal (extended to women in 1942) and mandatory. Thus, there was never any question that the democratic elections of 1962 would be held without literacy restrictions, and turnout was high.[17] Over the 1966–78 period, Balaguer was able to use the state to help construct a loyalty to himself, and through him to his party, which he largely ignored until the calendar demanded an electoral vehicle; it unquestionably helped him, though, that he could build on Trujillo's Partido Dominicano and on Trujillo's legacy within the rural, older, less-educated social sectors that became Balaguer's stable base of support. The PRD, in turn, was forged by a crucial electoral victory (though resulting in an ephemeral regime in 1963) and then by the further heroics of civil war and the subsequent repression under Balaguer; the struggle for democracy over the 1970s under these conditions and the hard bureaucratic work associated with it helped to build a strong organization, which continued to prosper in spite of Bosch's departure in 1973. Bosch, in turn, consciously sought to construct the PLD as an ideologically coherent and organizationally solid party, "a source of camaraderie and identity" with "tenacious socialization."[18]

The similarities with Venezuelan parties is especially germane because of the deep influence that many leaders of the Venezuelan AD party had on the PRD and on Peña Gómez, its secretary-general for many years. The PRD's factionalism can be understood by considering the nature of tensions generated between a president and his party's leaders in a neopatrimonial milieu. These tensions resulted because of three factors: the PRD's strongly centralized party structure and the country's partial approximation of a "partyarchy" (government by parties), the PRD's belief in no presidential reelection, and the partial autonomy of its major leaders from the president.

A partyarchy can be defined as a democracy in which the formal political process is monopolized by political parties and society is politicized along party lines. Its five characteristics include party control of nominations for public office; requirements that voters choose among parties rather than candidates; strong party discipline over legislators, reducing the autonomous role of the legislature in policymaking; the penetration of many organizations in civil society by the parties; and the politicization of the mass media (definition and characteristics from Coppedge 1994, 18–20).

The five characteristics of partyarchy do not fit the Dominican case as clearly as they do the Venezuelan one; but, as we briefly review here, there is no question that they are partially applicable. Dominican electoral law gives considerable powers to party leaders, rather than candidates: parties control nominations, and voters must choose among closed lists (not specific candidates) determined by parties.[19] A commonly expressed complaint was that because of the fact that party leaders selected candidates, sometimes through interfactional negotiations, voters rarely knew "their" legislator or municipal councilor. Indeed, as tables 5.2 and 5.3 highlight, the rates of incumbency reelection to both the senate and the chamber of deputies were remarkably low over this period. In the six electoral periods from 1970 to 1998, only 18 percent of both senators and deputies gained consecutive reelection. What is especially noteworthy are the low levels of consecutive reelection for the PRD, especially in the 1982 and 1986 elections, underscoring the importance of shifting factional control over party nominations.[20] On key issues, party leaders determined how legislators should vote; a break in party discipline, especially in the PRD and the PLD, usually presaged a serious factional split.

There are several indicators of the politicization of society, the fourth characteristic of partyarchy. Parties partially penetrated labor unions, student federations, and other organizations. Self-reported data by parties regarding primary votes leading up to elections highlight significant mobilizations. Elements of the mass media were frequently biased along party lines; some newspapers maintained an overt partisan bias, others permitted their journalists to receive additional "support" from party sources and sought a balance across journalists. Sparse survey data suggests that party identification may be declining countrywide from moderately high levels of partisan identification. Preelectoral surveys in May 1982 and May 1986 found 57 percent and 53 percent, respectively, of their samples stating a party membership (no apparent effort to distinguish degree of sympathy was made).[21] In a July 1989 poll, 43 percent of the sample stated a party membership; in turn, a November 1989 preelectoral poll found 86 percent of the sample expressing a party preference, of which some 44 percent stated they considered themselves a "member" of their party (i.e., around 38 percent of the sample). However, a poll carried out over seven weeks in early 1994, which was not preelectoral in nature, found only 18 percent of the sample stating they "belonged" to a party, though 52 percent responded that they "sympathized" with one.[22]

Table 5.2. Senate Reelection Rates by Party, 1970–1998

Term to Which Immediately Reelected	PR(SC) and Alliances		PRD and Alliances		PLD and Alliances		Total		
	N	%	N	%	N	%	N	%	
							Ratio of Incumbents Reelected to Total Elected		Reelected
	(Total Elected)		(Total Elected)		(Total Elected)				
Balaguer (PR, 1970–74)	4 (26)	15%	—		—		4/27[1]	15%	
Balaguer (PR, 1974–78)	7 (27)	26%	—		—		7/27	26%	
Guzmán (PRD, 1978–82)	5 (16)	31%	(11)		—		5/27	19%	
Jorge B. (PRD, 1982–86)	3 (10)	30%	1 (17)	6%	—		4/27	15%	
Balaguer (PR[SC], 1986–90)	4 (21)	19%	0 (7)		0 (2)		4/30	13%	
Balaguer (PR[SC], 1990–94)	5 (16)	31%	0 (2)		2[2] (12)	17%	7/30	23%	
Balaguer (PR[SC], 1994–96[3])	3 (14)	21%	1 (15)	7%	1 (1)	100%	5/30	17%	
Fernández (PLD, 1996–)									
Total number of reelected incumbents (percentage of reelected incumbents)	31 (86%)		2 (6%)		3 (8%)		36/198 (100%)	18%	

Note: The table provides information only on immediate reelection. Not included are three individuals (2, PRD; 1, PRSC) who returned to the senate after sitting out one or more terms. Research support from A. Liesl Haas in compiling data for this table is gratefully acknowledged.

[1] Five senators from MNJ party and one from MIDA.

[2] Senator Fernández Mirabal switched from PR(SC) to PLD for 1990 election.

[3] Congress elected for a four-year term; president's term shortened to two years by political pact and constitutional reform.

Table 5.3. Chamber Reelection Rates for the Same Province by Party, 1970–1998

Term to Which Immediately Reelected	PR(SC) and Alliances (Total Elected)		PRD and Alliances (Total Elected)		PLD and Alliances (Total Elected)		Total Ratio of Incumbents Reelected to Total Elected	Total Reelected
	N	%	N	%	N	%	N	%
Balaguer (PR, 1970–74)	18 (60)	30%	—		—		18/73[1]	25%
Balaguer (PR, 1974–78)	15 (86)	17%	—		—		15/91[2]	16%
Guzmán (PRD, 1978–82)	9 (43)	21%	— (48)		—		9/91	10%
Jorge B. (PRD, 1982–86)	9 (50)	18%	3 (62)	5%	0 (7)		12/120[3]	10%
Balaguer (PR[SC], 1986–90)	9 (56)	16%	9 (48)	19%	6 (16)	38%	24/120	20%
Balaguer (PR[SC], 1990–94)	13 (41)	32%	4 (33)	12%	9 (46)	20%	26/120	22%
Balaguer (PR[SC], 1994–96[4]) Fernández (PLD) 1996–	17 (50)	34%	4 (57)	7%	5 (13)	38%	26/120	22%
Total number of reelected incumbents (percentage of reelected incumbents)	90 (69%)		20 (15%)		20 (15%)		130/735	17%

Table 5.3. Chamber Reelection Rates for the Same Province by Party, 1970–1998

	PR(SC) and Alliances		PRD and Alliances		PLD and Alliances		Total	
	N	%	N	%	N	%	N	%
							Ratio of Incumbents Reelected to	
Term to Which Immediately Reelected	(Total Elected)		(Total Elected)		(Total Elected)		Total Elected	Reelected
Deputies re-elected in a nonconsecutive term	12		8		1		21	

Note: Not included are three cases of a consecutive election from PR to PRD in the same province and three other nonconsecutive elections from PR to PRD in the same province; also not included are one case of a consecutive switch from PRD to PRSC in a different province and one case of a consecutive election to a different province. Research support from A. Liesl Haas in compiling data for this table is gratefully acknowledged.

[1]In 1970 the other representatives were 11, MIDA; 15, MNJ; 3, PQD.
[2]In 1974 the other representatives were 3, PDP; 1, MVP; 1, MMP.
[3]In 1982 there was 1 representative from PAC (Campillo Pérez 1982).
[4]Congress elected for a four-year term; president's term shortened to two years by political pact and constitutional reform.

Turning to the second factor that helps explain PRD factionalism, PRD presidents were bound by a strong party tradition of opposition to immediate presidential reelection. This tradition grew out of the party's long struggle against Trujillo, and Bosch enshrined it in the 1962 constitution. However, because of Balaguer's removal of that limitation in 1966, PRD presidents were not restricted by a constitutional requirement. This fed ambiguity and distrust about the true intentions of the incumbents, Guzmán and Jorge Blanco, both of whom ended up supporting internal party candidates that ultimately lost the nomination to other party candidates.

At the same time, turning to the third factor, other major party leaders had sufficient autonomy from the president for significant executive-party conflicts to soon emerge under both PRD administrations, which rapidly translated into bitter executive-legislative conflicts as well. In both cases, it was the PRD leader in the senate that led the opposition to the president: Jorge Blanco versus Guzmán and Majluta versus Jorge Blanco. By the second time the conflict played itself out, the overlay of personal enmity and struggle for power overshadowed any ideological or programmatic differences.[23]

Thus, economic crisis and factionalism within the PRD paved the way for the electoral victory of Balaguer in 1986. Given his past patterns of political behavior, it is not surprising that Balaguer continued to govern in a neo-patrimonial fashion, evidenced both in his economic policies and political style; yet, Balaguer was forced to accommodate to dramatic changes in the Dominican economy imposed by changing international circumstances, even as he sought initially to ignore them (at least partially) and subsequently to profit politically from them as much as possible. Balaguer had clear ideas about policies that would enhance his stature and favor him politically focused on centralizing expenditures through his office, especially on public works; he bowed to international constraints as necessary and proceeded with his own agenda when feasible. Less concerned with constitutional formalities than the PRD, he had more success in managing economic policy for his political purposes. Paradoxically, this meant Balaguer combined economic misman-agement in terms of helping to provoke crisis conditions and impose a heavy burden on many Dominicans, with political shrewdness in terms of managing the tensions thus generated. In responding to the crisis conditions he helped provoke, Balaguer successfully enhanced fiscal revenues and demonstrated political adeptness at carrying out economic stabilization when required and taking advantage of initial restructuring policies. Yet, the cost of his mix of policies was increasing disorder and loss of capacity within the state; positive macroeconomic indicators in terms of growth and inflation were combined with high levels of inequality, low levels of expenditures in health and educa-tion (until near the end of his term), and continued high unemployment.

Balaguer was able to sustain his party as an effective electoral vehicle, in spite of occasional factional strife, his age, blindness, and failing physical abilities. He was aided in this by the fact he was not a lame-duck president. Though he did confront challenges to his leadership, he retained a solid base of support among certain rural and older voters, upon which he could build in beating these challenges back. Many in the party recognized him as the one undisputed leader. Because of this, and because of Balaguer's incredible drive for power, several politicians within the party failed in their calculations that they could develop a party base in order to launch a candidacy at the point when Balaguer was either too weak to renominate himself or ready to retire. However, it is telling that for the one election in which Balaguer was a lame duck, in 1996, the internal candidate he preferred lost the party nomination.

Balaguer was also helped by electoral rules. The fact that elections for congress were the same day as those for president and that there were no midterm elections enhanced presidentialism. The way the senate was elected also helped him. Only one senator is elected per province, and the winner need only win by a plurality (more votes than the next candidate, whether a majority or not). Although practically all electoral formulas tend to favor the plurality, or majority winner, somewhat, the system in the Dominican Republic often led to quite extreme results in favor of the plurality winner and made it very difficult for third parties to win seats. For example, in 1990, Balaguer's party and its allies officially received 35 percent of the vote, but achieved 53 percent of the senate (16 of 30); in that year, with 23 percent of the vote, the PRD only won 7 percent of the senate seats (2 of 30). As the country became more urbanized, the possibility of disproportionalities in representation grew even more.[24]

Tragically, historical patterns of neopatrimonialism were prolonged rather than weakened over the period from 1978 to 1996, even as additional formal institutional rules and informal norms also provided incentives for many of the political behaviors observable over this period.[25] These patterns can be summarized in the following points.

Within the state, the presidency has significant formal and vast informal powers. Formally, the Dominican presidency may be considered as weak because the Dominican constitution does not provide the office with strong budgetary or decree powers, a partial veto, or the ability to force referenda (cf. Shugart and Carey 1992, 146–58). However, this type of analysis risks confusing institutional formalism with reality. With important variations over this period, Dominican presidents have de facto assumed vast informal powers to establish taxes, set budgets by decree, and spend money with discretion, as well as ignore, sidestep, or abuse numerous other laws or presumed legislative prerogatives.

Informal presidential powers have been enhanced when there has been an absence of any effective check from the country's judiciary and when the legislature has been unable or unwilling to assume its constitutional responsibilities in lawmaking and in oversight of executive actions. The judiciary is named by the senate and has tended not to be an obstacle to executive discretion due to a combination of the country's extensive periods of authoritarianism, its civil law tradition, and the political nature of judicial appointments. This enhances the possibility for executive discretionality and for neopatrimonialism, especially when the executive is able to control a majority at least in the senate, if not in both houses. (As we shall see, PRD presidents often faced a more bitter intraparty opposition.)

The weak presence of a rule of law has permitted the use and abuse of state resources throughout the government and the bureaucracy for political and personal gain in the context of an unequal and weakly organized social struc-

ture. Although presidents can seek to establish a new pattern of behavior from above, effective monitoring and control over a porous, penetrable state is difficult.

Weak state institutions and the weak presence of the rule of law also increase the possibilities of prolonging political transactions, in that way often modifying outcomes initially determined by formal procedures. This was especially evident in the country's elections from 1978 to 1994, and frequently it has involved extensive transactions following the counting of the ballots, which often transformed (at least in part) the final results. Presidents also enacted major economic measures by decree when turned down by congress. Balaguer routinely violated the law regarding military promotions.

Finally, a major difference between the PRD and Balaguer revolved around the issue of presidential succession, given the nature of the country's parties and electoral system. *The constitutional possibility for unlimited reelection, as well as electoral rules strengthening the role of party leaders over candidates and of the presidential race over legislative ones have enhanced presidentialism and presidential power—especially for Balaguer.* These features in combination reinforced the Balaguer regime's neopatrimonial nature at a clear cost to democracy. *But, when the PRD was in power, the dynamic was of a president more challenged within his own party due both to the PRD's strong tradition of opposition to presidential reelection and to the tensions surrounding leadership-succession issues.* This tradition led other strong and ambitious PRD figures within the legislature to confront the president, leading to an intra-PRD struggle between "ins" and "outs," with initial ideological overtones degenerating into bitter government-party and executive-legislative strife, factional tension, and ultimately party division. Policy differences both within the PRD and across parties were overshadowed by a basic struggle for power, which was a consequence of international constraints limiting economic options and of the bitter conflicts over spoils, patronage, and power.

Conclusion

The period from 1978 to 1996 in the Dominican Republic did not lead to a sharp break with historical neopatrimonial legacies and institutions, a break that might have been facilitated either by certain kinds of socioeconomic change or by effective political leadership. Although the country did experience vast societal and economic changes over these eighteen years, there remained a potential social base for neopatrimonialism, with high levels of inequality, weak overall levels of organization within society, and pockets of authoritarian attitudes present in the country.

The country's political evolution was shaped by historical neopatrimonial legacies and inherited institutional structures, and it was constrained by the difficult international context. It turned out to be less modified by attempts to take advantage of opportunities for democratization opened up by the transition process. Particular political-institutional factors related to constitutional powers, electoral rules, and party structures served as additional independent obstacles to democratic consolidation. As a consequence of these various factors, neopatrimonial patterns only partially receded when the PRD was in power and returned in dramatic form when Balaguer reassumed power for another ten years in 1986.

At the same time, democracy was not fundamentally challenged either by the potential for a military coup or by popular rejection of democratic procedures. The military were removed as an overt threat to the democratic regime. They became a weak, personalized entity, too faction ridden to serve as an effective centralized potential instrument of the ruler, but far from the ideal of a professional, partially insulated, and mission-oriented institution.

Various rules and norms have been presented that help explain the inability of PRD leaders to change neopatrimonial patterns in the country over the 1978–86 period. These patterns were reinforced by Balaguer's return over the 1986–96 period and help explain his ability to retain power. In the next chapter, we will explore the tragic confluence of these rules and norms with international constraints, societal opposition, and policy errors in the eight years that the PRD governed the country following the 1978 democratic transition.

6 The PRD in Power, 1978–1986
A Missed Opportunity

The two presidencies of the PRD, of S. Antonio Guzmán (1978–82) and of Salvador Jorge Blanco (1982–86), ended badly. The first one was marked by the tragic suicide of the president near the end of his term; the second by a turn to neopatrimonial use of state power for political (if not personal) gain, especially in Jorge Blanco's last months in office, to be followed by corruption charges brought against the former president and a number of his collaborators after power was handed back to Balaguer in 1986. Each administration was marked by bitter intraparty division between "ins" and "outs" as the PRD increasingly lost its ideological moorings and its factions fought for power and spoils. These tensions spilt over into economic policymaking, whose evolution is the central focus of this chapter. Each administration also contained neopatrimonial elements—inevitably, given the state structure they inherited, the society they were governing, and the dominant set of cultural expectations. However, neither presidency possessed or sought the centralization of expenditures and power from above through contracts and patronage networks, and neither sponsored the mockery of administrative regulations that approximates the ideal-type of neopatrimonialism (and Balaguer's rule), though Jorge Blanco moved in that direction toward the end of his administration. Nor was the difference between public purpose and private gain blurred to the extent seen in more clearly neopatrimonial regimes (such as Balaguer's); nevertheless, issues of clientelist favoritism, nepotism, and corruption dogged both administrations and also had an impact on economic policymaking.

Seeking to project a moderate image, President Guzmán distanced himself from the PRD. Only four of the eleven members of his first cabinet were PRD party members. Yet, some thirty-seven immediate family members were appointed to high government posts, leading some to assert that instead of Balaguer's "personal government" the country now had Guzmán's "family government" (Atkins 1981, 130). Chief among those advisers were his daughter and son-in-law. They were often placed in the middle of the escalating feud between Guzmán and Jorge Blanco, who from the senate led the party in an often bitter opposition to the administration. Unproven, but widely circulated rumors and conspiracy theories tied Guzmán's family advisers to spectacular corruption, especially following the president's tragic suicide in July 1982, even as Guzmán himself may well have sought to prevent the president-elect Jorge Blanco from assuming power (Black 1986, 137; author's interviews with politicians and journalists, 1986).

At the time, the hope was that neopatrimonial patterns would experience a clearer and more dramatic break once Jorge Blanco assumed the presidency, given that he was going to govern with a PRD majority in both houses. Two dramatic events highlight Jorge Blanco's constraints and his limitations, respectively. In April 1984, sharp price increases mandated as part of an economic stabilization program approved by the International Monetary Fund (IMF) led to massive riots and scores of deaths; this badly tarnished the government's record in civil and human rights, one of the areas where the PRD had been able to project its sharpest difference with Balaguer. Then, in November 1985, a party primary that was intended to highlight the PRD's continued commitment to internal democratic procedures to select its presidential nominee ended inconclusively due to a shoot-out at the Concorde Hotel, where the ballots were being counted. Many observers believe that the vote count was interrupted because president Jorge Blanco's favored candidate, Peña Gómez, was losing to the president's bitter adversary in the senate, Jacobo Majluta. A few months later, in a pact among the three party leaders, Jorge Blanco simply named Majluta as the party's candidate and divided congressional and other candidacies among the party leaders' followers. The party's democratic nature suffered a blow from which it never recovered. Toward the end of his term, Jorge Blanco strayed even further from his initial promises of party-centered institutional government. For example, while maintaining a ban on the importation of private automobiles, he selectively gave away untold numbers of permits to import automobiles tax free, seeking to retain a base of support among certain middle-sector supporters. Indeed, in this area he even outdid President Balaguer's personalized gift giving.

The PRD governed the Dominican Republic during the 1980s, a period of dramatic economic difficulties imposed by the international system. The eight years of PRD rule, rather than leaving a legacy of lasting political and economic reforms and representing a move toward a more institutionalized form of politics, were a period of populist expansion followed by a complex period of delayed, wrenching economic stabilization, involving extensive negotiations with the IMF and other international creditors that did not lead to any signifi-cant economic reforms.[1] In the end, the party also divided and became cor-rupted in power. A first, unsustainable expansionary economic cycle was initiated by Guzmán,[2] leading his successor, Jorge Blanco to enter into negotia-tions with the IMF and ultimately to impose a severe economic stabilization plan in a protracted, painful manner. In 1985, for the first time since the 1965 civil war, the country actually experienced negative growth rates. More broadly, this eight-year period may be viewed as a missed opportunity for implanting a more institutionalized form of democratic politics in the country.

In explaining the evolution of economic policies during these two admin-istrations, PRD policymakers and sympathizers have tended to emphasize the negative international economic constraints and the pressures from external agencies and governments under which the Dominican Republic was forced to operate during most of this eight-year period. By this, they are referring to circumstances such as the sharp climb in oil prices following the second OPEC oil shock; the dramatic increase in international interest rates and declines in export volumes due to the international recession; sugar prices that fell in 1977–79 to increase in 1980 and fall sharply again thereafter; the reduction in the U.S. sugar quota; and declines in the prices of other Domini-can exports. They are also referring to pressures from the IMF and from the U.S. government. "If I had to place blame, I would say 70 percent external and 30 percent internal," one of Guzmán's policymakers told me (author's inter-view, Santo Domingo, 1986).

Critics of the PRD, in turn, have tended to emphasize questions of state capacity and political will under each of the PRD administrations. The Guz-mán administration's expansionist fiscal policies, exchange-rate policy, struc-turing and financing of public enterprises, and management of the country's external debt have all come under heavy criticism (see Stenzel 1986). Sim-ilarly, Jorge Blanco's management of negotiations with the IMF—particularly their protracted nature, the apparent corruption by some officials associated with his government, and his own turn to a more neopatrimonial style of governing toward the end of his term—also came under harsh criticism, espe-cially by conservative businessmen. "The PRD is a party of incredible voracity that entered government with no preparation or experience whatsoever," a leading industrialist has asserted (author's interview, Santo Domingo, 1986). Popular sectors, who had believed PRD governments would usher in a period of redistributionist policies, were instead met with harsh austerity policies and high inflation, which adversely affected government popularity.

However, one reason it was difficult for Jorge Blanco to implement an effective stabilization program was that there was no widespread perception by key political elites and organized sectors that it was both necessary and likely to be effective; rather, what political leaders saw were the risks, uncertainties, and high political costs. In addition, domestic socioeconomic and political constraints prevented certain actions to mitigate costs. The influence of powerful business groups as well as the divisive struggle for state spoils precluded effective fiscal reform. There was a clear disjunction between business and popular-sector interests and in their respective level and nature of societal organization and mobilization; moreover, PRD presidents were faced with bitter intraparty struggles that substantially complicated their abilities to sustain economic management.

Examining Economic Policymaking

Over the period from 1978 to 1996, the Dominican Republic confronted the problems of simultaneously managing economic policymaking and seeking to foster democratic politics: a set of problems faced by many other countries in the region and throughout the less-developed world. In this chapter, building on the comparative literature about the economic performance of new (more or less restricted) democracies, a simple scheme based on five clusters of factors is presented and is then employed to guide the discussion below and in the next chapter. Each is listed here in the direction in which it is most likely to help explain why governments have successfully initiated major measures of economic stabilization and structural reform, in spite of short-term risks for the incumbent president. (These five factors are derived from Nelson 1994a, 10–11; see also Nelson 1990, 1994b; Haggard and Kaufman 1995; and Haggard and Webb 1994.)

1. *Serious economic constraints*: the seriousness of the country's economic crisis; whether it has been preceded by a period of economic decline or instability.

2. *High levels of external pressure*: the effectiveness and nature of the pressure, of the conditionality requirements from external agencies and governments, and of their technical and financial aid.[3]

3. *Declining societal opposition, both structural and/or institutional*: the reduced political influence of interest groups and sectors (both in and out of the state) most tied to the older patterns of state intervention in the economy, whether this reduction is due to gradual changes in the economy generating competing interests, prolonged economic crisis and uncertainty, changed perceptions about the nature or causes of the economic crisis, or changes in the nature of political institutions or leadership.

4. *Greater state capacity and political support*: the incumbent administration's strong leadership capabilities; the cohesive nature, technical quality, and insulation of its economic team; its evident political bases of support. (A cohesive, technically competent economic team that is insulated, especially initially, but then is able to build bases of support to sustain and consolidate reforms is important.)

5. *Enhanced perception and political will*: a clear understanding, at a minimum by key government and economic leaders, that the crisis is not due to nonrecurring or merely cyclical phenomena, but to more deep-rooted ones and that other less painful options attempted in the past failed.

Given this list, it is not surprising that many of the problems and constraints of other smaller Latin American and Caribbean countries appear similar to those of the Dominican Republic. In many of them the impact of external constraints and pressures, the historical nature of state intervention in their economies, and the importance of clientelistic politics have been similar to the experience of the Dominican Republic, if not as extreme in their neopatrimonialism. Across all these countries, economic constraints have played a fundamental role in shaping economic policies, as have international organizations. At the same time, the Dominican Republic's neopatrimonial pattern of politics has affected a number of the factors listed above, impacting upon state policies. As we shall see in this chapter and the subsequent one, this is especially true of state capacity and political will and is partially true of societal opposition.

Building on this framework, this chapter and the next one accept that international factors may have been crucial in provoking the country's economic problems, but they also argue that to understand why policies evolved as they did the analysis must consider initial regime perceptions and policies, domestic societal constraints, international agencies, and political dynamics *in interaction* with each other. During the PRD years in office, international commercial and financial factors operated to worsen the country's economic situation. However, government leaders hoped these were short-term trends; the long-term nature of the problem was widely misunderstood both within Dominican society and among top political leaders, limiting the political support and political will necessary for painful economic measures. And, it is apparent that both the Guzmán and the Jorge Blanco administrations implemented policy decisions and political strategies that almost certainly made a bad situation even worse.

Patterns of societal and political opposition and support were also significant in explaining the evolution of policies during these years, interacting with the nature of the country's neopatrimonial, presidentialist system. The massive state resources and strongly presidential system of the country proved a strong temptation for both presidents. Guzmán was perceived at first by some as seeking his reelection in spite of the PRD tradition of opposition to immediate reelection; Jorge Blanco and some of his political collaborators were viewed as collecting a "war chest" from state funds to prepare for another run for the presidency, if not immediately. Whether these charges were true or not, it is undeniable that their intraparty opponents acted at the time on these perceptions and that both leaders sought to impose their preferred candidate unsuccessfully on the party. Their actions and the ambitions of presidential aspirants from their own parties in congress led to immobilizing executive-legislative conflicts. Both presidents found themselves constrained (to differing degrees) by their inexperience in state management; by pressures to use the state for partisan or personal benefit; by business interests attempting to protect their firms, benefit from speculative activities, and resist additional tax burdens; and by the dynamics of opposition politics in congress (not only from Balaguer's Partido Reformista but also, in some cases even more virulently, from members of their own party), which thwarted fiscal reform and international financing.

The Guzmán Administration, 1978–1982

Initial Political Goals and Evolution

Guzmán implemented a policy of enhanced public spending typical of populist programs elsewhere on the continent and for which there were substantial short-term political and partisan pressures. At least initially, there were few international constraints on his policies, though these were to grow dramatically over his term in office (see table B.2 for basic economic data, including figures on terms of trade and aid levels).

The initial strategy of the Guzmán administration was predicated on the notion that the private sector would strongly distrust his government and would thus be reluctant to invest. It was felt that the most logical policy was to increase effective demand by increasing public spending, leading in this way to increased private-sector investment, a strategy that was eventually given the name "induced demand." Top policymakers also desired to have a change in style from that of Balaguer, away from the neopatrimonial, personalized centralization of rule and the passive privatization of the economy, toward a more structured policymaking process and a more vigorous role for the state. This role would be carried out by more professional, technically prepared people in a more decentralized fashion. Similarly, there was a clear perception that industrial import-substitution was "exhausted" and that a renewed focus on exports, particularly on agro-exports other than sugar, was necessary.[4] This administration also believed the Dominican Republic had not fully taken advantage of the opportunity to take out loans from international, private commercial banks as other Latin American countries were doing, and it aggressively pursued that option.

There was an economic strategy, though not a fully developed one. Moreover, what comes through in interviews with major economic policymakers from the Guzmán administration is that the government was soon overwhelmed by crisis situations, to which its responses were subsequently given an ex post facto rationalization. This had much to do with the chaotic state of public finances they found, particularly in public enterprises; with party pressures for expanded employment; and over time with the political goals of the incumbent president.

The sense of crisis was exacerbated by the destruction wrought by major hurricanes in August 1979 (Hurricane David and then Frederick), estimated at around US$800 million. These hurricanes provided the initial justification for the government to rely on increased central-bank credit (called *inorgánicos*) for current expenditures. Government expenditures expanded dramatically and chaotically, though public investment remained flat. The years of 1979, 1980 (in particular), and 1981 were relatively healthy in terms of economic growth, but the expansionary process could not last. Public expenditures were financed in 1979 and 1980 primarily by recourse to external funds and in subsequent years primarily by domestic financing. Public-sector deficits jumped from 1.3 percent of GDP in 1977 to 6.5 percent in 1980—relatively modest figures perhaps by continental standards, but high in the Dominican context following the Balaguer years (see table B.4). The country's external debt grew from US$1.33 billion in 1978 to US$2.46 billion in 1982 (see table B.2). At the same time, because of the high import content of the expenditures that were generated (and increased fuel prices), there was a dramatic increase in imports by 1980. By May 1981, the central bank was also US$300 million behind in payments of letters of credit. All of this, combined with problems on the export front in 1982, led to serious balance-of-payments problems by the end of the term.[5] The Guzmán administration made the political decision that it would not negotiate a stabilization program with the IMF, though many economic policymakers within the government felt it was necessary.[6]

None of the economists associated with designing Guzmán's initial strategy had expected the extent of increase in public employment that occurred. The impact of this employment on public expenditures was magnified by long-overdue wage increases mandated by Guzmán in 1979 and again in 1980 (Inter-American Development Bank 1994b, B6).[7] Initially PRD pressures for access to the state, and subsequently (it was argued by some) reelectionist aspirations by the president, led to dramatic increases in public-sector employment, of 31.6 percent in 1979 and 10.1 percent in 1980 (see table B.4).

Perceptions of International Constraints and Opportunities

Guzmán was inaugurated with the strong support of the Carter administration, which had played an important role in insuring that a military coup in support of Balaguer would not be realized. Yet, U.S. economic assistance levels during Guzmán's presidency, particularly when compared with those under his successor, were relatively modest. At the same time, the temptation to borrow money from commercial banks was exceedingly strong in this period of petrodollar recycling—one of Guzmán's economic advisers affirmed during this period that the country had an unlimited capacity for foreign debt (Méndez 1994, 96). Many longer-term loans from multilateral and bilateral creditors could not be employed due to a lack of counterpart funds; as a consequence, in the Guzmán years seeing the most rapid debt growth, the country's debt structure emphasized short-term and medium-term financing at more onerous terms.

As was typical of many other governments in oil-importing Latin American countries, the Guzmán administration underestimated the extent to which oil prices would rise and was reluctant to adjust to the new reality. This error was facilitated by the eventually unrealized expectation of a major oil discovery and by the temporary increase in the world sugar prices. The economic situation ultimately deteriorated more than it needed to as a consequence of these misperceptions and of the unwillingness to recognize the fiscal limitations on the state. Yet, these limitations were not only the doing of the Guzmán administration.

Domestic Business Opposition

Guzmán represented the most moderate element of the PRD, and the party itself had become considerably less radical with the exit of Juan Bosch in 1973. Furthermore, significant tensions soon emerged between Guzmán and major PRD leaders in congress. Nevertheless, business groups still feared the consequences of Guzmán's coming to power. Most concerned was the group that had benefited the most from Balaguer's twelve years in office, the large industrialists and merchants of the capital city. As one businessman noted, "with the defeat of Balaguer, a political organization emerged with a different conception of what the country's correlation of forces should be; it had preestablished ideas regarding the country's development and the role of each productive sector which were worrisome to us" (author's interview, 1986). At the same time, though, there had also been growing discontent with the neopatrimonial, personalistic decision-making style under Balaguer, particularly by regional and smaller industrialists, who felt discriminated against. There was also resentment against the increased encroachment of high military officers into business areas. In the period 1966–78, with economic growth and diversification and with the proliferation of business associations representing regional and smaller businesses, it was inevitable that pressures to place relations between business and government on a more institutionalized basis would grow. Yet, in 1978, the immediacy, intensity, and direction of that drive were unmistakably colored by the coming to power of a figure from the PRD.

Shortly after the inauguration of the PRD government in August 1978, a group of leading Santo Domingo businessmen active in the AIRD decided to establish an effective peak business association. They opted to revitalize the essentially moribund CNHE.[8] Various models from other Latin American countries were considered, though the most important became the Consejo Coordinador Empresarial of Mexico. This was because of the aggressive role that organization had played in Mexico battling what was perceived as a similar challenge: a populist administration in charge of a massive state apparatus (the Luis Echeverría administration, 1970–76).[9]

The goal was to create a strongly united, ideologically self-conscious peak business association that could effectively dominate public debate. From 1979 on, an aggressive campaign to incorporate all existing business associations and major firms into the CNHE was implemented. This strategy began in earnest with a dinner of "business unity" in the summer of 1980; and it intensified further when the keynote speaker at that dinner, Luis Augusto "Payo" Ginebra, a conservative businessman closely aligned with Balaguer, assumed the association's two-year presidency in December 1980. The CNHE carried out open, confrontational attacks against the government, focusing on public employment, deficit spending, and price and import controls.

What this meant was that the intent of the Guzmán administration to woo the business sector through its policies, moderate discourse, and distance from perceived "radical" PRD elements failed. The government's vision clashed with the perception of business groups regarding what they needed to do in their own self-interest.

In policy terms, this opposition also helped prevent the Guzmán administration from addressing the public deficit, for which business groups so harshly attacked it, in ways that would have enhanced state capacity. One

cause of public-sector deficits was the nature and evolution of the tax structure. Tax revenue as a percentage of GDP steadily declined from 1977 to 1982;
that income, in turn, remained heavily dependent upon trade taxes, especially
on imports (see table B.4). The initial efforts by the Guzmán administration to
present a tax reform that would shift the country's tax burden away from trade
toward income, property, and sales—to approximate more the situation found
in other countries in the region—got bottled up in congress. One cause may
have been Guzmán's haughty rejection of negotiating with congress and
more purely political opposition (which will be discussed below), but there
was also intense opposition to shifts in the tax structure and to tax increases by
businessmen—and this was in a country that had practically no property taxes,
or even a capital gains tax on real estate sales. Business groups successfully
resisted efforts to impose changes in the tax structure, alleging that the state
should first enforce its current taxes. Yet, public revenues were falling (as a
percentage of GDP), especially because of a decline in import duties and
taxes. This was due not only to the growth in exempted food and oil imports
(as emphasized by business groups), but also to the country's broad and vague
system of exonerations, the major tool used to implement import-substituting
industrialization and a tempting resource for any president to employ for
short-term political advantage (World Bank, *World Development Report* 1985,
11; author's interviews with former Guzmán officials in 1985 and 1986).

Under these circumstances, Guzmán's response to the growing fiscal and
exchange crises was gradual. In mid-1980 and again in mid-1981, he declared
public austerity measures. He also shifted different import products from the
increasingly untenable parity rate (DR$1 = US$1) to the higher exchange rate
on the parallel market. Not surprisingly, the government's austerity measures
led to widespread popular protests. For example, the 1980 increase in gasoline
prices (induced by an OPEC price increase) provoked a strike by public-
transportation drivers which soon escalated into broader demonstrations, con-
frontations with the military and police, and the deaths of at least six demon-
strators. Peña Gómez played an important mediating role, harshly criticizing
Guzmán, while seeking to defuse the crisis (Rodriguez and Huntington 1982,
26).[10] As this underscores, tensions between Guzmán and several key leaders
of his own party continued to escalate.

Political Opposition

Guzmán found himself constrained by the fact that Balaguer's party retained
a majority in the senate (sixteen of twenty-seven seats).[11] Yet, Balaguer was
relatively restrained in his attacks on the government. The most significant

President S. Antonio Guzmán of the PRD (1978–82) giving a speech before congress. His most powerful congressional opposition soon came from his own party, led by then senator Salvador Jorge Blanco.

opposition to Guzmán eventually emerged from within his own party, led by Salvador Jorge Blanco, who had become president of the senate. By the end of Guzmán's term, PRD leaders were leading a ferocious opposition from congress. They became increasingly frustrated by his effort to distance himself from them (e.g., by naming non-PRD members to major cabinet posts), by some of his conservative policies (e.g., in foreign policy, where he refused to extend diplomatic relations with Cuba or to promote party positions vis-à-vis the Sandinistas in Nicaragua), and by his refusal to explicitly renounce any intention of reelection; they also attacked him for their own narrow political benefit as the government became more unpopular. The first formal break between Guzmán and the party came when Guzmán submitted a request to congress for emergency powers following the destruction of the hurricanes in 1979, in spite of the fact that the party's political commission had already stated its opposition. PRD congressional representatives initially turned Guzmán down.[12]

In spite of the PRD's strong anti-reelectionist tradition, Guzmán did not push for a constitutional reform to prohibit or limit reelection; furthermore, close associates advocated his reelection while he remained circumspect about his true intentions. For many party leaders, such as Peña Gómez, Guzmán was playing an ambiguous reelection game (ambiguous because it was never openly asserted) that was strenuously opposed (see Peña Gómez's May 1980 letter to PRD congressional representatives in Espinal 1982, 283–97). Even if Guzmán was not seriously intending to seek reelection, he may well have thought it advantageous to project such an image in an attempt to keep the allegiance of political followers and his own efficacy for as long as possible as a new election approached. Yet, several political observers believed that Guzmán's continuation of a policy of expanding public employment was directly related to his reelectionist aspirations, and some PRD factional groups accused the government of discriminating against them in its hiring practices (Moya Pons 1986, 26, 314; Espinal 1987a, 163–64, 182). At the same time, there is little question that the massive and unplanned influx of new employees helped lead to a further degeneration and disorganization of the Dominican state.

Intra-PRD opposition politics was ultimately destructive of many of the party's own goals, some of them economic. One example is tax reform, which in Guzmán's last year in office continued to be bitterly opposed by Jorge Blanco in the senate in spite of the fact that it would be the new administration that would benefit from the tax changes.[13] The most significant damage was probably to the PRD itself. Jorge Blanco and Peña Gómez were able to suffuse their opposition to Guzmán and to Majluta with an ideological content, in which they were seeking to promote a more autonomous, modern, and democratic country; however, questions of patronage, brokerage, and power politics lay just under the surface. In Jorge Blanco's administration, the factional strife in the PRD became reduced to a more blatant conflict over power and control of resources (see discussion in Espinal 1987a, esp. 153, 171; also Jiménez Polanco 1993, esp. 190).

At the same time, it is also evident that Guzmán opted to govern in a more constitutional and a less neopatrimonial fashion than Balaguer had previously or would upon his return to power in 1986. Guzmán viewed the role of the cabinet and his ministers more seriously (see table 4.2), and he did not employ presidential powers of dubious legality to manipulate budget expenditures or institute new taxes in the face of congressional opposition. His efforts at re-election and of budget manipulation were half-hearted compared to those of Balaguer, and there was nothing equivalent to the centralization of power and expenditures in the presidency experienced by the country during the Balaguer years. Congressional powers were more respected by Guzmán. Perhaps in sharpest contrast to Balaguer, Guzmán also treated with more respect his party's internal procedures, which ultimately led to the nomination of an individual, Jorge Blanco, whom Guzmán deeply distrusted and disliked.

The framework to change PRD rules toward proportional representation of factions in the party's central governing unit and toward greater participation by party faithful in the presidential-selection process was approved by the party convention of November 1979. In June 1981, party leaders agreed that a kind of party primary would select the party's nominee. In this way, party leaders hoped to avoid the possibility that government pressure or influence on a small number of delegates at a convention could determine the nominee.[14] Shortly after that decision, Guzmán also endorsed his vice president, Jacobo Majluta, for the PRD's nomination. Leading up to the vote, the party's secretary-general, Peña Gómez, stated several times his fear that the internal campaign was severely damaging the party and could lead to its division. Jorge Blanco's campaign slogan of "mano limpia" ("clean hands") was seen as a not-so-subtle attack on Majluta for corruption as head of the Corporación Dominicana de Empresas Estatales (CORDE, Dominican Corporation of State Enterprises); in turn, Jorge Blanco was accused of having dangerous radical ideas and of not really being a member of the PRD, while some of his sympathizers in the government were fired from their jobs.[15] Indeed, Guzmán went so far as to state that only Majluta guaranteed the continuity of democracy in the country. Jorge Blanco had created an additional electoral vehicle to capture non-PRD support, and there was some fear that if he did not gain the nomination he might leave the party.

The primary, held in November 1981, became polarized between Jorge

Blanco and Majluta, which the former officially won with 56.9 percent of the vote to the latter's 36.6 percent (minor candidates received the remaining votes). State funds were apparently not employed in large amounts to support Majluta's candidacy. Local base committees selected thirteen delegates to vote in their community for their preferred nominee. Delicate negotiations following the vote count were required to assure that Majluta would recognize the defeat. These negotiations assured Majluta that his sympathizers would be on certain key party lists and be given a strong representation within the party; Peña Gómez also formally stated he would not seek the party nomination in 1986, ostensibly paving the way for Majluta to gain the nomination for the next constitutional period.[16] In spite of these bitter internal party divisions, the PRD ultimately was able to win the May 16, 1982, elections, even gaining comfortable majorities in both the senate and the chamber of deputies.

The suicide of Guzmán on July 3, 1982, shocked the country and the party. Factors presented to explain the suicide include the following: isolation and a sense of abandonment by political collaborators as attention shifted toward the incoming administration of Jorge Blanco; concern that the grenade that had exploded at the Santo Domingo office of the JCE two weeks earlier with loss of life had come from a PRD leader; fear of retribution (based on corruption issues) against himself or family members by Jorge Blanco, whose inauguration he appeared unable to prevent; and a family history of depression, compounded by alcohol consumption and frustration over his inability to continue horseback riding (a favorite pastime) due to a hurt arm.[17]

The PRD's internal organizational unity and its democratic nature were both sorely tested by the executive-legislative conflicts and the nomination struggle. There were some ideological components "at the top" to the differences that distinguished Guzmán and Majluta from Jorge Blanco, which were also reflected in support for Jorge Blanco from certain labor unions and other organized popular-sector groups; yet, it remained true that much of the conflict revolved around factional and personal calculations and clientelist ties. Jorge Blanco's ability to win the party's nomination and ultimately the election were facilitated by his attacks on the Guzmán administration and by his ability to distance himself and the party from the government; the argument was that the bases of political democracy were established by the Guzmán government, but the next government would be more advanced and more in accord with party principles, more oriented to social democracy and economic justice (cf. Peña Gómez 1986a, 333–36). However, neither were these hopes realized nor the next cycle of intraparty strife to end so felicitously.

Guzmán sought to gain private-sector confidence by distancing himself from the PRD, asserting his was an administration independent from the party. In the end, he never fully achieved the former, while losing crucial party support. Although his technical and business supporters sought a more institutionalized, regularized, and decentralized decision-making process— goals that they partially achieved in contrast to the previous Balaguer adminis- trations—Guzmán's closest advisers were his daughter and his son-in-law, and his government was comprised overwhelmingly of business and personal asso- ciates from Santiago. Charges of corruption and of abuse of office emerged around some of them, even as the massive increase in state employment was viewed as part of a narrow personal project, rather than as a benefit to the party as a whole (Moya Pons 1986, 25). Many of Guzmán's top officials were also largely unknown by the powerful business groups in the capital city, who had been the bulwark of support for Balaguer and who distrusted both Guzmán and the PRD. At the same time, especially as the economy sagged and the government's popularity declined, the party-government conflict deterio- rated, and the most acerbic opposition to Guzmán's government increasingly came from within his own party, led in the senate by Salvador Jorge Blanco. Although there was bitter internal party strife, Guzmán did not openly seek to manipulate the selection process or the 1982 electoral process in the blatant ways that Balaguer previously had or subsequently would. However, Guz- mán's enmity toward Jorge Blanco was intense and, at a minimum, did lead him to insinuate to some Dominican military that the next president and some of his advisers were "dangerous." The Guzmán administration gradually shut itself off, and ironically, given how he began his term in office, Guzmán turned increasingly for solace and friendship to favored military officers. His administration had never gained business confidence, and it lost party and popular support. By the end of Guzmán's term in office, none of the original economic advisers were still associated with the government.

The Jorge Blanco Administration

The PRD entered the next presidential administration with some hope. Jorge Blanco, winner of the 1982 elections, claimed to be a champion of the party's true ideological doctrines and promised to be more willing to govern with the party. He also appeared to embody values of honesty and commitment to reform. And, unlike Guzmán, he had comfortable party majorities in both houses of congress. Unfortunately, international circumstances, societal re- sistance, internal party strife, and the new president's own leadership choices led to an administration very different from the one initially imagined.

In the months prior to his inauguration, Jorge Blanco's economic team began contacts with the IMF regarding a stabilization program and assistance.[18] Given the country's balance-of-payments problems, its small size, and the extreme difficulty of closing its economy, there were few realistic options for the country other than negotiating with the IMF. The social and economic consequences of unilaterally declaring a debt moratorium would have been devastating for the country, as private and official creditors would likely have responded harshly. Only if the larger debtor countries (Argentina, Brazil, Mexico, and Venezuela) could have been convinced to join a "debtor's cartel" might the smaller countries such as the Dominican Republic have hoped to form part of a moratorium; and in the 1982–86 period commercial banks successfully reached agreements with each of these major debtor countries (Devlin 1989, 182–235). With its historic ties with the United States and with close to 10 percent of the Dominican population living in the United States, an effective closing off of the economy would have been extremely difficult to realize. Similarly, a greater reliance on the state in a more closed economy would have been inhibited by the Dominican state's high levels of inefficiency and the absence of motivated and technically prepared professionals.[19]

Yet, an initial decision by Jorge Blanco to begin his term on a harsh note of austerity with the hope that in his last years he could pursue a more expansive policy, faltered as the full implications of the stabilization package became clear. Efforts to soften the blow of stabilization for key constituency groups of the PRD through delay meant the ultimate recessionary and inflationary consequences of the adjustment were probably greater. In the end, unable to implement even the political reforms he had promised, the president turned to reliance on the state for patronage and brokerage as his predecessors had, slightly expanding employment levels and providing benefits in a personalistic fashion while corruption charges swirled around other PRD officials in government.

There is tragic irony in the fact that when Jorge Blanco handed power to Balaguer at the end of his term, the social-democratic president prided himself that his principal achievements had been in the area of economic stabilization. He noted the Dominican state's fiscal discipline, the country's monetary stabilization, and its restructured external debt, even as he thanked the United States for its generous economic assistance (*Listín Diario*, August 15, 1986). In fact, after failing to meet its initial IMF agreement and after prolonged stasis as a consequence of urban riots and the scores of deaths that resulted from their poor management in April 1984, the government was left with no real option other than to go through with a harsh stabilization program in 1985. Long overdue measures (particularly devaluation and unification of the country's exchange rate) were finally implemented, and debt renegotiations with commercial banks and official creditors were judiciously and successfully realized. As a consequence of these measures and a drop in oil prices, Jorge Blanco did deliver a somewhat healthier economy to Balaguer than he had inherited; yet the costs were high. The burden of adjustment had fallen disproportionately on the poorer sectors of society. The desire of the government to retain some popular support had finally led it to implement crass clientelist measures, and the PRD's institutional basis, democratic nature, reputation for honesty, and extent of popular support had all been badly eroded.

Initial Policies and Changing Political Goals

Jorge Blanco began his administration on a note of austerity. In his inaugural speech, he spoke of the country's serious financial situation and implemented public austerity measures, primarily the cutting of public-sector salaries. Increasingly, this affected the state's ability to retain satisfied professional personnel (and in numbers apparently higher than in the past, many nominally worked for the state while holding one or more other jobs). This was followed by the signing of a three-year Extended Fund Facility agreement (worth US$400 million) with the IMF in October 1982, a program approved by the IMF's board in January 1983. The agreement called for a gradual transfer of imports from the increasingly fictitious parity exchange rate (DR$1 = US$1) to the higher free exchange rate,[20] increased public-sector revenues from a variety of taxes, strict controls of the growth of central-bank credit, and improved performance of public-sector enterprises. The government was also to seek to diversify exports by encouraging new agro-exports and by promoting expansion of industrial free zones.

It appeared that Jorge Blanco had accepted the argument that stabilization should be implemented fairly quickly. The government also sought to mitigate the costs of such a program. Because owners of land, real estate, and capital assets would be the principal beneficiaries of devaluation, the government proposed a series of taxes that would target them. Yet, neither a property tax, a tax on capital gains, nor proposed changes to corporate taxes gained congressional approval (Vega 1988b, 24). The government was only partially successful in acquiring passage of its tax measures, of which the most important was a value-added sales tax (ITBI, *impuesto a las transferencias de bienes industrializados*). Then, by making certain decisions and not others, by stealth rather than by any explicit statement, the government shifted its strategy. In August 1983, the country requested a rescheduling of official bilateral debt (also known as Paris Club debt) and then suspended payments. And, over the last quarter of 1983, as the governor of the central bank at the time subsequently noted, "the control of expenditures of the Central Government was lost" (Vega 1988b, 15); as a consequence, the government did not meet domestic credit and public sector deficit levels agreed upon with the IMF.[21] The result was a suspension of the program and extended negotiations regarding the second year of the program.

One of the historical and legal legacies that Jorge Blanco confronted revolved around the country's exchange rate. Many politicians and opinion makers had come to view the exchange rate not only as a proxy for inflation, but as a symbol of national worth. Thus, fluctuations in the exchange rate were always cause for newspaper headlines and national discussion. Legally, the country still operated as if parity between the Dominican peso and the United States dollar existed (indeed, as of mid-1997, the 1947 law that established parity between the two currencies had not been changed). The higher price for the dollar on the parallel or free market was not called an "exchange rate," but the "amount over" the official rate (*la prima*). All this led the president to state in his August 1982 inaugural speech that he would never submit a bill to congress devaluing the country's currency; evidently, he intended to carry out de facto devaluations as necessary, which he believed to be politically more palatable (Messina 1988, 28; see also 18–21).

Perceptions and Harsh Realities of International Constraints

The government's economic policymakers were divided regarding the pace of implementation of economic stabilization. Moreover, there was no agreement regarding the need for stabilization within the government itself, much less within the PRD or more broadly in society. Many of Jorge Blanco's advisers, whose own power relied on the continuing popularity of the president among key PRD constituency groups, preferred to defer the issue as much as possible. This was particularly true as the full inflationary impact of devaluation and the recessionary effect of curbing public spending were more fully understood.[22]

In turn, international creditors were much less forgiving of debtor countries in the earlier years of the debt-crisis period, when Jorge Blanco governed, than subsequently.[23] The World Bank, the IMF, and U.S. officials viewed the targets of the initial IMF program for the Dominican Republic as relatively "soft" and "realizable" (author's interview with World Bank officials, Washington, D.C., 1986), while the extent of funds made available and their terms were fairly generous. The agreement had specified a gradual schedule of dates in which key elements of the program would be realized, particularly regarding passage of remaining imports to the higher parallel-market exchange rate, rather than requiring they all be taken initially. Tensions between the IMF and the government heightened in late 1983 as a consequence both of government efforts to obfuscate the fact that the terms of the agreement with the IMF were not being met, especially with regard to the growth in government expenditures, and the government's desire to postpone final unification of the exchange rate. The IMF insisted that imported oil be transferred as agreed to the higher free exchange rate, which the government was reluctant to do. No agreement was reached, and the second year of the program was suspended. The government probably underestimated the IMF's reaction, as well as the extent of capital flight that would ensue. In the face of uncontrolled growth in government spending and deficit financing, the exchange rate deteriorated sharply in the last trimester of 1983 and particularly in early 1984 (see figure B.1). And the IMF decided that the disbursement of funds had actually helped reduce the urgency of reforms, rather than facilitated them, and thus that further funds could only flow after policy measures had been enacted.

The government wavered between attacking the IMF and determining what measures it needed to take to resume relations with it. It also postponed measures, hoping that the Reagan administration would provide additional grant or loan funds to ease the impact of the stabilization measures; yet, the U.S. administration was unequivocally committed to neoliberal (market-oriented) policies. Jorge Blanco essentially returned to the Dominican Republic from an official state visit to the United States empty handed, and the government's worst fears regarding a feared popular reaction to the stabilization measures were soon to be realized (cf. Messina 1988, 84–91).

That popular reaction came in April 1984. During Easter week, the government finally transferred all payments for imported goods—except for petroleum imports and payments on the external debt—to the free-market exchange rate. As a result of the de facto devaluation, the government also decreed price increases on numerous food items and other goods subject to price control. The government that had been attacking the IMF for months had suddenly instituted measures in search of an agreement. The process was poorly handled politically, and the security forces were disastrous in their management of the demonstrations that erupted to protest the price hikes. The government feared for its very survival as over one hundred deaths resulted from police and military overreaction to the "IMF riots," which had been planned demonstrations in some areas and had quickly spread as spontaneous actions, notwithstanding the government's unproven and probably unfounded conspiratorial rhetoric that state security forces were responding to provocations by organized armed bands.[24]

Violent riots protesting price increases in April 1984 led to scores of deaths and multiple arrests.

Talks with the IMF were suspended. Then, in July an exchange rate intermediate between the parity rate and the free-market rate was established for oil imports (except for the state electrical company) and gasoline prices were also increased around 70 percent. A so-called "shadow" agreement was reached with the IMF in the fall of 1984, though without the disbursement of IMF funds. A decision was finally reached to cancel formally the Extended Fund Facility program and replace it with a one-year standby agreement.

The government was gradually left with no maneuvering room. By late 1984, the central bank's foreign exchange liquidity reached a record low of only US$16.2 million, while large payments for key imports, especially petroleum, were due. The flow of U.S. and multilateral economic assistance funds halted, pending a formal agreement between the IMF and the country. The restructuring of private commercial and bilateral (Paris Club) debt also depended on such an agreement, and the IMF refused to sign an agreement unless the government first took the difficult final step of unifying the exchange rate and provided concrete steps to insure deficit reduction.

Finally, in January 1985, the Jorge Blanco administration unified the country's exchange rate for all transactions at the higher free rate, a move considered to be the most important one taken in the financial area since the Dominican monetary system was established in 1947. Reflecting the country's tradition of presidentialism and weak judicial oversight, Jorge Blanco was able to impose constitutionally dubious fiscal measures by administrative decree in the face of congressional opposition. A one-year IMF standby program (worth US$78.5 million) was finally signed in April 1985, at which time the government undertook to renegotiate for the second time its bilateral and private commercial bank debt, which it also successfully accomplished over 1985. With a less political and more technocratic economic team in place that controlled government expenditures more carefully, the government successfully complied with the IMF performance targets over 1985 and early 1986, receiving the final IMF disbursement in April 1986.[25]

The administration knew why it was reluctant to take the final step. The harsh stabilization program of devaluation, tight monetary policy, and control of public-sector expenditures induced a sharp recession. Real GDP declined by 1.9 percent; this was the first time the country's GDP had shrunk (in real terms) since 1965, the year of the civil war and U.S. intervention. Inflation shot up dramatically in the first half of 1985, slowing down in the second half. The annual rate for 1985 of 37.5 percent was the highest experienced by the country in this century to that date, though subsequent crises were to lead to even higher inflation rates. In spite of the devaluation, export performance was very poor, even though the country was helped by increased U.S. economic assistance as well as by the return of capital following the devaluation and the increase in domestic interest rates. The economic situation improved in early 1986 as a consequence of the economic measures taken and the drop in oil prices (for economic data, see tables B.2 and B.3). But, poor sugar prospects, little export diversification, and the deteriorated situation of state agencies and enterprises remained critical problems.

The brunt of the country's economic decline fell on the country's poorer groups, as business and middle-sector groups themselves took steps to minimize the effects of stabilization. At the same time, the actions of both business and political opposition served to heighten the government's blame for the stabilization program, while forcing it to enact economically short-sighted measures. By 1985, the government was crosspressured by executive-congressional deadlock on the one hand and its intent to sustain the austerity program agreed upon with the IMF (fearing the consequences of not doing so after having paid such a high cost already) on the other. The limitations imposed by the private sector had also been felt throughout Jorge Blanco's four years in office.

Domestic Business Opposition

The CNHE became embroiled in electoral politics as a consequence of the fact that its president and its executive director were both visible elements of Balaguer's unsuccessful reelection campaign in 1982. This confusion between associational and partisan roles was upsetting to a number of business groups, some because they openly supported Jorge Blanco's candidacy and others because they felt that a PRD victory was likely and that the strategy of public confrontation between the government and the CNHE had provided few dividends. Pressure to adopt a more conciliatory strategy grew and led to the imposition of a more compromise-oriented president of the CNHE in December 1982. It was also agreed that in the future any confusion between partisan and associational roles would not be permitted.

Although the Santo Domingo group had not been fully successful in creating an ideologically self-conscious, aggressive, and strongly united business association, it accomplished a number of its goals. It had unified business to a considerable extent, even though some associations left the CNHE, and it had insured that its agenda would be high on government concerns. A low-profile policy during the Jorge Blanco years, even with a more aggressive figure as president for the 1984–86 period, probably served the interests of the association and its member firms (it was also a policy urged on them by the United States, worried about regime stability). CNHE leaders justified their low-profile stance by arguing that in this way the business sector would not be blamed for the economic stabilization and that the negative social effects that stabilization generated would be blamed upon the government, whose popularity would thus be affected (author's interviews, Santo Domingo, 1986).[26]

As during the Guzmán years, efforts by Jorge Blanco to institute significant direct taxes failed. Similarly, measures to try to provide labor leaders and associations with minimum guarantees also failed to acquire successful passage in congress. Both of these were in large part a result of successfully mobilized business opposition in the legislature, though bitter factionalism within the PRD (discussed below) was also important.

At the same time, many businessmen did extremely well during the stabilization process. Some had prior knowledge regarding the timing of the transfer of products from the parity to the free exchange rate and were able to make windfall profits. Others profited from withdrawing their capital and returning it following devaluation. And many, particularly those who could maintain large inventories, benefited by immediately instituting price increases following devaluation. The economy became increasingly "dollarized" in the 1983–84 period.

By the end of Jorge Blanco's term in office, business groups perceived a tamed PRD. It had become more corrupt, perhaps, in government than they had expected, but it was now more bourgeois. Many still feared Peña Gómez, but others vigorously promoted the candidacy of Majluta, who eventually became the PRD candidate. As if to prove the ideological hegemony of business, Majluta, like Balaguer, also chose a businessman for his vice presidential candidate.[27]

Political Opposition

Just as business purposefully took a low profile during the stabilization process, seeking to defend its position, few politicians sought to be associated with a government forced to carry out such a harsh stabilization program. Both Balaguer and Bosch condemned any agreement with the IMF, and Bosch called for Jorge Blanco's resignation in January 1985 (Méndez 1994, 100–101).

Unlike Guzmán, Jorge Blanco had a comfortable majority in the senate (17 of 27) and a slim majority in the chamber (62 of 120); yet, he soon confronted congressional opposition from within his own party in a manner analogous to that which he had led against Guzmán and Majluta. The politically ambitious Majluta promptly created a separate movement, La Estructura (LE, The Structure), to help promote his presidential candidacy; this movement eventually became a distinct party. By July 1983, Peña Gómez was complaining that PRD militants were being absorbed by Majluta's incipient party. Followers of Jorge Blanco, in turn, plotted ways to weaken Majluta or force him out of the party. Jorge Blanco had led a party opposition to the government, but Majluta ultimately led a factional struggle that was to divide the party itself. After supporting an initial round of tax measures, Majluta blocked further tax legislation, international loans, and numerous other measures. Majluta also asserted that Jorge Blanco's administration was one of the worst the country had ever experienced.

Relations became more venomous over time, as a pattern of factional strife between "ins" and "outs" similar to that under Guzmán soon emerged. Jorge Blanco, however, several times stated he would not seek immediate reelection. In 1982 from the presidency, as in 1980 from the senate, Jorge Blanco formally submitted a proposed constitutional reform barring immediate presidential reelection. Majluta made no effort to promote it, whether because he did not wish to grant Jorge Blanco's government a "success" or because of his desire not to limit his own presidential ambitions.[28] Gradually, Peña Gómez, who was ideologically closer to Jorge Blanco, came to agglutinate the faction of the "ins" against the Majlutista "outs."

A critical turning point in intra-PRD relations came in mid-1984, when the senate refused to sanction a US$150 million IDB loan for the Madrigal dam and waterworks. This was intended to improve the seriously deficient water supply to Santo Domingo. Relying on various arguments developed by the senate's technical commission, the Majluta-led senate rejected the contract without conferring with the PRD's political commission. In spite of a subsequent formal request by the party to reconsider, Majluta and his followers refused to do so, breaking party discipline in congress. A tacit alliance with Balaguer and his party's senators assured the defeat of the loan request. The main reason for Majluta's rejection of the loan appeared to be his fear that funds from the loan would be siphoned off (by "commissions" and other questionable means) and used to block his presidential ambitions, while the project would enhance Jorge Blanco and Peña Gómez, his two major opponents within the party. In June 1984, in the face of Majluta's rejection of party authority, Peña Gómez announced he was creating his own faction within the party, a Bloque Institucional, and that he no longer felt bound by his past promise not to seek the party's nomination for the 1986 term (Peña Gómez 1986d, 45, 194, 203; author's interviews with leading PRD politicians of that period, 1986).

Congressional blockage was met by presidential assertions of sometimes extraconstitutional or extralegal power. Faced with implacable congressional opposition to any tax increase, the president enacted constitutionally dubious and commercially counterproductive fiscal measures by decree. In January 1985, the administration imposed a 36 percent tax on traditional exports and a 5 percent one on nontraditional exports (which it called an "exchange surcharge") to help finance the public-sector deficit and the increased costs of importing fuel at the higher exchange rate for the state electrical company.[29] The government was also forced to implement other revenue measures administratively, such as increased electric rates and gasoline price hikes. An increase in the public-sector minimum wage was paid for from resources for gold exports of the state-owned Rosario Dominicana (which more appropriately should have gone for capital expenditures, since these involved a nonrenewable resource). Only in the face of crippling job actions by middle-sector groups, such as engineers, teachers, nurses, and judges, did congress pass (indirect) fiscal measures in 1985 earmarked for wage increases.

Although Majluta's opposition tactics did tarnish the government's reputation, ultimately they did not serve his political ambitions; the actions of the PRD's three major leaders eroded the party's reputation for internal democracy as the factional strife was reduced more and more to a simple struggle for power and for control of the state and its resources. Majluta continued his

President Salvador Jorge Blanco (1982–86) and his close political ally in the PRD during his presidency, José Francisco Peña Gómez, in 1986. Behind them to the left is the secretary of state for the armed forces, Teniente General Manuel Antonio Cuervo Gómez.

active candidacy within the PRD, while building up La Estructura as a distinct party. The implicit threat was that even if he did not receive the PRD nomination, he would still run for the presidency. To determine the party's candidate for the 1986 elections, the PRD decided to hold a party primary in November 1985 throughout the country, with President Jorge Blanco supporting the candidacy of Peña Gómez against that of Majluta. The ongoing vote count in the Hotel Concorde apparently showed Majluta with a slight advantage when it was disrupted by a shoot-out (the *Concordazo*) between the two candidates' heavily armed followers, who marched off with ballots and prevented the completion of the process.[30] Instead of being selected through a democratic exercise as envisioned by the primary process, Majluta was ultimately named the PRD presidential candidate directly by President Jorge Blanco, "from above"; and like previous presidential candidates, Majluta was forced to accede to candidacies for other posts from the other factions. Thus, Majluta ultimately owed his nomination as the PRD presidential candidate to Jorge Blanco, yet he still sought to avoid overidentification with the administration he had been criticizing so sharply and whose lack of popularity he had sought to establish. Majluta was later to blame Jorge Blanco and Peña Gómez for torpedoing his campaign and causing his defeat (Majluta 1992). At the same time, the effects of congressional obstructionism were almost certainly to shift even more of the burden of adjustment onto groups in society least able to afford them.

In a comparative context, the electoral defeat of the PRD in 1986 was hardly surprising. The consequence of economic-stabilization programs following the oil-shock price increases and the continent's debt crisis had been the defeat of incumbent governments throughout the region. In the Dominican Republic, Balaguer prepared a more careful campaign in 1986, even as Bosch and the PLD gained strength in traditionally PRD urban and sugar-growing areas of the country. Given the country's electoral rules of a single-round plurality-winner presidential election, the PRD's loss of votes to the PLD simply helped give the presidency to Balaguer and his Partido Reformista Social Cristiano (PR[SC], Reformist Social Christian Party), who won by a slim plurality.[31]

The Failure to Modify Neopatrimonial Rule

In the end, the temptations of neopatrimonial, clientelistic politics proved too great for Jorge Blanco, even as they (in combination with other party and electoral dynamics) also deeply affected the PRD. Initially, Jorge Blanco sought to govern in a more institutional fashion than Balaguer; for example, he held regular cabinet meetings and also attended the meetings of the boards of the major decentralized institutes (see Espinal 1991a, 7–8). Yet, all his proposed political reforms were stymied in congress, and he was forced to employ executive decree powers to implement many major economic measures. There are also many signs that he was tempted to seek acquisition of a "war chest" through neopatrimonial means in order to leave a reservoir of good will among key electoral groups with an eye toward subsequent (though not immediate) reelection. Particularly toward the end of his term, Jorge Blanco relied on personalistic and brokerage politics, rather than seeking to sustain a more institutional presidential style. The hopes at the time of his election and inauguration were not realized. Especially in the period between

Balaguer's reelection in May 1986 and the turnover of power in August, Jorge Blanco "lost control of himself" (*se descontroló*), in the words of one sympathetic observer (author's interview, June 1987). Just prior to the May elections, the government lowered fuel prices by more than the decline in international prices. Subsequently, the export surcharge and a stiff US$20 tourist departure tax were lifted. Food subsidies through the deficit-plagued Instituto de Estabilización (INESPRE, Institute for Price Stabilization) were increased, even as INESPRE further delayed payments it owed the country's rice growers and as the state received advances on future sales of sugar and gold by state enterprises. The government also relied on central-bank credit and allowed arrears on payments to official bilateral creditors to develop.

More visible and publicly controversial were the massive numbers of import exemptions and exonerations that Jorge Blanco granted, apparently in an effort to build a solid business and middle-class base of support. While prohibiting the importation of automobiles, Jorge Blanco used presidential powers to grant massive numbers of exemptions for the importation of automobiles tax free, many of which were sold for cash by their initial recipients (author's interviews, 1986; cf. Espinal 1987a, 191). He also gave large-scale tax exemptions to close business associates for imports of industrial and commercial products and spare parts. Among other businessmen, these latter benefits bred intense resentment over "disloyal competition." Both import exemptions and exonerations had also been abused by Balaguer, especially during his 1974–78 term in office, though not to the extent they were now. Adding to the controversy of his final weeks in office, Jorge Blanco also passed out medals representing the nation's highest honors to close political associates. Balaguer, seeing Jorge Blanco as a major threat, would devote his first year in office to destroying him politically, primarily by successfully having corruption charges advanced against him and many of his close associates.[32]

Conclusion

A crucial opportunity to change the country's neopatrimonial style of politics was lost over the 1978–86 period, especially during Jorge Blanco's presidency. The social and economic failures of Jorge Blanco and of the PRD were not all of their making. They inherited serious structural, economic problems from the earlier Balaguer period and faced growing economic constraints (especially the drop in sugar prices and quotas, the increase in oil prices, and the collapse of international credit in the wake of the Latin American debt crisis initiated by Mexico in 1982), as well as sharp domestic opposition to tax and social reforms from powerful, newly organized business groups. Neither Jorge Blanco nor the PRD should bear the brunt of the blame for the country's limited economic options or economic decline, given the country's severe international constraints and private-sector pressures.

Yet, Jorge Blanco and the PRD cannot escape blame for the failures and excesses of his administration. Jorge Blanco's government, unlike the previous Guzmán administration, strongly identified itself with the PRD, and Jorge Blanco had campaigned as the alternative to Guzmán and Majluta's ostensibly more corrupt and clientelistic style of governing. Whereas Jorge Blanco had led a party-government split under Guzmán, Majluta fueled a bitter intraparty division under Jorge Blanco that would ultimately lead to a formal division. As a consequence of this strife, no social or even political reforms were enacted. The PRD was unable to reform the country's labor code, unchanged since the Trujillo era. Initial growth in organized labor under Guzmán languished under Jorge Blanco, as even the PRD-linked labor confederation fragmented along the lines of the factional party struggle. Although Jorge Blanco presented bills to congress calling for judicial reform and prohibiting presidential reelection, these simply died there.

It is Jorge Blanco and the PRD who must bear responsibility for not transforming the style of politics in the country. Should that failure be understood essentially as "destined," given the country's pathway? Alternatively, should it be viewed as structurally induced by the crisis and the constraints imposed by various domestic and international actors? Did individual leadership flaws play a role? I believe it is a mistake to view the failure simply as culturally overdetermined (as destined by the country's historical evolution)—in which case, even if Jorge Blanco's regime had confronted easier circumstances and had enjoyed more successes, he would have employed these same means to build a future political base. Of course we cannot be certain, but Jorge Blanco's initial rhetoric and actions do indicate he had the potential of being a leader who could have initiated the turn to a more regularized, accountable, and democratic politics. Moreover, the trajectory of the PRD demonstrated it was a party with significant democratic elements that could have helped start a new pattern of politics; thus, in the absence of severe crisis, some reforms might well have been instituted, even if there would not have been a total break with the past.

However, the failure, if not "destined," was at least in part path-dependent. The total impunity of past actors and the lack of effective institutional constraints against abuse of state resources precluded effective control over key elements of the state bureaucracy, even by a fully honest and dedicated top officeholder; and the dynamics of PRD factional strife, which were increasingly motivated by a struggle for control of state resources, also contributed to the inability of the PRD to advance the cause of democracy in the Dominican Republic at this time. Especially during Jorge Blanco's administration, the struggle for the presidency overrode nearly all other considerations of policy, ideology, and party coherence. The levels of corruption, of clientelist practices, and of infighting by PRD leaders under both Guzmán and Jorge Blanco suggest that the break with past political practices would at most have been partial even under more favorable economic circumstances.

Structural constraints probably played a role. It is plausible to view the multiple frustrations and failures generated by the country's severe economic crisis as inducing Jorge Blanco to return to the neopatrimonial methods that were institutionally entrenched in discretional presidential powers and in largely unaccountable institutions. These practices were culturally familiar and were no doubt also being urged on him by close associates. The mid-1980s was a difficult period for reformist human "agency" from the presidency throughout Latin America. A comparison of the lofty goals with the actual achievements of presidents such as Raúl Alfonsín in Argentina or Belisario Betancur in Colombia will attest to this. However, there is no sign that either of them "lost control of themselves" in the fashion that Jorge Blanco did, suggesting that personal characteristics also matter (Alan García of Peru may represent a situation more analogous to Jorge Blanco).

In the end, the PRD's policy errors and the excessive ambitions, divisive behavior, and apparent corrupt practices of some of its top leaders helped bring Balaguer back to power. In turn, Balaguer promptly demonstrated once again that in terms of this kind of politics and in terms of using neopatrimonial powers to manipulate the economy to his advantage, PRD leaders were rank amateurs compared to him.

7 Balaguer Returns, 1986–1996
The Tensions of Neopatrimonial Democracy

With the return to power of Balaguer in 1986, neopatrimonial patterns of politics and economic policymaking once again were starkly evident. Balaguer governed in a more democratic fashion than he had previously, especially in the first several years after he reassumed power in 1986. The military did not play an overt role in politics, and state-sanctioned repression and restrictions on public expression were lower. However, the democratic nature of the regime, especially regarding respect for political rights, eroded over the 1990s as Balaguer clung to power.

In chapter 1, we defined neopatrimonialism as a centralization of power in the hands of a ruler who seeks to reduce the autonomy of his followers by generating ties of loyalty and dependence, often creating complex patron-client linkages and, in the process, blurring public and private interests and purposes within the administration. In chapters 2 and 4, we related the various facets of this concept to the policies and behaviors of Trujillo (1930–61) and Balaguer (1966–78).

Now, consider some examples from President Balaguer's second extended period in office (1986–96). On typical evenings, the president personally heard reports by the appropriate officials regarding how much revenue the state had collected through customs duties and income and other taxes, as well as how much money the state had spent that day. The chief executive officer of Falconbridge, an exporter of ferronickel, was required to deliver in person a check in dollars to President Balaguer for the taxes the company owed the Dominican state. This check went into a special dollar account over which the president had exclusive control with no congressional or judicial oversight. Occasionally, expenditures from this fund were reported in monthly ads in the newspaper, but with no other accountability or explanation; for example, in July 1995 it was reported that US$26,000 toward an individual's studies at

Harvard University was paid from this account (*Hoy*, July 28, 1995). "Lucky guy," was the reaction of one Dominican when I pointed it out to him. But luck had much to do with connections, as this individual well knew: depending on who among his PR(SC) allies held which government post, this individual had sometimes simultaneously occupied two (technically full-time) government jobs, while continuing to work as a print and television journalist and a political media consultant.

The president carried out projects without congressional approval; for example, the state paid to renovate the residence and offices and to construct a tunnel connecting the two for the cardinal and archbishop of Santo Domingo, Balaguer's close political ally. The contract for the work was given to the architectural firm of the cardinal's brother. In 1991, a fairly typical year, 59.8 percent of the entire central government's expenditures flowed directly through the office of the presidency. In that year, the central government's expenditures were 32.3 percent over the amount initially budgeted, and the president had complete discretion over how to expend those funds, having in addition total control over US$150 million in the government's special dollar accounts. For several months in early 1994, the state electric company stopped receiving its monthly subsidy from the central government; it is widely believed that those, and other state, monies were used instead to help fund President Balaguer's reelection campaign, but there is no access to the accounting books to confirm or disconfirm this belief.

We have tied the failure to break with past neopatrimonial patterns in the country during the PRD administrations to several factors. These have included inherited institutional structures and incentives, international economic crisis and societal pressures, intraparty struggles, and failures of leadership. Under Balaguer, the question concerns how and why it was possible for him to pursue his favored political and economic strategies given the country's ongoing societal changes and continuing economic constraints. The brief answer combines personal, institutional, and structural aspects. Balaguer was a master at using constitutional and extraconstitutional powers and state resources to concentrate what power he had, expanding his margin of discretional power. He was often able to divide his opposition and to prolong conflicts and delay decision making to his advantage. He confronted a different intraparty dynamic because his own commitment to reelection was rarely in doubt. Unlike the PRD presidents, he was able to defeat his internal party challengers and retain control of his party. He was aided by the fact that Dominican society remained highly unequal and weakly organized and that, because of his historical trajectory, he retained an apparent captive electoral base, which he was able to augment sufficiently to help eke out narrow electoral victories. In sum, Balaguer faced dramatic international constraints and societal and political opposition, but he maintained greater political autonomy through neopatrimonial rule than had the PRD governments.

The various aspects of this answer, which also consider the costs to the country of his extended rule, are developed below. Given Balaguer's past patterns of political behavior, it is less surprising that he continued to govern in the neopatrimonial fashion evidenced both in his economic policies and political style. His policies in his first term in office generated high levels of economic growth and increased employment in the short term. However, they helped induce an economic crisis whose escalating rates of inflation and of devaluation and declining growth were even worse than those experienced under the PRD governments. Balaguer was eventually forced to accommodate dramatic changes in the Dominican economy imposed by changing international circumstances; he sought initially to ignore these changes (at least partially) and subsequently to profit politically from them as much as possible. He had clear ideas about policies that would enhance his stature and favor him politically (e.g., centralizing expenditures through his office, especially for public works); he bowed to international constraints as necessary and proceeded with his own agenda when feasible. Less concerned with constitutional formalities than the PRD, he ultimately had more success in managing economic policy, though he led the country into more severe economic problems than those experienced under Jorge Blanco. He was more politically adept at carrying out economic stabilization when required. The cost of his mix of policies was increasing disorder and loss of capacity within the state; positive macroeconomic indicators in terms of growth and inflation were combined with high levels of inequality, low levels of expenditures in health and education, and continued high unemployment.

In his last months in office, Jorge Blanco had already begun to undo some of the reform measures he had so painfully implemented earlier in his term. Those reform efforts had helped reduce constraints on government expenditures and had brought the regime some relief from external pressure. There was continued popular-sector dissatisfaction due to high unemployment and hopes for change generated by the electoral process. Business interests remained divided over the need for and the precise nature of market-oriented reforms affecting the internal market, while investments in export-processing zones and tourism continued. Balaguer was deeply skeptical of the political benefit of market-oriented reforms. Although during the 1986 campaign some of his associates had talked about privatization of some of the deficit-plagued state enterprises, he had never publicly identified himself with it. There was little political will, societal support, or effective international pressure for continued economic liberalization.

Balaguer moved quickly to reassert his neopatrimonial form of rule and to further divide and weaken his opposition during the period from 1986 to 1990, as explained in the first section below. He pursued economic policies very similar to those of his previous terms in office. Massive public expenditures on construction and public works were combined with constraints on other public spending by such steps as reducing public-employment levels, not increasing wages, and cutting back in social spending. Seeking to avoid international oversight and problems with congressional approvals of loans, Balaguer opted to fund his investment programs through unorthodox means, some of which were of dubious legality. Nevertheless, he found himself more constrained than in his previous twelve-year term, due to the changed nature of the country's economy and society and the existence of a more active political opposition.

A second policy period, over the second half of 1990 through 1993, involved economic stabilization and initial structural reforms. The contradictions inherent in his earlier policies generated bottlenecks, inflation, and increased external pressure. More elements of business favored stabilization and with growing economic diversification, some major domestic groups became more open to trade liberalization. Ultimately, Balaguer was forced to implement a stabilization program. He was able to delay it until after the 1990 elections, although he was now in a weaker political position because of the crisis-ridden nature of the electoral process and the protests that ensued. That year turned out to be worse than 1985, both in terms of the extent of decline in the country's economy as well as in terms of inflation, as the government implemented a serious stabilization program and took other economic measures. Once the measures were taken, Balaguer was able to reach agreement with the IMF in August 1991 for a nineteen-month standby agreement worth US$53 million. Over 1991–94, Balaguer was able to negotiate substantial debt relief. Balaguer became convinced that implementing certain structural reforms, such as trade liberalization, would enhance public revenues and benefit him politically. In 1992, congress also overhauled the country's tax code and, in the face of U.S. pressure, approved a new labor code. Major reforms in the financial sector regarding foreign investment were also introduced during this period.

In a third period, from 1993 until 1996, Balaguer put the country through a less extreme and more condensed version of the first two periods. He expanded public expenditures in late 1993 leading up to the 1994 elections, still focusing more on public construction efforts than on social service expenditures. Then, beginning in September 1994, he stabilized the economy and maintained the country's overall macroeconomic equilibrium as he handed power over in August 1996.

The discussion below is guided by consideration of the five clusters of factors identified in chapter 6 as important in explaining successful initiation of measures of economic stabilization and restructuring. Similarly, as in the previous chapter, each section below begins with a review of the administration's strategy, its initial policies, and the nature of international constraints and external pressure. It then turns to a consideration of domestic societal response before analyzing patterns of political support and opposition and their effect on the administration's understanding of its options.

Balaguer's Initial Program, 1986–1990

Initial Strategy and Diminished International Pressure

Upon assuming power in August 1986, Balaguer pursued a number of complementary economic and political strategies. He weakened the PRD and further fostered its internal divisions, bringing corruption charges against a number of its leaders and former officials, including former President Salvador Jorge Blanco. He cemented a close alliance with the Catholic Church, by ending steps toward the secularization of education that had been pursued by the PRD and by favoring the church with massive expenditures of public funds. His major method of economic reactivation revolved around dramatic increases in public investment, especially in construction and public works. Some of these were focused with an eye toward 1992, the 500th anniversary of what the Dominican Catholic Church and the government called the "discovery and evangelization of the Americas." Preparations included the construction of the Columbus Lighthouse, which was to shine a massive cross into the sky every evening upon its completion; the remodeling of Santo Domingo's Colonial Zone; and repairs and new construction for the church in Santo Domingo and throughout the country.

Balaguer's construction projects extended across the country. The largest ones included the Jigüey-Aguacate Dam, the Valdesia–Santo Domingo Aqueduct, and several major highway, bridge, road, and public-housing projects concentrated particularly in the capital. However, Balaguer spent money on multiple particularistic projects throughout the country and sought to reactivate agricultural production and to cement peasant support through modest land-titling efforts. These projects favored his cronies with huge contracts, generated employment, and provided visible evidence that his government was "doing something," unlike the previous PRD governments, which were being painted as both ineffective and corrupt. While augmenting the state's fiscal revenues, he kept business opposition in check through a combination of co-optative and coercive measures. Some leaders of organized business groups were intimidated by government threats, even as numerous other business leaders were favored by state contracts. During this initial period of reactivation, organized labor remained generally weak and divided. A nascent movement built around popular neighborhood associations was also weakened by a combination of selective repression, co-optation, and marginalization.

Balaguer dramatically expanded public expenditures, focusing them on construction projects, and concentrated direct control over expenditures in the office of the presidency. Table 7.1 shows the sharp growth in public expenditures from 14.4 percent of GDP in 1986 to 19.8 percent of GDP two years later, with modest and then more severe cutbacks over 1989 and 1990. The focus on construction is evident from the much higher GDP growth figures for construction than for overall GDP growth and from the data on reorientation of public expenditures toward capital expenditures in the table. As in his previous twelve years in office, Balaguer shifted the control of an overwhelming percent of government expenditures directly to the office of the presidency; the data in both tables 4.1 and 7.1 indicates that the percentage of expenditures committed to construction was over 90 percent for many years in his two different periods in government. Furthermore, the percentage of the central government's total expenditures represented exclusively by the office of the presidency averaged 53.5 percent over the 1987–95 period, compared to only 15.7 percent for the 1980–85 period of PRD governments.[1]

The president also retained impressive discretional powers over the budget. Based on a 1969 budget law, Balaguer was able to spend almost as he wished by undervaluing income in the official budget approved by congress; any extra revenues could then be spent by the executive almost entirely at its discretion (Tejada 1994). Balaguer also directly controlled several dollar accounts fed by certain trade and tourism taxes and refused to provide congress with a consolidated public-sector budget that included state enterprises, which steadily deteriorated over his ten years in office.

Balaguer funded his investments in several different ways over this period (1986–96). First, he saved in other areas. During his first year in office, he reduced public employment by some 16,000 people as real wages initially also declined (public-sector minimum wages were not adjusted from July 1985 until June 1988). He also eliminated or reduced subsidies from the central government to a number of state enterprises, including the CEA and INESPRE

Table 7.1. Public-Sector Expenditures, 1986–1995

	1986	1987	1988	1989	1990	1991	1992	1993	1994	1995
1.) Real GDP annual growth (%)	3.4	9.1	0.5	3.9	−4.8	0.7	7.9	3.0	4.3	4.8
2.) Real GDP annual growth in construction (%)	15.5	34.1	3.2	13.2	−19.2	−12.4	24.4	10.6	6.6	5.7
3.) Total public-sector expenditures (% GDP)	14.4	17.4	19.8	18.2						
				21.8	15.6	16.4	17.8	20.0		
4.) Central government capital expenditures/central government expenditures (%)	28.5	56.5	59.2	59.7	56.3					
						55.8	62.4	58.5	59.5	53.6
5.) Office of the presidency/central government expenditures (%)	31.9	53.7	52.6	53.9	50.7	59.8	53.3	52.6	53.5	51.8
6.) Office of the presidency/central government expenditures on construction (%)				79.8	92.8	92.7	97.1	97.6	96.2	96.7

Sources: Rows 1 and 2 (IDB 1994, 1997); rows 3 and 4, top lines (Santana and Rathe 1992, 129, 132); row 3, bottom line (World Bank 1995b, 5); row 4, bottom line (Banco Central, *Boletín Trimestral*, Oct.–Dec. 1995, 98; Apr.–June 1996, 98); rows 5 and 6 (ibid., Apr. 1991, 132; Oct.–Dec. 1993; Oct.–Dec. 1995; Apr.–June 1996). Series of numbers from different sources are not always strictly comparable.

(formerly a direct purchaser of domestic and imported foodstuffs, which it then sold at subsidized prices). Second, he increased revenues through a series of ad hoc measures. There were increased import duties and monetary surcharges, higher user fees, and windfall revenues from a boom in ferronickel exports. The government renegotiated contracts with three transnational corporations, of which the most important was one with Falconbridge, exporter of ferronickel, in May 1988. New revenues in dollars flowed to the government as a result of both the boom in world nickel prices and the new deal struck between the government and Falconbridge.[2] Third, Balaguer allowed public-sector deficits to grow as central-bank credit was widely employed as a funding mechanism (see table B.5). Finally, by mid-1989 he allowed debt arrears to accumulate, although the Dominican Republic was a more faithful payer of debt for a longer period than many of its continental neighbors.

The boom in construction and public works soon generated significant tensions in the economy. Public works tended to be import intensive, generating balance-of-payment and exchange-rate pressures, even as bottlenecks in the supply of domestic inputs also fed inflation. As the currency became increasingly overvalued, tensions with the tourism and EPZ sectors increased, since these desired low wages in dollar terms more than an expanded domestic market. Monetary policy was driven by Balaguer's investment program, even as the state became far more important in overall investment in the country. The contraction of public expenditures in other areas led to declines in real wages (made worse by the effects of inflation) and a decline in services in areas such as education and health. Another major problem was the state electric company, Companía Dominicana de Electricidad (CDE, Dominican Electric Company), whose growing inefficiency and inability to satisfy demand had three major results: growing power outages that disproportionately affected small businesses and the popular sector in urban areas; pressure on major businesses and wealthy Dominicans to invest in small private generators; and drains on public-sector revenues as the CDE required growing subsidies in the face of its own falling revenues.[3]

Balaguer sustained his favored economic program for as long as he could, and for longer than most economists thought possible. He was forced to cut back investment levels over 1988—a year of low growth, high inflation, and sharp fluctuations in the country's exchange rate (by historical standards; see figure B.1)—but he continued with his program in 1989 through to the 1990 elections. The means by which he managed the economy evolved over time. Balaguer was convinced that control over the exchange rate was imperative in order to control inflation, if not as a matter of national pride. He also feared the political fallout of a conditionality agreement with the IMF. Nevertheless, over 1987 and 1988 the government continued meeting payments on the country's multilateral and private commercial bank debt and sustained talks with the IMF.[4] However, Balaguer's desire for a surveillance program (which would permit renegotiation of the debt without providing any IMF funds), rather than a full standby program (which would impose stricter conditionality requirements while providing an IMF loan), was rejected by the IMF, especially given the government's evolving exchange-rate policies and fiscal and monetary policies.

During this period, Balaguer continued to delay policy modifications and to pursue his desired public-investment policies. The central bank moved unevenly from policies of multiple exchange rates, including a market-determined one, to more rigid exchange controls. In mid-1988, small exchange houses (bancos de cambio) through which flowed dollars uncontrolled by the central bank were closed; this move both favored the larger commercial banks and sent them a coercive message. In July 1988, the government then abandoned a dual-exchange system (with a market-determined free rate) for a formalized exchange control system. Temporary stability to the country's exchange rate was achieved through a variety of ad hoc measures, including a dramatic inflow of dollars resulting from the ferronickel export boom, modest and then more dramatic debt arrears, a willingness to use the central bank's dollar reserves, and intimidation and coercion within the business sector. Over the second half of 1988, the government also expanded import controls and began to restrict monetary growth. Increasingly frustrated, a central bank governor resigned in September 1989 in protest over the government's exchange policy.[5] In the first half of 1990 the central bank suspended the export licenses of more than one hundred local exporters, alleging they were not delivering their foreign exchange to the government; the government also pressed lawsuits against hotels, EPZ companies, and others to force them to deliver more of their dollars to the central bank at the (lower) official rate, even as the gap between that rate and the black-market rate continued to grow (see figure B.1 for a graphic representation of the sharp decline in the country's exchange rate during this period). Through these various measures, the government was able to retain its basic policies through the May 1990 elections without imposing a stabilization program, though it was forced to devalue the peso in April.

Domestic Societal Opposition

Overall, business groups tended to favor Balaguer over the PRD. However, they were soon to be bitterly disappointed by his government's policies, even as they found themselves too divided and too intimidated to be effective in pressuring for policy modifications over the 1986–90 period. During this first period of Balaguer's return, business played a relatively low-profile role. Few business leaders dared to confront Balaguer directly regarding his government's policies, in part out of fear of possible retribution and intimidation by government agents. The CNHE suffered in 1986 as a consequence of an effort by Ginebra, a past CNHE president close to Balaguer, to reimpose his own candidacy, whether to insure the loyalty of the CNHE to the government, for potential personal profit, or to further his own political ambitions. The move was temporarily beaten back, though Ginebra did become the CNHE president in 1988. The CNHE was unable to confront Balaguer institutionally, as it had the Jorge Blanco government. Indeed, Balaguer began his term in office by discreetly intimidating a leading member of the board of directors of the CNHE.[6] By 1989, business found itself in the uncomfortable position of tacitly supporting labor and popular-sector protests against the government and its policies, even as it was unwilling to endorse all of their demands.

Several different patterns of social protest were evident over the 1980s. Most significant was the emergence of urban, territorially based social movements. They were facilitated by greater democratic freedoms under PRD governments, and sometimes by the assistance of local church and other activists and by international aid. They were also fed by the economic crisis and by the growing disillusionment with the PRD and party politics in general. Their increased role gained dramatic national attention in the protest actions of April 1984; it was in neighborhoods where the protests were most significant that popular movements also tended to be most active subsequently (Ferguson 1992, 105). As a consequence of continued organization and in response to certain of Balaguer's policies, popular movement associations became particularly active over 1987 and 1988. Indeed, their protest actions over the 1980s overshadowed those of students, organized labor, and peasants, which had been more important in the 1960s and 1970s. The number and visibility of these urban movements increased under Balaguer in the late 1980s due to discontent about forced urban evictions, conducted to make way for new construction and other public-sector projects, and to demands for salary increases, price reductions for basic products, improvements in public transportation, provision of water and electricity, and street repair. Some regional and national level leaders emerged from these movements, but the vast number of protest actions did not call for a radical restructuring of society, and their political demands rarely went beyond a rejection of neoliberal economic policies and the IMF (for a detailed study, see Pérez and Artiles 1992, esp. 55, 60; see also Ianni 1990). At the same time, the combination of a dramatic increase of such protest actions along with the call for nationwide protests represented a growing challenge to the state, against whom the protest actions were organized.

Middle-sector professional unions and organizations represented another vigorous protest actor, though usually centered around specific demands. Quantitative data over the 1983–89 period indicates that protest actions by these groups took a sharp jump upward in 1985, probably as a consequence of the dramatic effect stabilization measures had on their standard of living. From then on, wage declines and deteriorating work conditions led to multiple protest actions by those professionals working for the state, such as teachers, health personnel, and agronomists. These protests sometimes led to wage increases (Pérez and Artiles 1992, 55). As noted in chapter 5, migration also emerged as an option for a number of Dominican professionals.

Organized labor remained weak and fragmented. The number of base-level unions officially registered with the ministry of labor did show a dramatic increase during the PRD years, although it declined subsequently in the first years of Balaguer's return. However, two other key indicators of labor strength were much more negative. The number of collective pacts signed annually over the 1978–87 period peaked in 1980 (at around seventy), but declined sharply to levels only in the mid-twenties by the end of the period. Finally, rather than growing labor unity, there was increased fragmentation at the top. In 1984, the country had four major labor confederations; by 1988 there were some seven labor confederations, with many unaffiliated unions, in a country in which the level of unionization reached only around 15 percent of the economically active population. Similarly, a growth in the overall number of local-level peasant associations was also linked with a decline in regional or nation-level, coordinated peasant protest actions over the mid-1980s (Ianni 1990; Espinal 1990a, 14; Núñez Collado 1993, 436–37; author's interviews in the ministry of labor, 1994–95).

The nature and intensity of protest activity intensified over 1987, 1988, and 1989 due to inflation, evictions, and complaints over services. In July 1987, there had been a partially successful one-day national strike. An appeal for a forty-eight-hour national strike in March 1988 by the Conferencia Nacional de Organizaciones Populares (CNOP, National Conference of Popular Organizations), an umbrella organization of popular neighborhood associations, was met with a cool response by sectors of organized labor—particularly by the Confederación Autónoma de Sindicatos Clasistas (CASC, Autonomous Confederation of Class-based Unions) and the Central de Trabajadores Mayoritaria (CTM, Majoritarian Center of Workers), the labor confederations closest to the PR(SC) and to the PLD, respectively. It was suspended after twenty-four hours as the church called for mediation. Ultimately, the church established a tripartite dialogue (government, business, labor) that marginalized the leaders of the popular-sector mobilizations. Thus, the labor confederations refused to join the call made by a new popular-sector group for another general strike in April 1988, and CNOP was again not permitted to join the tripartite dialogue. The parties to the dialogue signed an agreement on wages, social security, and taxes in May 1988; however, due to a lack of implementation of many of the measures, six of the labor confederations withdrew from further dialogue (only the PR[SC]-linked CASC stayed in). Popular-sector mobilizations declined over the second half of 1988, and the government also refused to address the demands of professional public-sector workers who went on strike (*Panorama* 1988; Espinal 1990a, 14; text of agreement in Núñez Collado 1993, 433–37). The country's attention was partially diverted by the spectacular trial against Salvador Jorge Blanco (in absentia) and a number of his collaborators held in November 1988.[7]

Discontent continued to grow as inflation levels increased, real wages declined, and the government did not change its basic policies in spite of promises to the contrary. In June 1989, there was a successful forty-eight hour general strike led by the CNOP. In the face of government intransigence, the church finally acquiesced in the action, and even business sought to use the strike to advance its own agenda. However, Balaguer shrewdly responded with very modest steps, and congress approved some limited reforms. Ultimately, these helped renew the division between some of the labor confederations and the CNOP and they also helped provoke a split within the CNOP itself.

By the end of 1989, many sectors of organized business were prepared to change from a conciliatory approach with the administration to a more direct one. The government's repressive efforts to sustain the multiple (and overvalued) exchange rates and to continue monetary growth to fund public construction programs, its refusal to deal with international financial institutions, and its capricious, neopatrimonial style provoked increased ire across various business groups. Balaguer's close friend Ginebra was replaced as president of the CNHE by a more independent figure, one whose multiple investments in various areas of the economy also allowed him to operate with greater independence in the face of possible government pressure. The March 1990 national convention of the CNHE, held just prior to the May elections, resulted in a wide-ranging series of resolutions calling for economic and social policy reforms, as well as for changes in different areas of state management to reduce the president's discretional powers (see Gran Convención de Hombres de Empresa 1990). That same month, small merchants protested over a reform in the collection system of the value-added tax, as Balaguer blamed "speculators" in business for unauthorized price increases and pressures on the exchange rate (Espinal 1991, 6).

Political Opposition

Balaguer confronted a fragmented political opposition. He was also able successfully to employ strategies of co-optation, intimidation, and division against the opposition, similar to those he employed with societal opposition groups. For the 1986–90 period, Balaguer had a comfortable majority in the senate (21 of 30 seats), although in the chamber he was just shy of a majority (56 of 120).

However, the PRD remained deeply factionalized, and its forty-eight representatives found it very difficult to cooperate with each other—much less with
the PLD's sixteen representatives.

The PRD had emerged from the 1986 elections badly divided. As noted,
Balaguer sought to destroy the strongest elements of the PRD, the Jorge
Blanco wing, by means of corruption charges and trials. The anticorruption
campaign was a huge political success for Balaguer. It helped sustain his own
image as an honest and effective leader and helped divert attention from the
country's ongoing economic problems. It also strengthened his position by
creating fear among opponents. The partisan cardinal and archbishop of
Santo Domingo preached a message of vengeance, even as the small movements of the left strongly supported the campaign, hoping to inherit part of
the PRD's constituency or perhaps betting on the possibility of "social chaos."
Once the political advantages of attacking his partisan adversary for not pursu-
ing legal, rule-governed behavior receded, Balaguer abandoned the theme, to
govern in ways focused far more on patronage than on ideology or respect for
the rule of law.

At the same time, over 1986–87, the factional strife within the PRD between the followers of Peña Gómez and Majluta intensified as two intraparty
governing bodies were formed. The JCE opted not to favor one faction over
another in a November 1987 decision, installing Peña Gómez as president
and Hatuey de Camps (allied with him) as secretary-general, while granting
Majluta a majority in the party's national executive committee. An independent group of professionals and elements of the church continued to seek to
mediate the conflict between the two over 1988–89 to prevent a party split.

Among those seeking to bring the PRD back together was the Movimiento
de Renovación (MODERNO, Movement for Renovation). This group of
professionals was comprised both of those interested in implementing neoliberal economic policies and those seeking a more institutionalized state and
more concerted social policies. The nature of Balaguer's regime and the
absence of a deep economic crisis permitted this heterogeneous set of interests
to come together. The desire to limit the discretionary power of the president
and to implement even the most basic state programs oriented toward education and health thus brought together individuals oriented primarily toward
market-oriented measures as a way of reducing abuse and discretionality with
those more focused on building state capacity and enhancing accountability,
transparency, and effective checks and balances on presidential power. What
united them at the time was a desire to avoid having either caudillo, Balaguer or
Bosch, assume the presidency in 1990, an effort in which they were ultimately
frustrated.[8]

Peña Gómez retained control over the PRD, with Balaguer's apparent tacit support.[9] Majluta launched his candidacy in January 1990 through a new party he had formed, the Partido Revolucionario Independiente (PRI, Independent Revolutionary Party). As a consequence of these internecine conflicts, the PRD was incapable of mounting an effective opposition to Balaguer's government. Going into the 1990 elections, Bosch and the PLD emerged as Balaguer's primary opponent.

The PLD's opposition to Balaguer, in turn, was steady, but not strident. For his eightieth birthday in June 1989, Bosch accepted a medal representing the nation's highest honor from Balaguer. And, as noted above, the PLD refused to join with other groups in protest actions against the state. Leading up to the 1990 elections, the PLD sought to moderate further its image within the business sector, while expanding its organization throughout the country. By 1989, in the face of the country's serious economic problems and the PRD's woes, survey polls gave the PLD a wide margin of victory. The party was so convinced of its victory that it refused to enter into alliances with other political groups. Last minute campaign errors by Bosch, a stronger than expected third place finish by the PRD, and probably some fraud helped Balaguer win a narrow victory in tense elections. The PLD attitude toward Balaguer was to change dramatically as a consequence of these elections, in which they were convinced that fraud prevented their victory. Thus, Balaguer was forced to implement an economic-stabilization program in the second half of 1990 under difficult conditions.

Balaguer Responds to Economic Crisis, 1990–1993

By mid-1990, it was clear that the country would need to implement a stabilization program. Foreign-exchange reserves were perilously low, nearly all international creditors had imposed a de facto embargo, and capital flight and disinvestment were increasing. Other problems included a drop in nickel prices, a drought, and an increase in world oil prices. Furthermore, the government faced the threat of U.S. trade sanctions because of complaints brought in Washington about the mistreatment of Haitian sugar workers and the lack of unions in the country's EPZs.

Once his electoral victory was secure, Balaguer agreed to a "solidarity pact" in August 1990 with business, labor, and other groups (for a summary of the key points, see Núñez Collado 1993, 156–58). He began to institute the measures necessary to stabilize the economy. Labor was also granted several concessions, including a modest increase in the minimum wage in October, representation on the boards of several state-owned enterprises, and the promise of a new labor code. Balaguer devalued the currency, unified exchange rates, increased fuel prices and electric tariff rates, cut public expenditures dramatically, controlled monetary expansion, and liberalized interest rates. The economy went into a sharp recession, especially the construction sector (see table 7.1). There was a dramatic surge in inflation, the highest rates the country had experienced this century (around 14 percent in September and around 10 percent on average from October through December) (Ceara Hatton 1993). In the first half of 1991, public investment in real terms was only about half of what it had been in the first half of 1990.

With these painful measures behind him, Balaguer reached a nineteen-month standby agreement with the IMF in August 1991. And, in July 1993, a few months after that agreement expired, a second nine-month agreement was approved by the IMF, which expired in March 1994, just before the scheduled May elections. During this time, Balaguer made substantial progress in renegotiating the country's foreign debt; debt as a percentage of the GDP declined from 92.8 percent in 1987 to 42.4 percent in 1993 (see table B.3). The country renegotiated its debt with its bilateral creditors, including a substantial repurchase of debt with Venezuela at almost two-thirds its nominal value. Finally, in February 1994, a debt restructuring with commercial banks was signed, which included a repurchase of around a third of the debt at a 75 percent discount and a swap of the balance at 65 percent of its value (Inter-American Development Bank 1994b, 77).[10] By this time, Balaguer was already dramatically expanding state expenditures with an eye toward winning the May 1994 elections.

Over the 1990–92 period, Balaguer also instituted a number of other far-reaching reforms in trade, taxation, and labor. Many other reforms were also proposed in areas such as foreign investment, monetary and financial reform, privatization and financial improvement of the state electric company, and privatization or closure of other state enterprises. Yet, when Balaguer stepped down from office in August 1996, with the exception of a law easing restrictions on foreign investment, all these other measures were still being debated. The reforms that Balaguer opted for had been widely discussed in the country by local economists and international agencies, advisers, and special missions. The UN Development Program, as a more neutral entity than the IMF or other international agencies, was an important policy mediator. It implemented a series of studies and helped bring in foreign missions. It played an important role, in conjunction with several local economists, in convincing a skeptical Balaguer to adopt the ostensibly market-oriented trade and tax reforms.

However, it is apparent that Balaguer largely agreed to enact the trade reforms and tax reforms because they would help provide him with additional fiscal resources (the former reforms doing much more than the latter, as explained below). Balaguer opted to avoid or to go much slower in other reforms that could erode his support base or prevent him from continuing to implement his favored strategies of public construction and public works. With regard to the economic reforms, Balaguer once again demonstrated his ability to proceed slowly and minimally, in ways that maximized his own goals while co-opting and dividing his opposition. As in the past, a great deal of the costs were borne by the poorest and least protected sectors of Dominican society for whom basic services in education and health continued to stagnate.

Trade

Without regard to legality, the Balaguer administration instituted a new trade regime for the country by decree in September 1990; with a few changes, it was finally approved as a law in August 1993 (for details on this, as well as on other subsequent minor changes instituted by decrees, see Dauhajre hijo et al. 1996, 189–90). The 1990 trade regime vastly simplified an extraordinarily complex set of taxes, duties, incentives, and exceptions into seven tariff rates, while reducing the maximum tariff from 596 percent to 35 percent over a gradual phase-in period. Many import bans were eliminated, as were special tax exonerations and exemptions based on law 299 (see chapter 4) and other incentive laws (except for those related to the EPZs).

To what extent the revised customs schedule actually represented a move toward trade liberalization is disputed among economists. According to the World Bank, the reform had little effect on reducing effective protection rates. Tariffs were lowered on imported inputs much more than on imported final products, and local industries were further helped by additional domestic excise and value-added taxes imposed on imported final products. In an additional effort to enhance revenues over the 1990–93 period, Balaguer's customs administrator also often vastly overvalued imported goods with absolute discretionality (World Bank 1995b, 11–15; Dauhajre hijo et al. 1996, 190–96).

A different study came to the contrary conclusion. This study compared prices of basic consumer goods in supermarkets in the Dominican Republic and in the United States and did not find significant differences, even as it provided data showing that domestic manufacturing firms went into recession in the early 1990s. Thus, it concluded the customs reform had affected domestic industry, contrary to the view of the World Bank. Because of the absence of computerized records in customs, only estimates of the average tariff rate on imported industrial inputs exist. In critiquing the World Bank methodology based on legal norms, this study also notes that the likely prevalence of extensive contraband and import underinvoicing has meant that imported consumer goods can often be placed for sale in the domestic market at rates substantially below those to be expected at official tariff and tax rates. Local industries have been forced to lower their prices in the face of this competition. Additional errors may also have been made by the World Bank in calculating the extent of domestic value added (Vega 1996).

Two key points, however, are not in dispute. One is that the reform increased state revenues. The reform became a revenue-enhancing measure in large part because import duties were now to be assessed based on the value of the imports at a market-rate exchange rate, rather than at some lower or even parity rate. Indeed, this change alone more than offset the tariff-rate reductions (World Bank 1995b, 14). Furthermore, in the context of the 1991 IMF agreement, a temporary 15 percent surcharge was imposed on many imports, as well as a 2 percent foreign-exchange tax (these were subsequently modified and lowered). The favorable impact this had on state revenues was dramatic: from 1990 to 1993, taxes on foreign trade jumped from 3.8 percent of GDP to 5.6 percent of GDP, representing a substantial portion of the increased revenues of the Dominican state during this period (see table B.5).

Another is that the reform did not seriously reduce the discretional power of the president. Even after the enactment of the reform, around one-third of the value of all imports still required prior import licenses, which were granted by the president (and thus usually necessitated "contacts" in the presidential palace). And the president retained the power to exonerate individuals or firms from the payment of customs duties for products ranging from industrial machinery to private automobiles.[11]

Taxation

Another major source of state revenue during this period was the differential on petroleum prices that resulted from the fact the government did not lower domestic fuel prices as international prices fell following the Gulf War. This tax generated revenues worth 2.0 percent of GDP in 1993 (see table B.5). At least one study indicates this tax has not had a regressive impact on income in the country (Dauhajre hijo, Achécar, and Swindale 1994, 7). Nevertheless, it has reflected and reinforced the discretional power of the executive and the ad hoc, crisis-response nature of the Dominican state.

In May 1992, a sweeping new tax code also attained congressional approval. The legislation lowered marginal tax rates from 70 percent to 30 percent (and to 25 percent in 1995), raised the deductible to exempt the bulk of wage earners from income tax obligations, incorporated an inflation adjustment for future years (a feature the government was illegally slow to implement), and expanded the goods and services required to pay the value-added tax (renamed ITBIS to include services). The way the tax was calculated on numerous goods and services was rationalized. The government also increased the value-added tax from 6 percent to 8 percent (it had originally proposed an increase to 10 percent) to the consternation of business groups, but it eliminated the double taxation of dividends. The new tax code also called for the gradual elimination of the import surcharge.

However, these sweeping tax changes were not reflected in increased revenues, primarily due to lax collection procedures. In spite of the reform, and reflecting the continuing erosion of state capacity under Balaguer, collections in this area actually fell from almost 6 percent of GDP to 5.1 percent of GDP over the 1990–93 period. There were extreme delays in generating the implementing regulations and any of the other administrative reforms essential for effective enforcement, such as sanctions for evasion and constraints on corruption. During this period, it was believed that state auditors were open to side-payments by business owners to reduce social-security or other tax burdens and that the superiors of these state employees, in turn, demanded a portion of these payments—thus practically institutionalizing these practices in the face of woefully low public-sector salaries (author's interviews, 1995–96). Only 8,000 of an estimated 28,000 registered businesses filed tax returns; of some 230,000 individuals liable to pay income taxes, only some 10 percent filed tax returns. In none of my visits to the country, did a gift-shop owner ever charge me the ITBIS as is legally required. Indeed, one study estimated that 67 percent of the theoretical ITBIS tax base evaded taxation (World Bank 1995b, 17n).

Labor

The third major reform that Balaguer instituted was an overhaul of the country's obsolete labor code, which had remained unchanged since the Trujillo era. Although such reform had been a demand of labor groups for decades, it was only in the face of imminent threat of U.S. trade sanctions that the government and local business interests acquiesced to institute the reform. Under various U.S. laws, a less-developed country that is able to import goods duty-free into the United States under the generalized system of preferences (GSP) or under the CBI may lose its right to do so "if such a country has not taken or is not taking steps to afford internationally recognized workers rights to workers in that country (including any designated zone in that country)" (cited in Government of the Dominican Republic 1993, 6). Other trade and investment benefits may also be lost. In May 1989, Americas Watch filed a petition for the lifting of such benefits with the Office of the U.S. Trade Representative (USTR) because of the abusive treatment of Haitian cane cutters. In April 1990 the USTR opted to extend the review for another year and consider as well the complaints by the AFL-CIO regarding the inability of workers to unionize in the country's EPZs. In April 1991, the USTR decided not to impose sanctions because of the "progress" that the Dominican government was making. Throughout this period, the Dominican government sought to institute enough measures to prevent a negative finding regarding both the treatment of Haitian workers and the rights of workers in the FTZs (on the issue of Haitian workers, see Americas Watch et al. 1991; del Carmen Ariza 1991; and U.S. Congress, House 1991). Responding to international pressure and to one of the pledges he made to labor confederations to insure they would not join a planned general strike in September, Balaguer promised to support modifications of the country's labor code. He appointed a commission of labor lawyers to revise the country's labor code in October 1990 and later convinced one of them, Rafael Albuquerque, in February 1991 to become secretary of labor to help usher through the new code.[12] In May 1992, after a long drawn-out process, the new law was enacted. Among other measures, it considerably expanded the rights of workers who sought to organize and established new courts to improve the resolution of labor disputes. Although many new unions were formed in the wake of the new labor legislation, few collective bargaining agreements were actually signed.

A law establishing a civil service and a public-sector career path was also approved by congress in 1991, and the required regulations from the executive branch were finally completed in 1994. However, as of mid-1996 only an extremely limited number of employees, primarily related to insurance and banking services, had been allowed to seek incorporation into the civil service (Oficina Nacional de Administración y Personal 1994; author's interview with government official, 1995; see also Consejo Nacional de la Empresa Privada 1995, 120–23). Indeed, without prior restructuring, professionalization, determination of qualifications, and improvement of salaries, such a law could conceivably end up complicating public-sector efficiency, rather than improving it, given the kinds of workers who would be guaranteed security of tenure.

Domestic Support and Opposition

Over the second half of 1990, as the effects of the stabilization program were felt most acutely, popular-sector protest grew. Balaguer continued to respond by granting at most partial concessions to split off parts of the protesting organizations and, in the end, by making a bold gesture—an offer to resign early—that confused and ultimately dissipated protest actions. Although the right to carry out protest actions was formally respected, abusive police behavior and, occasionally, targeted repression was common. The first major protest action following the May 1990 elections was in June 1990, when an umbrella group of popular organizations, the Colectivo de Organizaciones Populares (COP, Collective of Popular Organizations) called a two-day strike to demand policies, such as enhanced government subsidies, to lower inflation. Frustrated business groups tacitly endorsed the action as a way to pressure the government to change its policies, although of course they favored policies contrary to those of the protesting groups. The PLD then called for two days of "national civic mourning" on August 13 and 14 to protest Balaguer's inauguration on the 16th; the COP used this opportunity to protest against the solidarity pact the government had signed with business. An increase in gasoline prices led to a call by the COP for a seventy-two-hour general strike in late September; Balaguer was able to convince labor confederations not to join the protest action in return for a twenty-point agreement that made a range of promises, from a revision of the labor code and other legal changes in taxes, wages, and social security coverage to access to 1,000 units of public housing for some confederation members.

Divisions between, as well as within, popular-sector groups and labor confederations became even more apparent in November. The popular-sector groups were suggesting a five-day strike, though they were divided on whether the goal of the protest was to force Balaguer's resignation or to modify elements of the stabilization program; labor groups, in turn, sought a three-day action focused primarily on economic issues. On November 15, five days before the strike was to be held, Balaguer gave a speech in which he offered to hold elections at midterm in his period if there was so much opposition to his administration. This step helped defuse and divide the opposition, as discussion turned to the viability and seriousness of such an offer; thus the strike was not especially successful (see Espinal 1991).[13] Over the subsequent years, there were other major protests and many regional ones. For example, in July 1991, national strikes were held to protest the government's agreement with the IMF, but they were unsuccessful in forcing the government to change its policies; sixteen people died as a result of clashes with police. In October 1992, there were multiple marches and demonstrations surrounding the pope's visit and the "disappearance" of a leading human rights activist. Yet, with the return to moderate growth rates, with the successful control of inflation, and with popular hopes focused on the upcoming 1994 elections, the incipient popular-sector movements remained unable to move toward more effective, centralized, unified action (for a similar conclusion, see Ferguson 1992, 107–8).

As public-sector salaries and working conditions continued to deteriorate, strike actions by teachers, health personnel, and other public-sector workers continued. A four-month-long teachers' strike in 1991 prevented the academic year from ending; after extensive discussions and with the mediating help of Núñez Collado, an agreement was reached that lifted the strike, saving the 1990–91 school year and helping to initiate the new school year.[14] The agreement called for modest wage increases and set the stage for a more ambitious "Ten Year Plan for Education" with international assistance and advice.

By the time Balaguer began to institute economic-stabilization measures, most business groups widely recognized their need. The more organized business groups also favored a more extensive set of reforms, as spelled out in detail in their March document. Balaguer's jumble of policies and his lack of responsiveness in many areas also helped sustain tensions. However, differences between importers and groups more oriented toward the international marketplace, on the one hand, and producers for the domestic market, on the other, remained during this period. This not only provoked further division, it also inhibited effective joint action. The encouragement that a prominent importer gave to Balaguer to establish the new customs regime (unconstitutionally) by decree in 1990 provoked protest from other business leaders. In September 1991, Balaguer again modified the trade regime by decree. Yet, deeper economic tensions lay behind the conflicts over tactics, as the country's leading importers left the CNHE. In November 1991, sixteen business associations established the Unión Nacional de Empresarios (UNE, National Union of Entrepreneurs).[15] Domestic producers showed declining influence, as is evident in the outcome regarding the trade-liberalization law (a revised customs schedule). They believed that importers continued to undervalue their goods drastically, while other government policies and outcomes (such as high interest rates, the continuing crisis of costly electricity and frequent power outages, or unfavorable depreciation rates) prevented domestic industry from becoming more competitive.[16] However, the largest Dominican domestic enterprises were slowly beginning to change, diversifying their holdings and becoming more export-oriented.

Political Opposition

For Balaguer, the 1990–91 period was extremely tense, punctuated by protests, stabilization measures, and even his promise to resign early. He was largely able to retain his own party bases, in spite of the country's severe crisis. At the same time, party and societal opposition divided over the precise nature of their goals. Some sought an intransigent opposition, whereas others agreed to cooperate in achieving reform legislation like the new labor code. Ultimately, the opposition parties channeled the considerable anger and disappointment felt by many within the population into the 1994 electoral process.

In the 1990–94 period, Balaguer did not have as secure a majority in congress as in the previous period. Electoral vote counts and subsequent "negotiations" resulted in the PR(SC) retaining a narrow majority in the senate (sixteen of thirty seats); the PLD began Balaguer's new term with twelve seats, and the PRD held on to only two seats. In the chamber, once again, no party held an outright majority. The PR(SC) declined from forty-one to thirty-three seats, and the PRD fell from forty-eight to thirty-three seats. The PLD, in turn, expanded from sixteen seats to forty-six.

As a consequence of Balaguer's narrower grip on congress, opposition groups were more able to prevent the passage of some legislation and approval of other measures. However, principally because of his continued control over the budget and the judiciary, Balaguer retained considerable autonomy of action. Congress was saddled with a lack of resources and of professional staff, and the president was able to win over deputies on specific issues.

The PLD was extremely bitter following its 1990 defeat. Conflicts emerged between, on the one hand, those who had lost the internal debate prior to the election regarding the value of a coalitional strategy with smaller parties and, on the other, those who argued the PLD could and should win the elections unfettered by those alliances. There were also tensions regarding whether there should be any collaboration with Balaguer. The result was that in 1992 the party suffered a major split. The precipitating issue was the reform of the labor code. Nélsida Marmolejos, a prominent labor leader and PLD deputy, as well as several other congressional representatives broke with Bosch and with party discipline and voted in favor of the draft labor code in congress. The ultimate outcome was that one senator and twelve deputies left the party. This group, in turn, divided again, with one group supporting Peña Gómez in the 1994 elections. This fragmentation further widened Balaguer's margin for maneuvering in congress, even as informal collaboration between Balaguer and some PLD congressional leaders expanded.

In the meantime, the PRD was now firmly controlled by Peña Gómez. The PRD often played an obstructionist role in congress. At the same time, the party was in the midst of a process of reorganization, reunification, and coalition building in preparation for the 1994 campaign. With the PLD splintered and still led by the aging Bosch, the PRD sought to agglutinate as many political parties and movements as possible into an anti-Balaguer front. Early polls were now giving Peña Gómez a wide lead over the wily, officially undeclared candidacy of Balaguer.

From Electoral Largesse to Fragile Equilibrium, 1993–1996

This period comprises two subperiods. In the first one, leading up to the May 1994 elections, government economic policy was focused on the short-term goal of the elections, into which business and other groups in society also largely channeled their energies. In this period, Balaguer once again employed, and abused, the mechanisms of state power to help reassure his reelection. There is abundant evidence of the manipulation of the country's political economy with an eye toward the upcoming elections. The president changed both the governor of the central bank and the head of customs for political purposes.[17] Shortly afterwards, there was a surge in government spending facilitated by central-bank credit, as the public-sector deficit grew from 0.2 percent in 1993 to 2.9 percent of GDP in 1994 (see Dauhajre hijo et al. 1996, 13–14). Between April and November 1994, there was a sudden laxity in customs procedures; truckloads of goods slipped through at certain ports of entry without being declared and without paying the required taxes, apparently for side-payments. The extent of this traffic may well have gone beyond what even the president had intended, as indicated by a January 1995 audit. While business organizations clamored for greater institutionalization, numerous individual firms continued to play by the (somewhat perverse) rules of the game; after the scandal broke, though, several of the firms that could be identified were forced to pay back taxes on the imported goods.[18]

The backdrop of the second subperiod was the profound political crisis which followed the 1994 elections. The apparent fraud in the 1994 elections, in which Balaguer ostensibly defeated Peña Gómez by an even narrower margin than he had Bosch in 1990, generated a strong counterreaction by the U.S. government, organized business, parts of the church, and numerous other actors. The electoral crisis was resolved by the signing of the Pact for Democracy in August 1994 that led to a number of constitutional reforms, including the limitation of Balaguer's new term to only two years and the prohibition of immediate presidential reelection. The crisis helped mobilize efforts to strengthen civil society and further convinced many groups of the futility of working with the state as long as it was controlled by Balaguer. This view was enhanced over 1995 and 1996 as corruption scandals became public;

as harassment, phone tapping, and the intimidation of business, labor, and media actors viewed as anti-Balaguer became more widespread;[19] and as rumors about the extent and nature of corruption among Balaguer's coterie of followers, known as "the palace ring" (*el anillo palaciego*), grew.[20] The pact had been "witnessed" by different groups from civil society who later came together more formally in the Grupo de Acción por la Democracia (GAD, Group in Support of Democracy).

Nevertheless, in the second subperiod, beginning in late 1994, the state restabilized the economy. More professional management was brought back to customs and the central bank, and state expenditures were brought under control. By continuing to keep interest rates high, rebalancing fiscal accounts, and improving the supervision of the financial sector, Balaguer was able to keep inflation under control as moderate growth continued (see table B.3). A foreign-investment law that liberalized profit repatriation provisions and removed several archaic features from past laws was also approved in late 1995.

Yet, there was little progress in other areas. Government spending on education, 1.6 percent of GDP over 1991–93, was less than half the average spending for Latin America; the "privatization" of education continued to grow, reaching some 39 percent of all students in 1989. In health, the comparative figures are even worse; the government budget for health in 1995 was around 1.0 percent of GDP, compared to an average 5.2 percent for Latin America. In social security, the statistics are comparably as bad, less than 1 percent of GDP for the Dominican Republic, compared to around 5 percent of GDP for the rest of the region; the Dominican Social Security Institute, moreover, is probably the most inefficient in the region (Grupo de Acción por la Democracia 1996, 35, 43, 59).

And the decline in the country's state enterprises continued. Most of Trujillo's nationalized industries (managed under CORDE), the state sugar industry (CEA), and the state electrical company (CDE) were all significant money losers by the end of Balaguer's term. In January 1995, it was reported that ten of the twenty-three enterprises under CORDE were closed and owed the state Banco de Reservas over DR$400 million (*Revista Rumbo*, January 11–17, 1995). Corruption, clientelism, inefficiency, and disinvestment eventually led even enterprises that often had been profitable in the past to become plagued with deficits. Several state companies that had stopped operating by 1996 were still losing money because they had been unable to pay their workers benefits owed and definitely close their books.[21]

Both the CEA and the CDE steadily deteriorated over Balaguer's term in office. By the end of Balaguer's term the CEA was so inefficient that it could not even make a profit exporting sugar at the preferential quota rate, and its debts were continuing to accumulate; bad administration, clientelism, corruption, export taxes, and numerous other problems forced the central government to subsidize an entity that had provided Balaguer with resources in the late 1960s and 1970s ("CEA: El entierro," *Revista Rumbo*, June 26, 1995).

The circumstances of the CDE were even more dramatic. As Balaguer stepped down from office in August 1996, it was estimated that, of around 1.3 million users of electricity, 655,000 did not have metered service and that, of those, around 400,000 represented illegal connections. Losses in transmission and distribution of electricity were estimated to have climbed from around 21 percent in 1978 to 32 percent in 1986 to over 40 percent in 1995; thus, the company received payment for only 55 percent of the electricity that it sold in 1985, a figure that had declined to 45 percent in 1994. As a consequence, in the mid-1990s the more electricity the state company purchased from private suppliers to satisfy demand, the more money it was losing each month.[22]

Many reform bills languished in congress, while numerous studies and proposals collected dust on shelves. This lack of progress was due to several reasons. A central one, of course, was that Balaguer showed little interest in proceeding with many of the various measures, especially those that would enhance state institutionalization or accountability, limiting his discretional powers (see Santana 1995; Ceara Hatton 1995). Another was the existence of multiple divisions within the private sector, sometimes in association with individuals or groups in the state. There were conflicts between groups more oriented toward the export sector (such as EPZ firms and large domestic conglomerates with diversified holdings and a growing focus on exports) and those still dependent upon a protected domestic market; between some of these groups and importers; between private providers of health care and firms seeking to strengthen medical services provided by the state social security system; and between firms that had established contracts with the state (e.g., to provide electricity for the state-owned electrical company) and those that did not (and, in this specific example, sought a complete privatization of the state electric company).[23]

There was significant opposition in congress, both to the government in general and to the economic reforms. Balaguer managed only a precarious majority in the senate. The official 1994 results gave the PR(SC) 14 senators; the PLD, 1; and the PRD coalition, the remaining 16. However, Balaguer was able to win over one of the senators elected by the PRD coalition, which with the support of the PLD senator gave him the sixteen votes he needed. In the chamber, his party had 50 of the 120 seats, which, with the 13 deputies of the PLD, permitted occasional agreements on some measures. Yet, on major economic reforms, no consensus was possible, because of private-sector divisions and concerns by the parties. The PRD and the PLD were both fearful of the possible impact of privatization of electricity on tariff rates and on the vast portion of the popular sector that currently received service, as imperfect as it was, for free (through "informal" hookups). They were also reluctant to hand Balaguer either legislative victories or laws that could conceivably provide him access to more resources (such as would result from privatization).

Conclusion

The hopes that the Dominican Republic could become a more institutionalized democratic polity were not realized over the 1978–96 period. Factors that might have had an impact on reducing neopatrimonial trends in the country ultimately had only minimal effects. As this chapter and the previous two have underscored, there have been vast changes both in Dominican society and the Dominican economy with mixed results regarding the possibilities to help transform the style of politics. By 1996, there was a somewhat more mobilized and conscious presence of civil society, especially among business and middle-sector groups. At different times, popular-sector organizations demonstrated their ability to mobilize large numbers of people, but not to join together and forge a common program. Instead, they often fragmented as some of their leaders were co-opted. Migration and economic transformations also helped fragment or weaken a number of existing associations, even as overall levels of organization remained low and as high social inequality and expressed attitudes continued to favor clientelist forms of behavior. The expectation that the PRD governments, particularly that of Jorge Blanco, would help generate a new pattern of leadership, was not met. Instead, Balaguer was ushered back into power and unmistakably neopatrimonial patterns of leadership were reinstated.

Balaguer's second ten years in office left behind a decidedly mixed legacy. They were a period of expansion focused on construction, followed by stabilization, the initiation of some economic reforms, and the maintenance of macroeconomic equilibrium. Neopatrimonial forms of governing reemerged, yet under changed circumstances. State capacity and administration beyond basic functions of maintaining order, collecting revenue on trade, and distributing contracts deteriorated even further—even as these three functions were employed to help sustain Balaguer and his associates in power. Balaguer was able to sustain moderate growth rates and low inflation and to begin a number of economic reforms in the last years of his rule. Yet, in 1996 Balaguer handed over a state with a massive internal debt to contractors, with an overvalued exchange rate (sustained in part by high domestic interest rates), and with the bulk of the country's state enterprises in ruins. The task of constituting a state for both democratic and developmental purposes remains for his successors.

At the same time, as a consequence of evolving changes in Dominican political economy and as a counterreaction to Balaguer's rule, a variety of groups and organizations in the country with an increased awareness of themselves as part of a "civil society" that is independent from the state have emerged. By 1996, a consensus about the need to strengthen civil society and pressure for additional state reforms formed part of a proposed agenda for dialogue and action.

The discussion in this chapter exemplifies the way that the informal norms and formal institutions presented at the end of chapter 5 interacted to enhance neopatrimonialism. The vast powers of the presidency, the way informal powers are enhanced by the absence of effective judicial checks on authority or its abuse, and the discretional use of state resources have all been highlighted in the pages above. The contrast between the factional strife within the PRD and Balaguer's ability to avoid that within his party has also been noted. Despite growing difficulties, which will be examined in more detail in the next chapter, Balaguer managed to control his party, gain his renomination and reelection twice, and achieve crucial (if also increasingly) narrow majorities in the senate.

Similarly, at the beginning of chapter 6, five basic factors were presented as important in understanding why governments successfully initiate major efforts at economic stabilization or restructuring. In brief, these were serious economic constraints, high levels of external pressure, declining societal opposition, state capacity and political support, and enhanced perception and political will. As we have seen, these factors all explain elements in the process and evolution of economic policymaking under Balaguer. Neopatrimonialism, in turn, affected several of them, particularly by helping to divide and weaken societal opposition and by providing Balaguer with the will and the discretional state capacity to implement policies that would enhance state revenues over whose expenditure he then had substantial personal control.

Under Balaguer, as under the previous PRD governments, serious economic constraints and severe external pressure were important in forcing policy adjustments. Just as economic stabilization over 1984–85 could not be understood absent these pressures, the same is true over the 1990–91 period. Balaguer was aided by the fact that the terms of adjustment imposed by international creditors gradually eased from the early years of the debt crisis.

With a firm grip on the key levers of power and a keen sense of political timing, he also managed well the political tensions of adjustment, both in the early 1990s and following the 1994 election.

With regard to domestic societal factors, the picture in the country was complex because of contradictory tendencies. There was broader support for reforms oriented to improve state capacity and the judiciary, to reduce corruption, and to enhance investment in basic services than for more profound market-oriented reforms. Fortunately, unlike several Latin American countries that experienced hyperinflation (such as Argentina, Bolivia, and Peru), the Dominican Republic never experienced anything like the collapse of its economy. In those other countries, the severity of the economic crisis ultimately facilitated both business and more widespread societal support for deep market-oriented reforms. This support was still absent in the Dominican Republic, where a dramatic economic reorientation forced upon the country without major internal reforms led to significant out-migration and also to the gradual establishment of business interests more oriented toward the global economy and independent from the state. Nevertheless, many domestic manufacturers and agricultural producers remain aware of the profound costs of economic liberalization, while urban consumers have not yet been fully convinced of the benefits that might accrue to them. Over 1990–93, given the country's severe crisis, there was support by business groups for stabilization and reform; and since 1993, there has been an emerging consensus on the need for certain state and administrative reforms, as evidenced by church-mediated dialogues and other joint declarations. Overall, from the mid-1980s to the early 1990s, there was growing acceptance within the country of the need for IMF agreements in times of economic crisis and of the need to open and reorient the economy.[24]

Also important in the evolution of economic policymaking, however, was Balaguer's ability to employ neopatrimonial state powers to divide, intimidate, or co-opt potential opposition forces in society and within the political opposition; this was evident both when Balaguer was able to implement the policies he desired over 1986–90 and when he was subsequently forced to implement stabilization. The pages above have described Balaguer's ability to do this with business, labor, popular-sector, and political adversaries alike. Unlike the PRD presidents, Balaguer was able to maintain substantial (though not complete) control over his party and to manage his renomination twice from the presidency. The governing party existed primarily as a conduit for patronage and clientelism, and over time state enterprises became increasingly deficitary as state wages and working conditions declined.

Balaguer's administration provides additional evidence for the view that economic stabilization and initial restructuring is facilitated by a government with a strong, independent executive. Balaguer's neopatrimonial style of rule enhanced his state capacity and political support, though only in the limited ways required for the types of economic measures he took.[25] To the extent that certain restructuring measures could enhance state revenues, enable his favored policies, and facilitate his continuance in power, he favored them. Both because he did not believe in them and because he was able to avoid them absent an economic crisis as serious and as prolonged as in many other Latin America countries, Balaguer never embraced market-oriented reforms, unlike the emerging neopatrimonial or delegative presidents elsewhere on the continent (e.g., Carlos Salinas in Mexico, Carlos Menem in Argentina, and Alberto Fujimori in Peru following his 1992 *auto-golpe*).

Balaguer's wide discretion in employing presidential power was crucially enhanced by the fact that he controlled a majority of votes in the senate, where judicial appointments are made. As a consequence, his extraconstitutional actions never confronted an effective legal challenge—though even if they had, it is unclear how judicial decisions could have been effectively enforced. He was also occasionally able to muster a majority of votes in the chamber. Patronage and brokerage rewards were often crucial in sustaining his legislative support, though in areas such as labor reform he could build policy bridges with opposition politicians. One must remember, however, that the congress was not a site of policymaking and that individual representatives often obstructed and delayed measures seeking personal gain. It was Balaguer's ability to muster minimum support, especially in the senate, which permitted him to proceed without much concern for constitutional or legal requirements regarding legislative approval or judicial oversight.[26]

Yet, Balaguer's rule has differed from the turn to neopatrimonialism apparent in other Latin American cases. In the Dominican Republic, neopatrimonialism preceded, concurred with, and followed both Balaguer's return to power in 1986 and the economic crisis he helped lead the country into; limited economic restructuring was implemented largely to permit new resources to flow to the state for Balaguer's substantially discretional employment. Path-dependent factors and Balaguer's own political trajectory have played a stronger role in explaining the country's neopatrimonialism during this period than in these other Latin American countries, where delegative or neopatrimonial features emerged most dramatically in response to severe socioeconomic crises. In Argentina, Mexico, and Peru, respectively, Menem, Salinas, and Fujimori may have built on practices of clientelism and neopatrimonialism present in their societies, but their new governing styles materialized with the decline or substantial reorientation of corporatist relations and the weakening of organized sectors of society; and, they incorporated a neopopulist element of rule largely absent under Balaguer. These presidents also used vast presidential and newfound state powers facilitated both by these new weaknesses in society and by resources generated by the privatization of state enterprises (Vacs 1995; Cornelius, Craig, and Fox 1994; and Kay 1996). As the crisis recedes in these countries, the capacity to confront this style of rule may well also be greater than in the Dominican Republic with Balaguer, especially in a country like Argentina with a stronger civil society.

Balaguer's extended period in office also highlights the independent impact of political factors, even in the face of distinctly disadvantageous socioeconomic circumstances. The ten years under Balaguer represented a period of political stasis and blockage. Constitutional and formal institutional rules were combined with informal neopatrimonial institutions to sustain the aging ruler in power. These informal institutions had deep historic roots; perhaps only Balaguer—with his captive support base in society, an unparalleled knowledge of the levers of state power, and a willingness to use them—could have sustained power in this way in the face of continuing social change and international pressure.

His administrations also point out the risks of relying excessively on formal constitutional rules to determine political patterns. In a book filled with many useful insights but prone to this mistake of institutional formalism, Shugart and Carey (1992) assert that the Dominican Republic is an example of a country whose president has weak legislative powers because the Dominican constitution does not formally provide the office with strong budgetary or decree powers, a partial veto, or the ability to force referenda. They then argue this weakness helps to explain why the country is "among the most successful" of presidential democracies along with Costa Rica and Venezuela (177), success being defined simply as regime survival (the absence of breakdown). Yet, this chapter should make clear that regardless of the constitution, a president such as Balaguer has had *extensive* budgetary and decree powers, both by law and de facto in the absence of effective legislative action or judicial supervision.

Thus, especially under Balaguer, the absence of democratic breakdown in the Dominican Republic cannot be explained by the weak legislative powers of the Dominican president. Rather, what is apparent is that the quality of the country's democracy eroded as Balaguer employed a vast array of means to cling to power. An excellent way of discerning these tensions around neopatrimonialism and democracy is to examine the country's electoral processes, to which we now turn.

8 Parties, State Institutions, and Elections, 1978–1994

When can we consider political behavior to be neopatrimonial? Certain observable phenomena allow us to characterize political practices and the nature of political conflict as neopatrimonial, as discussed in chapter 1. One is that political oppositions often focus on legal, "rule-governed behavior" in an effort to gain power; however, once in power, these forces often fracture over the extent to which behavior should really shift from patronage toward ideology or the rule of law (Bratton and van de Walle 1994). Another is that political conflict is not easily or primarily identified along ideological or programmatic issues; rather, conflict is often better characterized as simply between "ins" and "outs" over spoils and patronage, blurring public purposes and private interests. Related to this, parties tend to be deeply personalized, putting an emphasis on clientelism and brokerage. A fourth characteristic is that presidentialism can easily slip into a pattern of clear presidential dominance, conveniently reinforcing patrimonial-regime attributes; and, because of its nature, neopatrimonialism inhibits the effective exercise of the rule of law, both with regard to the functioning of state bureaucracies and more broadly. In the previous two chapters, multiple examples of these features were presented that focused on development processes and economic policymaking.

Now, let us turn to an examination of elections and election campaigns. Contrast the "law-attentive" behavior of candidate Balaguer with the subsequent actions under President Balaguer. Candidate Balaguer wanted to win the 1986 elections, but he was concerned about the intentions of PRD president Salvador Jorge Blanco, of PRD candidate Jacobo Majluta, and of the administrative weaknesses and intentions of the judges of the JCE (Central Electoral Board). His concerns about the weakness of the JCE were shared by church and business leaders in the country and by the U.S. embassy. The solution was the creation of an ad hoc Commission of Election Advisers, chaired by the archbishop of Santo Domingo (Balaguer's strong ally), to insure that the election results would be respected. Neither Balaguer nor the archbishop complained then of any U.S. interference, even as the U.S. government actively supported the establishment of the commission; and Balaguer's party also assiduously sought support from international organizations and from Christian Democratic parties in other countries. Balaguer apparently had reason to be concerned about the probity of some members of the JCE in 1986. According to an eyewitness account by one of the commission members, only firm action by the commission prevented Ponciano Rondón Sánchez, the substitute president of the JCE, from twisting the vote count to provide PRD candidate Majluta with the victory in the days after the election; Majluta, in turn, already knew from the result of a quick count of which he had been informed that he was the probable loser in the election (author's field notes, 1985–86; Hartlyn 1987; Núñez Collado 1996).

President Balaguer in September 1992 nominated (and the senate confirmed) Leonardo Matos Berrido to an unexpected vacancy in the JCE. In this way, Balaguer was able to place a strongly partisan individual on the JCE, the entity responsible for overseeing elections and also the unappealable arbiter of all related legal claims. Matos Berrido had proclaimed Balaguer the Reformista (PR) presidential candidate in a fiery speech at a December 1973 convention, noting that the Reformistas would defeat the opposition through the unity of "pure" men (*Listín Diario*, December 3, 1973), and he continued to hold prominent posts within the party.[1] Matos Berrido was the government's central figure within the JCE in the implementation of a significant electronic fraud in the 1994 elections, sufficient to affect the result in Balaguer's favor, as detailed by a careful study of the 1994 elections. Associates close to Balaguer then helped launch a major "nationalist" attack against the U.S. government because of its condemnation of the flawed election process (Díaz 1996, 85–88, 171; author's interviews in 1994 and 1995).

Personalism and clientelism in party campaigns and within the major parties were also clearly evident. On May 1, 1990, I went along on a campaign trip by President Balaguer to Samaná. Balaguer flew in by helicopter and mounted a special Balaguer *móvil*. As the caravan moved slowly through the town, hats and baseballs were thrown into the crowd, and music emanated from a tremendous sound system powered by a portable electric generator mounted on a truck. Occasionally, people were allowed onto Balaguer's special car where they were given cash. Halfway through the march, Balaguer gave a short speech. On this labor day, he called for a free-trade unionism without party affiliation, which he said hurt the interests of workers. Then he proceeded to list the needs of Samaná that he promised to address: a free-trade zone, not just having factories and jobs, but with housing for the workers and day-care centers for their children; an expansion of the airport, which would become international; perhaps, as he had wished in his first twelve years as president, the transformation of Samaná into a free port; and improvement of the access roads to the city. He stated "progress has no end, it is infinite like life itself," as he promised also to expand the aqueduct, create new neighborhoods, and build schools. Then he called out to the crowd, "Are there any other needs?" To every need, he responded to strong cheers, "I promise you that, too." Then he asked his listeners to mark the photograph of the PR(SC) candidate on the ballot on May 16th. He reiterated at the end of his talk that "we have taken note of your other requests" (based on author's field notes, May 1990).

Building up to the 1994 election, Vice President Carlos Morales promoted the creation of an organization run by Alfredo Mota Ruiz. Its name exemplifies the central concept of this book, while capturing perfectly the nature of the Partido Reformista Social Cristiano (PR[SC]) at the time: Lo Que Diga Balaguer—What Balaguer Says. Unfortunately for Morales, on the final day to register candidacies, Balaguer said that someone else, Jacinto Peynado, would accompany him on the ticket. And, in the meantime, Lo Que Diga Balaguer had spun out of Morales's control and was accused of becoming a money-making enterprise.[2]

Although the PLD was a more formal and bureaucratic party than Balaguer's PR(SC), the dominant role of its founder, Juan Bosch, was clear. There had been the forced departures of Antonio "Tonito" Abreu and then of Rafael Albuquerque, individuals perceived as too ambitious and potentially threatening to the leadership of Juan Bosch within the party. By 1994, Bosch was aging, but was again named the PLD's presidential candidate. His vice presidential candidate, Leonel Fernández, characterized his own personal philosophy in the simple terms that undoubtedly helped earn him the trust of his party's leader and ultimately enabled him two years later to become the PLD's first presidential candidate other than Bosch: "I am the direct product (*fruto directo*) of Juan Bosch." In his speech accepting the presidential candidacy of the PLD for the 1996 elections, Fernández described himself as a "disciple" of Bosch, "the man . . . who was not only my guide and my conductor in the area of politics, but also my Teacher (*sic*) in the full humanistic sense of the term" (cited in Ozuna 1996, 147–48).

The existence of regular, free, fair, and open competitive elections is necessary for political democracy, even if not sufficient. Yet, genuinely competitive elections in the Dominican Republic and more broadly in Latin America have often been problematic. Primarily as a direct consequence of military coups or the illegal extension of presidential terms of office, elections have not always been *regular* occurrences. Even when held, elections have not always been fully *free*, either in permitting all opposition parties to participate or in the sense of assuring opposition forces the freedom to campaign and mobilize, access to the mass media, and no discrimination with regard to the use of state resources. Nor have they always been *fair* in terms of permitting all voters equal access to the polls on election day or in terms of accurately reporting actual vote counts. Even when the first three conditions may have been met, elections have not always been *open*, in the sense of being held in conditions of universal suffrage.

If a regime is neopatrimonial, the presence and the independent impact of neopatrimonial relations should be especially evident in election processes, when issues of political power are so clearly at stake. Neopatrimonial regimes may have elections that are regular and open—even those held in 1970 and 1974 in the Dominican Republic qualify; but there is greater variation regarding whether elections are fully fair and free. There may be more deviations than in consolidated democracies regarding whether they are fair in their vote access and count; and they may not be fully free, as the party in power may abuse its access to official resources or to the mass media. Furthermore, in the absence of firm constitutional guarantees and in the presence of highly unequal societal relations and a weak civil society, brokerage and clientelist relations may be especially marked.

Electoral processes touch on all three key defining aspects of democracy: contestation, inclusiveness, and rule of law. As discussed in the introduction, elections do not guarantee democracy. The more it is the case that elections are not the only process by which governments may be formed, that electoral discrimination is present, that effective oversight control or participation between elections is limited, or that the armed forces or some other group exercises a tutelary power or reserves certain areas of policymaking for itself, the less it can be said that the country is democratic.

Previous chapters have highlighted the limitations on the ability of the electorate to influence government policies in the periods between elections. This chapter focuses on the difficulties surrounding electoral processes in the years from 1982 to 1994. Elections permit one to examine what mix of appeals parties rely on in motivating voters, how parties in government use the state to buttress their support in society, and the commitment of different major political and socioeconomic actors to one of the most basic of the democratic rules of the game. This chapter seeks to demonstrate the logic of the behaviors of party leaders in the Dominican Republic, given both the incentives of neopatrimonialism within which they operate as well as those incentives generated by other electoral and institutional mechanisms. The political-institutional features presented at the end of chapter 5 will be supplemented by several specific to the nature of a critical state bureaucracy, the electoral oversight agency (in this case, the JCE). There are two central questions this chapter seeks to answer, with a focus on political-institutional factors. Why were these recent Dominican elections *in general* so crisis ridden? And why did they become *increasingly* so up to the 1994 elections?

Although neopatrimonialism and election rules help us understand a great deal about the nature and outcome of these elections, some additional issues are also important. Sections below will discuss three of these issues. First, in order to try to continue winning elections, political parties and leading candidates have had to respond to the dramatic changes in Dominican society and economy discussed in chapter 5. As the country has become much more urban, more educated, and more "linked" to the mass media, inevitably the social bases, policies, and appeals of parties have evolved as well. Over time, a more sophisticated use of opinion polling and of the mass media has emerged. Second, as has been true of all other processes analyzed in this book, international forces remain crucial. Party leaders, especially in the opposition, have actively sought out international support; and the role of international actors, especially the United States, has remained central throughout this period. Third, particularly in 1994 (and again in 1996) when Peña Gómez has been a leading candidate, the manipulation of ethnic and nationalist arguments has been important because of his Haitian ancestry.

The four elections from 1982 to 1994 examined in this chapter have operated under a common set of assumptions and institutional factors, some with profound historical roots and some set more by the example of the 1978 elections (the 1996 elections are discussed in the next chapter). These elections also became progressively more crisis ridden. As a result, they were symptomatic of serious problems with Dominican democracy and problematic for regime stability. At the same time, the fact that they were crisis ridden also generated increasing pressure from a variety of actors for changes that would insure freer and fairer elections. Following the disputed 1990 elections, certain important electoral reforms were enacted. The 1994 electoral crisis led to a further series of important constitutional and legal changes, while also further mobilizing societal and international attention. These helped lead to the two-round presidential election of 1996, discussed in the concluding chapter, whose outcome marked a sharp contrast with previous electoral processes and represented a new opportunity to break with the country's neopatrimonial patterns.

Political and Institutional Bases for Crisis-Ridden Elections

The four elections that followed the 1978 process have all been at least some-what crisis ridden. They have had a number of significant similarities. In each, the campaign period leading up to election day has been marked by wide-spread distrust, allegations of fraud, doubts about the administrative efficacy of the election agency, and by violence associated with campaign events. In addition to these matters, these elections have varied in two key respects whose combined assessment can provide a useful indicator of the extent to which elections in nonconsolidated regimes like this one are crisis ridden. One is whether or not the legitimacy and credibility of official results have been questioned by wide sectors of the population and especially by key domestic business and professional groups and influential international ac-tors, either because of apparent anomalies on election day (which may have been "arranged" earlier) or because the results are not presented in a timely fashion. Another issue is whether or not the results have been challenged as valid by the major losing candidate(s) and whether or not on that basis the loser is able to prolong and question the process. Naturally, the second can affect the first, but it is more likely to do so when there is a lower trust in the electoral agency and in circumstances that can raise further doubts, such as an incumbent president seeking reelection or a smaller margin of difference in the votes across major candidates.

This two-part conceptualization of crisis-ridden elections focuses on the extent of postelectoral conflict relating to the way in which fraud is perceived and acted upon, rather than upon the actual extent of fraud (which is difficult to know). In turn, this perception depends on the quality of the information regarding fraud that is presented and the nature of the standards against which it is being measured. Over this past decade, international standards regarding what is necessary for free and fair elections have probably tightened. Yet, the basic causes of crisis-ridden elections are not to be found in changing interna-tional standards but rather in domestic political processes. Four of these have been particularly important in explaining the evolution of electoral processes in the Dominican Republic.

Elections are crisis ridden because the presidency has had significant formal and informal powers. The importance of the presidency generated powerful incentives not to hold free and fair elections. Until the August 1994 constitu-tional reform, the winner of the presidential elections was determined by simple plurality in a single round. Thus, logic would suggest that presidential candidates sought to carry out a combination of two strategies: to divide their opposition without expending more effort than necessary and to agglutinate forces without relinquishing more power than required. These processes of fomenting division and seeking electoral coalitions of convenience, in which Balaguer proved himself to be a master, built on and further fueled the country's neopatrimonial politics of intrigue, distrust, and unstable alliances.

The continuing importance of the state sector and the country's strong presidentialism has meant that elections have had high-stake implications for many Dominicans. Given the considerable autonomy of the executive branch, the absence of competitive bidding for state transactions and the nonexistence (or since 1991, the nonimplementation) of civil-service legislation in a context of high unemployment, winning has been of considerable import to both wealthy and destitute party members as well as to sympathizers seeking contracts, spoils, jobs, or access to public housing. There are no controls over campaign financing and campaign spending, nor laws regarding access by the parties or the candidates to the mass media. Similarly, there is little effective control over the incumbent's use of state resources for partisan benefit.

Elections have been crisis ridden because of legitimate fears of presidential continuity being associated with fraud. The history of the country detailed in chapter 2 shows that Dominican leaders have often sought to continue their stay in office through violent, illegal, and unconstitutional means. More recently, in 1966, Balaguer modified the constitution shortly after reassuming power in order to reinstitute unlimited presidential reelection. As described in chapter 4, Balaguer further manipulated the elections of 1970 and 1974, in which ultimately most opposition parties pulled out; he attempted to do so again in 1978.

The opposition party, the PRD, has always had as a central tenet a rejection of unlimited, and especially immediate presidential reelection. Bosch's new party, the PLD, retained this principle. Yet, when it was in power, for reasons discussed in chapter 6, the PRD was unable to modify the constitution to limit presidential reelection.

Elections have been crisis ridden because party-leadership continuity has been strengthened by fraud allegations. The major Dominican political parties are national parties, whose leaders seek to perpetuate their control over their party organizations in order to gain the presidential nomination. In the elections from 1982 to 1994, as in the 1978 elections and those that preceded it, every party alleged fraud both during the campaign and after the election, whether they had won or lost. Alleging fraud or unfair practices and decisions is a mechanism that has enabled party leaders to minimize the potential role of their own faults or errors in the eyes of key party militants and sympathizers.

Linked to all of these factors, elections have been crisis ridden because of the weakness of the central electoral oversight agency. Institutional formalism might lead one simply to assume, based on constitutional and legal texts, that the mechanics of election management are unproblematic. One of the principal means devised to limit fraud and assure legitimate and credible election results has been the establishment of independent electoral agencies. Yet, in neopatrimonial regimes, the divergence between organizational form and substance lies at the heart of understanding how and why elections are only a first step, rather than the final step, of determining the outcome of struggles for power. As a consequence, one cannot assume the existence of strong, independent electoral oversight agencies, possessing such essential features as political independence, professionalism, technical capacity, and financial integrity.

In the Dominican Republic, elections have been overseen by the JCE and subsidiary municipal juntas. Tremendous pressures are brought to bear on the judges of the JCE and secondarily on those of the municipal electoral boards. These agencies combine administrative, regulatory, and judicial functions. The JCE is responsible for managing the voter registry list, regulating the campaign, and administering the elections; it is also the unappealable arbiter of all disputes related to the elections, with complaints being heard in the first instance by the municipal electoral boards. At the same time, the autonomy and credibility of the JCE has been affected by a number of factors. Its judges are named by the senate (or by the president if the senate is not in session and does not subsequently act) for terms coterminous with each electoral period and with political criteria often salient. The JCE has lacked budgetary independence, a stable personnel, and a steady work plan; like the rest of the state sector, it has paid woefully low salaries. Prior to 1994, the JCE also shared responsibility with the executive branch for the management of the offices that provide the personal identification cards that citizens must present along with electoral carnets disbursed by the JCE in order to vote. Particularly when an incumbent president has sought reelection, this has increased fears by opposition candidates that the electoral registry could be manipulated to favor the government party.[3] Building up to the 1994 elections, there were significant changes in the JCE, in the creation of a new identity card and registry, and in the organization of the elections. These changes were brought about due to the 1992 enactment of new electoral laws in the wake of the 1990 electoral crisis. However, the JCE remained an institutionally weak, politicized institution. As we shall see below, an imperfect alternative to a strong JCE was to have ad hoc mediating and support commissions or international observers or mediators.

Thus, a weak JCE has facilitated real fraud. This has been possible due to administrative incompetence or to open complicity of employees and JCE judges. Concerns could be more acute regarding the party of the incumbent president, especially when the incumbent himself was seeking reelection. This was because of the influence that party had in naming the members of the JCE and the budgetary and other pressures presidents could apply.

But, a weak JCE also has permitted parties to allege fraud during the campaign and afterwards. These accusations regarding fraud or the presumed bias or poor performance of the JCE have been employed in an effort to give parties "political advantage" over the JCE to pressure it to violate its own norms for party advantage (e.g., extending time to register people to vote or extending deadlines for candidate inscription); to prepare party militants to understand why a defeat might occur without blaming the leaders; and to delay and obfuscate publication of credible electoral results to enable time for "political negotiations" and "pressures" on the JCE that could favor the party making the allegations. These claims also have bred cynicism within business and other circles, permitting them even in the face of dramatic evidence of fraud to shrug it off by asserting either that "all parties do it anyway" or that the charges are exaggerated.

In essence, in the four elections that followed the one of 1978, election results were a consequence of a two-step process. First, ballots cast were more or less counted; second, political transactions and negotiations based on these "preliminary" results determined the final outcome. This second stage was especially important in the two elections when Balaguer was president, being least relevant in 1982.

A legitimate, accountable electoral agency, able to provide more credible oversight and results, could force that party leaders be more accountable for their failures to their followers. It would also require greater responsibility by the parties in recognizing the essential democratic rules of the game. Because the status quo favored the incumbent party so greatly, only the threat of serious political instability or international sanction would appear to force reform. Even party leaders elected on a reformist platform have been ambiguous about encouraging changes to the JCE once they were in the presidency, because they believed they could accrue advantage from a weak, penetrable board.

Constraints on Outright Authoritarianism

What prevented the Dominican Republic after 1978 from being an authoritarian regime? Why was this not simply a regime in which an incumbent president, having extensive constitutional and actual prerogatives, retained power by employing official resources and manipulating a weak electoral agency to carry out massive fraud, thus winning elections he might not otherwise have been able to win? As we saw in chapter 3, the 1970 and 1974 Dominican elections did somewhat resemble this scenario—although also important was military coercion against the opposition, which ultimately led them to withdraw from participation. Yet, unlike the situation under Trujillo, there was not large fraud in the counting and reporting of the votes, and Balaguer ruled more as a civilian; and following a tortuous process, Balaguer did oversee elections in 1978 that he ultimately recognized as having lost.

In the elections after 1978, the legitimacy of opposition parties and the roles of actors from civil society and from the international community were instrumental in pressuring for honest elections. Outright authoritarianism increasingly risked international opprobrium and economic crisis and would have required reliance on a military that grew weaker and more fragmented over time, and which civilian party leaders also deeply distrusted. For a pragmatic politician like Balaguer, it was better to seek to push the limits, while seemingly respecting the electoral rules of the game. Especially when they were in the opposition, candidates reached out internationally for support of a fair process and appealed for support from organized actors in civil society. This was the case for Balaguer in 1986, Bosch in 1990, and Peña Gómez in 1994. The fact that political forces believed they needed to appeal to international actors for support underscored the fragility of Dominican democratic processes and, in certain circumstances, may even have reinforced it. As election polling became more common, large-scale deviations from survey results could serve as a useful indicator of the presence of massive fraud. Nevertheless, when polls indicated that elections results would be close, as was often the case in the Dominican Republic, then massive fraud was not required to affect the outcome of the results.

These pressures turned out not to be completely sufficient. Over the 1986–96 period there was unquestionably slippage in terms of political rights, as the Dominican Republic became something of a hybrid regime with both authoritarian and democratic features. Aspects of this evolution were discussed in chapters 6 and 7. One effort to combine different qualitative measures into quantitative ones is represented by Freedom House indicators of political rights and civil liberties. On a scale where 1 is the highest score possible and 7 the lowest, political rights in the Dominican Republic declined from a 1 in 1989 to a 2 in 1990, a 3 in 1993, and a 4 in 1994; civil liberties, in turn, declined from a 2 to a 3 in 1984 (the year of the "IMF protests") and stayed at 3 throughout the time period. Freedom House ranks countries as "free," a proxy for democratic, when the two scores added together range from 2 to 5; under this guideline, the Dominican Republic slipped from a weak democracy over the 1990–92 period (with scores of 2 and 3, political rights listed first) to a more hybrid regime in 1993 (3 and 3) and 1994 (4 and 3) (Freedom House Survey Team, annual volumes 1978–95).

In sum, neopatrimonial legacies and how they are recreated by particular leaders in the presidency with its vast powers may produce powerful incentives for incumbents not to hold fully free and fair competitive elections; at the same time, if not a commitment to democratic rules of the game, then concerns about political instability, distrust of the military, and international and domestic pressure for honest elections generate contrary considerations. Not all presidents have been equally eager or able to seek their reelection or committed to holding free and fair elections. When parties have been in the opposition, they have tended more to desire a strong, coherent electoral agency; yet all parties have perceived some advantage from a weak, manipulatable agency. Only the threat of serious political instability, international pressure, or some combination of the two would appear able to force reform. It would take two crises and the forced withdrawal of Balaguer, however, to "get the reforms right."

Given all these various factors, when can we expect elections to be especially prone to crisis? The logic of the previous discussion explains why elections may be partially crisis ridden in any neopatrimonial democracy with strong presidentialism and weak electoral institutions. However, it points to heightened electoral tensions when a neopatrimonial ruler seeks to extend his rule through reelection and when an electoral oversight agency is weak, especially if election results are close.

The Elections of 1982, 1986, 1990, and 1994

There is no simple correlation between the country's socioeconomic context and the extent to which elections from 1982 to 1994 have been crisis ridden.[4] These elections have occurred in an overall structural context of high unemployment and of high levels of poverty, but in a variety of different short-term economic circumstances with no clear link to the nature of the electoral processes. This buttresses the validity of explanations based on political-institutional factors.

There is also no direct association between party-system fragmentation and crisis-ridden elections. As party-system fragmentation increased from 1982 to 1990, electoral crisis increased; then, as it declined from 1990 to 1994, electoral crisis still increased. However, as this section highlights, splits in the governing party have been weakly correlated with electoral crisis. Far more significant issues, as argued earlier, are whether an incumbent president is seeking re-election and the closeness of election results. At the same time, over the 1978–94 period, the country became more urban, more educated, and more linked by radio and television. As a consequence, party campaigns and methods also evolved, becoming more reliant on polling and targeted publicity.

Major Parties, Official Results, and Support Bases

In 1978, the country had two major parties. One was the PR, built around the caudillo figure of Balaguer and whose overwhelming strength was in rural areas of the country. Another, the PRD, was a more populist and urban-centered party. There were numerous other smaller parties, most representing personalistic movements led by individuals who had broken with one of the two major parties (see del Castillo 1981; Campillo Pérez 1982). The most important of these smaller parties was the PLD, which combined a radical ideology and a rigid institutional structure with a strong loyalty to its leader, Juan Bosch. The period from 1978 to 1994 saw an increase in abstention and party fragmentation through 1990, with a slight return to bipolarization and increased participation in 1994 (see table 8.1).

Over time, the PR(SC) sustained its rural base and expanded somewhat in urban areas, while the PRD's urban base eroded in the face of both PR(SC) and PLD growth. Data on election results by level of urbanization in appendix A highlight this evolution. The PR(SC) base has consistently remained rural, with correlation coefficients between vote and urbanization oscillating between −.23 (in 1990, using 1993 census data) and −.51 (in 1982) over this time period. Its electoral victories in 1986, 1990, and 1994 were facilitated by sustaining its rural base, slightly increasing its urban vote, and dividing the opposition vote. In 1994, as in earlier elections, PR(SC) voters tended to come from "the more stable, status quo segments of the electorate—women, older voters, and both ends of the social class structure," as well as from agricultural workers, especially older ones (Hamilton and Strother 1994, 67).

The strongly urban base of the PRD declined over time, although its rural support appeared to remain roughly constant (in terms of average percentage vote for the PRD by municipality); the table in appendix A indicates that PRD urban support was eroded by both the PR(SC) and the PLD, as its total support fluctuated sharply over the 1986–94 period. Thus, the correlation between PRD vote and urbanization declined from .40 in 1978 to a statistically insignificant .18 in 1994. In 1994, the PRD's strongest appeal was among men, younger voters, and middle-sector and working-class groups (Hamilton and Strother 1994, 67).

Table 8.1. Official Results for Presidential Elections, 1978–1994

Parties and Party Alliances	1978 (% Vote)	1982 (% Vote)	1986 (% Vote)	1990 (% Vote)	1994 (% Vote)
PR(SC)	42.2	39.2	40.5	33.5	na
PR(SC) and allies	—	—	41.5	35.0	42.3
PRD	51.7	46.7	33.5	23.0	na
PRD and allies	—	—	38.8	23.2	41.5
PLD	1.1	9.9	18.4	33.8	na
PLD and allies	—	—	—	33.9	13.1
PRI	—	—	—	7.0	2.3
Valid votes[1] (thousands)	1,658	1,818	2,112	1,934	3,016
Null votes (%)[2]	5	3	4	3	5
Observed votes (%)[2]	3	3	1	1	1
Total votes (thousands)	1,744	1,922	2,195	1,973	3,082[3]
Abstention (%) (by electoral registry)	24	26	28	40	14 (estimated)[3]
Abstention (%)[4] (by estimated population over 18)	26	31	38	51	24

Sources: Brea Franco (1991); Monción (n.d.); Junta Central Electoral, Boletín Electoral No. 22, in *Listín Diario* (20 May 1994). Estimated population over 18 for 1994 of 4.07 million from *El Siglo*, 9 September 1993.

Party names and presidential candidates: PR, Partido Reformista (1978, 1982), PRSC, Partido Reformista Social Cristiano (1986, 1990), Balaguer (all elections).

PRD, Partido Revolucionario Dominicano, Guzmán (1978), Jorge Blanco (1982), Majluta (1986), Peña (1990, 1994).

PLD, Partido de la Liberación Dominicana, Bosch (all elections).

PRI, Partido Revolucionario Independiente, Majluta (1990, 1994).

[1]Party vote percentages based on valid vote totals.

[2]Based on preliminary vote count; subsequently, some observed and null votes are validated for specific parties.

[3]Based on preliminary and incomplete vote count.

[4]This rough estimate also includes individuals legally ineligible to vote such as foreigners, military and police personnel, and convicted criminals.

The PLD gained strength over the 1980s in areas of high labor concentration, such as the sugar-growing regions of La Romana and San Pedro de Macorís, as well as in the country's two major cities, Santo Domingo and Santiago. Its base was among industrial workers, middle-sector professionals, and youth (del Castillo 1986, 19). As appendix A shows, the correlation between PLD vote and urbanization grew from 1978 to 1982 ($r = .36$ in 1978 and .48 in 1982), to decline somewhat over the next three elections, even as the party's overall vote declined sharply from 1990 to 1994.

Candidates and Campaigns

The bitter struggles within the PRD for the presidential nomination in 1982 and in 1986 were described in chapter 6. President Guzmán ultimately gave up on his own ambiguous personal aspirations and, like Jorge Blanco after him, sought instead to impose a preferred candidate on the party. Both were ultimately unsuccessful. Guzmán favored his vice president, Jacobo Majluta; instead, the party nominated Jorge Blanco for the 1982 election. Jorge Blanco, in turn, favored José Francisco Peña Gómez, but ultimately the PRD nomination went to Majluta in 1986.

In 1982, Jorge Blanco ran a much more sophisticated campaign than had previously been the case in the country. He carried out a poll just of PRD members prior to the party convention to aid him in his strategy to gain the party's nomination, pledging to run an honest administration. He carried out a selective publicity campaign, targeting specific types of voters, rather than making a single basic appeal; he relied on polling data during the campaign to adjust his message; he employed television systematically; and he created an organization, La Avanzada Electoral, to help bring the large numbers of independent voters into his campaign—even while his central campaign theme, "A New Generation to Power," did not identify him with the party. Last-minute campaign spots targeted at warning potential PLD voters that they were "wasting" their vote and could end up electing Balaguer apparently led to a 5 percent decline in the PLD vote; this was aided by the fact that PLD voters tended to be younger, urban, and more educated than average and slightly more male (del Castillo 1986, 16; Vega 1986a, 25). Jorge Blanco's campaign was also helped by the fact that Peña Gómez agreed to be the PRD's candidate for mayor (síndico) of Santo Domingo, where polling data showed that other proposed PRD candidates were not nearly as popular. His victory was aided by the fact that dissident voters in urban areas turned to Bosch and the PLD, rather than to Balaguer and the PR.

In 1982, Balaguer again ran for the presidency. However, from his perspective, the more democratic convention process that he permitted in the party was counterproductive (del Castillo 1986, 17). It ultimately led to the nomination of Fernando Alvarez Bogaert as his vice presidential candidate, with which he was very unhappy. Balaguer had named Alvarez as his vice president in 1978 as a counterweight to politically ambitious military, who at that time ultimately forced Alvarez to resign. Alvarez continued to campaign for support within the party after 1978. In 1982, Balaguer actually withdrew from the presidential race for several days in an unsuccessful effort to force Alvarez's resignation, as the party lost valuable time in internal struggle; nevertheless, in spite of a lackluster campaign and a lower vote in percentage terms, Balaguer came in a strong second (see table 8.1).

In 1986, unlike four years earlier, Balaguer acted as if he sought to win. He supported the merging of his party with the existing minor Christian Democratic parties, opening the way for the integration of the newly named PR(SC) (Partido Reformista Social Cristiano) into the international Christian Democratic Union. As with the link between the PRD and the Socialist International, this association brought the PR(SC) international visibility, financial and technical assistance, and the promise—never realized—of an ideological basis for the party. Balaguer revitalized the party through a series of local-level conventions, focused especially on the candidates for mayor. A number of the conventions actually nominated candidates that Balaguer had not initially desired. Balaguer carefully renewed his ties with conservative figures who had previously broken with him and even successfully wooed General Wessin y Wessin, who had tried to overthrow him in 1971 and who now headed the small PQD. He reached out to independent voters and youth and incorporated extraparty candidates for key positions—including Carlos Morales Troncoso, a politically unknown businessman, to serve as his vice president, and Rafael Corporán de los Santos, a dynamic entertainer, as candidate for mayor in Santo Domingo.

Bosch and the PLD, in turn, further moderated their policy positions in 1986, continuing to move away from anti-imperialist and Marxist rhetoric attacking foreign investment, the U.S. government, and the oligarchy. Rather, Bosch ran principally on the promise of honest, efficient administration. He bitterly attacked Majluta, the PRD's candidate, thus indirectly, but purposefully boosting Balaguer's candidacy. As table 8.1 and appendix A indicate, Balaguer's victory in 1986 was based on a marginal increase in his percentage of the vote (due especially to growth in urban areas), a doubling of the PLD vote (with greatest absolute growth also in urban areas), and the erosion of the PRD's urban support base with a decline in its percent of the total vote.

The 1986 campaign lacked serious discussion of issues. Both Balaguer and

Jacobo Majluta campaigning for the presidency in April 1986, accompanied by José Francisco Peña Gómez. Growing tensions between the two led to a formal split within the PRD by the next election.

Majluta ran flashy campaigns that were also characterized by considerable infighting and disorganization. They swapped charges of repression and corruption, and their extensive television propaganda combined upbeat messages occasionally targeted to specific groups with biting negative advertisements. The PLD campaign was much more tightly organized, but lacked the financing and the rural outreach of the other two parties.

As he equivocated regarding reelection in 1990, Balaguer faced a challenge for the presidential nomination within the PR(SC) from Fernando Alvarez Bogaert. Negotiations between Alvarez and Balaguer in February 1990 for a single PR(SC) list failed, and Alvarez held his own PR(SC) convention. Not surprisingly, the JCE ruled that the incumbent president's nomination was the legal one, and Alvarez gave Balaguer a pro forma endorsement so he could not be blamed if Balaguer were defeated. Balaguer retained Morales as his vice president. He also successfully forged a number of alliances with minor parties, including most significantly the PQD. Another minor party that supported Balaguer was LE, Majluta's personalist vehicle of 1986; its leader, Andrés Van der Horst, had been given a cabinet position by Balaguer after the 1986 elections.

Balaguer's main messages continued to resonate among the same broad sectors of the population to which he had appealed in the past. His main slogan was "Balaguer: A Route without Danger," which sought to emphasize Balaguer's experience as head of state, while playing on fears of Bosch's background (whether of radicalism or of shifting ideology) and of his relative inexperience in public administration. He also continued his unabashed promises for more public works. Yet, the PR(SC) approached the campaign in apparent disarray, because of the internal conflicts within the party, the lack of clear national coordination, and the apparent unpopularity of certain local-level candidates.[5]

The factional struggle between Majluta and Peña Gómez between 1986 and 1990 ended in a formal party split, with Peña Gómez successfully retaining the party name and symbols. Peña Gómez and especially Majluta—with his hastily organized PRI—approached the 1990 campaign from weakened positions.

Following the party's strong finish in 1986, the PLD began to prepare a strategy for an electoral victory in 1990. This involved relaxing the organizationally rigid structure of the party to make it more accessible to the population as a whole, reaching out to regions of the country—especially in rural areas—where its presence was weak, and seeking accommodation or at least dialogue with the church, with business groups, and more guardedly with the military and the U.S. government (author's interviews with PLD campaign strategists, May 1990). Bosch's campaign sought to project an optimistic, upbeat message: "Bosch: A Better Future"; and to convince the population that he could win and take power: "Bosch Now." With Balaguer's government losing popularity due to inflation and to electricity and water shortages, and with the PRD in disarray, the PLD appeared well situated to gain an electoral victory. Bosch had apparently comfortable margins of victory in polls taken in January and February; however, this was before it was clear whether and under what party banners Peña Gómez and Majluta would run and before Balaguer became an official candidate.[6]

Bosch then incurred a number of serious campaign errors. One mistake was hubris: the party refused to ally itself with any other party or movement. Bosch then became unnecessarily embroiled in a conflict with members of the church hierarchy. In response to a question at a gathering of Protestants, Bosch asserted that in a future PLD government Catholicism would no longer be referred to as the "official religion" and that chaplains of different denominations would be available for the military and police and in jails and state hospitals. This opened the door for several church leaders antagonistic to Bosch to question whether the concordat with the Vatican would be retained in a PLD administration. Bosch also went beyond his party's platform to call

Election crises were not the result of the Dominican people, who turned out in large numbers and waited with patience and dignity to vote. This picture is from May 16, 1990.

for extensive privatization of state sugar mills. The issue of privatization generated fears among public employees, and even members of the PLD's own labor confederation expressed their opposition to it. PR(SC) leaders argued they opposed such measures, because even though the enterprises incurred massive deficits, the employment they generated served a "social function."

But not all of the damage was self-inflicted. The PR(SC) president of the senate charged that if Bosch were to win he would install a communist regime. Other negative campaigning raised the specter of a communist takeover because of former or active leftists in the PLD and raised questions about Bosch's mental abilities. In fact, given Bosch's testy temperament, his campaign sought to shield him from direct questioning by the media as much as possible.

Peña Gómez's campaign, in turn, focused on his popular roots and sought to convince former PRD adherents to return to the fold. As Bosch's problems with the church grew, Peña Gómez emphasized his own religiosity. Polling data suggests that in the last weeks of the campaign, Peña Gómez's vote increased somewhat, largely at Bosch's expense. Official results, listed in table 8.1, give Balaguer a narrow victory over the PLD due only to party alliances, especially with the PQD. The historically high rate of abstention is probably due to several factors, especially the country's difficult socioeconomic conditions and the weakness of the PRD following its recent division. The inability of some internal migrants to vote because they had not reregistered in their new place of residence and the absence of others who had migrated overseas might also have increased abstention levels.

In 1994, Balaguer's strategy was based less on ceding candidacies to form links with other parties, as in 1990, and more on a recovering economy; on focusing public expenditures and appeals on urban areas and among younger voters, where historically he had been weakest; and on massive abuse of official resources for electoral purposes.[7] It was also based on polarizing the electorate around ideologically charged issues of national identity, especially salient because of Peña Gómez's Haitian ancestry and because of U.S. desires for greater Dominican compliance with an embargo against the Haitian military government in order to reinstate Jean Bertrand Aristide to power in Haiti. Balaguer has always alluded to Dominican identity in terms of its Hispanic, Catholic, white essence, in contrast to Haiti's "pagan," African, black roots. Dominican sensitivities had increased in the years leading up to the election due to growing Haitian migration into the country and heightened international focus on the Haitian military government. Peña Gómez's ancestry became a major campaign issue, as his opponents implied that the country's cultural identity, economic well-being—and even its very existence as a sovereign state—would all be threatened by his victory. As Peña Gómez turned to international actors for support, these issues became even more enmeshed.

As in the past, Balaguer equivocated regarding reelection, making references to his age and his health. Speculation regarding Balaguer's intentions intensified over 1993. In October, the pattern of expanding public investments, trips to inaugurate new public works, renewed subsidies for agricultural crops, and his public statements made it apparent that Balaguer intended to seek his reelection. Moreover, foreshadowing what was to become a major element of the negative campaign against his main opponent, Balaguer began talking of a presumed international conspiracy to force the union of Haiti and the Dominican Republic. Major alternative candidates within his party fell silent, except for Fernando Alvarez Bogaert who retained popularity with many party loyalists. Alvarez's antagonistic relationship with Balaguer and Balaguer's "palace guard" meant it was unlikely Alvarez would be granted the vice presidency or other significant access to power; given the apparent growth in his movement, though, it appeared risky not to incorporate him (Díaz in *Hoy*, November 17, 1993).

Balaguer was officially proclaimed the presidential candidate of the PR(SC) on January 6, 1994, and was given freedom to determine his vice presidential candidate and the candidates for major congressional and mayoral posts. Two critical deadlines loomed, and for the PR(SC) as for the other major parties, they led to a bargaining process that once again appeared little rooted in programmatic or ideological issues.[8] According to the new electoral law, by February 16 all party alliances needed to be determined and by March 16 all candidacies needed to be registered with the JCE. Given election rules and the precedent that in 1990 the PR(SC)'s narrow victory had depended upon party alliances, the issue of alliances retained saliency; given Balaguer's age and health, the question of the vice presidency appeared crucial. Fernando Alvarez Bogaert did not wait for what would have been an unlikely nod. On January 19, he was proclaimed the presidential candidate of the small Unidad Democrá- tica (UD, Democratic Unity Party), which had been allied to the PLD in 1990; his next step, elaborated below, was to become Peña Gómez's vice presidential nominee. However, by the February deadline, the PR(SC) had reached al- liances with eight minor parties.

As in the past, Balaguer chose several key candidates at the last minute, and there were several last-minute substitutions. Unceremoniously dropping Carlos Morales Troncoso, his vice president for eight years, Balaguer opted for Jacinto Peynado as his vice presidential nominee, choosing an independent figure within the party. Peynado, the grandson of a past president (under Trujillo) and a wealthy businessman, had twice served as senator for the crucial Santo Domingo, or National District, area (which now represented around 30 percent of the national vote) where he had built his own impressive political machine.

The other parties had selected their presidential nominees and most of their other major candidates long before Balaguer and the PR(SC). The first to define its presidential ticket was the PLD. As in the PR(SC), it was clear that the nomination "belonged" to the party leader unless he explicitly re- jected it; in 1994 neither the PR(SC) nor the PLD practiced internal democ- racy, although the PLD had more elaborate institutional forms and rules. In December 1992, a full seventeen months before the elections, Juan Bosch was renominated as the party's presidential candidate (in spite of serious concerns regarding his physical stamina and mental acuity raised by several family and close party associates). And, in September 1993, the party chose the young, dynamic figure of Leonel Fernández to join Bosch on the ticket.

At the same time, the PLD assiduously sought alliances with other parties and movements, creating what it called the Patriotic Electoral Front. The most important and the most logical alliance—with the PRD—was out of the question for personal reasons, in spite of their ideological proximity.[9] Bosch had retained a deep animosity against Peña Gómez since 1973, when the latter stayed with the PRD rather than accompanying Bosch to the PLD. This animosity intensified in 1990 when Peña Gómez did not side with Bosch in the days following the elections. The PLD also did not consider an alliance with Majluta due to Bosch's firm refusal.

Then, in December 1993, the PLD reached a surprising electoral agreement with the Fuerza Nacional Progresista (FNP, National Progressive Force), whose leader, the outspoken lawyer Mauricio Vinicio "Vincho" Castillo, became the senatorial candidate in the National District for the PLD. Castillo had often been a close ally of Balaguer and was identified with conservative nationalist and anti-Haitian ideas; what he had in common with the PLD was a dislike of the PRD and a commitment to attacking corruption. In the end, the PLD had alliances with only two other parties that had legal recognition by the JCE, as well as with some independent figures in other provinces.

Within the PRD, Peña Gómez's strong showing in the 1990 elections made him the clear nominee for the 1994 elections. From the first reported poll, in May 1991, Peña Gómez was the front-runner, with 41 percent of those polled who intended to vote expressing their support for him. The polls showed a remarkable consistency in his percentage of electoral support. Peña Gómez was officially proclaimed the party's candidate in a convention held in early July 1993. Party primaries subsequently determined a number of the key mayoral and senatorial candidates, though Peña Gómez was also given the freedom to select a number of candidacies. The PRD also assiduously sought alliances with other parties and movements. Although in the end no deal was reached with Majluta, alliances were made with a number of minor parties and movements, including ex-leftists and former PLD leaders.

Most striking was the alliance made by Peña Gómez and the PRD with Fernando Alvarez Bogaert. The Acuerdo de Santo Domingo (Santo Domingo Accord), signed on February 13, 1994, gave Alvarez the vice presidential nomination, ceded seven senatorial candidacies to followers of Alvarez, and assured their placement on congressional lists in fifteen provinces and other candidacies. Peña Gómez defended the ideological coherence of the alliance by noting it was between "the liberals and progressives of the Partida Reformista, [and] the moderates of the left and the moderates of the PRD." He also noted the personal connection that existed between Alvarez and himself.[10] Public opinion polls suggested the new alliance initially had a favorable impact. In the end, the PRD went to the polls on May 16 allied with five other minor parties that had gained legal recognition from the JCE.[11]

On basic socioeconomic policies, there were no fundamental differences across the major candidates. There was broad agreement on the country's overall developmental strategy, which focused on tourism, free-trade zones, and agro-exports, while exploring different future integration options. All noted the need to improve certain state administrative functions, particularly the administration of justice; to reform the social security system; and to expand state expenditures in education and in health. The PR(SC) program focused more on the benefits of sustaining macroeconomic stability, while the PRD emphasized the need to modernize the state in order to assure sustained and equitable growth.

The most important differences between the PR(SC) and the opposition parties involved issues of governing style, of emphasis in public programs and expenditures, and of expressed commitment to constitutional and political reforms. The two major opposition parties, the PRD and the PLD, both promised to govern in a more institutional fashion, with a less patrimonial presidentialism and with greater respect for the oversight powers of the other branches of government. They also criticized the PR(SC)'s emphasis on public-works expenditures and indicated they would expand programs and expenditures more quickly in education, in health, and more broadly in "human capital." Both the PRD and the PLD attacked corruption, though it was a stronger theme of the latter party. Both also talked more insistently of the need to address issues of poverty and inequality.

The PR(SC) had several, almost parallel, campaign efforts.[12] Positive, upbeat campaign themes suggested that Balaguer represented "A Road without Risks, without Deviations, without Disagreeable Surprises, A Familiar Road" ("Un Camino sin Peligros, Sin Desviaciones, Sin Sorpresas Desagradables, Un Camino Conocido") and "Change from Above" ("El Cambio desde el Poder"). PR(SC) publicity noted how he had stopped inflation, stabilized the exchange rate, fostered growth, and carried out multiple public works, such as dams, schools, hospitals, and housing projects. In campaign appearances over the first three months of 1994, Balaguer promised the construction of more than 17,000 public-housing units, five aqueducts, three highways, hospitals, sewers, stadiums and sports fields, schools, and more (Revista Rumbo, April 11, 1994, 21).

There were three major negative campaign themes. One tied Peña Gómez to the corruption, violence (particularly the 1984 "IMF riots," which led to scores of deaths), and economic failures of past PRD governments, particularly that of Salvador Jorge Blanco (1982–86). The second negative theme suggested that Peña Gómez was a temperamental and unstable individual.[13] A third tied Peña Gómez's Haitian ancestry to potential threats to Dominican cultural identity and even to its national integrity in the face of a presumed international plot to force the integration of the two islands. Truths, half-truths, and outright lies were mixed together in a potent mix intended to appeal to Dominican fears of Haiti. Right-wing nationalists claimed one million Haitians now lived in the country (Balaguer even claimed in 1989 that two million did); but academic experts estimate the figure for Haitians *and* Dominicans of Haitian descent (whose citizenship rights have commonly been denied) to be around 500,000 to 700,000. They have also noted that much of that migration has taken place while Balaguer was president and that the Dominican state—because of its demand for Haitian cane cutters and construction workers—has itself been a major promoter of that migration (see Lozano 1992; Corten and Duarte 1995; Vega, interview with author, 1994).

The United States did want the Dominican Republic to enforce the embargo against the Haitian military, although it was reluctant to apply too much pressure before the elections. Balaguer was not eager to enforce the embargo, for a complex set of motives. One was a fear that too effective an embargo would lead to increased Haitian migration into the Dominican Republic (parallel to any prodemocracy concerns the U.S. government might have held, it also wanted to restrict Haitian migration to the United States—and in that sense it was much less concerned about potential migration to the Dominican Republic). Some Dominicans feared that the UN High Commissioner for Refugees would establish Haitian refugee camps on the Dominican side of the border, although reports about these appear to have been grossly exaggerated. More important were Balaguer's traditional anti-Haitian attitudes and his intense dislike of Aristide. Relations between Balaguer and Aristide had been very bad prior to the latter's overthrow in September 1991, and links between Dominican and Haitian military had always been close (see Cuello H. 1997; Lozano 1992). Neither the PR(SC) nor conservative nationalists in the country favored Aristide's return to power (author's interview with high-level PR[SC] leader, May 1994).[14] Also, breaking the embargo was a new, major source of profit for Dominican military near critical border crossings. The complex web of truths and half-truths about U.S. policy toward Haiti and its migration policies were then mixed together with an alleged international "old integrationist project" between the two countries, for which no evidence was ever forthcoming.[15] Then, because of Peña Gómez's ancestry and his "ties" to Washington "liberals," his candidacy was viewed as favoring this project.

At a large demonstration in Santiago one week before the election, Bal-

Milagros Ortiz Bosch, a leading politician within the PRD, was the only woman elected senator in the 1994–98 period. She is shown here giving a speech to a national youth congress on April 24, 1995.

aguer brought these various messages together. He focused on how he could promise greater peace and tranquility and could insure continued public works to benefit people. Then, after noting that the elections would determine whether or not "international pressures . . . to fuse the two countries that dispute control of the island" would continue, he added that "whether or not we will continue or not to be Dominicans will depend, most definitely, on these elections."[16] Indicating the importance of Santiago and the Cibao valley region for his electoral victory, Balaguer campaigned on a permanent basis in the region for a week, returning just before election day to inaugurate a new airport at Puerto Plata and to extend a new baseball franchise.

Peña Gómez and the PRD, in turn, promised a government that would be more institutionalized and that would focus more on people than on public works. Their main campaign theme was that Peña Gómez would "invest first in people," that he would form a "shared government that would invest in people" ("un gobierno compartido que invertirá en la gente"). Balaguer's penchant for focusing on public works and monuments like the Columbus Lighthouse was criticized, while the PRD promised greater attention to issues such as employment, education, and health. Negative themes and advertisements linked Balaguer to Trujillo, focused on repression that had taken place in the 1966–74 period when Balaguer had been president, and criticized the tight circle of collaborators (known as *el anillo palaciego* or "the palace ring") who surrounded Balaguer and were suspected of corruption.

Both the PRD and the PLD emphasized the need for political and constitutional reforms to limit presidential autonomy, enhance congressional oversight, strengthen the state's administrative abilities, and enhance the administration of justice. Other reforms, such as prohibiting immediate presidential reelection, calling for a second round in presidential elections, reapportioning congressional seats to reflect provincial population levels more adequately, and holding presidential elections on a separate date from congressional and municipal-level elections had been agreed upon in a multipartisan forum in which the PR(SC) had representation, though it ultimately did not sign the final document (Fundación Siglo 21, 1994).

The PLD focused its campaign around the theme "The True Change" ("El Verdadero Cambio") and repeated a number of social, economic, and anticorruption themes from its previous campaign. In this election, however, it attacked Peña Gómez directly, and through its alliance with "Vincho" Castillo, focused more on the issue of Haitian migration than it had previously. Bosch often appeared weak or rambling in his campaign appearances, which were limited, and the party continued with low standings in the polls.

As this description of the candidates and campaigns indicates, the incumbent president—Balaguer—sought reelection in 1990 and 1994. Table 8.2 summarizes information with regard to presidential reelection and margins of victory. Based on these two issues, we would expect that the least problematic election would be that of 1982, since Guzmán was not seeking reelection and the margin of victory of Jorge Blanco over Balaguer was still substantial, if less

Table 8.2. Factors Favoring Crisis-Ridden Elections

Election Year	1978	1982	1986	1990	1994
Margin of victory (%)	9.5	7.5	2.7	1.1	0.7
Incumbent seeking reelection	yes	no	no	yes	yes

than the margin present in 1978. In turn, we would expect the most problematic elections to be those of 1990 and 1994, as in both cases Balaguer sought his reelection and the margins of victory increasingly shrunk. The 1986 elections would be in an intermediate category, because although Jorge Blanco was not seeking reelection there was a narrow vote margin.

Political-Institutional Factors and Degrees of Crisis: Comparing the Four Elections

The experience of the Dominican Republic with elections following the 1978 transition was not a felicitous one. The narrative above has addressed issues relating to the socioeconomic context and to the major parties, their internal conflicts, and presidential candidate selection. Centralized party leaderships, patronage, and clientelism have predominated. Each election process has had problems, and the pattern has been largely a discouraging one of increasing problems and crises. Yet, it is important first to underscore what factors became less relevant. In spite of the mistrust that sectors of economically dominant groups felt toward the PRD and the PLD—especially toward Peña Gómez and Bosch—by the time they were viable electoral contenders they were also acceptable to most of these groups; and, although there was occasional military unrest, the military were not an important political actor.

Another crucial factor to underscore is that election results did not deviate significantly from what preelectoral surveys projected they would be, although their deviations favored Balaguer. In each election since 1982, the number of quality polls surrounding each election has gradually increased. Unfortunately, most polls are financed by the parties and candidates, leading to an occasional manipulation of their results. There has been very limited polling by independent news sources. Many voters who responded "undecided," "don't know," or "no opinion" to the various polls have apparently subsequently voted for Balaguer, which has been explained by the fact they also tend to be less-educated, older, female, and rural voters skeptical of polls, but also fitting a common profile of a Balaguer supporter. With these considerations in mind, the difference in percentage terms between the opinion surveys just before the elections and the electoral results have either been within the margin of error or close to it, although Balaguer has always had a last-minute "jump" in support (even when in the opposition) (for analyses of polls in different elections, see Vega 1990a; Vega 1994b; and Brea et al. 1995).

Presidential Continuity and Electoral Fraud

Presidential reelection does not have to create a crisis in a democracy. However, it is a problem if done continuously, which is why nearly all presidentialist democracies have imposed some kind of restrictions on reelection. In the Dominican context it has been especially problematic because of the extent of presidential powers and the ability and willingness of the incumbent seeking to remain in office to employ a wide variety of means to do so. An additional factor in this case is that the crises of presidential reelection present in 1990 and again in 1994 all revolved around a single individual. With each reelection bid the perceived stakes grew greater.

The JCE's Lack of Institutional Autonomy

Elections are intended to choose leaders—and even to resolve crises, not to create them. One reason they have created crises in the Dominican Republic has been due to the weakness and low legitimacy of the JCE. Two key reasons for the JCE's low legitimacy have been the way its judges have been named and its lack of budgetary autonomy. The nomination of JCE judges has favored their politicization, rather than their professionalization. Until 1992, the JCE was comprised of three judges and their replacements, named by the senate for terms coterminous with each administration. Lawyers with experience in electoral matters, but with little administrative or managerial capabilities were typically selected, and their partisan bias was a relevant factor.

For the 1982 elections, Balaguer's senate controlled the process of naming the JCE judges. However, Balaguer ran a lackluster campaign from the opposition and was clearly defeated. The process of naming new JCE judges leading up to the 1986 elections was problematic. A new JCE president was selected in September 1982, but the two other judges were not. The previous ones finally resigned in July and August of 1983. After five months the president finally named the other two members by decree. The Majluta-controlled senate confirmed the designations, but named the three replacements (*suplentes*). Tensions between Jorge Blanco and Majluta were evident (Brea Franco 1987, 42–43).[17]

For the 1990 elections, the opposition parties refused to participate in the nomination process of the judges, claiming it was biased. In April 1987, the seventeen senators of the PR(SC) met alone and nominated the three JCE judges. The judges stated their willingness to have their nominations reconsidered, but this was never done; and after six months they withdrew their offer. Although the three judges were viewed as sympathetic to Balaguer, the president of the JCE was also considered to be an independent, strong-willed individual. In his view, the opposition parties preferred not to be a part of the process, so they would be freer to attack the credibility of the JCE (Tavares 1993, 70).[18]

In 1994, the naming of the JCE judges was done under a different law. In response to the criticisms of the JCE as an institutionally weak and partisan body, dependent upon the executive, a new law was passed in May 1992, which only partially addressed these concerns. One of the changes was an expansion of the membership of the JCE from three to five members. However, the JCE remained an entity that uneasily combined administrative, regulatory, and judicial functions. Its members were still chosen by the senate in a fashion that did not ensure them long-term tenure or a nonpartisan disposition. The JCE was also not provided with budgetary autonomy. Even more disturbing was the fact that, less than two years from new elections, complex new responsibilities had been given to a JCE whose main members had still not been named.

Finally, on June 17, 1992, the JCE was formally integrated by the senate. The PR(SC) had control over three of the nominations, including the top position, and the PRD and the PLD each proposed one name. Manuel García Lizardo, at age seventy-eight, resigned as attorney general (*procurador general*) to become the president of the JCE.[19] Considered a respected and honest man of conservative instincts, including a traditional view of authority, he had also served as president of the JCE for the 1982 elections. None of those named were openly partisan, though their political sympathies were clear. Subsequently, one of the PR(SC)-sponsored judges died and was replaced by Matos Berrido, discussed above. In sum, though at least the PRD and the PLD now had representation within the JCE, this institution remained a highly politicized body and one in which the PR(SC) retained a majority of votes.

Another continuous theme throughout this period has been the lack of autonomy of the JCE vis-à-vis the executive in a number of respects, ranging from finances to control of agencies having a direct impact on the JCE. Manipulation and delays in funding JCE activities have been constant complaints of JCE presidents. Prior to the 1990 process, the JCE president even publicized the establishment of a foundation to provide the organism with funding. The 1992 law did not assure the JCE greater financial autonomy;

rather, it limited JCE expenditures to no more than 1.5 percent of the national budget, although it specified that JCE expenditures had priority over other state expenditures. Leading up to the 1994 elections, the JCE president several times had to make public appeals to President Balaguer for funds.

The low institutionalization of the JCE and the ability to make allegations regarding fraud strengthened the hands of the traditional party leaders. A weak, manipulatable JCE also helped the parties to resolve problems that were a consequence of their internal disputes and problems. For example, in 1986 the PRD pressured the JCE to maintain the voter registry open beyond the original deadline; due to the bitter dispute between Majluta and Peña Gómez, the party had not been able to carry out registration activities. In 1990, chaos ensued at JCE sites in Santo Domingo and throughout the country as the parties scrambled to register their candidates by the legal deadline at the end of February. The JCE was required to provide a filing extension, and then for both the PR(SC) and the PRD to determine which of two presidential nominees presented was the legal one. The JCE was also forced to decide who were the legal candidates in many congressional and municipal races.

The JCE, Ad Hoc Commissions, and Real and Potential Fraud

All democracies confront continuing problems regarding fraud, but rarely in consolidated democracies does it affect the outcome of major, national-level elections. Serious allegations of fraud would be investigated, and political parties would not continuously make unproven allegations. In the Dominican Republic, fraud during elections—sometimes on a massive scale, sometimes more targeted—has in fact been the norm for much of its history. It reached its apogee under Trujillo, under whom the legally constituted JCE published official results that were absurdly false.

More recently, just as common have been sometimes exaggerated and often unsubstantiated allegations of fraud. During the campaign, nearly all the parties make the accusations; following the election, the losing party does—a "fraud syndrome" as one set of authors have argued (del Castillo and Tejada 1992). Balaguer's Partido Reformista alleged that massive manipulation by computer with the voter registry lists gave the PRD their victory in 1978 (see chapter 4). In 1982, in spite of the fact that opinion polls strongly favored a PRD party and the vote count demonstrated a loss by a substantial margin, Balaguer's party again alleged that fraud had significantly affected the outcome of the elections. It insisted on these allegations even though the JCE judges had been named by a senate controlled by the PR. The PR legally challenged election results in over two dozen municipalities, and even published its *White Book* (*Libro Blanco*) regarding the irregularities of the elections (del Castillo 1986; del Castillo and Tejada 1992; Partido Reformista 1983). And, during one of the hearings, under still unexplained circumstances that helped spawn conspiratorial theories, a grenade exploded in the main JCE building, causing several casualties (see chapter 6, note 17). However, the final results were widely viewed as legitimate and credible.

In the subsequent three elections, issues of potential fraud, real fraud, and electoral crisis gradually became more intertwined. Fraud allegations in the 1986 preelectoral period included such issues as the accuracy of the electoral registry, the extension of the period to register to vote, the quality of the ink intended to prevent multiple voting, the nature of party alliances, and the format and manner of use of the new single ballot. The incredible weakness of the JCE in 1986 soon became evident. As the preliminary vote count in favor of Balaguer widened two days after the elections, and with only 8 percent of the voting stations (*mesas*) yet to be counted, Majluta forced a stop to the vote count and recused two of the JCE judges. He alleged fraud and irregularities.[20] Whether due to complicity, cowardice, or other factors, the judges immediately stepped aside, bringing into the presidency of the JCE an individual abjectly identified with Majluta—whose victory he immediately sought to bring about. Recused in turn by the PLD and the PR(SC), the new JCE president refused to step aside and prolonged the halt in the vote count.

In that year, the electoral process was aided to a successful conclusion by the existence of an ad hoc Comisión de Asesores Electorales (CAE, Commission of Electoral Advisers), presided over by the archbishop (a strong Balaguer supporter). The formation of the CAE was demanded by Balaguer and agreed to by Jorge Blanco. Following the crisis provoked by Majluta and the installation of a new JCE president, only the presence of the CAE gave confidence and legitimacy to the process. The CAE became the neutral, stabilizing force that the JCE should have been, declaring that the votes had been counted honestly and then challenging the dubious, stalling tactics of the new JCE head. The CAE called for the electoral results to be respected and was immediately supported by business, professional, and labor organizations; the PR(SC) mobilized Christian Democratic leaders from around the world. Finally, after a political agreement between Majluta and Balaguer (allegedly involving payment of some campaign debts, among other issues), Majluta recognized Balaguer's victory—eleven days after the election (Hartlyn 1987; Núñez Collado 1996; author's interviews, 1986).

Throughout the 1990 campaign, the PLD and the PRD also presented numerous allegations of potential fraud. The major issues were the accuracy of the electoral registry; illegal voting by members of the armed forces, noncitizens (especially Haitians), or underage citizens; vote buying or preventing sympathizers of opposing parties from voting by buying or "renting" their voter identity cards (*cédulas*) on election day; fraud at electoral polling booths (*mesas electorales*); PR(SC) domination of municipal electoral boards; and manipulation of the vote count by the computers of the JCE. The PLD went further and asserted that its victory could only be prevented by fraud. But Bosch was unable to appeal to the church as a neutral arbiter (as had occurred in 1986) because of his conflicts with it. Thus, he approached Jimmy Carter and requested that the former U.S. president head an international delegation to observe the 1990 elections.

The weakness of the JCE during the vote count again became evident. The count following the election proceeded very slowly; the fifth bulletin, transmitted around 8 A.M. the next morning, gave the results of only 155 *mesas*. Initially, the main problem was in Santo Domingo, where the preprinted, computer-coded tally sheets previously prepared for each *mesa* had been erroneously distributed in a large percentage of cases, leading to massive delays in data entry. The JCE feared that any explanation of the delay would foster further distrust—particularly given that, beginning with the sixth bulletin, the lead had shifted from Bosch to Balaguer. Carter was asked to help legitimize the JCE. Midmorning on Thursday, Carter agreed to make a joint television appearance with the president of the JCE in which he provided his own assurances that the vote count was being undertaken fairly and that the delay was caused by a technical problem that was being corrected.

However, as the narrow margin for Balaguer maintained itself, Bosch accused the government and the JCE of a "colossal fraud" and said the PLD was prepared to take to the streets with the people. Yet, on the day after the elections, no one knew who had won. The parties' own computer centers still had incomplete results, and late that night the JCE had still not even received the tally sheets from 1,000 *mesas* around the country. Nor were there any obvious indications of massive fraud. For these reasons, Peña Gómez and the PRD refused to support Bosch in his claim of victory. As negotiating efforts, particularly by Peña Gómez, began to falter, Carter was approached as a neutral mediator and guarantor of the electoral process. He helped defuse the immediate postelectoral crisis atmosphere, but after his departure the process of verification and review of the vote count soon broke down.

The PLD was never able to provide convincing proof of fraud, and the small international delegations had not clearly witnessed any.[21] Nevertheless, there was a widespread perception throughout the country that there had been fraud, generated by the multiple irregularities, the weakness of the JCE, and incessant PLD charges. And, in the months and years after the election,

The entrance to the Junta Central Electoral (JCE—Central Electoral Board) on May 21, 1990, reflected the country's tense situation at the time. A heavy military presence provided security, and a sign warned that admission to the building with any weapon was prohibited, without exception.

Dominican researchers asserted they found clearer evidence of the purchasing of identity cards to prevent people from voting in poor, probable pro-Bosch neighborhoods; of military voting; and of duplicate identity cards allowing multiple voting (Moya Pons 1992, 584–85).[22]

Prior to election day in 1994, there were some reasons to believe these elections might not be as crisis ridden as earlier ones. One of these was that in contrast to previous elections, each of the major political parties seemingly had representation within the recently expanded JCE. Another was that identification cards newly issued by the JCE were the basis for voting. A "pact of civility" was signed by all the major candidates, except Bosch, six days before the elections, in which the candidates pledged not to claim victory prior to an official proclamation by the JCE (a similar pact had been signed in 1986). The pact was witnessed by a commission of church and civic leaders, led by Monsignor Agripino Núñez Collado, and this commission soon established itself as an additional institutional support of the JCE and a mediator among the political forces (for the text of the pact and the signatories, see *Listín Diario*, May 11, 1994). Additionally, there were several dozen international observers, who had placed themselves throughout the country and made extensive contact with local leaders.

However, similar to past elections, the campaign was marred by violence, negative campaigning, and widespread charges of potential fraud. The new identification cards had been distributed in an incomplete and hasty fashion, and many had been issued with errors. The uncertainty and confusion generated by the process intensified the various charges of potential fraud. The fact that the president of the JCE did not go to his JCE office due to illness for over a month in January and February only made matters worse. Majluta suggested that the elections should be postponed for two months. Even more incredibly, just before the elections, Balaguer expressed the view that people should be allowed to vote with the old identification cards, as well as the new ones. All the parties expressed fears that there would be many null votes due to unwitting errors by voters, who were being requested to mark three separate ballots (one for the presidency, one for congress, and one for local positions) and to place them in three separate ballot boxes. Given the tardiness with which the JCE began a voter-education campaign regarding the new form of voting, many of the parties urged a return to the old system (*El Caribe*, April 15, 1994). At the same time, intense debates continued about all other issues related to the electoral process: the quality of the indelible ink, the quality of the paper, the printing of the ballots, and the nature and reliability of the vote-counting computer system.

The central problem in 1994, though, was with the electoral registry. As elsewhere in the region, this has been a key area of weakness in the Dominican Republic. Before 1994, the JCE shared responsibility with the executive branch for the management of the offices that provide the personal identification cards required to receive the electoral carnets citizens must present to vote. The potential for abuse was naturally very great. President Jorge Blanco refused to allow the offices related to identity cards to be placed under the control of the JCE for the 1986 elections. And, leading up to the 1990 elections, Balaguer named a staunch PR(SC) loyalist to direct the offices that distributed the identification cards (Brea Franco 1987, 44; Tavares 1993, 142).

A critical point of dispute in each of these elections was whether voters with apparently valid identity cards should be allowed to cast a ballot at a *mesa* if their names did not appear on the official electoral registry. In 1978, the JCE issued a ruling, on the midmorning of the election, that citizens in those circumstances could vote "observed" (*votos observados*), which required them to leave their identity cards as well as their ballot in a separate envelope. In

1982, the JCE produced a similar decree, but this time issuing it one week before the elections. In 1990, the JCE members spent most of the two days prior to the elections debating among themselves and with party delegates whether and how such individuals should be allowed to cast their ballot. The opposition parties were concerned that the government party had padded the electoral rolls; thus, they feared that if such votes were permitted, even as *votos observados* in contested fashion by placing the documents and ballot in an envelope for later certification, that this could provide a potentially fraudulent margin of victory. On the morning of election day, newspapers finally published the JCE resolution permitting *votos observados* in specified circumstances. In fact, the number of such votes was low, numbering 14,442 in 1990 (even fewer than the 27,843 observed votes noted in the 1986 preliminary count).

Then, in 1994, in the context of newly distributed identity cards and a new voter registry list, and with the concurrence of all the parties, the JCE decreed well in advance of the elections that voters in such circumstances would not be allowed to vote. However, by midmorning on election day, it was clear there was a significant problem, related to the parties' insistent fear that there could be changes in the voter lists (what was often referred to as *dislocación*, or dislocation of names). Opposition parties began receiving complaints from candidates and sympathizers that their names were not on the official voter registry list at their *mesa*, even though their names did appear on the lists that the opposition parties had and though their identity card specified they should vote at that particular *mesa*. Throughout election day, this problem was largely not evident in the National District, but was noted personally by international observers in approximately a dozen different provinces (see Solarz and Soudriette 1994).

In spite of the tensions between them during the campaign, on the morning of election day, the PRD and the PLD (along with the other opposition parties) requested that the JCE issue a decree permitting such voters to cast a ballot freely. By a 3–2 vote, with the PR(SC) sympathizers on the board voting together, the request was rejected late in the morning, though a formal resolution rejecting the proposal was never made. Following extensive meetings with the heads of the international observer teams, members of the ad hoc Civility Commission, and party leaders, the JCE ultimately emitted a resolution twelve minutes after the polls closed at 6 P.M., extending the voting until 9 P.M. and permitting those to vote "observed" whose identity cards specified they were to vote at a specific *mesa*, but whose name did not appear on the voter registry list. By issuing a resolution, the JCE admitted there was a problem of disenfranchisement; by its timing, the JCE showed it was ineffectual or cynical, impacting the institution's credibility. The JCE resolution was largely ignored throughout the country, for such reasons as partisanship, malice, administrative ineptitude, fatigue, and the lateness with which official word finally reached some of the *mesas*.[23]

In 1994, unlike 1990, there was more extensive international participation and a formal domestic mediating group. International advisers had been working with the JCE for some time. There was a major delegation to observe the elections from the OAS, and other delegations from the NDI and the International Foundation for Electoral Systems (IFES). A domestic ad hoc Commission to Observe the Pact of Civility was created. On election day, irregularities and discrepancies between the official voter registry rolls and those earlier given to the parties were personally witnessed by many of the international observers. The major international observer groups denounced the issue soon after the election.[24] Their charges were soon echoed by the mainstream U.S. press and by the U.S. government, which was generally more attentive to issues of democracy due to Haiti.[25]

Over the next several weeks, the PRD did an outstanding job of document- ing the manipulation of voter rolls throughout the country, in spite of nu- merous obstacles. Key domestic groups remained unwilling to challenge the ability of the JCE to proceed with an honest vote count, either out of a naive faith in the good will of the president of the organization or because they actually favored Balaguer's reelection over a Peña Gómez presidency. Nev- ertheless, under pressure, the JCE established an internal commission with participation by some members of the ad hoc commission. The report of this JCE commission essentially substantiated the fraud; it admitted a significant problem with disenfranchisement among the small numbers of voting stations it was able to review and also pointed to incredible anomalies in the manage- ment of the JCE computer and official voter registry rolls.[26] The JCE simply ignored its own internal report; it also dismissed the July 22 decision to nullify the elections of the electoral board of Santo Domingo.

Balaguer was officially declared the winner on August 2, 1994. As in the past, though, Balaguer also desperately sought to control the senate. One step in that direction was achieved by dealing with the PLD. A legal loophole regarding proper notification of party alliances was invented to enable the JCE to give the PLD one senate seat that otherwise would have gone to the PRD coalition, which thus ended up with fifteen of thirty senators; three chamber seats were similarly affected (Díaz 1996, 179–87). The second step, which came later, was to win back the allegiance of a former Alvarez sup- porter who had been elected senator on the PRD alliance ticket.

With his proclamation as president secure, Balaguer intensified complex "dual-track" negotiations with both the PRD and the PLD, as strong pressure from the United States to hold new elections also continued.[27] Given their party's poor electoral performance, and the intense animosity at the top between the PLD and the PRD, PLD leaders believed they had much to gain through effective negotiations with Balaguer. On August 9, Balaguer offered to divide his four-year term with Peña Gómez, although of course with the first two years for Balaguer; Peña Gómez asked for time to reflect on it. Ultimately he opted to reject it; the head of the OAS delegation and Monsignor Núñez Collado also believed the offer would make a mockery of the electoral process. Tortuous negotiations followed with apparently differing agreements contracted between Balaguer and the PLD and Balaguer and the PRD.

A Pact for Democracy was signed in the presidential palace in an elaborate ceremony with dozens of witnesses on August 10, which approximated more the agreement contracted between Balaguer and the PLD. The pact promised new elections in eighteen months and several constitutional reforms, including the banning of immediate presidential reelection. The old 1990–94 congress ultimately approved a series of significant constitutional reforms in an accelerated fashion, completing the process just hours before Balaguer was inaugurated president again on August 16, 1994. These reforms included the prohibition of immediate president reelection, the holding of new elections in two years (Peña Gómez had originally agreed to eighteen months), and the requirement that a second round be held among the top two vote holders if no candidate received more than 50 percent of the vote in the first round (Peña Gómez had agreed to a 40 percent threshold, and this seemingly minor change was to seal his fate two years later). Other reforms extended the right of Dominicans to hold dual nationality, a long-term request of overseas Dominicans (Graham 1996), and called for the establishment of a special council consisting of representatives from the three branches of government and from different parties (Consejo Nacional de la Magistratura) to name supreme court judges. This reform also extended lifetime tenure to all judges, a move that was poorly thought through, but with the good intention of seeking to help professionalize and depoliticize the judicial branch. Finally, the constitution was reformed to require that all future elections be held by a system of closed voting stations (*colegios cerrados*), which would require voters to remain at their polling places until they had voted as a means of preventing double-voting.[28] There was also a stated consensus that a new JCE should be nonpartisan. The PR(SC) and the PLD divided up control of congress, marginalizing the PRD, which was boycotting the sessions in protest.

Throughout the 1994 process, the role of the United States loomed large.

Indeed, without international pressure, Balaguer most likely would not have felt it necessary to accept the constitutional reforms and promise new elections. The PRD, in turn, probably would have opted more for a strategy of strikes and protests, akin to the PLD in 1990. The efforts of the United States to favor free and fair democratic elections were invaluable. Yet, as in past occasions reviewed in earlier chapters, major political actors in the Dominican Republic were required to develop a strategy with regard to the United States, either seeking to involve it as a tactical ally or accusing it as an interventionist adversary.

Conclusion

Over the period from 1978 to 1994, neopatrimonial politics surrounding electoral processes was evident. The elections became increasingly crisis ridden, as defined by the criteria of credibility and opposition acceptance. In table 8.3, whether the election results were viewed as credible has been scored on a scale ranging from 0 (credible) to 2 (not credible). Opposition acceptance, in turn, has been scored on a scale ranging from 0 (yes) to 3 (strong, clear no) because of the tremendous disruptive potential of an opposing candidate not accepting the results, regardless of the views of others. Thus, crisis-free elections would score 0, whereas the most crisis-ridden elections would score 5. The "crisis score" of the Dominican elections gradually increased from 1 in 1982, to 2 in 1986, to 4 in 1990, to the highest possible score of 5 in 1994.

The discussion above elaborates the links to crisis-ridden elections from the political-institutional factors discussed at the beginning of the chapter—strong presidentialism and presidential reelection, party-leadership continuity, and weak electoral oversight. Dominican elections were more crisis ridden when a president sought reelection and, given weak electoral oversight agencies, when victory margins were narrow. Both of these conditions overlapped with Balaguer's ultimately successful efforts to reelect himself in 1990 and 1994. By 1994, neopatrimonial politics, presidential continuity, and fraud had seriously impaired the democratic nature of the Dominican political regime.

At the same time, in seeking to win elections, parties also adopted at least some modern campaign strategies. They partially modified their messages and their strategies to accommodate to the country's changing social structure and to take advantage of polls and modern technologies (and not just for sophisticated computer fraud). The first clear example of this was Jorge Blanco's campaign in 1982. By 1994, Balaguer's campaign combined basic

Table 8.3. Crisis-Ridden Elections, 1982–1994

Election Year	(A) Results Credible?	(B) Accepted by Losing Candidate?	(C) Score
1982	Credible (0)	Weak no (1)	1
1986	Credible (0)	Strong initial no, then yes (2)	2
1990	Weak credibility (1)	Strong no (3)	4
1994	Not credible (2)	Strong no (3)	5

Note: (A) "Are the results viewed as credible by the population at large and by key domestic and international actors?" Credible (0); weak credibility (1); not credible (2).
(B) "Are the results accepted by the losing candidate?" Yes (0); weak no (1); strong initial no, but then acceptance (2); strong consistent no (3).
Adding the two together, the range is from 0 (crisis-free elections) to a maximum of 5 (crisis-ridden elections).

patronage appeals with upbeat television ads addressed to potential new voters in urban areas as well as its more captive segment of the rural vote. Targeting Peña Gómez's Haitian ancestry, Balaguer's campaign also sought to invigorate a sense of nationalism and resentment, polarizing the electorate around fears of Haiti and of U.S. intervention. The PLD in 1994 also sought to evoke anti-Haitian sentiment in the population.

Throughout the years, the U.S. government sought to support "free and fair" elections in the country, while not appearing excessively interventionist. This was not always easy to do, either because domestic actors sought U.S. involvement or because the United States sought to prevent or to correct what it saw as a (potentially or actually) flawed process. The 1994 electoral process, in particular, cast the United States (and the OAS) as a major—but not determining—actor in the Dominican Republic's domestic political processes.

Taken as a whole, these electoral processes dramatize the extent to which neopatrimonial politics, presidential continuity, and fraud impaired democracy in the Dominican Republic. Given the country's vast social changes and the initial hopes raised by the PRD period, the extent of political stasis represented by Balaguer and exemplified in his manipulation of the 1990 and 1994 elections has been remarkable. This ability built upon a stable, if minoritarian, base of support in society. Balaguer was then able to abuse his presidential powers and state resources and encourage and take advantage of divisions within opposition parties. He was also able to take advantage of the overall weakness of and divisions within Dominican civil society.

Time—both biological and historical—appeared to be running out for Balaguer.[29] It has done so later and in a fashion more controlled by him than anyone would have ever predicted. In the concluding chapter we examine how changes and reactions induced by the electoral crises examined above and Balaguer's absence from the presidential race permitted a relatively crisis-free election in 1996 and what may be viewed as a new transition in the country, as well as implications for the future of neopatrimonialism and of democratic politics in the Dominican Republic.

9 A New Transition
Prospects and Conclusions

What we can hope to do is to defend and extend over time the powers to choose for ourselves, individually and locally, how we will act and make our own lives, and defend, too, the political framework which has best secured this opportunity over the last two and a half centuries.—John Dunn, Democracy

On March 26, 1996, Dominican newspapers ran stories about the country's beauty contest. The articles were less about the winner, though, and more about the process of selection. As one account explained, members of the jury had cast their votes for one candidate, but the organizers of the contest had crowned someone else. One of the organizers told a journalist, "Why are you making so much noise protesting? [*¿qué tanto yun yún es el que ustedes hacen?*] This is common to contests all over the world." The Dominican friend who sent me the newspaper clipping commented in the margin: "Not even a beauty contest can be held here without the ingredient of fraud. What can one expect on May 16 [election day]?"

Earlier that month on a trip to the country, I had visited an electoral training workshop for young people in the town of Azua. The workshop was preparing them to teach other youth how to go out in their communities to explain to voters the new constitutionally required system of *colegios cerrados*. This system, intended to prevent the possibility of double voting, now required women first to register and then to vote in the morning and then men to do the same in the afternoon. After a brief presentation, the first question asked by an earnest young man was, "What do we tell people who ask us *if* there will be elections on May 16?"

Leading up to the 1996 presidential elections, there was an unmistakable atmosphere of diffuse fear about the intentions of President Balaguer, his close associates, and other antidemocratic actors in the Dominican Republic. Yet, the fears were not realized in what turned out to be watershed elections. These were the first elections since 1962 in which neither Juan Bosch nor Joaquín Balaguer were presidential candidates, and the first since 1966 in which Balaguer had not been a candidate. They were the result of a political transaction to resolve the 1994 postelectoral crisis—which cut Balaguer's last term in half and instituted other constitutional reforms—including the prohibition of immediate presidential reelection and the requirement of a second round if no candidate received over 50 percent of the vote in the first round. These elections resulted in the victory of PLD presidential candidate Leonel Fernández in the second round, following a remarkable short-term electoral coalition between Balaguer's party and Bosch's party supporting Fernández's candidacy. Prior to the elections, there was a much more concerted and organized effort by key sectors in civil society to work for honest elections and prepare against fraudulent ones. International pressure also played a significant role in easing the exit of the eighty-eight-year-old Balaguer in 1996, though this role was of a different nature than in 1978. Finally, unlike recent past elections, the 1996 process was largely *not* crisis ridden. Near-final results were known the morning after the election, and, even more crucially, they were accepted by the loser, Peña Gómez, who conceded his defeat only hours subsequently.

Thus, the struggle for democratic politics in the Dominican Republic began a new chapter in 1996. In the first section below, the 1996 electoral process and results are presented, and changes in the major factors explaining why past elections were crisis ridden are linked to an explanation of why the 1996 elections were not. Then, the new transition represented by the 1996 elections is contrasted with that of 1978 on the basis of the framework for analysis presented in chapter 3. The final section provides a review and summary.

The 1996 Elections

I want to get out of the logic of conspiracy. I want to believe in people. I want to believe in the authorities of the JCE. I want to believe the candidates. I want to believe that here the logic of decency will impose itself.—Jorge Prats,
Hoy, *April 1, 1996*

The 1996 elections were a contest among candidates from the country's three major parties in a first round on May 16, 1996, and then between the top two on June 30.[1] The front-runner in the polls going into the first round was Peña

Gómez of the PRD and the Acuerdo de Santo Domingo. This time, however, the fifty-nine-year-old was the oldest of the three leading candidates—rather than the youngest as he had been in 1994. In spite of substantial discontent within his own party, Peña Gómez kept Fernando Alvarez Bogaert as his vice presidential candidate. The unhappiness was fed by concerns regarding Peña Gómez's declining health and by ambitions within his own party (in fact, in September 1996, Peña Gómez was required once again to undergo cancer surgery). The second candidate was Leonel Fernández of the PLD, who had been Bosch's vice presidential candidate in 1994. Fernández, aged forty-two, selected another relatively young figure from his own party, Jaime David Fernández Mirabal (nephew of the Mirabal sisters killed by Trujillo), to be his vice presidential candidate. The third candidate was the fifty-five-year-old Jacinto Peynado of the PR(SC), the country's vice president. He named María Isabel Gassó, a politically unknown businesswoman from the Cibao region of the country, as his vice presidential candidate.

In chapter 8, crisis-ridden elections over the 1978–94 period were linked to three issues: presidential continuity, party-leadership continuity, and weak electoral oversight. The 1994 elections also underscored the tremendous weakness of the elements of Dominican civil society committed to democratic institutions and outcomes; the few relevant groups in 1994 had poured their energies and their hopes into a central electoral board (JCE) that had ultimately defrauded them.

Significantly, all of these features changed for the 1996 elections. Presidential continuity was no longer an issue, as President Balaguer could not constitutionally succeed himself. Vice president Jacinto Peynado won the tough primary struggle for the PR(SC) presidential nomination; yet, from the beginning Peynado found little support from Balaguer, who supported the PLD candidate, Leonel Fernández (at first only informally). As the PLD had scarce representation in congress, Fernández would need PR(SC) congressional support and Balaguer's cooperation to govern, if he wished to do so democratically; if Peynado were to win the presidency, then Balaguer's power within both the executive and his party would be more clearly displaced. As a further consequence, there was little access to state resources in support of Peynado's candidacy for the first round. Indeed, state media bias and other state support were more evident for Fernández in the second round, although to a much lesser degree than the abuses evident in the 1994 race. Underscoring his rejection of Peynado, President Balaguer did not cast a vote in the first round, although voting is obligatory under the Dominican constitution. For the second round, Balaguer actively campaigned for Fernández and voted. For Balaguer, retaining party leadership now required insuring the defeat of his own party's candidate.

Doubts, like those expressed by the young man cited above, about whether the elections would really take place were common. Most informed observers believed that if he could find a way, Balaguer would remain in office. A number of his close advisers made ambiguous statements about whether the elections were truly necessary or not. There was real concern that Balaguer might take advantage of a chaotic situation either between the first and second rounds of the elections or between the second round and the inauguration to cling to power.

Another difference from past elections, however, was the professionalism, dynamism, integrity, and political independence of the judges of the JCE. A top PRD leader, in giving the background of the four men and one woman and how they came to be named, described each of them as "serious" (author's field notes, May 1996). In the past, other criteria had been more important. The parties had initially been satisfied with a weak JCE, from which they could seek to extract political advantage. Following the 1990 crisis, the opposition parties had sought to insure party representation within the agency to protect their interests. Then came the 1994 crisis, which taught the parties the risks of the strategy of a partisan-based JCE and also provided the domestic and international pressure necessary to name an independent, professional JCE for the 1996 elections. Throughout the process, the president of the JCE, César Estrella Sadhalá, and his fellow judges demonstrated their commitment to well-managed, honest elections. Furthermore, the process of renovation of new judges also took place among many municipal-level boards. The JCE carried out a significant effort to improve the electoral registry, eliminating to the extent possible people with more than one identification card, people who were deceased, and military and police personnel who improperly had ID cards since they were legally prohibited from voting. Although some problems remained, the JCE also provided all the parties with computer copies of the electoral registry for their examination weeks in advance, unlike what took place in 1994. There was also a dramatic improvement both in the training of the officials who worked at the individual voting stations and in the seriousness with which they accepted their responsibilities.

A final difference was a concerted effort by the country's major organized business, labor, civic, educational, and church groups to play a more visible role in seeking clean elections. At one level, this comprised an effort to engage the parties and candidates in substantive discussions about policy issues. The umbrella organization GAD was formed; many of its members had been signatories of the Pact for Democracy signed in August 1994. The group brought together the country's major business, labor, educational, and civic leaders. It established a network of over seven hundred organizations in forty-three different municipalities to discuss what the country's priorities should be; it also encouraged the country's business, labor, nongovernmental organizations (NGO), and other sectors to contribute suggestions.

Thus, leading up to the 1996 presidential elections, the GAD helped elaborate a national agenda generated by consultation with all these groups and focused on ten key priorities. It also worked to establish municipal-level networks of groups within civil society to articulate local-level goals and priorities, and established or supported various programs of civic education and election observation to help insure a transparent election process (Grupo de Acción por la Democracia 1996; author's interviews with members of the GAD, 1996). The ten priorities represented a blueprint of action for the country. They symbolized not only long-term developmental challenges for the country, but particular problems that had become worse as a consequence of Balaguer's neopatrimonial rule and the nature of his interaction with other political and social forces in the country. The priorities included economic goals such as employment generation and improvement in the provision of electricity; social and environmental goals related to education, health, social security, the provision of housing for lower-income groups, and the protection of forests and other natural resources; and goals oriented to making the state more effective and accountable, such as modernizing and institutionalizing the state apparatus, imposing an effective rule of law, and improving democratic access to the state by decentralization and other reforms.[2]

At another level, the effort from civil society was focused on the dual goal of supporting the JCE while providing additional outside checks on the quality of its work and the veracity of its results. Parts of the GAD and other groups were active in providing electoral and civic training leading up to the elections. They also helped develop a network of domestic election observers, the Red Ciudadana de Observadores Electorales (Citizen Network of Electoral Observers). This network was intended to observe and critique the election process as well as generate an independent "quick count," which would serve as an additional valuable source of information in a potential crisis situation.[3] A number of the top leadership of the main organization overseeing the effort to organize the domestic observer network and the quick count, Participación Ciudadana, were perceived to favor Peña Gómez.[4] Like the GAD, Participación was also receiving extensive financing from the U.S. government, through the Agency for International Development (USAID). As a consequence of these issues, while continuing to attack Peña Gómez on presumed

A banner in the town of Peralta, Azua, urges people to "Join the Network!" of nonpartisan electoral observers. This was one of many efforts from civil society designed to help insure that the 1996 elections would be free and fair.

nationalist (anti-Haitian) grounds, the pro-Balaguer group of conservative nationalists attacked what it called "international intervention" in Dominican domestic affairs and also pressured the JCE to restrict the number of allowable domestic observers. The cardinal even stated in early March that he believed the Catholic university should cut off all its ties with USAID, as the university was the conduit for aid money being used to support many of the activities of the GAD and of Participación Ciudadana.

Yet, in general, the campaign was much less bitter and negative than in 1994. The cardinal's charges gradually died down and later that month there was a state visit by the newly inaugurated Haitian president René Preval to the Dominican Republic, where he was met cordially by President Balaguer. In the weeks before the May 16 elections, the PLD threatened to object to any "Haitian-looking" voter, claiming that the PRD had illegally registered thousands of Haitians to vote, but the party backed away from that position in the face of both domestic and international objections. Other allegations of potential fraud, similar to those in past elections, were common. The most insistent claim by parties was the "purchase" or "renting" of their voters' *cédulas* by opposing parties to prevent them from casting their ballot.

In addition to the significant changes in these factors from the past, there was also an important constant from 1994. That constant was international attention and pressure.[5] The U.S. government played a critical role in financing and supporting the GAD and Participación Ciudadana, though both also had some other bases of support. The NDI, which had supported civic electoral networks in several other countries in the region and around the world, provided initial support to Participación; however, given the NDI's prominent role in 1994, which had been attacked by conservative nationalist forces linked to Balaguer, it pulled back in favor of other international advisers for the 1996 elections. The elections were once again held under extensive international observation, from the OAS, the NDI, and other organizations, in addition to the domestic observation efforts.

As in past elections, the electorate behaved in an exemplary and dignified fashion, as it was often forced to wait for many hours in long lines to vote. Concerns that the complicated voting mechanism decided upon to implement the requirement for *colegios cerrados* would dramatically increase both abstention and confusion were not realized. In each of the past elections, a new voting system of some kind had been introduced.[6] As a consequence, all the parties had raised fears of both high abstention and potential tricks by their opponents to prevent voting while also encouraging their own faithful to vote early. Participation rates in the 1996 elections approximated historical averages in past "normal" elections (compare table 9.1 to table 8.1).

The results of the first-round election demonstrated the importance of electoral rules for the final outcome. In 1994, Peña Gómez had indicated his support for a second-round election if no candidate had received more than 40 percent of the vote in the first round; however, the final accord struck between the PLD and the PR(SC), which was approved as the constitutional reform, specified a threshold of 50 percent. Peña Gómez won the first round with 45.9 percent of the total vote. Fernández received 38.9 percent, and Peynado came in a distant third, with 15.0 percent (see table 9.1).

Given this gap, how can we explain that Fernández won the second-round election with 51.3 percent of the vote forty-five days later? There appear to be three main explanations: active support for his candidacy from Balaguer and the PR(SC); the fact that many of these voters were already predisposed to support Fernández over Peña Gómez as their second choice; and the ability of Fernández to broaden his coalition without generating large-scale defections to Peña Gómez among his first-round supporters.

Fernández received concerted support from Balaguer and the PR(SC),

Table 9.1. Official Results for the 1996 Presidential Elections

Parties and party alliances (Candidate)	First round, May 16 (% Vote)	Second round, June 30 (% Vote)
PR(SC) (Jacinto Peynado)	15.0	—
PRD and allies (José Francisco Peña Gómez)	45.9	48.7
PLD (Leonel Fernández)	38.9	51.3
Valid votes[1] (thousands)	2,904	2,861
Null votes (%)[2]	1.5	.1
Observed votes (%)[2]	.0	.0
Total votes (thousands)	2,951	2,879
Abstention (%) (by electoral registry)	21	23
Abstention (%)[3] (by estimated population over 18)	37	38

Sources: Junta Central Electoral and *Gaceta Oficial*, vol. 154, no. 9938 (Santo Domingo, 10 November 1996). The assistance of Isis Duarte in acquiring the data for this table is gratefully acknowledged.
[1]Party vote percentages based on valid vote totals.
[2]Calculated from total vote; some observed and null votes were subsequently validated for specific parties; the total number of observed votes was only 2,399 in the first round and 1,078 in the second round.
[3]Based on population estimates provided by the Instituto de Estudios de Población y Desarrollo (IEPD, Institute for the Study of Population and Development), which includes individuals legally ineligible to vote, such as foreigners, military and police personnel, and convicted criminals.

formalized by an open pact between them. This also led to state support for his candidacy. The Frente Nacional Patriótico (National Patriotic Front), as it was called, was similar in name to the agreement the PLD had struck with other parties in 1994; the phrase reflected themes of nationalism and anti-Haitianism intended to raise doubts about Peña Gómez. Following a historic rally in June, which found Balaguer, Bosch, and Fernández sharing the same platform, the use (and abuse) of state funds in support of Fernández also increased, as did blatant media bias by state-supported television.[7] Another form of state support may have partially backfired on Balaguer and the PLD. Balaguer had named General Pérez y Pérez as head of police on May 13,

President Balaguer openly supported Leonel Fernández, the presidential
candidate of the PLD, following the first round of the 1996 presidential elections.
Shown on the stage in front of a massive rally in June 1996 are, from left to right:
Fernández; Juan Bosch, PLD founder; President Joaquín Balaguer; and Jaime
David Fernández Mirabal, the vice presidential candidate. Fernández defeated
José Francisco Peña Gómez of the PRD in the second round.

shortly before the first-round elections. Leading up to the second-round elections, the PLD stepped up charges that the PRD was "buying" or "renting"
cédulas from PLD supporters to prevent them from voting. The national
police began demanding to see identity cards, arresting those that did not have
them in their possession and at other times confiscating cards from other
individuals; the PRD believed its sympathizers were being unfairly targeted
and protested domestically and internationally. A June 6 letter of protest from
former president Carter was followed on June 7 by a statement from PLD
candidate Fernández asserting that the arrests were also affecting his party's
sympathizers and asking the police to desist from further action. On June 11,
President Balaguer replaced the chief of police.

The support offered Fernández by Balaguer and the PR(SC) was effective because of the high levels of distrust against Peña Gómez that already existed within significant portions of the population that had supported the PR(SC) candidate in the first round. Many business groups provided Fernández with generous financing from early on. Significant sectors of the population distrusted Peña Gómez due to their concerns about what was perceived as his volatile temperament, sometimes combined with a racist anti-Haitian component. No preelectoral poll had ever shown Peña Gómez with over 50 percent support, while many surveys showed that an important segment of the electorate rejected him. Thus, Fernández was able to maintain his PLD base of support, while adding new voters.

There were not apparent significant differences between the programs of Peña Gómez and Fernández. Fernández argued the main difference was that in the Dominican Republic the populist, social-democratic, statist model of the PRD had failed. At the same time, the neoliberal model was also a failure, as there was a gap between rich and poor, which meant that the state had to play a role in fostering social equity. While rejecting a social-welfare model as not viable for the country, what he sought was an equilibrium between the state and the market, not the hegemony of either one. Peña Gómez explained that the variations in the government programs were not large, as they were inspired by similar philosophies. However, he argued, Fernández had allied himself with Balaguer, who represented an antiquated economic model and an authoritarian style of government, and if Fernández were to win he could find himself a hostage to Balaguer (based on candidates' responses to questions by NDI delegate members, May 1996). Thus, the central issue revolved less around programmatic issues and more around who would have the opportunity to govern. In the end, the coalition of the PLD and the PR(SC) achieved a slight majority.

Regardless of the electoral results, the country could be satisfied with the process itself. Significant changes in the factors identified as leading to crisis-ridden elections in the country over the 1978–94 period explain why the 1996 elections were different. President Balaguer was not seeking reelection, the JCE moved toward a model of nonpartisan professionalism, and there was a more concerted engagement in support of the electoral process on the part of domestic societal groups, including domestic observers on election day. International pressure remained significant throughout. Peña Gómez's concession the day after the election was aided by the fact that the margin of victory was sufficiently convincing and that the vote count was consonant with those generated by independent and party quick counts. It also reflected Peña Gómez's continuing restraint in electoral periods, which he has shown since at least 1978.

Yet, questions remain about what would have occurred if Peña Gómez had been the victor in 1996. What kind of reaction would there have been from Balaguer and his close collaborators and from those business leaders who still distrusted him? At a minimum, the transition period would have been far more tense. With Fernández as president-elect, Balaguer was willing to vacate the presidency, reassured that he would have significant guarantees of continuing influence and that he and his close circle of collaborators could avoid serious judicial or other types of investigation or retribution.

The 1996 Elections as a New Transition

The inauguration of Leonel Fernández in August 1996 raises hopes in the Dominican Republic for a more regularized and formally institutionalized regime and, in that way, for a more democratic regime as well. Given the deterioration in the democratic nature of the regime as its neopatrimonial elements were enhanced over the 1986–96 period, the handing over of power by Balaguer again in 1996 can also be examined as a new transition for the country, especially as compared to 1978.

The circumstances in 1996 are contrasted to those of 1978 in table 9.2. The table is organized in terms of the same three clusters of factors discussed in chapters 3 and 4 (cf. tables 3.1 and 4.3). Overall, the three factors are more favorable in 1996 than they were in 1978. In 1996, with regard to the preexisting regime, Balaguer governed more of a hybrid regime than an authoritarian one. Although distrust about Balaguer's intentions ran high in 1996, he was not an open candidate for reelection as he had been in 1978, and he was now eighty-eight years old rather than seventy.

Balaguer's ties with major military, economic, and political actors all also reflect significant differences between the two periods. One of the most important was with regard to the military, which was no longer a significant actor in 1996. In spite of the fears raised by the naming of General Pérez y Pérez to the national police during the electoral period, the military were divided regarding their partisan loyalties, even as they were an unprofessional force, largely distrusted in terms of their ability to govern by sectors in society. Balaguer's distant and more disdainful relationship to the military in 1996 was different from the more dependent link he had to them in 1978, when there were several politically ambitious officers in service to him and his campaign. Peña Gómez and the PRD had sympathizers within military circles; Fernández's father was a retired military officer, which also provided the president-elect with important channels of communication into the armed forces.

Table 9.2. Comparing Transitions, 1978 and 1994–1996

	1978	1994–96
I. Preexisting authoritarian regime		
	Neopatrimonial and authoritarian	Neopatrimonial and hybrid
Military:	Somewhat autonomous, visible cliques	Weak, somewhat autonomous; divided but no visible cliques
Societal organizations:	Weak, but some present	Somewhat stronger, more active, and visible presence of a prodemocratic, antineopatrimonial civil society
Political opposition:	Opposition parties tolerated	Opposition parties widely recognized as legitimate actors
Economic allies:	Weak, but increasing autonomy	Few economic allies outside of close cronies
II. International geopolitical and economic context		
Hierarchy of U.S. policy goals:	No visible communist threat; democracy important goal	Democracy and free elections a central goal in the post–Cold War era
Extent of U.S. involvement:	High-level, diplomatic, and economic means	High-level, diplomatic means
III. The transition process		
Mode of transition:	From above, negotiated with guarantees for departing ruler; tacit political pact	From above, August 1994 constitutional reforms as a political pact, more effectively instituted by a watchful civil society and parties with international support; 1996 presidential election results provided guarantees for departing ruler
Institutional changes and continuities:	Inherited constitutional framework of presidential dominance; but some power sharing; military purged	Constitution now precludes immediate presidential reelection; president with little congressional support and complex electoral calendar; military not a perceived threat

By 1996, Balaguer had alienated more economic actors than had been the case in 1978. Unlike 1978, in 1996 many of the country's leading economic groups were openly seeking a replacement to Balaguer through their engagement with the electoral process. Business leaders were much more familiar with both of the major presidential candidates; many insisted they had "learned" from their experience with Guzmán, and this time business associations would not seek to attack and isolate a new administration (author's field notes, May 1996). Although societal organizations were still weak and fragmented, there was a more vigorous, incipient effort to organize a civil society, which called for greater institutionality and an atmosphere of tolerance. The political opposition in 1996 was widely recognized as legitimate, and all major parties had representation in congress and in municipal-level governments.

The international geopolitical context was also more favorable to democracy in 1996 than in 1978. This reflected the greater engagement of a wide variety of international NGOs and other movements in fostering democracy, the end of the Cold War, and a more emphatic U.S. policy in favor of free elections. The country's political economy was also more vulnerable to the effects of potential political instability because of its greater international openness, especially with regard to tourism and investments in export processing zones.

At the same time, the kind of economic transition the country was being impelled to make toward a more open, market-driven economy—in large part due to changes and pressures emanating from the international economy—was itself a challenge to democratic rule. The central debate regarding market-oriented reforms is whether or not they are in fact critical over the medium term for democratic consolidation because they establish the bases for successful, sustained economic growth that would not otherwise be possible; because they provide for the diffusion of economic resources both away from the state and more broadly throughout the society; and because they permit the reconstitution of a capable state (building on Nelson 1994a, 21). The painful dilemma for countries like the Dominican Republic, apparent over this period, is that whereas these reforms may indeed be necessary to foster sustained growth, they have yet clearly to do that, to diffuse resources away from the state or within society, or to lead to a stronger (if "leaner") state. As we saw under both the PRD and the Balaguer administrations in the 1978–96 period, the process of economic transition is extraordinarily difficult to manage politically; Balaguer also demonstrated how partial implementation of economic reforms can be employed to enhance neopatrimonialism. The challenge of reconstituting a state and formulating a strategy for growth will "ultimately hinge on whether political institutions allow for effective management of a market economy while remaining accountable to the interests and aspirations of competing social and economic interests" (Haggard and Kaufman 1995, 310).[8]

For the Dominican Republic, as for any democratic country, these two tasks of economic management and democratic accountability are challenging to implement simultaneously. They will require deft political direction, the ability to communicate to the population at large, critical support from key societal and business interests, and the ability and willingness to forge political agreements around particular issues. In a number of other countries in Latin America, the consequences of economic crisis have been market-oriented reforms implemented by "delegative" presidents, thus enhancing neopatrimonial elements of their democracies at the expense of more regularized and accountable mechanisms. Especially given the Dominican Republic's historical trajectory, related types of processes cannot be ruled out. Indeed, in early 1997, one of the main Dominican intellectual authors of the package of economic reforms was openly calling for President Fernández to implement them by decree if necessary, flaunting democratic procedures.

With regard to the third cluster of factors, the transition process, there were some similarities with 1978. The 1996 mode of transition could again be considered as occurring "from above," with guarantees for Balaguer and his henchmen due to the balance of political forces and the nature of the judiciary following Fernández's inauguration.[9] The results of the 1994 congressional elections and the 1996 presidential elections combined to strengthen Balaguer's position. The weak presence of the PLD in congress means that President Fernández must negotiate with the PR(SC) and the PRD, assuming respect for formal institutions. Thus, Fernández never provided a public accounting to the country of the conditions in which he found the state's finances, and his administration confirmed that it did not intend to address corruption issues of the past administration.

How can we assess the greater likelihood of change in the Dominican Republic following this transition compared to 1978? The overwhelming element of continuity apparent in political patterns and outcomes over the 1978–96 period was explained by a number of factors. These focused on the vitality of path-dependent neopatrimonial political-institutional patterns and incentives, ultimately strengthened by the timing of the transition with regard particularly to the impact of international economic issues. Also important were features of the country's political-party system and electoral laws, which enhanced factional strife within the PRD, and the confrontational and restraining responses of powerful domestic societal groups. Both significant societal change, impacting the structural bases of neopatrimonialism, and political agency from above, helping to induce a new and more democratic pattern of culturally expected political behaviors, were viewed as having either failed or not been sufficiently present in the country over this time period to diminish neopatrimonialism. Hope for a change in political patterns ended with Balaguer's return to office in 1986.

In 1996, after Fernández's inauguration, there was modest hope that both societal change and political agency from above could have more of an impact in constraining neopatrimonial patterns of behavior. The continued effects of urbanization and migration, the increasing internationalization of the country's economy and society, the increased mobilization of a more self-conscious civil society, and generally lower expectations about what a change in government might mean all point to elements of societal change that could be helpful. Both the high costs of a sharply confrontational style adopted by business in the Guzmán years and the costs of living under the kind of policy style adopted by Balaguer might help induce a more conciliatory style of negotiation, especially by business sectors, which now perceive that it is the state that must defend its role as long as the structural power of business and the legitimacy of the market's role are high. With Balaguer's expected (but, as of mid-1997, not yet realized) passing from the political scene, it is unlikely that anyone else with an equal commitment to neopatrimonial domination of the state will be able to sustain the abiding loyalty of a significant (if still minority) percentage of the country's population. And, in partial contrast to international pressures in the 1980s—which were more single-mindedly in favor of market-oriented reforms—international organizations in the 1990s are focusing on "governance" issues, on the need to build viable, accountable state institutions as a part of any successful process of economic liberalization. Yet, as the preceding discussion indicates, expectations for political transformation have now become decidedly more modest.

Reflecting this, assessments of President Fernández were mixed as of mid-1997. Some of President Fernández's actions during his first months in office indicated that he sought to establish a different standard of presidential conduct than followed by Balaguer. Fernández was governing in a more institutional fashion; for example, he ended the practice of maintaining separate, special dollar accounts, and he was granting more autonomy to his cabinet ministers. He promptly fired an air force general who challenged his authority, even as he permitted the development of an investigation into one of the more notorious "disappearances" of a noted journalist during Balaguer's first twelve years in office.

Yet, given his weak congressional base and his attempts to play more "by the rules" than Balaguer, Fernández's administration appeared blocked. Many of his major legislative initiatives, especially those related to economic reform, remained stymied in congress due to opposition from both the PR(SC) and the PRD (there were also disagreements within his own party). He was unable either to gain accords with Balaguer or Peña Gómez or to win over enough individual congressional votes; but this inability also reflected continuing divisions across business and labor groups about the extent, nature, and timing of the reforms discussed in chapter 7 (the key elements of the proposed reforms and a justification are in Dauhajre hijo and Aristy Escuder 1996 and Dauhajre hijo et al. 1996). At the same time, advances in other areas were being made. For example, the Dominican congress finally approved a loan with the IDB, seeking to modernize its own structures, and a law against domestic violence was finally approved (see the interview with Milagros Ortiz Bosch in *Revista Rumbo*, May 5, 1997, 29–33).

Elements of the old style of politics clearly remained. Fernández cleverly managed a conflict over the budget between the executive and the legislative to permit him considerable discretion over expenditures for 1997. Over early 1997, congressional figures, especially from the PR(SC), sought to engage him in a "deal" that would extend their term in office for another two years (to be concurrent with the presidential term) in return for a constitutional reform allowing his reelection; after some equivocation, he turned it down (at least as of June 1997). As of mid-1997, resignations of some of the JCE judges had been accepted, and it was unclear if they would be replaced and by whom, raising new fears about the weakness of the electoral oversight agency. The PR(SC), in particular, had reason to fear the midterm elections, based on election polls.

There are reasons to be hopeful that Fernández's commitment to respect democratic and constitutional norms will continue. As of mid-1997, combined with his lack of control over congress, this commitment has substantially reduced abuses of the informal powers of the presidency, in contrast to Balaguer. How Fernández manages the process and responds to the outcome of the 1998 congressional election will be one key measure of the nature of his leadership. At the same time, actions by the opposition parties are also crucial. Potentially acrimonious and divisive conflicts over presidential nominations for the year 2000 could confront all three parties—based on Balaguer's age and health (in 2000 he would turn 93), on Peña Gómez's own severe health problems, and on the fact that Fernández cannot succeed himself absent constitutional reform. In none of the three parties are there obvious heirs. Leadership successions in the three parties could lead to a more invigorated process of internal democracy and of open competition; or they could degenerate into bitter struggles for power. In sum, expectations for continued modest changes in political patterns and trajectories were realistic, although not assured.

Neopatrimonialism and Democracy

This book has had three primary theoretical goals. It has sought to establish the value of a mode of analysis centered on historical-institutionalism and path-dependency, to provide evidence for the independent (but not exclusive) impact that political and institutional factors have had on significant political outcomes in the Dominican Republic and to demonstrate the analytical utility of the concept of neopatrimonialism in the Dominican and similar contexts. It has pursued these goals while seeking to provide a basic review and analysis of the struggle for democratic politics in the Dominican Republic, especially from 1961 to the present.

The neopatrimonial pattern of politics experienced in the Dominican Republic inhibited the creation of formal institutional rule and a democratic polity responsive to societal demands and needs within international and other constraints. Although the explanation of how neopatrimonial patterns of politics emerged in the Dominican Republic presented in chapter 2 was particular to that country, it was cast in the general terms of historical-institutionalism and path-dependency. It emphasized the importance of such factors as fragmented economic elites, poverty, war, and the impact of foreign intervention on the creation of a strong military in helping to lead to neosultanism, rather than linking its emergence to an ineluctable destiny of the country traced from its colonial past.

The kind of politics represented by the terms "neopatrimonialism" or "neosultanism," which has so dramatically marked the Dominican Republic, is hardly unique to that country or to countries of Hispanic culture. More than one kind of path can lead to this kind of politics, though it is more likely to appear in countries with the features noted in the previous paragraph. Neosultanism has been found in countries throughout the globe (see Chehabi and Linz 1998). And key traits of neopatrimonialism (presented in chapter 1) found useful in understanding political patterns in the Dominican context, particularly under Balaguer, were derived from analyses of African politics, though they could also have been drawn from other countries or regions (Bratton and van de Walle 1994; Brynen 1995; Hutchcroft 1991).

The evolution of Dominican politics strongly suggests that democratic transitions are affected by the nature of the preexisting authoritarian regime, and particularly that transitions from neosultanistic regimes like that of Trujillo are more difficult than from less restrictive neopatrimonial regimes. Similarly, the 1996 transition from a Balaguer who led a hybrid authoritarian-democratic regime was fraught with less crisis than that of 1978 from an authoritarian Balaguer regime. These findings are consonant with those of a review of recent transitions in Africa, which concludes that the prospects for political democracy are more promising "in transitions from regime types, and in world regions, *other* than neopatrimonial ones" (Bratton and van de Walle 1997, 273). At the same time, given their focus on a set of countries from a single region in a narrow time frame, these authors may well underplay the differing kinds of roles that international actors may play in transition episodes. As discussed in chapter 3, the extent of success of the transition from the Trujillo regime as well as its ultimate outcome were linked in significant ways to the nature of relations with the United States. And although an explanation for the success of the 1978 transition focused primarily on U.S. intervention was rejected, chapter 4 did explore the ways in which the United States and other international actors and processes contributed to the transition.

The above chapters have also provided additional evidence for the independent impact of political factors and for disjunctive (rather than simple) causal links from socioeconomic changes to political outcomes. As seen in chapter 6, though economic difficulties induced internationally and exacerbated domestically were obviously important factors in explaining PRD failures over the 1978–86 period, at the same time, neopatrimonial temptations, intraparty factional disputes in this context, and failures of leadership were also important in explaining the PRD decline and its inability to change the country's style of politics. The kinds of political-institutional incentives presented by neopatrimonialism, as well as those specific to the PRD and the kind of party system in which it operated (presented in chapter 5), helped explain aspects of the party's factional strife. Balaguer's ability to sustain himself in power over the 1986–96 period, as discussed in chapter 7, was strongly associated with the informal norms of neopatrimonialism, rather than with economic successes (especially over 1990–91). Formal constitutional and political rules, though important, were a poor guide by themselves in understanding the major patterns and behaviors of key actors. Under Balaguer, the increasingly corrosive impact of neopatrimonialism on democracy became evident. This was particularly evident in the electoral processes examined in chapter 8.

The analysis of neopatrimonial politics in the Dominican Republic in these chapters also pointed to the risks of institutional formalism, of an exclusive focus of political analysis on formal institutions and rules (as important as these may be). In many countries with authoritarian, hybrid, or nascent democratic regimes, the assumption that formal rules are the only guide necessary to understanding the nature of bargaining across political actors is often wrong. Similarly, an exclusive focus on how political actors seek to change or defend formal constitutional or electoral laws may miss the key point that since the central issue is power and control of resources, formal domestic democratic rules are only one of several arenas in which the political struggle is realized.

In a regional perspective, though, it is important to recognize that the Dominican Republic avoided the extremes of political polarization and of violence that afflicted a number of its Central American and Caribbean neighbors. As a member of the PLD and also a noted sociologist told me in 1990 (paraphrasing), "I could never admit it publicly, but Balaguer has been a key factor of stabilization in this country." What could he have meant by this? The difference between the Dominican Republic and more conflict-ridden countries in the region was that in the island republic social inequalities did not lead to political polarization between an extreme right with ties to the armed forces and a guerrilla left. An extreme right in the Dominican Republic, centered in a military-landowner alliance, did not form historically, first, due to the way the armed forces were created during and emerged from the era of U.S. occupation and, second, due to the nature of the Trujillo regime. Subsequently, structural factors related to the absence of a powerful landowning class and the ability to (hyper)exploit Haitian labor were also important. Yet, returning to the observation of the PLD leader, Balaguer also played a somewhat moderating role, occupying the space on the right and effectively blocking the possible emergence of a conservative group more rooted in or associated with the country's armed forces either during his rule or subsequently. The fact that Balaguer governed as a "civilian" ruler over 1966–78 (and subsequently) facilitated the subsequent removal of more politically oriented military leaders; Balaguer's return to power obviated any perceived need for a conservative alliance with the military.[10]

In the same vein, Balaguer's major, historical political opponents, Bosch (with a hiatus in the late 1960s and early 1970s) and Peña Gómez, have also ultimately had more of a depolarizing than a polarizing impact on Dominican society. They have done so by channeling dissent through partisan channels and elections and helping to diffuse anger through organized protest, while continuing to engage in politics. At the same time, given the weaknesses of organized labor (or of the popular church) the PLD had limited bases on which to build a stronger radical party in the country, also limiting the bases for greater pressure toward more participatory forms of democracy.[11] But, both Bosch and Peña Gómez also had their democratic limitations; Bosch, and eventually Peña Gómez within the PRD, supplanted formal notions of internal party democracy for that of uncontested party leader. Bosch's moderating role could be seen in the case of Caamaño's invasion in 1973 and also, more ambiguously (though ultimately), in the 1990 electoral crisis. Peña Gómez's role was clear building up to and throughout the 1978 electoral process, as well as in 1990, 1994, and 1996, when he ultimately helped to defuse rather than to polarize circumstances.

In 1996, the Dominican Republic faced a new opportunity to break with historically embedded neopatrimonial patterns and forge more formal, regularized, accountable, and democratic institutions. Many of the same types of challenges faced in preceding decades—from the international economic arena, from domestic societal actors and expectations and from political dynamics and informal norms—remained, though attenuated by secular changes and recent experiences. Yet, throughout Latin America to date, the initiation of far-reaching, structural, market-oriented economic reforms has required concentrated executive authority. And, few countries have been able to move toward a more clearly accountable executive while consolidating both economic reforms and democracy. Whether the Dominican Republic can implement crucial, but painful economic reforms through a more consensual, negotiated process, remains to be seen.

The other two major options are unilateral executive actions, with neopatrimonial overtones, or policy stasis and economic decline. As Balaguer demonstrated and other Latin American countries have also highlighted recently, neopatrimonialism is an option for political rulers in seeking to resolve the inevitable tension between governability (which seeks to maximize efficient decision making, if not consensus) and democracy (whose exercise involves the expression of multiple interests and conflict). This could be especially true for a country like the Dominican Republic in which it has such deep historical roots. The temptation to return to strong presidentialism, especially if the country's party system becomes more fragmented, could be strong. In another disturbing scenario, effective centralization of power may decline, to be overshadowed by policy immobilism, corruption, clientelism, prebendal politics, and a weak and easily penetrated state; policy could then be easily influenced by powerful societal actors, whose direct influence would override formal rules or organizations, while political actors in a decentralized fashion also raided the state. This would be a recipe for crisis and decline. The fact that international creditors and investors appear less willing to support these types of excesses perhaps limits its likelihood more than in the past.

Overall, the features of the country's current constitutional framework and electoral calendar appear to complicate governance in the country more than to enhance it. The prohibition of immediate presidential reelection may help inhibit the emergence of a neopatrimonial figure (assuming it is not changed). And, holding congressional elections at the midterm of the presidential term, rather than concurrently with presidential elections may lead to the selection of politicians more responsive to their constituencies and less beholden to the party leaders who placed them on congressional party lists (as noted above, to date, party lists have often been confected by top party leaders on their own or as part of negotiations over presidential nominations). Yet, another consequence of this new institutional combination is that it is more likely that presidents may never achieve effective governing majorities. Given the abuse of presidential powers that possessing such majorities represented under Balaguer, many may perceive that as beneficial for the country. The opposing risk of immobilism and ungovernability as a consequence of executive-congressional deadlock, however, is a real one. A lame-duck president might have an especially difficult time managing relations with a congress elected at midterm and looking toward the new presidential elections. Such a president would probably also be challenged to manage effectively the relations within his own party; the kinds of factional strife that the PRD experienced over the 1978–86 period may well affect the current governing party in a few years time. Rethinking the electoral calendar while implementing other kinds of reforms, such as democratizing party nomination procedures, could help lead to congressional representatives with more meaningful ties to their local constituencies, enhancing the likelihood of governance.

Indeed, constitutional reform was high on President Fernández's agenda as he was inaugurated. Parties and many groups in society had already held extensive discussions on several reforms that the country appeared to need badly, beyond those adopted in the crisis circumstances of August 1994. These included reforms to limit the bias produced in senate elections in which each province, regardless of its size, elected one senator; to facilitate connections between voters and individual congressional representatives, especially in the larger urban areas; to achieve more effective decentralization; and in many other issues (cf. Fundación Siglo 21, 1994; Brea 1994). Yet, as noted in the previous section, as societal groups pondered the kinds of constitutional and political reforms that would enhance representation and accountability and the legal reforms that would assure them more access to government and assurances of equal treatment, many members of congress were simply advocating an extension of their terms to the year 2000, when the next presidential election was to be held.

Much of what has been said in the pages above about political parties and the nature of their ties to the state and to society has highlighted their limitations and constraints on democratic practices. Does this mean that the struggle for democratic politics in the Dominican Republic should seek to sidestep political parties entirely? Throughout contemporary Latin America, there is "widespread public unhappiness with parties," as Conaghan (1995, 458) argues for the case of Ecuador. For many in the mass public as for some social activists and intellectuals (with significant subregional variations), parties represent weak, clientelized, corrupt, impure entities that ought to be replaced by other types of "civic" organizations. Yet, what Gamarra and Malloy (1995) argue with regard to Bolivia and its party system could also be said for the Dominican Republic in the period since 1978: "parties have always been in effect the main source of the problem of governance in Bolivia and at the same time the only real source of any potential solution" (421). Efforts to construct a more democratic state and more responsive parties are essential, given their centrality to democratic politics. It is also true that pressure from a stronger, more vigorous, and more egalitarian civil society, equally committed to playing by the democratic rules of the game, will also remain important and that such a civil society must also continue to be constructed and expanded.

Democracy—as ideology and as utopia—is about translating hope and fear into the ability to be able to speak for oneself, to be heard and to let that have real consequences for one's life (Dunn 1992, 265–66). At the same time, democratic *politics* is about the painful working out of those aspirations within existing and evolving societies, states, and institutions. In a valuable article on the French Revolution, Fontana (1992) describes two fundamental ways to consider the role of democracy in the French Revolution. The first emphasizes the role and impact of the surge of "participation from below" and the emerging political and social identities of the new collective agents. The second examines instead how the emerging political system was defined by its procedures, instruments, and institutions. There is an inevitable tension, she argues, between the expression of political participation by large social groups and the determination of a set of rules that would allow for the delegation of that power to be exercised by political agents (109). In focusing on the struggle for democratic politics in the Dominican Republic, this book has chosen to emphasize the second of these two critical issues.

The Dominican Republic over the period from 1961 to 1996 exemplifies a country that did not move smoothly from democratic transition to habituation and consolidation. The consolidation of democratic politics is not inevitable, is not assured once achieved, and is itself in fact a process of becoming better or worse, especially in a world in which notions of statehood, sovereignty, and citizenship continue to evolve. Yet, I continue to believe it is desirable even as I believe that historical paths which to our contemporary eye may appear to zigzag may also eventually lead not only to democratic politics, but to democracy more broadly.

Appendix A
Election Results by Level of Urbanization, 1962–1994

Table A.1. *Election Results at the Municipal Level by Party and Level of Urbanization, 1962–1994*

1962

% Urban 82	Number of Municipalities	%PRD—Number of Votes	%UCN—Number of Votes
0–20	21	58.81—108,973	30.06—53,349
20–40.1	29	55.01—163,510	26.84—102,138
40.1–60	15	59.90—109,378	29.19—61,476
60–80	10	65.69—78,244	28.16—58,263
80–100	2	63.27—159,396	32.73—42,110
		Pearson's r/p-value .134/.24	Pearson's r/p-value .000/.99

1966

% Urban 82	Number of Municipalities	%PR—Number of Votes	%PRD—Number of Votes	%PLD—Number of Votes
0–20	21	64.78—147,692	30.55—63,923	
20–40.1	29	65.90—264,844	29.48—129,970	
40.1–60	15	60.97—150,736	32.53—70,741	
60–80	10	53.45—102,697	41.02—71,902	
80–100	2	27.24—94,188	63.34—158,034	
		Pearson's r/p-value −.410/.000	Pearson's r/p-value .383/.001	

1978

% Urban 82	Number of Municipalities	%PR— Number of Votes	%PRD— Number of Votes	%PLD— Number of Votes
0–20	21	53.03—121,663	41.27—99,898	0.46—979
20–40.1	29	51.13—228,248	43.29—217,287	0.54—3,578
40.1–60	15	49.88—128,953	45.09—133,934	0.50—2,072
60–80	10	46.55—89,092	48.42—123,250	0.98—2,880
80–100	2	24.68—130,207	69.65—281,396	1.58—8,866
		Pearson's r/p-value −.364/.001	Pearson's r/p-value .397/.000	Pearson's r/p-value .359/.001

1982

% Urban 82	Number of Municipalities	%PR— Number of Votes	%PRD— Number of Votes	%PLD— Number of Votes
0–20	21	45.81—126,418	44.02—114,391	4.47—11,361
20–40.1	29	42.85—215,554	43.64—226,172	5.91—40,456
40.1–60	15	37.79—124,264	50.32—146,891	5.13—22,936
60–80	10	34.53—80,560	49.05—116,903	9.40—39,988
80–100	2	19.78—121,380	53.06—250,511	21.88—65,108
		Pearson's r/p-value −.514/.000	Pearson's r/p-value .316/.005	Pearson's r/p-value .477/.00

1986

% Urban 82	Number of Municipalities	%PR(SC)— Number of Votes	%PRD— Number of Votes	%PLD— Number of Votes
0–20	21	48.82—138,146	37.20—107,579	9.63—25,512
20–40.1	29	46.34—256,698	39.87—214,816	11.35—81,941
40.1–60	15	44.97—163,859	41.28—143,581	10.47—56,141
60–80	10	40.93—106,350	39.43—96,676	16.65—79,675
80–100	2	29.45—209,194	35.88—237,881	33.41—144,744
		Pearson's r/p-value −.497/.000	Pearson's r/p-value .066/.571	Pearson's r/p-value .399/.000

1990

% Urban 82	Number of Municipalities	%PR(SC)—Number of Votes	%PRD—Number of Votes	%PLD—Number of Votes
0–20	21	37.41—94,849	25.04—62,607	26.63—72,586
20–40.1	29	34.79—175,242	24.56—123,099	29.97—181,499
40.1–60	15	37.38—116,684	24.50—77,428	26.35—107,474
60–80	10	34.90—84,895	26.12—57,087	30.68—112,017
80–100	2	25.72—175,946	23.59—123,865	43.08—179,702
		Pearson's r/p-value −.209/.068	Pearson's r/p-value .018/.878	Pearson's r/p-value .199/.082

1994

% Urban 82	Number of Municipalities	%PR(SC)—Number of Votes	%PRD—Number of Votes	%PLD—Number of Votes
0–20	21	46.03—150,453	38.80—128,324	9.41—31,397
20–40.1	29	43.98—315,718	38.61—275,895	10.91—95,762
40.1–60	15	43.17—223,191	41.38—203,570	9.35—60,071
60–80	10	42.03—186,846	40.70—171,241	12.24—76,751
80–100	2	38.01—386,471	39.87—409,380	17.81—131,812
		Pearson's r/p-value −.273/.016	Pearson's r/p-value .152/.184	Pearson's r/p-value .251/.028

1990 (with 1993 Urbanization)

% Urban 93	Number of Municipalities	%PR(SC)—Number of Votes	%PRD—Number of Votes	%PLD—Number of Votes
0–20	11	40.66—46,670	24.58—30,011	22.27—28,496
20–40.1	26	34.41—141,865	25.51—102,920	30.13—156,889
40.1–60	30	35.98—202,159	24.77—140,021	28.05—183,455
60–80	7	36.76—77,369	24.17—44,838	30.48—101,590
80–100+ StoDom	3	25.65—179,553	22.67—126,296	44.47—182,848
		Pearson's r/p-value −.233/.041	Pearson's r/p-value −.041/.723	Pearson's r/p-value .249/.029

1994 (with 1993 Urbanization)

% Urban 93	Number of Municipalities	%PR(SC)— Number of Votes	%PRD— Number of Votes	%PLD— Number of Votes
0–20	11	50.43—72,962	35.58—56,191	8.30—10,889
20–40.1	26	42.32—258,284	39.97—239,071	11.00—86,727
40.1–60	30	43.48—366,229	40.46—332,538	10.28—100,010
60–80	7	44.81—172,548	39.37—144,782	10.73—65,367
80–100+ StoDom	3	37.53—392,656	40.72—415,828	17.26—132,800
		Pearson's r/p-value −.305/.007	Pearson's r/p-value .179/.120	Pearson's r/p-value .235/.040

Note: Percentage was calculated as mean average of percentages for municipalities in each category. Since there are great variances in number of voters in each municipality, it is possible for one party to have a higher average percentage yet fewer votes than another party. This data is available from the author and will be archived at the University of North Carolina's Institute for Research in the Social Sciences.

Appendix B
Socioeconomic and Public-Sector Data

Table B.1. Comparative Socioeconomic Data

Country	Year	Gross Domestic Product per Capita	Illiteracy Rates (15 years and up)	% Labor in Agriculture	TVs per 1,000 Inhabitants	Air Passengers per 1,000 Inhabitants
Colombia	1960	927	27.1	50.1	19 (1965)	1,528
	1970	1,157	19.2	39.3	39	3,010
	1980	1,273	12.2 (c)	34.2	87	4,589
	1990	1,416	13.3	26 (1992)	108 (1989)	5,267
Costa Rica	1960	1,435	15.6	51.2	35 (1965)	155
	1970	1,825	11.6	42.5	58	256
	1980	1,759	7.4	30.8	106	403 (g)
	1990	1,667	7.2	24 (1992)	136 (1989)	467
Dominican Republic	1960	823	35.5	63.7	13 (1965)	43
	1970	987	33	54.7	23	129
	1980	761	31.4 (d, f)	45.7	72	392 (g)
	1990	716	16.7	33.9 (1992)	82 (1989)	718
El Salvador	1960	832	51	61.5	12 (1965)	37
	1970	1,032	42.9	56.0	26	138
	1980	1,325	32.7 (a)	43.2	63	266
	1990	1,091	27	35.5 (1992)	87 (1989)	525
Guatemala	1960	1,100	62.2	66.5	12 (1965)	62
	1970	1,420	54	61.2	14	113
	1980	1,085	44.2	56.9	25	119
	1990	892	44.9	58.1 (1993)	45 (1989)	156
Honduras	1960	619	55	70.3	1 (1965)	152
	1970	782	43.1	64.9	8	296
	1980	1,015	—	60.5	13	510
	1990	880	26.9	53.9 (1992)	70 (1989)	610

Table B.1. Continued

Country	Year	Gross Domestic Product per Capita	Illiteracy Rates (15 years and up)	% Labor in Agriculture	TVs per 1,000 Inhabitants	Air Passengers per 1,000 Inhabitants
Jamaica	1960	1,610	18.1	41.5	—	31
	1970	2,364	3.9 (a, e)	33.2	—	279
	1980	1,341	—	31.3	—	757
	1990	1,401	1.6	27.3 (1991)	—	1,004
Nicaragua	1960	1,055	50.4	61.8	9 (1965)	27
	1970	1,495	42.5	51.5	27	107
	1980	1,097	—	46.5	63	—
	1990	505	13 (1985)	35.4 (1992)	61 (1989)	130
Panama	1960	1,264	23.2	51	53 (1965)	72
	1970	2,017	18.7	41.6	—	307
	1980	2,287	12.9	31.8	112	364 (h)
	1990	1,938	11.2 (b)	23.7 (1992)	165 (1989)	205
Venezuela	1960	3,879	37.3 (d)	33.3	72 (1965)	804
	1970	4,941	23.5	26	—	757
	1980	3,851	15.3	16.1	114	5,144
	1990	3,038	10.2 (b)	10.2 (1991)	156 (1989)	6,847

Sources: GDP: *Statistical Abstract of Latin America*, vol. 30, pt. 2, 1993 (Los Angeles: UCLA Latin American Center, 1993). Based on national series converted to constant 1988 US dollars. Illiteracy rates: UN Economic Commission for Latin America, *Statistical Yearbook for Latin America and the Caribbean 1994* (Santiago, Chile: 1995). Percentage labor in agriculture (1960, 1970, 1980): UN Economic Commission for Latin America, *Statistical Yearbook for Latin America 1990* (Santiago, Chile: 1991). Percentage labor in agriculture (1990): *The Europa World Year Book 1994*, 2 vols. (London: Europa Publications, 1994). TVs: *Statistical Abstract of Latin America*, vol. 30, pt. 1, 1993 (Los Angeles: UCLA Latin American Center), 1993. Air passengers: *The Europa World Year Book 1994*. 2 vols. (London: Europa Publications, 1994).

[a]UNESCO estimate.
[b]1990 census.
[c]10 years and older.
[d]Excludes indigenous population living in forest.
[e]No schooling counted as illiterate.
[f]5 years and older.
[g]Refers to first nine months only.
[h]Does not include data on INAIR airline.

Table B.2. Selected Economic Indicators, 1976–1986

Indicator	1976	1977	1978	1979	1980	1981	1982	1983	1984	1985	1986
GDP growth, constant market prices	6.7	5.0	2.2	4.8	5.7	4.0	1.3	5.0	0.3	−1.9	3.0
Inflation, annual average	7.9	12.8	3.6	9.1	16.7	7.5	7.3	5.1	27.0	37.5	9.7
Real wages, average annual growth rate	na	na	na	na	−6.5	−7.4	−6.9	−6.5	1.5	−2.0	7.0
Merchandise, terms of trade index (1970=100)	100.2	89.5	85.5	86.6	103.2	106.0	72.7	78.9	83.4	na	na
Merchandise, terms of trade index (1980=100)	na	na	na	na	100	114.4	87.9	87.8	89.8	78.2	83.1
Export of goods (US$ million)	—	—	—	869	962	1,188	768	785	868	739	722
Import of goods (US$ million)	—	—	—	1,094	1,520	1,452	1,257	1,279	1,257	1,286	1,352
Exchange rate	1.0	1.0	1.0	1.0	1.0	1.0	1.0	1.0	1.0	3.6	2.9
Real effective exchange rate	—	—	—	—	100.0	98.7	97.4	102.9	140.9	128.8	137.7
Disbursed total external debt[1]	—	—	1,332	1,602	1,967	2,256	2,462	2,896	3,056	3,276	3,288
U.S. assistance, grants, and loans[1]	—	—	7.0	75.4	70.1	43.1	87.9	69.7	104.6	179.8	107.8

Table B.2. Continued

Indicator	1976	1977	1978	1979	1980	1981	1982	1983	1984	1985	1986
Assistance from international organizations[1,2]	—	—	—	—	—	119.9	na	168.4	119.2	193.3	na

Sources: (UN/ECLAC = United Nations, Economic Commission for Latin America and the Caribbean; SALA = *Statistical Abstract of Latin America* [Los Angeles: UCLA Latin American Center]). GDP growth: UN/ECLAC, *Statistical Yearbook* (1981, 1121 for 1976–79; 1988, 64 for 1980–84; 1992, 68 for 1985–89; 1994, 72 for 1990–93). Inflation: UN/ECLAC, *Statistical Yearbook* (1981, 153 for 1976–79, Santo Domingo only; 1988, 94–95 for 1980–84; 1992, 98–99 for 1985–91; 1994, 102–3 for 1992–93). Real wages, Inter-American Development Bank (1994, 75 for 1984–93). Government employment excludes CDE and CEA, from World Bank (1987b, 250); second row from Alemán (1994, 80). Terms of trade (1970=100): UN/ECLA, *Statistical Yearbook* (1983, 510–11 for 1975–77; 1985, 528–29 for 1978–84). Terms of trade (1980=100): UN/ECLA, *Statistical Yearbook* (1991, 498–99 for 1980–83; 1992, 510–11 for 1984–86; 1994, 518–19 for 1987–93). Exports and imports: Inter-American Development Bank (1982, 233 for 1979; 1990, 94 for 1980–83; 1994, 75 for 1984–93). Exchange rates: Inter-American Development Bank (1990, 94 for 1980–83; 1994, 75 for 1984–93). External debt, 1978–86: Inter-American Development Bank (1988, 580). U.S. assistance: SALA (vol. 31, pt. 2: 891). International assistance: SALA (vol. 31, pt. 2: 883).

[1]Current US$ million.
[2]The World Bank, the Inter-American Development Bank, the United Nations, and the United Nations Development Program.

Table B.3. Selected Economic Indicators, 1986–1993

Indicator	1986	1987	1988	1989	1990	1991	1992	1993
GDP growth, constant market prices	3.0	8.4	1.5	4.1	−5.0	0.5	6.8	2.3
Inflation, annual average	9.7	15.9	44.4	45.4	59.4	53.9	4.6	4.8
Real wages, average annual growth rate	7.0	−2.3	4.0	−11.0	−4.6	6.0	15.0	5.0p[1]
Minimum wage:								
FTZs—Nominal	250.00	288.75	436.25	527.00	804.05	1,040.00	1,144.00	—
FTZs—Real (1980)	107.55	107.18	112.11	93.13	89.13	74.92	78.79	—
Public sec.—nom.	250.00	250.00	336.25	418.00	559.25	780.00	780.00	—
Public sec.—real	107.55	92.79	86.41	73.87	62.00	56.19	53.72	—
Merchandise, terms of trade (1980=100)	83.1	78.8	85.6	74.3	60.3	59.1	53.8	51.4
Export of goods (US$ million)	722	711	890	924	734	658	566	530
Import of goods (US$ million)	1,352	1,592	1,608	1,964	1,793	1,729	2,178	2,115
Exchange rate	2.9	3.8	6.1	6.3	8.5	12.7	12.8	12.7p
Real effective exchange rate	137.7	164.9	196.9	157.7	152.8	142.8	142.0	136.7p
Disbursed total external debt[2]	3,687	3,923	3,991	4,053	4,387	4,494	4,649	4,024
Debt as % of GDP	77.9	92.8	80.6	69.6	67.8	52.6	52.7	42.4
U.S. assistance, grants, and loans[2]	107.8	42.7	60.0	83.9	33.6	33.9	24.2	—
Assistance from intl. organizations[2,3]	—	142.7	108.4	200.7	8.0	140.6	4.9	—

Sources: Same as appendix B.2, except (1) disbursed total external debt: Inter-American Development Bank (1994, 75 for 1984–1993). This more recent source cites higher debt levels for the Dominican Republic for each year reported than in Inter-American Development Bank (1988), cited in the previous table. And (2) debt as percentage of GDP: Inter-American Development Bank (1994, table 7). Minimum wage data from Inter-American Development Bank (1994, table B.5).

[1]p = preliminary.
[2]Current US$ million.
[3]The World Bank, the Inter-American Development Bank, the United Nations, and the United Nations Development Program.

Table B.4. Selected Public-Sector Indicators, 1976–1986

Indicator	1976	1977	1978	1979	1980	1981	1982	1983	1984	1985	1986
Public-sector accounts as % GDP (next 3 rows)											
Current revenue	28.0	25.2	23.2	22.6	25.2	25.0	21.4	23.1	24.2	25.7	—
Current expenditures (wages, goods, and services)	7.9	7.2	8.5	9.7	10.1	10.0	9.6	9.6	8.6	8.2	—
Capital formation	6.0	6.2	5.2	5.1	5.4	4.6	4.2	3.5	3.7	4.7	—
Total fiscal surplus or deficit	−0.7	−1.3	−5.4	−5.1	−6.5	−5.8	−7.1	−5.3	−3.5	−0.8	—
Office of the presidency/ central govt. expenditures (% GDP)					13.7	14.9	11.5	15.8	12.3	26.2	31.9
Tax revenues (% GDP)	13.6	12.8	11.7	11.3	10.8	10.4	8.5	9.1	9.7	15.1	13.9
Taxes on imports (% of total taxes)	34.7	34.9	38.4	35.6	31.9	24.5	25.9	29.7	29.6	24.1	27.2
Taxes on exports (% of total taxes)	12.6	15.4	7.2	8.7	8.3	11.7	1.5	0.8	1.8	28.1	10.7
General government employment (thousands)	116.7	122.0	129.2	170.0	187.2	193.9	201.3	204.3	210.6	219.2	218.2

Source: World Bank (1987b, 242); tax income from Dauhajre hijo (1989, 87–89); presidency and central government expenditures from Banco Central, *Boletín Mensual*, various issues.

Table B.5. The Public Sector under Balaguer, 1986–1994

	1986	1987	1988	1989	1990	1991	1992	1993	1994
Public-sector revenues (% GDP)				17.0	12.6	14.9	17.2	18.2	—
Tax revenues (% GDP)					9.6	9.3	12.1	12.7	—
Foreign trade taxes					3.8	3.9	5.7	5.6	—
Petroleum differential					—	1.9	1.7	2.0	
Fiscal balance (% GDP)				−7.4	−4.7	0.1	1.3	−0.2	−2.9
Public-sector employment	218,084	201,910	195,302	191,302	188,500	186,998	—	253,949	266,945

Sources: Fiscal balance: Dauhajre hijo and Aristy Escuder (1996, 12). Employment: Alemán (1994, 80 for 1986–91); "BC Dice Gobierno Tiene 266,326 Empleados," *El Caribe* (Aug. 11, 1996, 9A for 1993–94). Public-sector revenues and tax revenues from World Bank (1995b).

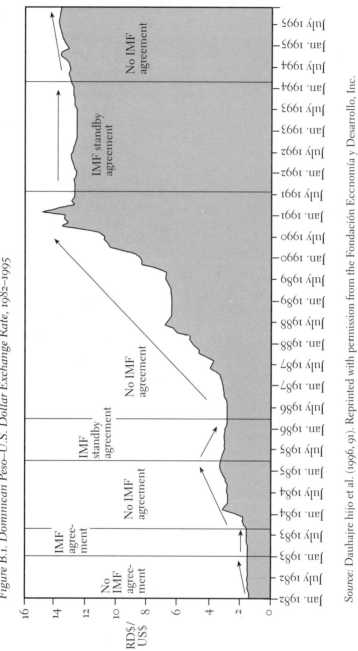

Figure B.1. Dominican Peso–U.S. Dollar Exchange Rate, 1982–1995

Source: Dauhajre hijo et al. (1996, 91). Reprinted with permission from the Fondación Eccnomía y Desarrollo, Inc.

Notes

Chapter 1

1. See the discussion in Collier (1993) and in Ragin (1987). Collier reviews literature about how the usefulness of case studies may be expanded by making "within-case" comparisons and how, in these and other circumstances, case studies may be employed to test hypotheses as well as to generate them. Ragin notes the tension inherent in seeking explanations "that are general but also show an appreciation of complexity." As he writes: "An appreciation of complexity sacrifices generality; an emphasis on generality encourages a neglect of complexity. It is difficult to have both" (54). Case-oriented research focuses more on complexity, whereas variable-oriented research focuses more on generality.

2. Most of the explanations that have been actor- and process-centered and emphasized agency over structure in the recent literature have focused on democratic transitions. In particular, see O'Donnell and Schmitter (1986). Criticisms of this literature include Bermeo (1990) and Remmer (1991). Karl (1990) has emphasized the need to bring the two together. Within the international relations literature, there are excellent discussions of agency-structure problems (see Wendt 1987; Dessler 1989; and Mahoney and Snyder 1993).

3. Although it seeks to integrate both structure and agency, this is a somewhat more "voluntarist" approach, as it does not presume that structural factors determine political behavior; it also views structures, institutions, and culture as providing opportunities for action as well as constraints. A good discussion of different types of "voluntarist" and "structuralist" approaches is in Mahoney and Snyder (1993).

4. An excellent synthesis of some of this research is Brea et al. (1995); for a similar observation about the need to transcend these kinds of approaches, see Espinal (1987a: 11–13). See also the list of scholars in the preface and works by them cited in the reference section.

5. A useful definition of a "political regime" (or "regime" for short) is found in Collier and Collier (1991, 789): "The formal and informal structure of state and governmental roles and processes. The regime includes the method of selection of the government and representative assemblies (election, coup, decision within the military, etc.), formal and informal mechanisms of representation, and patterns of repression." They go on to note that a regime is distinguished analytically from the individuals who occupy key posts, from the coalition of groups that supports it, and from the policies adopted by them.

6. This definition comes from Hartlyn and Valenzuela (1994). With regard to the

dimensions of public contestation and inclusiveness, it is indebted to the influential work by Dahl (1971). See also the discussion in Linz (1978) and O'Donnell and Schmitter (1986).

7. With regard to the first and third of these tensions, using another conceptualization, Rueschemeyer, Stephens, and Stephens (1992) discuss the need to maintain two different "balances of power" for democracy: within civil society and between the state and civil society. The analytical point is similar, though. As societies evolve, these relations will be in a continual process of change, and efforts to attain "optimum" balances will be ongoing.

8. For an extensive review and careful analysis of various ways of defining democracy and creating subtypes, see Collier and Levitsky (1997). The definition of democracy presented above most closely approximates what they consider to be a procedural, minimum definition that has been expanded to incorporate "the criterion that elected governments must have effective power to govern" (434). The central empirical issue distinguishing the expanded definition from the basic one usually concerns whether elected officials have a reasonably effective control over the military.

9. This definition does not preclude the need to examine whether and how inequalities in society or in weak states with an impoverished rule of law may impact the possibility of political democracy or its nature. The links across imperfect democratic regimes, weak states, and unequal societal structures are complex, and advances and regressions across these three dimensions are not necessarily synchronized with each other.

10. My conceptualizations of neopatrimonial and hybrid regimes build upon writings focused on cases other than the Dominican Republic to preclude making what could be construed as circular or tautological arguments.

11. For O'Donnell's valuable concept of "delegative democracies," see O'Donnell (1992; 1994). In these articles he applies this concept to a number of South American countries, such as Argentina, Brazil, and Peru, historically marked by both neopatrimonial and corporatist features, where the former have been strengthened and the latter dramatically weakened as a result of the collapse of the import-substitution model of industrialization, the debt crisis, economic globalization, and the prolonged crisis of the state. To the extent that the concept of "delegative democracy" also embodies a theory regarding its emergence (based on a response to a critical juncture of multiple crises in these cases), it is less applicable to the Dominican Republic, where historical path-dependent elements are more important. The Dominican Republic's historical trajectory is marked both by more extreme neopatrimonial features and the near absence of corporatism in an overall context of much weaker popular-sector actors and of a weaker state than in these South American countries. Thus, contemporary neopatrimonial features in the Dominican Republic are much less tied either to declines in levels of social organization or to efforts to regain state capacity in the context of socioeconomic crisis than in the countries discussed by O'Donnell. As explained in the text below, analyses of key social, structural, and political features of African neopatrimonial regimes provide valuable insights for the Dominican case.

12. Hybridization may take more the form of consociational, restricted democracies, where constraints on contestation more than military impositions on civilian authority

are the central issue; nonconsolidation of democratic regimes may result less from "delegative" regime features and more due to a crisis of the state as the regime seeks to further democratize. For both of these, Colombia would serve as an empirical example (see Hartlyn 1988).

13. The relevance of the concept of neopatrimonialism to an understanding of the Dominican Republic has been noted by other authors, particularly with regard to the nineteenth century (e.g., see Hoetink 1982; and Cross Beras 1984). On the more recent period, see Oszlak (1984); employing the term in a somewhat different manner, see Corten (1993, esp. 186, 202–5) and also Brea (1995, 26–29).

14. This conceptualization is derived from Bratton and van de Walle (1994); Theobold (1982); Snyder (1992, 379); Medard (1982); Eisenstadt (1973); and Brynen (1995). To the extent neopatrimonial regimes base their legitimacy on law, regime actors are vulnerable to accusations of corruption. For a useful discussion and conceptualization of corruption—viewed broadly as the deviation from public norms (usually understood as "laws") for private gain—see Scott (1972, 3–9).

A number of analyses tend to focus more on the second attribute of neopatrimonialism noted in the text relating to public authority that blurs public roles and private purposes, downplaying the issue of effective centralization of authority through personalized power (e.g., Hutchcroft 1991). Certainly, a common historical route toward neopatrimonial regimes (or the more extreme neosultanistic ones discussed below) is to emerge from, build on, co-opt, and/or dominate these more decentralized patronage networks (as Hutchcroft discusses for the Philippines under Ferdinand Marcos, and as is also relevant for the Dominican Republic). And, if a neopatrimonial ruler begins to lose control (or even if in a transition period another type of ruler seeks, imperfectly, to impose more of a rule of law), a possible outcome is toward a more decentralized form of plunder from the state. Furthermore, in some countries, there may be significant and long-lasting regional variations regarding the importance of clientelist relations and patronage networks in dominating political relationships and state-society relations. As crucial as it is to incorporate these neopatrimonial elements into the political analysis of these countries or regions, it would stretch the concept excessively to characterize lacking a central personalized neopatrimonial authority as also having neopatrimonial regimes, though some more intermediate characterization might be appropriate.

More problematic are those analyses that have focused on the issue of personalized central authority, without considering whether there is the lack of any kind of rule of law and the blurring of public and private roles. This would stretch the concept excessively in the other direction. Regimes that do not possess this second characteristic are not fruitfully considered neopatrimonial. For that reason, I reject the characterization of General Augusto Pinochet in Chile as a neopatrimonial ruler, in the otherwise often insightful article by Remmer (1989). Further reason for this rejection may be found in the way the transition from Pinochet's rule was realized—with considerably more respect for the rules, however arbitrary and undemocratic they were, by both the exiting regime and the incoming administration than was the case in the Dominican Republic (for a brief discussion of the Chilean transition, see Linz and Stepan 1996, 205–18).

15. The analysis in chapter 2 also highlights how these factors can help explain the emergence of different types of neopatrimonial regimes.

16. On the impact of the rule of law on how bureaucracies should function, see Bendix (1962, 423–30). For a valuable discussion of how, "beyond the issue of inequalities and social cleavages (as against the democratization of access to power)," clientelism can continue to prosper in the absence of protected constitutional rights, based on the Italian case, see Rosetti (1994, quotation on 87). In neopatrimonial regimes, all of these social, political, and legal problems are present.

17. This may help to explain why so many narratives of Dominican politics have focused on individuals as the key explanatory variable, and also why this text does so at different points.

18. Linz's initial inspiration for differentiating the more institutionalized form of authoritarianism, for which Spain was his paradigmatic case, from this other type of authoritarian rule—which he termed "sultanism" building on Weber—came in part from information about Trujillo and the Dominican Republic from Jesús de Galíndez (Chehabi, 1995). Galíndez was a Spanish exile who had lived in the Dominican Republic from 1940 to 1946; his March 1956 abduction from New York and assassination on Trujillo's orders following the completion of his critical doctoral dissertation at Columbia University on the Trujillo regime helped galvanize international opposition to Trujillo.

19. Because these kinds of regimes in the twentieth century inevitably have had elements of legal-rational order and of a legitimizing ideology, rather than being perversions of traditional rule, it is not appropriate to retain the term "sultanism." For a view that concurs with the former point but argues for keeping the term unchanged, see Chehabi (1995).

20. These issues are further elaborated in the discussion of the framework for analysis of transitions presented in the opening pages of chapter 3.

Chapter 2

1. By the seventeenth century the Spanish were referring to the island more as Hispaniola, rather than Española, as before; and they called the eastern section Santo Domingo, in keeping with their practice of calling islands and colonies by the name of the major port city (Knight 1990, 54).

2. This population consisted overwhelmingly of free mulattos and poor whites. Decades of poverty, combined with recent war and devastation, had "relegated the racial problem to insignificance. . . . The important thing was not to be wholly black—or, at least, not black enough to be taken for a slave or a Haitian" (Moya Pons 1985, 252).

3. Haiti's policies toward the eastern half of the island were induced in part by international financial pressures. In return for French recognition of Haitian independence in an 1825 treaty, Haiti promised an indemnification of French settlers of 150 million francs as well as commercial concessions. This soon forced Haiti to borrow money from French banks and led to efforts at domestic taxation and export promotion that were strongly resisted on both sides of the island.

4. The British abolished the slave trade in 1808 and legally abolished slavery in all

their colonies in 1834. France and Denmark did so in 1848 and the Dutch in 1863. Spain abolished slavery in Puerto Rico in 1873 and in Cuba only in 1886. Once slavery was abolished in Cuba, legal slavery came to an end in the Caribbean (Knight 1990, 167).

5. La Trinitaria was a movement based on three-person cells, but its name clearly evoked the Holy Trinity. Its motto was *Dios, Patria y Libertad* ("God, Country and Liberty"), and the movement's flag and shield had a cross and an open Bible—all of which became national symbols. Dominican nationality became defined in religious and Hispanic terms, which permitted contrast with Haiti. Perhaps because the Catholic Church was relatively weak in their country and because the country's principal enemy was the anti-Catholic and non-Spanish-speaking Haiti, Dominican liberals too were largely pro-church, in contrast to their counterparts in the rest of Central and South America (Martínez-Fernández 1995, 71–75).

6. Two excellent sources for this period are Hoetink (1982, 287–98) and Moya Pons (1983, 281–426 passim). Santana, the country's first military caudillo, served as president from 1844 to 1848, for a few months in 1849, from 1853 to 1856, and, after overthrowing Báez in coalition with forces from the Cibao (whom Santana eventually marginalized), from 1858 to 1862, a period during which Spain reannexed the country with Santana's urging. Báez served as president a total of five times, including the periods of 1849–53 and 1856–58.

7. Hispaniola lay in a very strategic location for several critical passageways in the Caribbean, and this fact affected Dominican history for the rest of the nineteenth century. Dominicans, believing Samaná Bay in the northeastern part of the island was attractive to major powers as a naval base and coaling station, sought to employ it as a bargaining asset in negotiations regarding protection or annexation. Samaná was briefly leased to the United States in 1869, when annexation was being debated, but it never became a naval base. Dominicans, including Trujillo, took a long time in recognizing its declining value in the twentieth century.

8. On Báez more generally and on why Hispanophile Dominican historians have tended to favor Santana over the mulatto Báez, see Sang (1991, esp. 187–99). As one historian has noted, in three key instances (the 1844 independence movement, an insurrection against Báez in 1857–58, and the "War of Restoration" to oust Spain in 1863–65) northern Cibao liberal intelligentsia played a major leadership role. Yet, leaders from the Cibao, economically the country's most dynamic region, ultimately failed to control the central government which fell into the hands of figures from the southern and eastern parts of the country, who were better able to develop military power through their patron-client relations (Martínez-Fernández 1993, 594).

9. Heureaux used large numbers of spies to control the country's population; co-opted or bribed many of his opponents, sending others into exile or murdering them; arranged for enemies overseas to be murdered; and massively enriched himself and his coterie through extensive corruption. See Wiarda (1975, 221); for a useful biographical sketch, see Cross Beras (1984, 145–53), and for a somewhat less harsh assessment and periodization of his rule, see Sang (1996b).

Numerous others have noted the similarities between Heureaux and Trujillo, beginning with none other than Heureaux's son, who published the "first great panegyric to Rafael Trujillo, in which he pointed out the similarities between the latter and his father" (Hoetink 1982, 122–23, esp. quotation on 122). For a fascinating fictional dialogue between Heureaux and Trujillo, see Vega (1988a).

10. As Hoetink notes, this confusion between the president, the state, and the country in both political and economic terms was not unique to Heureaux's regime; he also cites Weber's concept of patrimonialism (1982, 81). The rest of this paragraph is drawn from Hoetink (1982, 74–77).

11. The country's first modern sugarcane operation, for example, was established by a Cuban exile in 1875 and involved a capital expenditure considerably larger than the Dominican national budget of that year (Murphy 1991, chap. 2). An excellent review of these changes over the period 1890–1930 is Abel (1985).

12. For details on Heaureaux's financial dealings and the scandalous behavior of nearly all the actors involved, see Cross Beras (1984, 173–239).

13. Perhaps the first of many subsequent U.S. or international election-observation missions designed to help insure free and fair elections in the country had taken place in the previous elections of December 1913. The U.S. minister had arranged a truce in October between warring factions and had extracted their pledge to hold elections for local offices and a constituent assembly, to which the United States ultimately sent three official delegates and three dozen additional observers over the protests of many of the candidates. The United States declared that if these elections were not carried out properly, it would assume direct control of the subsequent ones. Indeed, the subsequent planned presidential elections could not be realized due to continuing rebellions, which ultimately led the United States to take the actions described in the text (see Campillo Pérez 1982, 148–52).

14. Dominican historians and social scientists continue to debate when it can be argued that the Dominican state emerged and consolidated. For example, Betances (1995a; 1995b) emphasizes the importance of socioeconomic and political processes dating from the mid and especially the late nineteenth century; and Catrain and Oviedo (1981) assert that consolidation occurred during the period of the U.S. occupation. Building on Lowenthal (1969b) and especially on Espinal (1987a, 39, 47–48), I would acknowledge the periods of Heureaux and of U.S. occupation as important for state building, but would argue the national state was consolidated under the Trujillo era.

15. The strategic issue in the Dominican Republic is highlighted by Moya Pons (1983, 472); in a careful analysis of U.S.-German relations in the first decades of the twentieth century, Nancy Mitchell (1996a; 1996b) explains that U.S. strategists and top leaders feared German expansion into the hemisphere and that these fears were accentuated by the actual strength of the German navy and the ambiguity of pronouncements by German leaders, but that, in fact, German actions in the region were extremely cautious. Calder (1984, 259–60, n. 69) notes the lack of reference to the German question until after the occupation. On liberal interventionism, see Calder (1984, 22–23); see also Hunt (1987, 125–35) for a discussion of the common roots, differences, and "strikingly similar direction" (131) of the Latin American policies of Presidents Theodore Roosevelt and Woodrow Wilson. As Knight (1990, 224) notes, U.S. policy toward the Dominican Republic and Haiti diverged because of racist attitudes—in the words of one State Department official, "counsel [rather] than con-

trol" was possible in the Dominican Republic because of the "preponderance of white blood and culture," whereas Haiti would require "as complete a rule by Americans as possible . . . for a long period of time" because the Haitians "are negro for the most part . . . and almost in a state of savagery and complete ignorance."

16. See Calder (1984, xix) and also Schmidt (1971, esp. 13–16). Schmidt notes the "American policy of pragmatic, materialistic uplift in Haiti was conceptually rooted" both in the Progressive reform movement in the United States as well as in "enlightened British colonial experience" (13). Yet, he also notes this "materialistic approach fit the methods and priorities dictated by selfish American purposes, and also conformed to American prejudices, which held that Haitians were incapable of political and intellectual achievements" (13). The hope was that progress in terms of self-government would follow eventually once the necessary material bases for civilization had been established. On U.S. expansion into sugar, see Murphy (1991, chap. 2).

17. Crassweller (1966, 69–70); electoral figures from Galíndez (1973, 19). As mentioned in Crassweller and cited in Galíndez, the U.S. minister in the country at the time asserted Trujillo's vote total exceeded the number of voters in the country. In fact, subsequent elections under Trujillo would never admit to the abstention rate reported for these elections.

18. See Gleijeses (1978, 20); Moya Pons (1983, 491). Sumner Welles was well aware of the risk (Welles, 1966). He wrote circa 1928: "Because of its efficiency the Policía Nacional is a body far more potent than the old army ever was" (908). Yet, he saw that risk more from the civilian side: "It is only through the settled conviction of the governors of the country that their own interest as well as the safety of the nation lies in the maintenance of this branch of the service completely apart from politics, that the national security of the Dominican Republic may be assured" (909). See also the discussions in Goldwert (1962) and Atkins and Wilson (1972, 44–46).

19. In contrast, President Roosevelt agreed to see Trujillo, but only in a private meeting; Trujillo's meeting with Secretary of State Cordell Hull was also quite formal (Vega 1985, 159–60; Crassweller 1966, 172–75).

20. The following pages are derived from Hartlyn (1998b).

21. See Vega (1992, 464; 1986c, 860). The increasingly corrupt and venal qualities of these types of regimes as their sultanistic tendencies increase over time mean they often are unable to respond adequately to natural disasters, which has a profound negative impact on their stability (on Somoza and the 1972 earthquake in Nicaragua, see Booth 1995). In contrast, in 1930 Trujillo dealt effectively with the cyclone, even as he was able to employ it to his political advantage, centralizing power and resources.

22. His penchant for statues of himself in public places has already been noted in chapter 1. When he served as president in the 1950s, he was officially referred to as "His Excellency, the Generalissimo, Doctor Rafael Leonidas Trujillo Molina, Honorable President of the Republic, Benefactor of the Nation, Restorer of the Financial Independence of the Country, and Commander in Chief of the Armed Forces."

23. See Moya Pons (1990a, 511–12). It should be noted that the ability of Trujillo to become the richest man in the country after only four years reflected in part the relative poverty of the country's oligarchy as much as the effectiveness of Trujillo's efforts.

24. In 1956, the vast holdings of the U.S.-owned West Indies Sugar Company were purchased by Trujillo in his name for US$35.8 million, including an initial US$10 million down payment, which drew upon state resources. The public debt of the two major state banks increased dramatically, helping to stimulate further deterioration of the country's economic situation at the time. See Vega (1990b, 602).

25. For a discussion of "elections" under Trujillo, see Galíndez (1973, 94–101).

26. The March 1956 kidnapping and assassination of the Spanish (Basque) exile Jesús de Galíndez who had completed a doctoral dissertation at Columbia University harshly analyzing Trujillo the month before, became an international cause célèbre— even as Galíndez's manuscript, one copy of which evaded Trujillo's agents, became a best-seller throughout Latin America. In 1957, following the December 1956 murder of the U.S. pilot who had transported Galíndez to the Dominican Republic, the case became a source of growing tension between the United States and the Trujillo regime.

27. The U.S. naval attaché ended a 1940 report on the Dominican military on this note. See Vega (1992, 243).

28. The record year for military expenditures was 1959, as the regime found itself increasingly besieged. In that year, even as the overall government budget contracted (from DR$164.9 million in 1958 to DR$155.7 million), 26.4 percent of the total budget was earmarked to the armed forces and an additional 9.6 percent to the police (DR$56 million total). In the subsequent two years, as the government budget continued to contract (to DR$143.7 million in 1960 and DR$137.2 million in 1961), the amounts devoted to the armed forces and police did as well (to DR$44.1 million in 1960 and DR$40.6 million in 1961). Data from the Oficina Nacional de Planificación (1968, 445, 459, 480).

29. Vega (1992, 353, 372 on promotions; 227, 240, 307 on plots); see also Crassweller (1966, 130).

30. Bernardo Vega (letter to author, September 1994) has lowered his original estimate of the number of deaths from 12,000 to less than 5,000.

31. Following the massacre, important intellectuals at the service of Trujillo, such as Manuel Arturo Peña Batlle and Joaquín Balaguer, articulated an anti-Haitian rhetoric. For example, in an essay written in 1944 and translated into English, which never mentions the 1937 massacre, Joaquín Balaguer (1949) provides an extensive defense of Trujillo as the organizer of Dominican nationality and statehood because of his essential efforts in the areas of population, territory, and sovereignty. The first two are related basically to the issue of Haiti, and the book includes a section as an appendix entitled "Invasions and Acts of Vandalism Perpetrated by Haiti Against the Dominican Republic." The book explains why the Dominican authorities wanted to stem Haitian immigration, including such reasons as "the loss of its national character," "the disappearance of its customs and the undermining of its morality," "the danger of totally losing the purity of its original appearance," and the hopes the authorities had that they could attract "a powerful migratory stream formed of Caucasian elements" (145). Many of these charges and others were repeated some thirty-five years later (Balaguer 1983).

Trujillo's obsession with race even led him to use face whiteners to lighten his skin (he had Haitian, Afro-Caribbean ancestry through his maternal grandmother) (Crassweller 1966, 84–85; Murphy 1991, 132).

32. For a valuable analysis of the major themes of "Trujillo's ideology" and of the key intellectuals behind them, see Mateo (1993). See also Moya Pons (1990a, 517); Espinal (1987a, 51–77); Sáez (1988, 89–104); Murphy (1991, 129–44).

33. President Vásquez, prior to 1930, usually sought to obtain U.S. approval in advance for all expenditures for capital improvements. Crassweller (1966, 182).

34. The Dominican Republic was the last country in which the United States retained a customs receivership, and even after the treaty was signed, all funds collected by Dominican customs were deposited in the Dominican branch of a U.S. bank representing foreign bondholders, to distribute the funds between them and the Dominican government. In a careful review of Trujillo's actions, Bernardo Vega (1990b, esp. ii–iii, 451) deflates much of the nationalist aura that still pervades common views of Trujillo's financial actions. He argues that these actions during the 1930s probably prevented the debt from being paid off before 1947 (and perhaps even at discounted rates and with additional commercial concessions), and that Trujillo left the country saddled with extensive debt that was not greater primarily because the United States refused several loan requests from his regime. Both the 1940 convention and the 1947 cancellation of the country's debt imitated steps taken by Haiti, in the first case some six years earlier, in the second some five days before. Although the monetary system established in 1947 was solid, Trujillo was able to manipulate it for his own personal benefit. See also Moya Pons (1990a, 516–17).

35. See Wiarda (1975, 439–54); Moya Pons (1986, 65–68). Moya Pons estimates that Trujillo's material beneficence toward the church was worth around US$26 million. As explained below, in the 1980s and 1990s, Balaguer was also to receive the sometimes crucial support of the archbishop of Santo Domingo (and eventually cardinal), and he rewarded him and the official church with extensive construction and other projects.

36. All the country's constitutions and numerous other government and literary documents were published in 1944 as part of the "Trujillo Collection" during the centenary of the country's independence from Haiti. For the constitutional texts, see Gobierno Dominicano (1944).

37. An extremely rare successful strike broke out in the sugar lands of La Romana and San Pedro de Macorís in January 1946. The leader of that strike, Mauricio Báez, was killed apparently on Trujillo's orders four years later while in exile in Cuba.

In spite of Trujillo's initial opposition, Dominican sugar mills continued to exploit Haitian labor to cut cane, bringing Haitians across the border for the harvest and then returning them. This contrasts sharply with the case of Cuba, where beginning in 1933 the cheap foreign labor was gradually deported and Cubans, increasingly organized and better paid, began to cut cane: one thing that made this possible was that much larger quantities of Cuban sugar entered the U.S. market under a preferential price. See Vega (1990a, 115–26).

38. To make matters even more confusing, there is an alternative form of the argument, cast in the language of path-dependency by the economic historian Douglass North (1990). He argues that the one kind of critical discontinuous change is that which results from conquest or revolution, and that the evolution of North America

and Latin America differ radically from the beginning of their colonization because of the imposition of very different institutional patterns from the mother country upon the colonies: "persistence of the institutional pattern that had been imposed by Spain and Portugal continued to play a fundamental role in the evolution of Latin American policies and perceptions and to distinguish that continent's history, despite the imposition after independence of a set of rules similar to the British institutional tradition that shaped the path of North America" (103). This same kind of view is evident in Putnam (1993, chap. 5), which also presents path-dependency as a form of an "iron law of history," not dissimilar in consequence from other kinds of idealist or materialist "destined-pathway" interpretations. In a panel discussion at the 1994 convention of the American Political Science Association, Putnam acknowledged that though he would still argue that the weight of history matters for outcomes today, his argument should have paid more attention to potential turning points, as history does not move in a straight line. I am much more sympathetic to this latter view of history and to the notion, advanced at the same panel by Stephen Krasner, that history is often important because the past is a key source of salient cultural solutions, not because the past ineluctably imposes a "tradition."

39. In Valenzuela's view, Chile's constitutional formula succeeded at an early stage in substituting—in Weberian terms described in chapter 1—rational-legal authority (an elected president, whose power in office was derived from law) for traditional authority (a hereditary monarch, whose power was inherent by generations-old, divinely ordained practices), marking a sharp institutional discontinuity with its colonial past. This contrasts with others' arguments that what set Chile apart was that "exotic liberalism" was avoided and that a Spanish patrimonial state was "recreated" with only minimal concessions to Anglo-French constitutionalism (Morse 1964, 163–64, cited in Valenzuela 1989, 173). In a comparative perspective, there may not be a total contradiction between these views. Morse (1964) may overplay the degree of continuity with the past and miss the radical shift in the basis of legitimation of authority in Chile, but it *is* important that in Chile (as in Costa Rica) "liberalism" (whether exotic, exaggerated, or otherwise) did not initially overreach and fail dramatically, beginning a cycle of "failed liberalism" that so marked the history of other Latin American countries, including the Dominican Republic.

40. The contrast between more deterministic "destined-pathway" arguments and "path-dependency" ones is discussed in Mahoney and Snyder (1993), building on Fulbrook and Skocpol (1984).

41. See Levine (1989, 250–52). Renewed attention is being paid to the potential role of warfare, geopolitics, and forms of military organization in inhibiting democratic evolution in the very different European context as well. Downing (1992), in an argument that rejects a culturalist or idealist view of democratic evolution in Europe, asserts "medieval European states had numerous institutions, procedures, and arrangements that . . . provided the basis for democracy in ensuing centuries . . . [but] constitutional countries confronted by a dangerous international situation mandating extensive domestic resource mobilization suffered the destruction of constitutionalism and the rise of military-bureaucratic absolutism" (9).

42. For one of the best analyses of this type, focusing on the "overdetermining

influence of imperialism" on the Dominican Republic, see Cassá (1979, quotation on 17); for his own subsequent critical self-reflection on the need to "overcome reductionist explanations," see Cassá (1996, quotation on 25).

43. Haiti became (after the United States) the second independent state in the Western Hemisphere. But independence for the rest of the Caribbean would be a difficult, protracted affair. The Dominican Republic was the next Caribbean state to gain its independence, whether dated from 1844 or 1865 (see Knight 1990, 211).

44. The issue of the 1965 U.S. intervention will be examined in more detail in the next chapter.

45. The Cuban case is an intermediate one in this scheme. It is one in which initially strong sugar elites were devastated by war and then, over the first three decades of the twentieth century, increasingly sold their interests to U.S. investors; in turn, the U.S. was important in helping to establish the Cuban military, but Batista was never a neosultanistic ruler. Indeed, compared to Trujillo, his rule in the 1950s was not especially repressive; compared to those he overthrew, it was not much more corrupt (based on Louis Pérez, personal communication, 1995).

46. In the introduction to Chehabi and Linz (1998), Linz has defined "semi-opposition" as "those groups that are not dominant or represented in the governing group but that are willing to participate in power without fundamentally challenging the system."

Chapter 3

1. From 1899 to 1905, there were ten governments: four that lasted a month or less and two others that survived less than a year. The president who entered office in December 1905, Ramón Cáceres, was assassinated in November 1911, unleashing a new wave of political instability (see Ventura 1985, 35–44).

2. Background structural factors will be mentioned here, but not highlighted. As noted in chapter 1, relatively low levels of economic development and high levels of societal inequality often mutually reinforce neopatrimonial political patterns; these socioeconomic patterns were clearly present in the Dominican Republic. However, the central thrust of this and the next chapter is to examine the links from regime, institutional, and international geopolitical patterns to the success or failure of democratic transitions; those links from socioeconomic factors to institutional patterns will be considered in chapter 5.

3. The following discussion builds especially on Hartlyn (1998a); Linz and Stepan (1996); Snyder (1992); O'Donnell and Schmitter (1986); Karl and Schmitter (1991); Shain and Linz et al. (1995, esp. 28–40); and Bratton and van de Walle (1994).

4. See Dahl (1971) for the simple yet profound observation that the prospects of a democratic transition are enhanced the more the costs of repression increase while the risks of toleration decrease. By focusing almost exclusively on the "endgame" part of the transition process, some of the initial transitions literature (e.g., O'Donnell and Schmitter 1986) underplayed the role of mass actors even in transition processes "from above."

In their analysis of transitions from neopatrimonial regimes in Africa in the early 1990s, Bratton and van de Walle underscore the fact that the transitions often originate from mass protests as a result of economic crisis and the exclusionary nature of political patronage, which is often centered on kinship or ethnic ties (1994; 1997, 83–84). The extent of fiscal profligacy in the Dominican Republic was considerably less than in the cases they describe. Past excesses in the Dominican Republic had led to international intervention in the first decades of the twentieth century; the historical memory of that intervention, and the continued hegemonic presence of the United States, led Trujillo (except toward the end of his rule) and subsequent Dominican rulers to be more prudent in general than their African counterparts. See also the discussion at the end of chapter 4.

5. Most of the authors who analyze transitions from above and from below cited in the text do not actually go this far; and several, in fact, have elsewhere emphasized distinctly different themes. Karl and Schmitter (1991, 269) do state their belief in the assumptions that the mode of transition may determine to a significant extent the type of democracy, its possibilities of consolidation, and possible consequences for social groups in the long range, though they leave analysis of these assumptions to future work.

6. These three factors are analogous to the mechanisms specified by Collier and Collier (1991, 30–31) in their framework identifying "critical junctures." The first factor is analogous to their "constant causes," the second to their "mechanisms of reproduction," and the third to their "mechanisms of production." Yet, it is doubtful that democratic transitions, by themselves, meet the stringent requirements of a "critical juncture," which are initiated by a major cleavage or crisis. Over this past decade, however, because democratic transitions have been combined with sustained socioeconomic crisis and state collapse, leading to vast modifications in state-society relations as well as in changes in political forms, many Latin American countries may in fact be in the midst of a "critical juncture."

7. In Hartlyn (1998a), I argue that *differing modes of transition may not necessarily have opposing consequences* (which I illustrate by comparing transitions in Argentina and Brazil in the 1980s) and that *similar modes of transition may not necessarily have the same effects* (which I illustrate by comparing the evolution of Colombia and Venezuela following their similar kinds of transitions in the late 1950s).

8. Six months after May, the rest of the Trujillo family was forced into exile; two months later, Balaguer was also finally forced into exile and a provisional government representing a clear break with the Trujillos was formed.

9. From 1958 to 1960, military and police forces grew from 18,014 to 31,000. See Vega (1992, 225, 428–53; 1991, 221–24). One of the paramilitary groups, a "foreign legion," had a small number of foreign mercenaries. Other advisers of Trujillo, such as Balaguer, tried to encourage him to seek reconciliation with the church and the United States rather than confrontation.

10. For the United States, there were two key issues. On the one hand, the Eisenhower and then the Kennedy administrations wished to embark on a more interventionist policy against the perceived growing threat of Fidel Castro in Cuba, and Latin American support for a shift away from noninterventionism against Cuba required a willingness for the United States to act against rightist dictators as well. On the other hand, after the fall of Batista, the United States also began to believe that political

democracy and social reform might serve as stronger bulwarks against communism than dictators such as Trujillo. This, too, called for a more interventionist U.S. strategy.

11. The strong mutual enmity between Trujillo and Betancourt dates back at least to the 1940s, when many Dominican exiles plotted from Venezuela with sympathy from the Betancourt government against Trujillo. Trujillo, in turn, tried to support a plan, which failed, to overthrow Betancourt in November 1946. (See Ameringer 1974; 1996).

12. The measure barely passed, as Argentina, Brazil, Guatemala, Haiti, Paraguay, and Uruguay abstained (Slater 1967, 193–94).

13. Gleijeses (1978) asserts that at least twelve of the fourteen conspirators "were motivated by fear for their own security and privileges . . . and by desire for a revenge that at last seemed possible" as well as by hopes of power and riches; social reform and political democracy were of little interest to them (303). The United States, which at first had strongly encouraged the conspirators, became nervous following the Bay of Pigs debacle. It feared that a power vacuum in the country if Trujillo were to be killed could be taken advantage of by Dominican radicals with ties to Fidel Castro.

14. Guerrilla movements failed to establish themselves in rural areas, the peasantry was successfully wooed by moderate and conservative forces, and in fact some Dominican conservatives viewed leftist forces as so weak that they purposefully bolstered them for their own purposes (all this contrasts sharply with the situation in Cuba in 1959 and Nicaragua in 1979; cf. Wickham-Crowley 1992, esp. 320).

15. Presaging key emphases he would employ subsequently, Balaguer's rhetoric at this time focused on the central importance of order in the face of the threat of chaos and anarchy, of reconciliation in the face of *apetitos desbocados y recriminaciones gratuitas*. He tried to feed into people's fears—of a vacuum of authority, of communism, of another bloody dictatorship, of potential societal dissolution, of loss of life and property (see Brea 1991).

16. Following his resignation, Ramfis Trujillo went on a three-day drinking orgy, personally killed the six remaining imprisoned assassins of his father (two were never captured) who had been brutally tortured, and then left on the family yacht, with his father's body and reportedly $90 million (see Gleijeses 1978, 44–46).

17. Martin's detailed and frank memoirs provide historical background on the country and a detailed analysis of the events he both witnessed and helped to shape so intimately following in the footsteps of past U.S. diplomats. Indeed, Martin wrote unself-consciously that his goals and policy objectives were exactly the same as those of Sumner Welles at the end of the U.S. military occupation in the 1920s: "His task foreshadowed mine forty years later. . . . He succeeded and so did I. But before he succeeded, he encountered nearly every obstacle I encountered" (Martin 1966, 30).

This highlights a recurring theme of interventionism in U.S.-Dominican relations, ultimately problematic for the establishment of autonomous political practices and democracy in the country. These diplomatic achievements were significant, reflecting considerable intelligence, skill, and effort. Yet, success at this level covered up the fundamental fact that the United States could not simply establish the Dominican Republic as a consolidated democracy. If it could, then Martin would not have needed to carry out decades later the same tasks as Welles. Nor would a military coup have put an end to constitutional government only months after Martin's efforts and a few short years before a U.S. military intervention would require yet another unquestionably intelligent, skilled, and dedicated U.S. diplomat, Ellsworth Bunker, to seek to achieve the same three goals of supporting a provisional government, helping it hold elections, and insuring a transfer of power (see Hartlyn 1991).

18. Four of the seven members of the council were UCN sympathizers, including Rafael Bonnelly (its head), Nicolás Pichardo, Eduardo Read Barreras, and Donald Reid Cabral (who replaced Balaguer when he went into exile). The fifth was a church figure and apparent UCN sympathizer, Monsignor Eliseo Pérez Sánchez (cf. Martin 1966, 246–81; and for an acerbic assessment of Imbert and Amiama, Gleijeses 1978, 60–63, 77).

Ambassador Martin saw neither the UCN nor the PRD as "ideal." For him, the "UCN was too upper-middle-class, too heterogeneous, too politically naive, and lacking in real understanding of the people's needs." In turn, the PRD leadership was "too ideological, too theory-ridden" with its "lower ranks . . . filled with some of the worst elements in Dominican political life, the remnants of the old PD [Trujillo's former party]" (Martin 1966, 206).

19. For this period, in terms of English-language sources, Gleijeses (1978) is one the best on the Dominican left and Wiarda (1975) is one of the best for the PRD and U.S. policy.

20. Critical in the organization of FENHERCA and in subsequently advising Juan Bosch was the figure of Sacha Volman. Behind his thick accent and conspiratorial air, lies the fact that he was part of a group of individuals who supported social-democratic efforts throughout Latin American in this time period with CIA funding. For example, over 1960–61, Volman was director of the Costa Rican Institute for Political Education, where Bosch and former Costa Rican president José Figueres taught and where some forty-five Dominicans received training, including José Francisco Peña Gómez and Norge Botello. The institute received funds from Norman Thomas, whose own institute was unwittingly funded by the CIA, which used the Jacob Kaplan Fund as a conduit from January 1961 to September 1963; Thomas had not known the true source of the funds. Leading up to the 1962 elections in the Dominican Republic, Volman played an important role in training peasant leaders and helping to set up FENHERCA (Volman, interviews by the author; Wiarda 1975, 1:618–20; Black 1986, 32–34; and especially, Vega 1993a, iii, 531–32). Volman was also active during the Bosch government in the establishment of another think tank, the Centro Internacional de Estudios Económicos y Sociales (CIDES, International Center of Economic and Social Studies), which also received CIA funds. Following the 1963 coup it was shut down by the military, who accused it of being a communist front!

Wiarda (1975, 1047) also notes that, because Bosch never called for a massive effort to "de-Trujilloize" the country, regional military commanders in a number of areas may well have supported his candidacy over that of the UCN (subsequently, of course, they were to support Balaguer).

21. For an excellent analysis of the full array of political parties and movements leading up to the 1962 elections, see Wiarda (1975, esp. 1035). Much of the information in these next paragraphs is derived from this source. See also Martin (1966).

22. Until the last minute Bosch had insisted on the need to hold the August elec-

tions, in spite of the fact it was clear that this was administratively impossible. Apparently, what he wanted and ultimately achieved was removal of the constitutional requirements that to be elected president of the country one needed to have lived in the republic for the past five years and that at least one parent had to be Dominican born (Bosch's father was Spanish and his mother was Puerto Rican). Ambassador Martin concludes his discussion of this incident by noting: "We could not trust Juan Bosch. For President he would not do. . . . he was a reckless political plunger, willing to risk everything, including the democratic system itself, to gain a personal political objective" (Martin 1966, 201).

23. In seeking the pact, Martin cited the precedent of a pact agreed to by the candidates in the 1924 Dominican election, under the watchful eye of Sumner Welles. Like the council of state, the provisional government appointed in October 1922 also confronted numerous obstacles, particularly revolving around charges of bias and questionable procedures in the upcoming elections. As described by Dominicans and North Americans alike, the electoral campaign involved brutal, nasty tactics, with a willingness by some political leaders to do almost anything for personal political advantage (even at the risk of continuing the occupation) and an unwillingness to compromise among certain nationalists; an assassination plot by nationalist forces against the presidential candidates, Welles, and others was even uncovered. Nevertheless, the elections went off as scheduled in March 1924, with effective measures implemented to insure their fairness. Horacio Vásquez and his party emerged as clear victors, a result recognized after some protest by his principal opponent, Francisco Peynado. Vásquez was inaugurated president in July 1924 and the last U.S. marine left the country in September of that year (see Campillo Pérez 1982, 165–72; Calder 1984, 232–37; Moya Pons 1983, 488–91).

24. Although it should be obvious to the reader, it may be useful to emphasize the difference between political pacts that are generated and almost imposed from abroad, such as this one or its 1924 predecessor, and pacts that are generated by the internal motivations of the central political actors themselves, such as the pacts that led to the establishment of the National Front in Colombia and the Pact of Punto Fijo in Venezuela. It also contrasts, as discussed in chapter 4, with the somewhat more ambiguous "pacting" in the Dominican Republic some sixteen years later. Indeed, Martin (1966) reports that when he suggested such an agreement to the members of the council of state, reminding them that a similar agreement had been reached in 1924 (under the stewardship of Sumner Welles), "all broke out in loud laughter" (222). It is also true that in the Dominican context, socioeconomic and military actors were not represented through the nascent party structure, and separate agreements would have been needed to be struck with them that were not. Bosch's short-lived government of 1963 was more analogous to the tumultuous *trienio* period of Venezuela, when a majoritarian Acción Democrática party (AD, Democratic Action) tried to impose radical reform and was bitterly opposed by socioeconomic, military, and church actors, than to the Betancourt government that was trying to help him gain his election at the time; the major difference was probably the modesty of Bosch's proposed reforms and the extent of his opponents' recalcitrance. Shortly after he was overthrown, Bosch (1965, 39) argued that the "country needed a revolution to bring it up to

at least the twentieth century," not Cuban style à la Fidel Castro, but Cuban style à la Grau San Martín, "that would permit us to advance in a few months to at least the point Venezuela reached in 1945, when Betancourt first came to power."

25. Balaguer sought to run for the presidency, but was blocked by the council of state, with U.S. assistance, from returning; they feared his continued support within military circles and his unknown electoral base. The JCE eventually rejected his candidacy "on a technicality," and Balaguer was prevented from taking a flight back to the country in mid-November (Martin 1966, 262–64, 271–72).

26. Again in this instance, comparison with the case of Venezuela is instructive in a number of respects that buttress the various arguments presented here. As with Bosch and the coup of 1963, the issue of majoritarian, hegemonic political control by what dominant actors perceived as a radical reformist force factored into the 1948 military coup against the AD party. Like Bosch, the AD had been able to rewrite the constitution as it desired, had won the presidency, and had gained majoritarian control of congress. The 1948 coup, by a coalition of socioeconomic, church, and military actors, put an end to that country's first experience with democracy. Unlike the Dominican Republic, Venezuela was undergoing much more dynamic and fundamental socio-economic transformation as a consequence of oil exports. However, the difficulties of immediate transition from neosultanistic rule and the potential role of nonsultanistic authoritarian rule in facilitating the emergence of independent political and social organizations is also evident in the Venezuelan case. Following the death of the neosultanistic Juan Vicente Gómez in 1935, two increasingly more politically liberal authoritarian regimes allowed limited activities by independent social and political organizations leading up to the short-lived *trienio* of 1945–48 (see Ewell 1984).

27. "The Consejo was created to overthrow Juan Bosch" is what José Ernesto García Aybar, its first president, told Frank Moya Pons (Moya Pons 1991, chap. 3, 6n).

28. Specific issues irritating the industrialists included the unwillingness of Bosch to promote a new industrial incentives law (instead, he preferred to grant tax exemptions on a case-by-case basis), the imposition of a sugar export tax as world prices increased, and the threat of a new bill focused on properties linked to Trujillo and another imposing a value-added tax on real estate (Moya Pons 1991, chap. 4, 14–17).

29. Although in his first analysis of why he was overthrown, Bosch emphasized domestic factors (Bosch 1965), subsequently he has argued that the United States played a central role in his overthrow because it feared he might discover the extent of U.S. involvement in plots from Dominican soil to overthrow Duvalier (see Grimaldi 1985). The issue of Dominican-Haitian-U.S. relations during this period remains murky, although it is evident that at different times Bosch, members of the Dominican military, and the U.S. government supported plotting by sometimes overlapping and sometimes different Haitian groups in ultimately vain efforts to overthrow Duvalier. It is most unlikely that this was the issue that led to Bosch's overthrow, especially given the array of domestic actors against him and the coup coalition they were able to construct (see the discussion in Vega 1993a, iv–v, 97–111, 145–46). Bosch's subsequent emphasis on this point must be understood in terms of domestic politics and his desire to reach out to industrial and commercial elites, even as his first book also was written

very much with a domestic Dominican audience in mind, particularly middle-class and professional groups.

30. The U.S. labor attaché, Fred Somerford, worked hard to support a labor confederation that would be strongly anticommunist, but also "apolitical"; his efforts were important in preventing labor unity in support of Bosch's government. Somerford believed Bosch and Miolán were "thieves and gangsters," and that the PRD was "probably Communistic" (Wiarda 1975, 555).

31. Bosch did little to mobilize efforts to help him retain power at the time, Lowenthal (1972) argues, noting that "Bosch seemed to lack the fundamental optimism and singleminded determination necessary to let the experiment [in democracy] proceed" (193n).

32. Martin (1966) writes that he told Bosch as the coup was imminent: "I don't think the military really want to do this. . . . The cívicos have convinced them you're handing the country over to the Communists. I know it isn't true, you know it isn't true, but you've got to prove it isn't true. You can do it now. . . . Call a special session of Congress. Tell them first, to enact something like our Smith Act. Second, tell Congress to stop travel to Cuba—pass a law making it a crime to violate passport restrictions. Third, tell them to enact a law permitting deportations" (562). For a variety of reasons, and in a passive manner, Bosch rejected the advice (Martin writes, "[Bosch] kept saying, 'The revolution is frustrated,' and 'I can do nothing'") (564).

33. On how the triumvirate and first cabinet were named, see Guerrero (1993, 237–54). Reid Cabral replaced the first head of the triumvirate, Emilio de los Santos, who resigned in quiet protest following the killing of fifteen captured guerrilla members of 1J4, including the group's leader Manolo Tavárez. Inspired by the Cuban example, but misreading the Dominican situation, 1J4 had opened six guerrilla focos in late November, which were quickly dismantled. Reid's naming also led to the withdrawal of four miniparties from the governing coalition; in April 1964 the other two parties, including the UCN, also resigned (Gleijeses 1978, 108–16, 123).

34. Imports surged from the previous year's record high of US$165 million to US$202 million in 1964 (including an estimate for contraband); the country ended the year with a balance of trade deficit of US$23 million (Oficina Nacional de Planificación 1968, 424). On military corruption, see Moya Pons (1991, chap. 4) and (Wiarda 1975, 1476).

35. Preliminary results from a CIA-sponsored poll in April 1965 indicated that Reid had the support of only 5 percent of the potential Dominican electorate, compared to around 25 percent for Bosch and 50 percent for Balaguer (Lowenthal 1972, 48–49).

36. AID provided US$31.1 million in 1965 to pay the salaries of government employees and AID, and the OAS provided an additional estimated US$54.8 million in emergency assistance that year (Oficina Nacional de Planificación 1968, 500).

37. Gleijeses (1978) argues that in 1966 Bosch was a reluctant candidate, torn between a desire to win and a realization that his victory would be followed by a new and more bloody coup (281). Others argued he made few public appearances because he feared for his life.

38. That Balaguer carved out a support coalition distinct from that of the UCN in

1962 is evident from the relatively low correlation of election results at the municipal level between the 1962 UCN vote and the 1966 PR vote (0.25, p < .05). The subsequent PR vote remained fairly consistent at the municipal level; for example, the correlation of municipal electoral results for the PR from 1966 to 1978 was 0.74 (p < .001). In 1966, Balaguer also clearly affected PRD strength in rural areas; in 1962, the PRD had not confronted a neo-Trujillo candidate. One indicator of this is that the equivalent PRD vote correlation at the municipal level from 1962 to 1966 of 0.56 (p < .001) was considerably lower than that for the PRD between 1966 and 1978 (0.72, p < .001). See also the election results in appendix A.

39. Many Dominicans viewed their armed forces as "really controlled by 'the Pentagon,'" and others probably believed that U.S. economic assistance would be more forthcoming for Balaguer than for Bosch; thus, those who desired "peace and stability" would vote for Balaguer. By provoking nationalism, the intervention should have encouraged some voters to turn to Bosch. Yet, given the negotiated surrender of the pro-Bosch forces and Balaguer's active campaigning in contrast to Bosch, this effect may well have been muted (Slater 1970, 180–81; also, author's interviews in 1985 with U.S. policymakers from that period).

40. In this sense, they presaged a number of the elections in El Salvador and in Guatemala in the 1980s.

41. On demonstration elections in the Dominican Republic, El Salvador, and Vietnam, see Herman and Brodhead (1984). One problem with the term "demonstration elections" is that it directs attention away from the domestic consequences of elections held in part to assuage international opinion or the domestic opinion of a foreign power.

42. Some feel fraud, particularly in more remote rural areas, may have inflated Balaguer's total somewhat, though not enough to change the overall results (Wiarda 1975, 1799; cited also in Herman and Brodhead 1984, 40).

43. It certainly was a success for President Johnson domestically. Johnson had very high, immediate domestic popular support for his actions in the Dominican Republic, which were presented as involving the use of military force to prevent the communists from gaining power and to save American lives. Harris surveys taken in February and July 1965 show a 10 percent jump in the U.S. public's approval of Johnson's handling of foreign policy (from 50 percent to 60 percent); the July 1965 poll found 71 percent agreeing that U.S. troops should stay until "there is a stable government." If there had been high levels of U.S. casualties, opinion might quickly have shifted. Instead, in a December 1965 poll, 52 percent of the sample agreed that Johnson was right to send troops to the Dominican Republic (with 21 percent saying it was wrong and 27 percent having no opinion); 32 percent of this same sample agreed that this action probably hurt relations with other Latin American countries (26 percent believed it helped, 12 percent thought it made no difference, and 30 percent had no opinion). And college-educated respondents in this sample were even *more likely* to agree it was right to send troops (63 percent), even though they *also* agreed it probably hurt relations with other Latin American countries (48 percent).

In contrast, Reagan's invasion of Grenada in October 1983, confounded with the deaths of over 225 U.S. marines in Lebanon, did not possess the same degree of support at the time or even some months after the event: it led to a 15 percent jump in the approval rating of his foreign policy (from 31 percent in August 1983 to 44 percent in October to 46 percent in November before starting to decline again); in August 1984, 34 percent agreed it was right that the United States invaded Grenada and 38 percent believed it was wrong (17 percent took an intermediate position, and 11 percent were undecided). (Harris Polls are archived at the Institute for Research in the Social Sciences, University of North Carolina at Chapel Hill; the research assistance of Margaret Commins is gratefully acknowledged).

Chapter 4

1. For a brief discussion of the cycles or waves of democratization in Latin America from the late 1920s to the early 1990s, see Hartlyn and Valenzuela (1994, 158–61). That article also discusses how the surge in military governments in Latin America in the 1960s helped spawn these new, more pessimistic views in reaction to the excessive optimism of the early modernization literature. The "third wave" of world democratization, of which the Dominican Republic was an early harbinger, has resparked what I would consider an excessive re-embracing of modernization literature by some authors (e.g. Pye, 1990), without sufficient attention either to international economic, geopolitical, and ideological issues or to domestic political and institutional ones.

2. In this regard, because the Dominican Republic is viewed by all three of these sets of arguments as a least likely case for democratization, the country can be considered a "critical case study": one that particularly impairs these perspectives, because although it is most likely to follow the path predicted by advocates of these approaches it does not do so (cf. Eckstein 1975; Collier 1993). At the same time, to the extent that these three perspectives provide arguments about prospects for democratic consolidation, more than for transition, the subsequent chapters will provide some qualified support for more nuanced presentations of some of these views: on economic dependence, see the valuable discussion in Rueschemeyer, Huber Stephens, and Stephens (1992, esp. 71–75, 219–22, 261–68, 277–81); on political culture, see Diamond (1993, 1–27) and Muller and Seligson (1994); and on the U.S. role in promoting democracy in Latin American, see Lowenthal (1991a).

3. For two valuable analyses with a similar focus to mine, but which play down the roles of the United States and of the PRD more than I do, see del Castillo (1981) and Espinal (1986); and for one that especially highlights class and organization dynamics, see Conaghan and Espinal (1990).

4. Among several useful analyses of Balaguer's twelve years, see Cassá (1986) and Lozano (1985). The ensuing pages will further clarify why I believe it is appropriate to consider Balaguer's regime as neopatrimonial—which helps to clarify both the elements of historical continuity and change and the nature of the regime's relations with the military and with domestic political and social forces—rather than as "bonapartist," which is Cassá's interpretation. The terms partially overlap in that in both cases regimes are understood to sustain an important element of state autonomy from dominant economic interests. However, the bonapartist characterization in this work paints issues of state autonomy with too broad a brush, and its efforts to draw structural

links between dependent capitalism and Balaguer-style bonapartist rule are so general they are unable to explain the differences with other bonapartist regimes of the same era and region—such as the military regime that came to power in Peru in 1968, which clearly did not pursue the requisite types of "conservative policies" envisioned in this analysis. Other crucial aspects of the regime, including the nature of its political ties, are also downplayed (cf. Cassá 1986, esp. 266–72).

5. For a fascinating and careful treatment of this entire process, see Moya Pons (1991). This study details the extensive maneuvering by leading industrialists—overwhelmingly from Santo Domingo—leading up to the promulgation of law 299 of April 1968, which established the legal framework for further import-substituting industrialization, while circumscribing the role of foreign investment to protect established industries. The law discouraged further investments in sectors where the country already possessed sufficient installed capacity—thus protecting the monopoly or oligopoly position of established domestic interests, who had direct representation on the board that determined whether tax exonerations should be permitted or not. Over the years, Dominican industrialists generally favored foreign investment unless it competed directly with them; Balaguer tended to have a more open attitude, leading to several significant clashes.

6. On government employment levels and low expenditures on health and education, see World Bank (1978b). A review of civil-service legislation may be found in Jácome-Martínez (1981, 208–15). Initial civil-service legislation was passed under the U.S. military occupation of 1916–1924 and changed several times thereafter, but was never truly implemented; it was actually *abolished* under Trujillo in 1951.

7. From 1968 to 1976, the contribution of taxes on foreign trade to total current central government revenues ranged from 42.7 percent to 52.2 percent (World Bank 1978b, 75).

8. The value of partially or totally exonerated imports as a percentage of the value of total imports grew from 47.3 percent in 1970 to 71.8 percent in 1976; although as much as half of this may have represented discretionary exemptions of high tariffs on the importation of private automobiles, the rest was associated with the country's industrial policy. This encouraged industrial activities based on imported equipment and inputs, rather than the development of local products and exports. Over 1974–76, Balaguer was able to accommodate this by expanding taxes on exports, as world sugar prices hit record highs (World Bank 1978b, 74).

9. Over 1966–67, Gulf and Western gradually bought out the South Porto-Rico (*sic*) Sugar Company holdings in the country; during that period, a radical union linked to the PRD was destroyed, and several labor leaders were killed. It seems evident that the U.S. government perceived the presence of Gulf and Western as beneficial in a potentially volatile country emerging from a civil war; increases in the U.S. sugar quota granted to the Dominican Republic helped the company. At the same time, Gulf and Western's tourist operations in the country were apparently losing money, and negative publicity generated by progressive Christian organizations focusing on the company's treatment of Haitian cane cutters led corporate managers to sell off holdings in the country after Charles Bludhorn's death in 1983. Bludhorn, the founder

and president of the company, had seen the Dominican operation as a special, personal project. In October 1984, the Cuban-American Fanjul brothers took control of Gulf and Western's sugar operations both in the Dominican Republic and in South Florida, as well as its Dominican tourist complex (see Murphy 1991, 30–31; Frundt 1979).

10. See Plant (1987, 161–67) for a copy of the 1980 contract and Cuello H. (1997) for a detailed analysis, copies of the contracts, and much additional valuable documentation. As Cuello H. (1997) discusses, the contract system finally collapsed dramatically in 1986, although the issue of Haitian migration to the Dominican Republic continued to grow in importance.

11. When Trujillo was killed in 1961, there were twenty-two generals or admirals in the Dominican armed forces; this number was down to six on active duty when Balaguer was inaugurated president in July 1966, but it had increased to forty-eight by the time he departed power in August 1978 (Atkins 1981, 46).

12. For the first estimate, see Latorre (1975, 330–31); Vilas (n.d., 7), based on Alcántara Almánzar (1971); Campillo Pérez (1982, 265–66); and Gutiérrez (1972, 11). See Moya Pons (1995, 392) for the second estimate. The formal name of La Banda was the Frente Democrático, Anti-Comunista y Anti-Terrorista de Juventud Reformista (Democratic, Anticommunist and Antiterrorist Front of Reformist Youth). According to one U.S. senior diplomatic official who met Peña Gómez in Washington in August 1971, the United States informed Balaguer that it would be hard for his friends in the State Department to help him with aid requests in the U.S. Congress if these repressive activities weren't curtailed (interview with author in 1986). Nivar had been a key pro-Balaguer military officer conspiring against Reid in 1965 and had been forced into exile by Reid; at that time, he and Peña Gómez had conspired together, but inconclusively, their mutual desire to be rid of Reid not sufficient to overcome their differing political loyalties (Gleijeses 1978, 149). The extent and nature of U.S. military and police assistance to Dominican security forces, especially during the early Balaguer years, is an area where many details have yet to be made public.

13. A direct claimant to Trujillo's mantle and potential challenger to Balaguer, Trujillo's son Ramfis, died in an automobile accident in Spain in December 1969.

14. The captive was released unharmed after Balaguer agreed to release twenty political prisoners who flew to Mexico. By 1978, nineteen of the twenty were dead (Atkins 1981, 26).

15. A close associate of Balaguer at the time of the 1974 elections explained to me that as the elections approached and a defeat appeared more probable, Balaguer urged the military to apply more pressure against the PRD-led coalition with the hope that they would abstain in 1974, as they had in 1970. He noted that Balaguer's style was indirect, so the historian is unlikely to find any written directives from the office of the presidency on this issue (interview in March 1985). Balaguer also miraculously survived a helicopter crash six days before the elections (Campillo Pérez 1982, 270–78; Atkins 1981, 25).

16. General Nivar also toyed with conspiratorial politics, though in the view of one close observer, more to keep track of the various conspiracies than to participate in

them (author's interview in May 1986). On the PRD and leftist groups leading up to the 1970 elections, see del Castillo (1981, 23–25), Gutiérrez (1972, 67–72, 115–29), and Gautreaux Piñeyro (1994, 75–80). On the MPD's establishment and early years, see Gleijeses (1978, 321–27). Over 1969, as it worked with Wessin y Wessin, the MPD often carried out urban terrorist acts (see Hermann 1983, 392; and the interview with Bosch in Gutiérrez 1972, 90–91). For a review and critique from a leftist perspective of the emphasis by the MPD on armed struggle and coup plotting with right-wing, military, anti-Balaguer groups over popular organization during the Balaguer period, see "Análisis del movimiento . . ." (1978, 13–53); this article also critiques other leftist groups during this period, including a failed insurrectional strategy by parts of the 1J4 and the Dominican Communist Party.

17. As a former follower of Bosch notes, whether consciously or not (and some figures close to him at that time, although not when I interviewed them in 1986, argued it was indeed not consciously), Bosch's expulsions from the PRD was a way of identifying these individuals—several of whom were subsequently assassinated—as "communists" (Gautreaux Piñeyro 1994, 118).

18. One observer close to Bosch at the time believed Bosch was also crafting a new civil-military conspiracy that was intended to lead to a coup d'état and to his coming to power, a plan that had to be shelved by Caamaño's failed invasion (author's interviews in 1986).

19. It appears that Castro sought unsuccessfully to dissuade Caamaño from what was likely to be a suicide invasion (see Gleijeses 1978, 414–15, n. 34). There is much that remains unknown about linkages and conspiracies across Bosch, Peña Gómez, Caamaño, and other parties of the left during the 1966–73 period. For the view that Bosch saw Caamaño as a potential threat to his leadership of the opposition and that he knew of Caamaño's invasion ahead of time, see Gautreaux Piñeyro (1994). Caamaño was disappointed that Bosch and the PRD did not mobilize in his support; but Bosch has argued that by asserting Caamaño had not entered the country, he saved the lives of dozens of Dominican youth who might have died trying to join his hopeless struggle—which could well be true. A few of the survivors tried again in June 1975, which led to another wave of arrests of opposition leaders. For a picture of the Dominican military's efforts to confront Caamaño's incursion as "particularly inept," see Atkins (1981, 68–71).

20. Over October and November 1969, Bosch had traveled to China, North Korea, and North Vietnam; subsequently he had written an extremely favorable review of these visits while also strongly criticizing the United States (see Bosch 1992, 39–73, originally published in the Dominican Republic in 1970, as well as the other articles and speeches from that period compiled in the book). In addition to Caamaño's presence in Cuba, followers of Bosch had also been sent for training to China and other socialist-bloc countries following Bosch's trip, which may further explain Peña Gómez's references (see Gautreaux Piñeyro 1994, 103; and author's interview with ex-PRD activist in 1986).

21. This conclusion is based on a systematic review of the compilation of summaries and texts of Peña Gómez's speeches in the archives of Sara Peralta de Rathe, to which I

was kindly given access. Only the compilations of Peña Gómez's more recent speeches have been published. Subsequent discussions of Peña Gómez's speeches from this period also rely upon these archives.

22. This may be the only case in Latin America in which a radical splinter from a populist party is led by the original leader of that party, rather than by disgruntled figures from younger generations—for example, consider the cases of Betancourt of AD in Venezuela and Haya de la Torre of APRA in Peru in the 1960s as their parties experienced splits. It is also true that from a mass perspective, Bosch's radicalism was less apparent, since in the months leading up to the division he was actively promoting a coalition with anti-Balaguer forces that spanned the ideological spectrum; in turn, his decision to leave the PRD was widely perceived as hurting that coalition and the prospects of ousting Balaguer (on both of these points, see del Castillo 1981, 75–80). Bosch chose the name of the party because of the similarity in sound of the PLD acronym with that of the PRD (Gautreaux Piñeyro 1994, 135). Although no one has done more to obfuscate the matter than Bosch himself, at least one careful student of Dominican political parties asserts, after a careful evaluation of Bosch's writings and the references he makes to Marx and Lenin, that the PLD was founded with a Marxist-Leninist ideology (Jiménez Polanco 1994, 244).

23. Fifteen years later, Bosch would argue that he feared gaining the presidency in 1974 at the head of the PRD because it lacked trained cadres (cited in Jiménez Polanco 1994, 181). Another argument was that Bosch feared that he would win the 1974 elections, provoking a military coup led by General Pérez y Pérez that could be worse than the Balaguer regime (Cuello 1984, viii). Both views reflect a certain "structural pessimism" evident in Bosch as far back as the 1962 campaign. Other sources for this paragraph include Espinal (1982, 70–74); González Canahuate (1985, 58–67); del Castillo (1981, 68–70); and the author's interviews with ex-PRD activists and close observers of that period in 1986.

24. The other two parties of the Santiago Agreement, respectively on the left and the right, were the PRSC and a fraction of the small UCN.

25. This "fear" of accusations from the left, is cited by Espinal (1982, 76); del Castillo (1981, 73); and was also evident in interviews with ex-PRD leaders in 1986. Many businessmen and party leaders interviewed in 1985 and 1986 felt that the PRD abstention in 1974 was a large mistake, even though the PRD may not have attained the presidency, for it meant Balaguer confronted no opposition in congress; however, these views do not consider what the sociopolitical implications of massive governmental postelectoral fraud or direct military interference might have been.

26. From the perspective of several senior U.S. diplomatic personnel in the country, Guzmán's candidacy was the best of all the likely PRD candidates, and it greatly facilitated convincing "Washington" to act in defense of the electoral results (author's interviews in 1986).

Following Guzmán's inauguration and Vance's retirement from the State Department, Vance (an attorney) was hired by Gulf and Western to negotiate a settlement with Guzmán regarding the company's abuse of state funds on the sugar futures market under Balaguer, a settlement which appeared to be extremely favorable to the company and which was never fully concluded by the Dominican state—indeed, by the time of the Jorge Blanco administration, the file had apparently disappeared from state archives (author's interview with high-level official in the Jorge Blanco government, 1986). Although there are important differences between this kind of "sequential" employment of a person who occupied a public role for subsequent private purpose (and expected gain), as opposed to a "simultaneous" blurring of roles, many Dominicans felt Guzmán was placed in a difficult position.

27. In August 1984, Peña Gómez explained that he had had "great doubts that [Guzmán] could be a competent ruler" because he lacked sufficient intellectual knowledge, which is why he had believed it was necessary to generate new leaders and a primary competition, but that Guzmán proved him wrong (Peña Gómez 1986d, 255–56).

28. Balaguer's efforts to take advantage of flattering statements by Carter at the signing of the Panama Canal Treaty in September 1977 regarding his administration and the forthcoming elections led PRD supporters in the U.S. Congress to demand greater U.S. government impartiality. As it turned out, with Guzmán as the PRD candidate, the U.S. government was impartial. Furthermore, unlike previous elections, this time major multinationals, including Gulf and Western, which owned sprawling sugar lands, a major sugar mill, and tourist facilities, opted toward neutrality in the electoral contest (author's interviews with businessmen and political leaders, 1986).

29. Those involved in the kidnapping and in Alvarez's forced resignation included the secretary of the armed forces (General Juan René Beauchamp Javier) and the chiefs of staff of the army (General Marcos Antonio Jorge Moreno), of the navy (Vice Admiral Francisco Javier Rivera Caminero), and of the police (General Neit Rafael Nivar Seijas), who were among the more "politically" oriented military. This group did not include officers from the Pérez y Pérez group (as identified by Atkins 1981). According to a figure in the incident, Alvarez held off for eight days, but after being told by Balaguer that if he did not resign there would be no elections and a possible bloodbath, he agreed to do so. The politically motivated military were convinced that Balaguer was in poor health and that Goico was less of a threat to them (Atkins 1981; Gómez Berges 1985; and author's interviews in late 1985 and early 1986).

30. For examples of Balaguer's use of a polarizing rhetoric of fear in the campaigns of 1990 and 1994, though not directed toward the armed forces, see chapter 8.

31. In fact, the replacement was a result of a U.S. Justice Department investigation of Hurwitch involving the misuse of embassy funds. Hurwitch was indeed close to Balaguer, and the PRD believed he was even receiving support from him. Statements of the incoming ambassador regarding U.S. support for free and open elections in the country were viewed as a repudiation of past policies. In fact, however, under Hurwitch's supervision, the embassy had already prepared a contingency plan for any attempt to subvert the elections; in retrospect it is unlikely that U.S. policy would have been different if there had been no change of ambassador. Balaguer delayed the presentation of Yost's credentials until just before the election, so a picture of the two of them together would appear in the newspapers on election day. However, since the new ambassador now was officially recognized by the Dominican government, he

was able to act far more effectively in the postelectoral crisis (author's interviews with U.S. diplomatic personnel and former high-level PR and PRD figures, 1986; Atkins 1981, 94).

32. Atkins (1981, 109) asserts that army chief of staff, Jorge Moreno, and the head of presidential security, Marte Pichardo, were also heavily involved, whereas the navy chief of staff, Admiral Rivera Caminero, in spite of an extreme distrust of Peña Gómez, was not; however, an individual close to the military and to Balaguer in that period argued that Rivera Caminero was involved and that the military probably acted because someone close to Balaguer, perhaps a member of his family, told them to proceed (author's interview, 1986). This minor discrepancy might be resolved by the views of a key U.S. diplomat of the period who noted that Rivera Caminero was not as central a player as others and was a key contact for the U.S. military advisory group in the country (author's interview, 1986). Story regarding the *actas* of Santo Domingo and Galo Plaza told by Hatuey de Camps to the National Democratic Institute (NDI) delegation (May 1996). Regional harassment of the PRD is mentioned in Campillo Pérez (1982, 288) and in numerous interviews in 1986 by the author with PRD candidates of the period.

33. Several people told me that the PLD received support from the government during the campaign, in the form of money and vehicles. Bosch was in contact with Balaguer indirectly to let him know he would not oppose (and thus, in effect would support) a coup. This information is based on the author's interviews (in 1986) with close observers of Bosch and the 1978 campaign and with an individual close to Bosch in 1978.

34. During the Trujillo era, except for a brief period from 1955 to 1958, U.S. civilian diplomats sought to keep their distance, while U.S. military personnel largely embraced Trujillo. The civilian-military "dual track" was also somewhat visible in the tense months leading up to Bosch's overthrow in 1963.

35. For a more detailed discussion of the role of fraud and accusations of fraud in Dominican elections, see chapter 8. Certainly, these were unlikely to have been "perfect" elections, although the major suspect of manipulation would have to be the government. Of the neutral Dominican and foreign observers that I interviewed, none had seen credible evidence or believed the accusations of fraud (sufficient to affect the outcome of the election), and most Balaguer supporters acknowledged the president's unpopularity and the PRD's intelligent campaign in 1978.

36. Readers may also wish to turn back to table 3.1, which summarizes in general terms the ways in which each of these clusters of factors may be more favorable to democratic transition.

37. This set of comparisons does not allow us to make a more definitive statement. With extensive U.S. efforts, democracy progressed further following Trujillo's demise than might have been expected. But it is telling that in spite of these efforts, Bosch was overthrown in 1963. What we cannot know is what might have occurred had communism not been an issue or had the United States or international organizations sustained high levels of involvement in the early to mid-1960s. Contemporary El Salvador might become a more telling test of the effectiveness of measures under these circumstances, albeit from a different kind of authoritarian regime.

38. These are explored by Bratton and van de Walle in their article (1994) and in a book published as I was reviewing the copyedited manuscript (1997).

Chapter 5

1. This explanation builds upon and, thus, "tests" (in the Dominican context) the arguments presented in chapters 1 and 3 about neopatrimonial path-dependency and about the transition process representing both constraints and opportunities. This explanation also relies on comparative literature on democratization during this period, which has highlighted the impact of international economic constraints and the problematic nature of certain kinds of political-institutional arrangements on consolidation. The Dominican Republic is not unique on the continent either in its difficulties in achieving consolidation during this period or in some of the kinds of problems that it has experienced. Yet, what the analysis of these several chapters seeks to underscore is how comparable important aspects of its political experience are, not only to certain other Latin American cases, but also to African cases of neopatrimonialism, without at the same time "reducing" the entire explanation of what has occurred in the country to neopatrimonialism or stretching excessively the observed points of similarity.

2. The Caribbean Basin Economic Recovery Act (CBERA) became law in August 1983. For twelve years (subsequently extended indefinitely by the CBI II legislation), it provided Caribbean countries duty-free access to the U.S. market, while also promising increased flows of U.S. aid to the countries of the region (Paus 1988, 193–94). The 1986 legislation exempted qualifying nations such as the Dominican Republic from all quota agreements, such as the Multifibers Agreement, while requiring that all raw materials either originate from the United States or from qualifying nation suppliers (this became known as "Super 807," or "807a," as it lifted restrictions imposed under clause 807 of the trade act that had initially fostered assembly-abroad operations by charging duty only on the value added by assembly while at the same time subjecting such imports to quotas and other restrictions). The CBI II law, in turn, eased the restriction regarding raw materials by permitting the use of non-U.S. materials if they were not produced in the United States, while allowing for some processing of the material (for example, cutting and layout) to occur in the qualifying Caribbean-basin country (Kaplinsky 1993, esp. 1854–55). Of lesser importance has been section 936 of the Internal Revenue Code of 1986, under which U.S. companies based in Puerto Rico could carry out part of their production process in a CBI country while still retaining their U.S. federal income tax exemption (Willmore 1995, 530). While these trade measures were being enacted, the U.S. sugar quota was experiencing a dramatic drop. The total quota for 1984 was 1.1 million tons, of which the Dominican Republic was given slightly over half (535,392 tons); by 1987, the total quota had dropped to 349,770 tons, of which the Dominican share was 160,160 tons (Paus 1988, 201–20). In some subsequent years it increased somewhat, but never to the 1984 level.

3. Employment levels are estimates; other sources differ regarding precise numbers, but not general trends—for example, Kaplinsky (1993) or Willmore (1995, 530), which

states that EPZ employment is now greater than in the protected domestic manufacturing establishments.

4. Dauhajre hijo and Aristy Escuder (1996, 51) give a surprisingly high 1995 estimate for FTZs of 180,000 jobs and net exports of US$795 million.

5. See Economist Intelligence Unit (1994, 25) for 1980–92 data. Puerto Rico grew from around 1.6 million to 2.6 million during this same period. For 1995 data, see Banco Central (1995b, 19) and Economic Intelligence Unit (1995, 20–21).

6. International pressure regarding the labor code also reflected growing attention to the plight of Haitian cane cutters and other Haitian workers in the Dominican Republic. As Dominicans became more sensitive to the treatment of Dominican migrants in the United States, it was also inevitable that focus on Haitians in the Dominican Republic would also grow. Complex structural dynamics—of inequality and dramatic poverty within Haiti, of a lack within the country of alternatives to departure—fed Haitian migration to the Dominican Republic, and the only long-term solution to the mistreatment of Haitian cane cutters is probably a dramatic reduction in Dominican sugar production. For analyses of the complex interplay of relations across the United States, Haiti, the Dominican Republic, and international NGOs over the 1980s and 1990s, and for debates over the social or political implications of analyzing the mistreatment of Haitians as "slavery" or probably more accurately as "forced labor," see Lozano (1992), Corten (1993), Corten and Duarte (1995), Murphy (1991), and Cuello H. (1997). As many of these analyses underscore, denying basic citizenship rights to a substantial portion of a population living within the Dominican Republic's borders clearly restricts the scope and ultimately the viability of democratic politics (in terms of contestation, inclusiveness, and the rule of law), yet the building of democratic coalitions across the Dominican Republic and Haiti to address this problem in all of its structural, cultural, and political dimensions is likely to be a difficult and protracted process.

7. Preliminary results of the 1993 Dominican census (which was fraught with problems) estimated that the country's second largest municipality of Santiago had around 488,300 people, of which 364,900 lived in the urban area (Oficina Nacional de Estadística 1994, 30).

8. Out-migration is a widely perceived option; in a 1994 survey, 25 percent of the sample said that to make progress in their lives they may have to leave the country (Duarte et al. 1996, 180). Large-scale migration is hardly unique to the Dominican Republic; indeed, it is extensive throughout the Caribbean. According to one source, for Cuba, some 10 percent of Cuban-born individuals live abroad; for Puerto Rico, 40 percent; Jamaica, 21 percent; Barbados, 25 percent; Trinidad and Tobago, 20 percent; and Haiti, 20 percent; this source gives a figure of over 10 percent for the Dominican Republic (Vega and Despradel 1994, 204).

9. Graham (1995, 22); and author's interview with U.S. consular official in Santo Domingo, 1996, for the first and last estimates. The 1992 estimate is based on a household survey which showed that nationally 6.3 percent of Dominican income came from overseas remittances and that in urban areas 6.0 percent of income did (Dauhajre hijo, Achécar, and Swindale 1994, 10–11).

10. Comparisons of this nature are fraught with risks and should probably be treated only as rough approximations. Indeed, in comparison to studies by other Dominican economists, the poverty indices by Dauhajre et al. (1996) are conservative.

11. For example, 76 percent of the sample (91 percent of the rural subsample) agreed with the statement "a good president should be like a father to whom one must go to resolve problems," and 50 percent of the sample (59 percent of the rural subsample) agreed with the statement "a strong leader would do more for the country than all the laws and institutions together"; on the other hand, 79 percent of the sample also agreed that "the presidency of the republic has too much power." For tabulations of these and other questions by socioeconomic strata, level of education, age, residence, and gender, and for a valuable discussion also of ethnic and racial issues raised by the questionnaire, see Duarte et al. (1996, 46–51, 184).

12. This survey did not ask about specific political preferences, but from other survey studies it is clear that Balaguer's strongest base of support has typically come from rural, older, less-educated, and women voters (cf. Hamilton and Strother 1994).

13. More research is also needed to determine the actual and potential impact of return migrants. Even as migrant communities abroad were important bases of financial support for some political parties (especially the PRD and the PLD), some believed that many return migrants brought not only investment capital, but a rejection of nondemocratic and neopatrimonial norms. Gaining more notoriety and attention were the small minority involved in the narcotics retail trade in New York (see Graham 1996).

14. Guzmán was definitely more conservative than Jorge Blanco; accusations that Jorge Blanco was "surrounded by communists" circulated among domestic and foreign business circles in 1981 and 1982 (Peña Gómez 1986b, 19). In a speech on September 11, 1981, Peña Gómez remarked that some in "the government" were more opposed to Jorge Blanco than even to Balaguer and might not accept his victory, specifically noting the suspicions that some military held of Jorge Blanco (Peña Gómez 1986a, 128–29). Majluta, who became president following Guzmán's suicide in July 1982, played an important role in easing tensions between the military and the incoming Jorge Blanco administration and insuring a smooth transition (Peña Gómez 1986c, 323–28; Moya Pons 1995, 412). As one interviewee told me, military officers had asked Majluta if he really intended to hand power over to Jorge Blanco, whom Guzmán had told them was a communist surrounded by dangerous radicals and whose campaign Guzmán believed was supported in part by the Cuban government (author's interview in February 1986).

15. This practice, of which several examples were cited to me, was not limited to top military and appeared to riddle the government bureaucracy.

16. The problems of relying on "partisan balance," rather than on partially insulated, professional agencies and individuals in another critical state institution—the electoral oversight agency (the JCE)—is a central theme of chapter 8. Nevertheless, at least with regard to the military, Dominican administrations since 1978 have prevented the emergence and consolidation of an armed forces that were too corporate and too autonomous with regard to civilian oversight and control. However, a few months after his inauguration in 1996, President Fernández dramatically fired the

head of the air force, who appeared to be acquiring a personal following and a taste for political power and who was challenging civilian authority. The fact that the incident passed without major turmoil underscores the weakness of the military institution and the lack of societal support for military incursion into politics.

17. This may be contrasted both with Brazil, where literacy requirements were not lifted until 1985, and with Ecuador, where such restrictions were in place until the late 1970s (Conaghan 1995, 445). On women and the vote under Trujillo, see Mota (1976).

18. On Ecuadorian parties and the inability to forge strong parties, see Conaghan (1995). The descriptions applied here to the PLD are borrowed from Conaghan's descriptions of the strongest Ecuadorian parties (447). See Mainwaring (1995) on Brazilian parties; for a parallel discussion of Dominican and Ecuadorian parties, see Conaghan and Espinal (1990, 569–71).

19. The electoral law only permits one list to be registered by party by province or municipality for the positions in question (representatives to the chamber of deputies or municipal *concejales*; note that only one senator is elected from each province or the national district); that list is called "closed" because individuals are elected based on the order in which their names are placed on it. Throughout this period, there were complex and changing rules regarding party alliances. The fact that legislative elections were always held concurrent with presidential elections also helped accentuate the party and its top leader over local candidacies. In 1986, voters were even unable to split their ballot.

20. For the 1986 elections, of the country's 147 legislators, only 33 (22.5 percent) were renominated by their party; within the PRD, only 14 (18 percent) of the party's 79 senators and deputies were renominated (*Hoy*, April 7, 1986).

21. In the May 1982 and May 1986 polls, the PRD was the party with the highest level of expressed membership by the samples: 31.0 percent and 30.2 percent, respectively. Breakdown by party was not available for 1989 (Brea et al. 1995, 202).

22. First three polls cited in Brea et al. (1995, 202); third from *El Siglo*, November 7, 1989; last from Duarte et al. (1996, 66). The contrast with countries like Ecuador remains dramatic; a 1989 survey in Ecuador's two major cities found no more than a third categorizing themselves as either militants or sympathizers of any party and more than 70 percent as either independent or indifferent (Conaghan 1995, 451).

23. For a detailed analysis of how in the context of partyarchy, factionalism and splits emerged in the Venezuelan AD party because of tensions over the internal selection of its principal leaders and over executive-legislative relations (which clearly hurt its prospects in general elections), see Coppedge (1994).

24. As Brea Franco noted (1991), it was theoretically possible for a party with plurality victories in sixteen rural provinces—which together contained only 20 percent of the country's population—to win control of the senate (cited in Brea et al. 1995, 154–55). See Brea et al. (1995, 151–63) for a useful summary of Dominican scholarship on problems of disproportionality in chamber as well as senate elections.

Further evidence of the centralizing impact of election rules is found in Mitchell (forthcoming). As he notes, although in four of the six national elections from 1962 to 1990, ticket splitting was possible, few voters did. In 1994, however, when ticket splitting was further facilitated by actually having three separate ballots, there was evidence of somewhat greater ticket splitting; in that year, the PLD's local candidates received 3.7 percent more overall votes than did the PLD's presidential candidate.

25. A number of these patterns were modified by constitutional reforms carried out in August 1994 as discussed in chapter 8; among other measures, these reforms restricted immediate presidential reelection and called for the creation of a special council formed by the three branches of government to name supreme court justices, who, in turn, would name all other judges.

Chapter 6

1. Although measures taken during the PRD years facilitated the country's economic reorientation toward services, many of the exchange-related and other reforms painfully taken in the context of an IMF stabilization plan were undone by the subsequent Balaguer administration.

2. Guzmán committed suicide on July 3, 1982, and his vice president Majluta completed the remaining weeks of his term in office. For simplicity, I refer to the entire period (1978–82) as the Guzmán years.

3. Some scholars see a double-edged nature to the influence of such aid—especially in smaller countries, where large amounts of aid may reduce the urgency of reform as much as the pain of adjustment (see Nelson 1990a, 206).

4. As we saw in chapter 4, criticisms of Balaguer's import-substituting industrialization strategy began almost from its inception; Balaguer's insistence on retaining it in the face of its economic costs appeared to be based on his reliance on industrialists as a core support group. Under Balaguer, in spite of high levels of economic growth (11.1 percent average from 1969 to 1973, 6 percent average from 1974 to 1976, and somewhat lower subsequently), open unemployment exceeded 20 percent, and agricultural output stagnated with growth at less than 2 percent per year (see Moya Pons 1986; and World Bank, *World Development Report*, 1985).

5. Terms of trade and export levels had improved in 1980 and 1981 because of high gold and silver prices, but declined subsequently due particularly to a fall in sugar prices.

6. One of the first major debates in the country regarding the likelihood, the nature, and the timing of negotiations with the IMF took place in October 1981 in a formal debate on the external sector organized by the Forum organization. See Moya Pons (1982), especially the presentation by Bernardo Vega (one of Jorge Blanco's key initial advisers as governor of the central bank and a proponent of the need for a stabilization program).

7. The other major factor overlooked by this strategy was the impact that increased public expenditures would have on the country's import levels, and thus on its balance of payments.

8. The CNHE had been created in 1963 as part of the efforts of different business groups to conspire to overthrow Bosch. Four interest associations controlled the CNHE, and until 1978 they had a "gentlemen's agreement" that the presidency would rotate among them. Of these four, the association that dominated the organization and paid most of its budget was the AIRD. Yet, until 1978, the CNHE had no office of

its own, no staff, no publications, and no services for its member firms; it was allowed to operate out of the Chamber of Commerce, Agriculture, and Industry of Santo Domingo (author's interviews with a number of the central actors, Santo Domingo, 1986).

9. A secret agreement was signed with the Mexican organization, whereby it provided the CNHE with technical assistance to help establish an office to track the ideological tendencies of the press and of politicians, in part to attempt to determine likely future economic policies.

10. For a more extensive discussion of trends in the evolution of popular-sector organizations, labor unions, and social protest, see chapter 7. Valuable analyses of why there were only limited gains by popular-sector organizations and by labor during the PRD years include Cassá (1995); Espinal (1985, 1987b); Ferguson (1992); and Ianni (1987, 1990). The author's personal visits to the country's major labor confederations and interviews with union leaders (over 1985–86 and in subsequent visits) highlighted the constraints under which they operated, their relative weakness, and the fact they were often unable to escape from the neopatrimonial logic of the larger political framework in which they operated. A clear example is the rise, division, and decline of the PRD-linked labor confederation.

11. As already noted, as the senate was responsible for appointing judges, in effect this gave Balaguer control over the judiciary. Numerous Balaguer officials were accused of corruption before the courts, but none of the judicial processes prospered.

12. As one PRD senator at the time subsequently told me, given the use Trujillo had made of emergency powers following a cyclone (see chapter 2), the party could never agree to granting such powers to a president (author's interview, 1985). An example of how the ideological tensions between the president and party leaders surfaced is that after the hurricanes, Peña Gómez, Jorge Blanco, and other party leaders traveled to the airport to meet a shipment of aid from Cuba, which they and not the government had requested. Furthermore, Jorge Blanco from congress promoted an amnesty law and a law permitting Dominicans to travel to socialist countries that Guzmán was slow to act on. For other examples of ideological and political tensions between Guzmán and the PRD, see Rodriguez and Huntington (1982).

13. Guzmán's problems with congress were also magnified by Balaguer's decision in mid-1980 to oppose any new fiscal measures and to block required congressional approval of new international loans. Since his Partido Reformista maintained a majority in the senate, this was a significant move, assuming party discipline could be maintained.

14. See González Canahuate (1985, 86–87, 104–5); and Moya Pons (1986, 26, 314), who wrote that the more open selection method had the consequence, which was not immediately evident to Guzmán, of increasing the number of eligible PRD voters beyond even the employment capacity of the Dominican state.

15. Although an audit of CORDE under Majluta's management was indeterminate, at a minimum it is clear that Majluta "ran his campaign" out of his CORDE offices until he stepped down months prior to the primary date; during his months as head of CORDE, public resources were almost certainly employed to further his own faction's possibilities.

16. The position of mayor of Santo Domingo was promised to a Majluta sympathizer. Ultimately, however, on the basis of surveys which showed all the proposed candidates to be unpopular, Jorge Blanco opposed them. Thus, Peña Gómez, who originally was going to run as PRD candidate for senator from Santo Domingo, ran for mayor, and Majluta himself became the PRD candidate for senator from Santo Domingo. Peña Gómez's popularity in Santo Domingo helped assure a comfortable margin of victory for Jorge Blanco in Santo Domingo, offsetting losses elsewhere, and assuring his win.

17. The most widely repeated account of the tragic event focuses on charges of corruption against Guzmán's daughter and son-in-law and Guzmán's fear of retribution by Jorge Blanco, with whom he had a bitter enmity; however, this would be an insufficient explanation in itself, as most individuals in similar circumstances would not choose to kill themselves. More conspiratorial versions focus on the accidental explosion of the grenade at the JCE, not as an embarrassment, but as an aborted coup attempt by Guzmán or his daughter to seek to prevent Jorge Blanco's accession to power (see Black 1986, 137). I have been unable to sort out fully the various accounts, though I doubt the veracity of the more extravagant ones. Based on the interviews I carried out, the text provides the set of factors that appear to me to be the most likely to have played an important role in this tragic event; here, as elsewhere in the book, future revelations might lead me to revise the text.

Accusations of massive corruption by members of the Guzmán family were repeated to me, but with little specific evidence. In interviews, I was given limited examples of abuse of power and of the use of state resources for private gain, such as the private use of official aircraft or state equipment. Guzmán's widow, her daughter, and her daughter's family returned to Santiago, where they continued to reside. What is clear is their continuing personal resentment as well as their sense of ideological distance from Jorge Blanco and from Peña Gómez; in 1996, they openly endorsed Peña Gómez's opponent, Leonel Fernández, for the presidency (author's interviews with important figures in the Guzmán administration and with PRD leaders, 1985 and 1986; 1996 press reports).

18. The contacts began following the suicide of Antonio Guzmán, while Jacobo Majluta occupied the presidency.

19. This was even more true of the Dominican Republic that it was of Jamaica, where it turned out to be a critical stumbling block for the Manley regime (see Huber Stephens and Stephens 1986, 310–14). There is much to criticize regarding specific actions of international actors and the policies they sought to impose on debtor countries, but the analysis here (as in the book in general) is focused more on domestic political processes and actors in the face of these international constraints and demands.

20. By early 1983, 46 percent of total imports remained in the official (parity exchange rate) market, as compared to 65 percent in 1978. Around 90 percent of these imports were raw materials, primarily oil or oil-related (World Bank, *World Development Report*, 1985, 53).

21. An IMF document of March 1985, to which I was provided access, noted that the major area of "slippage" was in public finance and was heavily concentrated in the last months of 1983. It stated that the country's fiscal deficit/GDP ended the year at 5.6

percent, in contrast to the program target of 3.9 percent (author's field notes, 1986). The World Bank later estimated the fiscal deficit to be 5.3 percent of GDP (see table B.4).

22. For one version of the internal debates in the face of extraordinarily difficult international circumstances, see Messina (1988); for a contrasting one, that also argues that a "shock treatment" was not feasible due to its total lack of acceptance within the government, the party, and the country, see Vega (1988b, esp. 26).

23. For evidence on this, see Devlin (1989, 181–235); Jorge Blanco also makes this point in an August 1991 interview with Rosario Espinal, see Espinal (1991a, 6).

24. Ferguson (1992, 93) notes that protests began as a demonstration by neighborhood associations in the poverty-stricken Capotillo area of Santo Domingo, requesting a rollback of the price increases, a repeal of the agreement with the IMF, improved public utility services, higher minimum wages, and other demands. Met with harsh repression, crowds fought back, and demonstrations soon spread across Santo Domingo and to some thirty other urban areas. Ferguson cites 112 civilian deaths, 500 wounded, and 5,000 arrests over the period from April 23 to April 25, 1984, with nearly all of the casualties due to actions of the country's security forces.

25. The country was not alone in having an IMF agreement. In February 1986, the Dominican Republic was one of twenty-nine countries that had standby agreements with the IMF, while an additional two countries had extended agreements.

26. The way in which the banks in Mexico had been blamed for that country's economic problems and how they were nationalized by López Portillo in 1982 was mentioned in two of the interviews with business leaders.

27. In fact, as will be discussed in the next section, electoral statistics indicate that the PRD suffered proportionally greater losses from its left flank, as the PLD doubled its vote.

28. For the text of these failed reforms and for a full description of the process of constitutional reform, see Brea Franco (1983b, 55–62, 82–83, 345–61). Some cooperation from PR congressional representatives would have been required, as constitutional amendments must be passed by a two-thirds vote of both chambers meeting together.

29. In the spring of 1986, the exchange surcharge on traditional exports was reduced to 18 percent, and its application to nontraditional exports was eliminated.

30. The interpretation of events that appears most plausible to me now is that security officials linked to Jorge Blanco's government sought to stop the vote proceedings as the outcome appeared to favor Majluta (see Majluta 1992; see also Espinal 1987a, 195–96).

31. For the 1986 election, the Partido Reformista (PR) united with several minor Christian Democratic parties, including confusingly the Partido Revolucionario Social Cristiano (PRSC) to become the Partido Reformista Social Cristiano. For ease of exposition for the period from 1986 on, Balaguer's party is abbreviated as PR(SC).

32. "Vincho" Castillo, a lawyer close to Balaguer, brought the corruption charges; and, at least initially, Balaguer did not interfere overtly in the judicial process. Even those sympathetic to Jorge Blanco do not deny there was corruption, but in interviews with the author over 1987 and 1988 they asserted that his administration was "no more corrupt" than Balaguer's earlier governments, whereas Jorge Blanco at least did not

order any assassinations, was more respectful of civil liberties, and tolerated accusations levied against him to an extent Balaguer never would have.

Corruption under Jorge Blanco probably grew over time and may well have been more visible than under the previous Balaguer years for three reasons. One was that those acquiring wealth during the PRD governments were from more modest backgrounds, whereas under Balaguer those who may have been enriching themselves illegally were already quite wealthy. Another is that corruption tends to be more visible during periods of economic decline. Finally, Jorge Blanco explicitly campaigned on a pledge of honest, open government, making the contrast even starker (see Hartlyn 1989, B482–83).

Chapter 7

1. Averages calculated from tables 7.1 and B.4. As the data in table B.4 indicates, Jorge Blanco dramatically increased expenditures through the office of the presidency from 12.3 percent in 1984 to 26.2 percent in 1985. Since 1986 was a transition year (Balaguer was inaugurated in August), I have not included it in the averages for either Jorge Blanco or Balaguer, though it continued to show an upward trend, to 31.9 percent. This is consonant with the argument (presented in chapter 6) that Jorge Blanco turned increasingly to neopatrimonialism toward the end of his term in office.

2. Nickel exports grew from US$78 million in 1986 to US$115 million in 1987 and then jumped to US$309 million in 1988 and US$372 million in 1989 before falling to US$228 million in 1990 (IMF, *International Financial Statistics*, various issues).

3. See Ceara Hatton (1993) for an excellent discussion of the tensions inherent in Balaguer's economic policy. The IDB estimated that in 1989 one-half of the country's electric power was provided by these small-scale generating units. This represented the most inefficient de facto form of privatization imaginable, leading to further foreign-exchange expenditures—both for the oil to run the generators and the machines themselves, which were more inefficient than an effective national power grid could tolerate (Inter-American Development Bank, *Economic and Social Progress*, 1990, 95 ff.).

4. In December 1987, the then governor of the central bank wrote a letter to President Balaguer warning him that, given the country's precarious reserves and the dollar demands of the ambitious public-investment program, he could not preclude a collapse of the country's exchange rate without access to additional external resources; he noted that the country actually had a negative net flow with both the World Bank and the IMF in 1987 (reprinted in Dauhajre hijo 1990, 537–43). At year end 1988, the government had around US$540 million in debt arrears, principally to bilateral (Paris Club) creditors. In an April 1989 column, one economist claimed that the Dominican Republic "must be one of the best payers of external debt in Latin America" (Dauhajre hijo 1989, 231).

5. This underscores the fact that the country's central bank has not had autonomy relative to the presidency, even as powerful elements of the private sector have also had important access. The bank's governor, its personnel, and the members of the bank's governing body, the monetary board, may be replaced by the executive branch

and do not need to be full-time economists. Although Balaguer may have intervened more openly in central-bank operations than did the PRD governments, one of Guzmán's central-bank governors also resigned (in March 1980) in protest over the government's decision to continue funding public-sector deficits through central-bank credits (i.e., monetary expansion). When Robert Triffin first helped establish the country's central bank under Trujillo in 1947, he saw the only possible counterbalance to Trujillo's power as coming from the private sector, to which he gave strong representation on the bank's board (see Vega 1990a, 149–54). Throughout this period, the most powerful economic groups and families in the country have been able to influence policy and inform and protect themselves more adequately than other firms or social sectors in the country. As of mid-1997, this structure had not changed, though steps toward greater bank autonomy were being discussed. Dauhajre hijo et al. (1996, 77–89, 719–22) provides further comparative evidence of the remarkably low autonomy of the country's central bank, whether calculated on an index created by Cukierman (which indicates low autonomy, but which could still overstate the Dominican bank's autonomy given that the law is not always complied with) or based on the average tenure of central-bank governors. With an average tenure of only around twenty to twenty-one months, the Dominican Republic had the second lowest average of the sample of fifty-eight countries (only Argentina was lower). The two PRD governments over 1978–86 had five different governors and Balaguer over 1986–96 had six, with "political" ones (especially responsive to his dictates) in place for the electoral periods (September 1989 to June 1990 and August 1993 to September 1994). Balaguer did name a professional governor in September 1994 (who reduced the bank's workforce by over 600 employees in a four-month period) and who was not replaced by the incoming Fernández administration in August 1996.

6. As one leading businessman explained, Balaguer was able to "coerce" the country's business sector "in a way that no one else could." Business leaders could be open to intimidation because of the fact that, given the way "you have to do business in this country, no one is squeaky clean." For this reason, some businesses avoid government contracts and seek to minimize all contacts with the public sector. Another interviewee noted that Balaguer "knows the origins of all Dominican fortunes," which gave him greater capacity to control the business sector and maintain his independence from it (author's interviews, May 1990).

7. Following a long interrogation session and an order for his arrest on corruption charges relating to illegal commissions on the purchase of equipment for the armed forces, Jorge Blanco fled to the Venezuelan embassy on April 31, 1987, requesting political asylum. A heart spasm led to his internment in a Santo Domingo clinic, even as the Venezuelan government opted not to respond to his asylum request. Jorge Blanco was allowed to leave for the United States for medical treatment after acknowledging there was a warrant for his arrest. He returned in 1989 and, as required by law, a new trial was held at that time. He was found guilty again, and as of mid-1997 the case was still languishing on appeal while he was out on bail.

8. The movement foundered over whether it should remain a pressure group or seek to transform itself into a political party, and it eventually disappeared. Many of its former members, however, have remained influential in ongoing debates on eco-

nomic liberalization and political and state reforms. The movement presaged the growing emphasis of international financial institutions such as the World Bank and the IDB on the need to join market-oriented reforms with enhanced state capacity and "democratic governance."

9. Balaguer's support was imputed by observers at the time from the coincidence of the timing of certain judicial decisions that permitted Jorge Blanco supporters to vote in key intra-PRD conflicts in support of Peña Gómez. Balaguer's apparent electoral calculation was that Peña Gómez in control of the PRD would hurt Bosch and the PLD more in the upcoming 1990 elections, whereas Majluta in control of the PRD would probably hurt Bosch less and Balaguer more (author's interviews, 1990).

10. The Dominican economist Bernardo Vega argued in the late 1980s that the foreign-exchange bonanza generated by the brief boom in nickel prices should have been used to retire the country's debt at what were then very favorable prices on the secondary market; if that had been done, the country would have come out much better than it did with the 1994 renegotiation. Instead, those boom funds were used to pay for construction and infrastructure projects with total presidential discretion, rather than relying for these projects on loans from multilateral development banks, which would have come with oversight conditions and required congressional approval (see Vega 1991, 97–99; 1994a).

11. Oil and agricultural products and agricultural inputs largely remain under license (Vega 1993b). I was given one example of how a "contract" to import foodstuffs was granted as a political favor to an individual who knew nothing about agricultural marketing: a woman who had once been the outspoken leader of a popular-sector organization that had given Balaguer serious problems was given a lucrative contract to import garlic (author's interview with a journalist, 1995).

12. Albuquerque was a noted labor lawyer who had been a prominent leader in the PLD until he was ousted by Bosch. He founded his own small party and formed political alliances with other groups at different times while continuing his legal work. In 1990, Albuquerque was a failed senate candidate for Majluta's new party; in 1994, he remained allied with Balaguer as he continued to serve as his secretary of labor; in May 1996, he quit Balaguer's government to work with PLD candidate Leonel Fernández.

13. The move would have required a constitutional amendment and, given how problematic the 1990 elections had been, there were reasons to be skeptical about organizing an unscheduled electoral process. The proposal bought time for Balaguer, as he intended, and was eventually forgotten, as so many of his past promises and proposals.

14. As in other areas, such as labor and electoral reform, Monsignor Agripino Núñez Collado played an important mediating role across labor and business interests and between these interests, congress, and the president in reaching agreements and helping to enact legislation (see Núñez Collado 1993).

15. The UNE did not consist solely of importing interests, though it was a strong proponent of neoliberal reforms. For example, construction interests joined the UNE because of their interest in sidestepping protected local industries to be able to import

cheaper cement and building material. In contrast, some importers, such as auto-mobile distributors and pharmaceuticals, stayed with the CNHE (author's interviews with business leaders, 1996). See also Espinal (1998).

16. The contrasting points of view are starkly presented by the president of the industrialists' association, Marranzini (1995) and the president of UNE, Dauhajre (1995).

17. Balaguer changed the customs director, in his own words, "because we are in a preelectoral period and changes are necessary to improve the situation of the mili-tancy of the Partido Reformista" (quoted in *Revista Rumbo*, January 11–17, 1995, 28).

18. Shortly after this scandal, another major problem with embezzlement of funds in the ministry of education was made public, seriously affecting progress on the consensually arrived at "Ten Year Plan for Education."

19. Relevant here are three anecdotes based on the author's trips to the Dominican Republic over 1995 and 1996. One interviewee, active in the GAD, explained he had to unplug his phone during our conversation because a tap that worked through the phone wires had just been discovered in his office. At another time, a U.S. government official explained to me, "You know, you just don't talk on the phones in this country." Finally, a journalist reporting on the 1994 electoral fraud received death threats. Phone taps were apparently not just carried out by state agents; Balaguer's strategists for his 1994 campaign in the United States assert their faxed strategy memos were intercepted by the opposition (Hamilton and Strother 1994, 43).

20. Based on the not unreasonable assumption that 15 percent of government ex-penditures were lost to corruption, Dauhajre hijo et al. (1996, 750, 754) estimated that the Dominican Republic had the highest level of corruption in Latin America and that, of a worldwide sample of countries, only Nigeria and Pakistan had a higher "corruption index."

21. These included enterprises such as the state airline, forced to suspend flights in early 1995, and companies that produced products such as edible oils, paint, and hardware. The journalist Minerva Isa analyzed the extent, nature, and causes of the financial crises of the umbrella holding company CORDE and of many major enter-prises in a series of articles published in *Hoy*, from August 19 to September 2, 1996. For dramatic examples of corruption and mismanagement, see especially Isa (1996a; 1996b).

22. It was estimated that the CDE owed private energy suppliers around DR$1,300 million for past debts and was spending or accumulating debts of around DR$635 million each month (of which DR$332 million was to private suppliers), but was receiving only DR$300 million monthly from customers (Araujo 1996).

23. See the sharply opposing visions presented by Marranzini (1995), representing domestic industrialists, and Dauhajre (1995), giving the point of view of importers. For example, several leading organizations stayed away from the special national conven-tion that was held in November 1995 and that resulted in the publication of a "Busi-ness Agenda for Integrated Development" (Consejo Nacional de la Empresa Privada 1995). At the convention, in recognition of the increasing role of women in business and to move toward gender-neutral language, it was formally decided to change the

name of the umbrella organization from the Consejo Nacional de Hombres de Empresa (CNHE, National Businessmen's Council) to the Consejo Nacional de la Empresa Privada (CONEP, National Council of Private Enterprise).

24. Scant survey data is consonant with this view. A 1984–85 opinion survey, showed 15.4 percent of the sample agreeing that the "government was right to sign an agreement with the IMF"; to a similar question in 1992, 29 percent of a survey agreed. To the question of whether government should stimulate foreign investment, 41 percent said yes in a 1983 poll, compared to 63 percent in a 1992 poll; to a question regarding whether tourism was good for the country, 68 percent agreed in 1986, and 77 percent did in 1992 (poll data cited in Brea et al. 1995, 231).

25. Factors at the individual level also play a role. Balaguer is unquestionably a skilled politician, which emerged time and again in his management of such issues as gasoline-price increases.

26. With regard to possessing some control over congress, Balaguer was similar to the above three presidents. In spite of the numerous corruption charges surrounding Menem and his entourage, he remained untouched because the Peronists controlled congress. In turn, Collor's impeachment on corruption charges in Brazil clearly related to the fact he did not control a majority in congress.

Chapter 8

1. Another side of his personality emerged in 1982. In what was described as a "crime of passion," he killed his wife who was seeking a divorce; he spent a few months in jail in preventive detention before being released on bail, and in a 1985 trial the judge dismissed all charges against him (Díaz 1996, 86–87).

2. For Mota's lyrical description of the organization, see *Listín Diario*, August 3, 1992, 7; ministries and government agencies, in turn, reportedly complained of being forced to purchase large blocs of tickets for receptions and dinners sponsored by the organization (author's interview, 1994).

3. Beginning in the early 1970s and imitating other Latin American countries, and in fact with the assistance of Chilean and other electoral experts, the JCE began to elaborate a formal electoral registry (established by law 55 of 1970). Voters were able to cast ballots in the 1962 and 1966 elections by presenting their identity cards, as voter registry lists did not exist. Problems with the pre-1994 Dominican registry identified in del Castillo and Tejada (1992) include the lack of deletion of deceased individuals; the lack of deletion of individuals on active military or police duty (constitutionally unable to vote), or of those condemned of crimes; and the possibilities of duplicate ID cards and of foreigners having ID cards. A conservative estimate is that these names comprised 10 percent to 15 percent of the electoral registry. Some substantial additional number represented Dominicans who had migrated overseas. At the same time, many hundreds of thousands of Dominicans had never registered to vote. In sum, this study estimated perhaps a 60 percent to 75 percent validity of the electoral registry prior to the issuance of new identity cards in 1993.

4. Material on these elections is derived from the author's personal observations of the 1986, 1990, and 1994 elections and interviews with many key actors. This chapter is

based in part on earlier articles, Hartlyn (1987; 1990; and especially 1994). Other useful analyses of Dominican elections include, among others, Espinal (1990b; 1992); Murphy and Santana (1983); Jiménez Polanco (1994); Brea et al. (1995); Mitchell (forthcoming); Latorre (1995); Campillo Pérez (1982); and works by Julio Brea Franco, José del Castillo, Frank Moya Pons, Adriano Miguel Tejada, and Bernardo Vega, cited below or elsewhere in this book.

5. As had happened before and was to occur again, the closed nature of candidate selection, especially within the PR(SC), was such that after the filing date potential candidates appeared at JCE sites around the country to determine if and where on the list they had been registered (cf. Hartlyn 1987; del Castillo 1986, 17–18).

6. A Gallup poll showed the following support levels (in percentages) for Bosch, Balaguer, Peña Gómez, and Majluta, respectively: 34, 24, 13, and 12; a Penn and Schoen question based on the party scenario that occurred in May, reflected the following percentages for the above four, in the same order: 36, 26, 19, and 12 (*El Siglo*, February 21, 1990; *Listín Diario*, February 21, 1990).

7. Some of these abuses have been discussed in chapter 7; for additional examples and details, see also Díaz (1996, 123–39).

8. For example, see "Alianzas determinarán triunfo comicial 94," *Listín Diario*, November 14, 1993; "Enigma de alianzas domina puja electoral," *Listín Diario*, January 16, 1994; and "Alianzas, claves del actual proceso electoral," *Ultima Hora*, January 15, 1994.

9. When questioned by the NDI delegation about the major differences between the PLD and the PRD on May 15, 1994, Leonel Fernández explained the two parties had many areas of agreement, but the "major difference is [the PRD's] past political behavior, . . . they are corrupt, inefficient, and unpopular. We believe we deliver with a behavior in concordance with what we say" (author's field notes, 1994).

10. At the age of fifteen, Peña Gómez, from a modest background, had been hired by Alvarez's grandmother, a devout woman from a prominent and wealthy family, to educate the poor children she took under her care. The text of Peña Gómez's speech is reproduced in "Peña Gómez expone alcances Acuerdo," *Hoy*, February 16, 1994.

11. For a listing of the minor parties and their alliances for 1994, see Hartlyn (1994); for previous elections, see Jiménez Polanco (1994). In 1994, there were two other candidates. Jacobo Majluta of the PRI, after considering or trying to ally himself with each of the three other major parties, ultimately went to the polls on his own. The pragmatic, ambitious politician of conservative instincts found himself isolated. As another reflection of ideological and programmatic inconsistency, Majluta chose José Francisco Hernández as his vice presidential candidate. Hernández had been Bosch's vice presidential candidate in 1990, and before ultimately joining Majluta he had considered joining the PR(SC) effort ("Hernández, un vice de dos políticos muy opuestos," *Ultima Hora*, March 17, 1994). Majluta passed away just before the first round of the 1996 elections, for which he had intended to support Peña Gómez.

The fifth candidate was a popular priest from the Jarabacoa region, Antonio Reynoso Reynoso (Padre Toño), at the head of a coalition of popular organizations, Movimiento Independiente de Unidad y Cambio (MIUCA)–Nuevo Poder (Independent Movement for Unity and Change—New Power). He attacked the traditional personalistic and clientelist style of politics in the country, corruption, and disregard for the needs of the poor. Limited organization, personnel, and budget and the compelling logic of winner-take-all presidential elections limited his ability to project an effective national candidacy.

12. Problems of overlapping and competing efforts were evident also in the other parties. See "Los equipos de campaña: desunidos para ganar," *Revista Rumbo*, April 18, 1994.

13. In late April, anticipating the PLD's release of a copy of the videotape in their possession, which followed a few days later, the PRD showed a videotape apparently filmed in 1983 of Peña Gómez participating in a session in which a Brazilian "spiritualist" removed a tumor from an individual with a pair of scissors. The videotape was employed to suggest that Peña Gómez was involved in satanic cults. Subsequently, videotapes of Peña Gómez saying that his supporters would rise up in violent protest causing the country to burn if he was assassinated and aggressively confronting a heckler during a speech were also aired, and similar kinds of newspaper ads were published.

14. In 1993, the cardinal and archbishop of Santo Domingo denounced efforts to reinstall Aristide in Haiti as a "big mistake" (as quoted in Corten and Duarte 1995, 105). In May 1992, President Bush had ordered the direct repatriation of Haitian refugees headed for the United States, a policy President Clinton reaffirmed shortly after inauguration in January 1993, for which he had enlisted Aristide's support by promising harsher measures against the Haitian military. An oil and arms embargo against Haiti was imposed by the United Nations in July 1993; lifted soon thereafter, when an agreement had seemingly been reached; and then reimposed in October (see Perusse 1995, 160–61; and Dupuy 1997, 175–80).

15. For example, see M. A. Velázquez Mainardi, "Proceso electoral y crisis haitiana," *El Nacional*, May 8, 1994, 11.

16. See "Balaguer alega presionan fusión RD con Haití," *El Nacional*, May 8, 1994.

17. As a foreign political observer at the time noted to me, "the JCE is weak because the senate names weak people to the agency so the parties can negotiate politically if they desire to do so" (author's interview, 1986).

18. Opposition parties were later to change their view regarding Tavares's autonomy, claiming that preferential treatment by the Dominican judicial system of his son who had been arrested tainted his ability to be impartial (author's interviews, May 1990).

19. The previous JCE president, Tavares, notes that he had rejected an offer to become president of the supreme court because of the low salary. As president of the JCE, he was permitted to continue working on his own legal affairs and thus to continue earning additional money, even during the elections and even in legal processes before the state! (Tavares 1993, 67–68, 128).

20. Subsequently, Majluta blamed his defeat more on the lack of effective support from either President Jorge Blanco or Peña Gómez (see Majluta 1992).

21. Author's field notes (1990); see the report by the Council of Freely Elected Heads of Government (1990).

22. In interviews (1990–91), others asserted a crucial element that gave Balaguer his margin of victory was computer fraud related to the vote in Santo Domingo. They

pointed to three factors: the seemingly anomalous jump in Balaguer's vote count in the city from 1986 to 1990, given the social discontent expressed against the government; the initial massive administrative problems related to the distribution of the election material; and irregularities in the transmission of election results by fax from the Santo Domingo Junta to the JCE. For some it was more than just coincidence that Luis Taveras—the former general manager of IBM in the country, who had been a key computer adviser at the JCE for the 1990 elections—was granted the plum job of director of CORDE by the subsequent Balaguer administration. In a survey poll in early 1994, 57 percent of the respondents stated they did not have confidence in the 1990 election results (Duarte et al. 1996, 209).

23. In some areas of the country, military sympathetic to the PR(SC) sought to end the balloting early as word that the JCE might pass a resolution extending the voting leaked out; some of the municipal juntas made no effort to enforce the ruling; some presidents of *mesas* simply refused to extend the voting out of apparently partisan reasons while others refused because they had already begun the vote-counting process (these conclusions are based on behaviors observed by or reported to international election delegation members, author's field notes, May 1994).

24. The first international delegation to do so on May 18th, in a carefully worded statement, was that of the National Democratic Institute, led by the former New York congressman Stephen Solarz (and of which I was a member). Solarz and the delegation believed that they, as international observers, had to tell what they saw and that the burden of proof in disentangling the causes and the impact of the disenfranchisement should rest with the JCE (a view held by NDI in Washington, D.C., as well). They reached this conclusion after listening to what individual NDI delegates around the country had actually observed, confirming that other individual international observers had witnessed the same troubling phenomena and deliberating for many hours on the appropriate course of action. They also did so in the face of considerable pressure from domestic leaders and the head of the OAS delegation, influenced by the domestic leaders, who feared that even a cautious statement could be "putting a match on oily waters" (i.e., favoring an outbreak of violence), legitimizing Peña Gómez in his belief that the elections were stolen, and discouraging a process of negotiation between Balaguer and Peña Gómez (author's field notes, May 17, 1994; see also Díaz 1996, 196–97, 280 n.6).

25. Much remains to be known about how internal U.S. government dynamics on the issue of Haiti may have constrained policy toward the Dominican Republic during this period. In Washington, D.C., and within the U.S. security and intelligence apparatus, Haiti had considerably more priority than the Dominican Republic given its high domestic salience. At the same time, the U.S. Embassy and AID missions in Santo Domingo were able to sustain considerable diplomatic pressure around the Dominican elections.

In the weeks prior to the Dominican elections, Clinton's policies toward the Haitian military junta and Haitian refugees were being harshly criticized, leading the administration to modify its policies toward the refugees and to take additional steps to pressure the Haitian military. Only five days after the Dominican elections, on May 21, the United Nations levied an even more comprehensive embargo against the Haitian military government. And on May 26, William Gray, President Clinton's newly appointed special envoy to Haiti, met with President Balaguer. Following their meeting, it appeared that the Dominican Republic was complying much more strictly with the embargo against Haiti, as check points and major roads on the border were closed. This series of events led to speculation about an informal "deal" between Balaguer and the U.S. government (see Wiarda 1994). Yet, the Dominican embargo remained "leaky," and if there had been any agreement to allow Balaguer to remain in power in return for greater cooperation from him with regard to Haiti (for which I was unable to find any evidence), it appeared to have unraveled by July and August, as U.S. pressure on the Dominican Republic to hold new elections further intensified. U.S. forces landed in Haiti in September 1994 after a complex series of events, including last-minute negotiations involving former president Jimmy Carter; Aristide returned the following month to reassume the presidency (Perusse 1995, esp. 89, 161–63; Dupuy 1997, 153–62, 181–83; author's interviews with U.S. Government and international officials, 1994, 1995).

26. For a critical period just prior to the election, when the official voter registry rolls were printed, the international advisers were not allowed access to the computer center. What is reported in the JCE document is that the computer log was mysteriously erased, that the JCE had no copy of the official voter registry list employed on election day (only the copy given to the parties), and that the disenfranchisement took place either by switching names that were always of the same gender or, in some cases, by substituting new names.

27. Following the JCE's declaration of August 2, the U.S. Department of State declared it was "disappointed" by the JCE decision and stated that "the United States believes that new elections are the right idea, and urges Dominican authorities to take immediate steps in that direction." Extremely blunt language was employed in private meetings with Dominican officials.

28. Puerto Rico had once held elections under this method, which was the apparent inspiration for the PLD to suggest it. It was also lauded by the Partido Reformista's *Libro Blanco*, protesting the "irregularities" of the 1982 elections (Leonel Fernández presentation to the NDI delegation, May 1996, in author's field notes; Partido Reformista 1983, 287–88).

29. The caution in this phraseology reflects the fact that few would completely rule out a political comeback until Balaguer is deceased.

Chapter 9

1. By election day, two minor candidates had dropped out leaving only one, Abinader, who received less than 1 percent of the vote. It has been argued that the logic of two-round presidential elections with a 50 percent threshold is likely to encourage minor-party candidates to enter the first round and to stimulate party-system fragmentation; that it did not do so in this election in the Dominican Republic speaks to the strength and vitality of these three major parties (cf. Shugart and Carey 1992, 288–92; Espinal and Hartlyn 1995).

2. See Grupo de Acción por la Democracia (1996). With regard to specific recom-

mendations by the different business, labor, NGO, and municipal groups, there were often tensions, if not outright contradictions. The publication also lists eight additional priorities, ranging from social goals such as gender equity, pensions, and child-welfare policy; to economic goals focused on public spending and policymaking; to urban areas, peasant agriculture, and foreign trade.

3. The "quick count" consists of a parallel vote tabulation by independent observers of a carefully drawn, preselected sample of voting stations; in this case, from three subsamples (Santo Domingo, other urban, and rural). Six hundred voting stations from a total population of almost 10,000 were preselected. By midnight on May 16, the "quick count" had tabulated results from 505 of the 600 voting stations and was extremely close to the final results published by the JCE; this success was repeated in the elections of June 30 (author's field notes, May 1996, July 1996).

4. Not surprisingly, as in other countries where domestic civic observation networks have been created, the leadership has often come from middle-class intellectuals, professionals, and business figures who are in many cases alienated by government abuse of power and therefore more sympathetic to opposition movements promising greater democracy and transparency. Yet the organization was committed to the democratic process rather than to a specific result. The group's quick-count results in both electoral rounds proved remarkably close to the official JCE results, including the victory of Fernández over Peña Gómez in the second round; although there were tensions within the organization that election evening, professionalism ultimately reigned.

5. Whether President Aristide in neighboring Haiti would attempt to stay in office past his constitutional five-year term (three years of which he spent in exile), and what U.S. policy toward that would be, were also carefully watched in the Dominican Republic. It was widely believed that if Aristide remained in office, Balaguer would seek to do the same. When Aristide hinted in late 1995, prior to the scheduled December elections, that he might reconsider his agreement to leave office in February 1996, the United States responded with firm pressure (Dupuy 1997, 172).

6. In 1986, for the first time, the country voted using a single ballot that did not permit split voting (until then, there were separate ballots for each party, which had facilitated vote-buying practices); in 1990, voters were given a single ballot, but they could vote differently for president, for senate and chamber candidates, and for municipal-level candidates; in 1994, voters were asked to mark three separate ballots (for president, for senate and chamber of deputies, and for mayor and municipal council) that were placed in three different ballot boxes. For a discussion of ticket splitting in the country's major urban municipalities, see Mitchell (forthcoming).

7. This statement is based on impressionistic evidence and conversations with journalists and political activists. Participación Ciudadana did not study the issue of potential bias in the mass media for several reasons. One was that it believed that observing the vote was the single most important priority, given scarce human resources and limited funds. Another, as explained by a top leader of the organization, was that since 1994 important sectors of national opinion had wanted to demonstrate that the organization favored one candidate (i.e., Peña Gómez); given the importance of state media and its possible bias against that candidate, the organization could find

itself having to defend its credibility as a neutral election observer (author's field notes, May and June 1996).

8. More generally, for a nuanced review and critique of both neoliberalism and its critics, see Haggard and Kaufman (1995, 309–34).

9. The Consejo de la Magistratura, established by the 1994 constitutional reform, was unable to be formed during Balaguer's last two years in office due to conflicts over the makeup of its members among the parties. The PR(SC) and the PLD were eager to speed the process along and to guarantee the tenure of judges favorable to them already in place; the PRD had the opposite goal and was successful in blocking the formation of a Consejo with limited PRD representation. Stalemate, though, favored the PR(SC) and, to a lesser extent, the PLD, as it was a senate dominated by the PR(SC) that had last played a significant role in nominating judges. Under President Leonel Fernández, the Consejo was finally able to be formed, though it was not until August 1997 that new members of the supreme court were named. The excruciating delays were extremely frustrating to the business, professional, and middle-sector groups of civil society eager to improve the professionalism and the functioning of the country's judiciary, but the new supreme court was widely viewed as professional and nonpartisan. Twelve of the sixteen judges who were named had been nominated by groups from civil society, and though political agreements in the Consejo appeared to favor the PR(SC) (four judges were viewed as favorable toward it), the court was no longer considered controlled by Balaguer. Yet, further critical judicial reforms remained stalled in congress as of mid-1997 (interviews with figures in the country's judicial reform efforts, 1997; *Revista Rumbo*, August 6–12, 1997).

10. In the polarized Cold War world of the 1980s, the Dominican Republic was also aided by geography. Due to its island status and thus its distance from ongoing guerrilla or *contra* struggles, U.S. military aid and involvement was minimal, in contrast to a number of Central American countries in the 1980s.

11. Cf. the emergence of the Partido dos Trabalhadores (PT—Workers' Party) in Brazil at around the same time as the PLD emerged (Keck 1992).

References

Newspapers and Magazines

El Caribe
Hoy
Listín Diario
El Nacional
Panorama: Noticioso Mensual Dominicano
Revista Rumbo
El Siglo
Ultima Hora

Other Sources

Abel, Christopher. 1985. "Politics and the Economy of the Dominican Republic, 1890–1930." In *Latin America, Economic Imperialism and the State*. Edited by Christopher Abel and Colin M. Lewis. London: Athlone.

Alcántara Almánzar, José. 1971. "Grafoanálisis de la violencia en Santo Domingo." Unpublished manuscript.

Alemán, José Luis, S.J. 1994. "Empleo y apertura externa en la República Dominicana." *Estudios Sociales* 27, no. 97: 67–89.

Alemán, José Luis, et al. 1976. *Economía dominicana 1975*. Santo Domingo: Fondo para el Avance de las Ciencias Sociales.

——. 1978. *Economía dominicana 1977*. Santo Domingo: Fondo para el Avance de las Ciencias Sociales.

Alvarez, Julia. 1994. *In the Time of the Butterflies*. Chapel Hill, N.C.: Algonquin Books.

Americas Watch, National Coalition for Haitian Refugees and Caribbean Rights. 1991. *Half-Measures: Reform, Forced Labor and the Dominican Sugar Industry*. Washington, D.C.: Americas Watch.

Ameringer, Charles. 1974. *The Democratic Left in Exile: The Antidictatorial Struggle in the Caribbean, 1945–1959*. Coral Gables, Fla.: University of Miami Press.

——. 1996. *The Caribbean Legion: Patriots, Politicians, Soldiers of Fortune, 1946–1950*. University Park: Pennsylvania State University Press.

"Análisis del movimiento revolucionario dominicano: bases para la unidad." 1978. *Realidad Contemporánea*, nos. 6–7: 13–53.

Araujo, Fausto. 1996. "La crítica situación de la CDE." *El Nacional, Semana*, October 13: 6–7.

Atkins, G. Pope. 1981. *Arms and Politics in the Dominican Republic*. Boulder, Colo.: Westview Press.

Atkins, G. Pope, and Larman C. Wilson. 1972. *The United States and the Trujillo Regime.* New Brunswick, N.J.: Rutgers University Press.

Balaguer, Joaquín. 1949. *Dominican Reality: Biographical Sketch of a Country and a Regime.* Mexico: n.p.

———. 1983. *Mensajes al pueblo dominicano.* Santo Domingo: Industrias Gráf, Manuel Pareja.

———. 1989. *Memorias de un cortesano de la "era de Trujillo."* Madrid: G. del Toro.

Banco Central de la República Dominicana. Various years. *Boletín Mensual.*

———. 1994b. *Principales indicadores económicos.* Santo Domingo: Banco Central.

———. 1995b. *Informe de la economía dominicana: Enero–junio de 1995.* Santo Domingo: Banco Central.

Bendix, Reinhard. 1962. *Max Weber: An Intellectual Portrait.* Garden City, N.Y.: Anchor Books.

Bermeo, Nancy. 1990. "Rethinking Regime Change." *Comparative Politics* 22, no. 3 (April): 359–77.

Betances, Emelio. 1995a. "Social Class and the Origins of the Modern State: The Dominican Republic 1844–1930." *Latin American Perspectives* 22, no. 3: 20–40.

———. 1995b. *State and Society in the Dominican Republic.* Boulder, Colo.: Westview Press.

Betances, Emelio, and Hobart A. Spalding, Jr., eds. 1986. *The Dominican Republic Today: Realities and Perspectives.* New York: Bildner Center for Western Hemisphere Studies.

Black, Jan Knippers. 1986. *The Dominican Republic: Politics and Development in an Unsovereign State.* Boston: Allen and Unwin.

Booth, John. 1989. "Costa Rican Democracy." In *Democracy in Developing Countries: Latin America.* Edited by Larry Diamond, Juan Linz, and Seymour Martin Lipset. Boulder, Colo.: Lynne Rienner Publishers.

Booth, John A. 1995. *The End and the Beginning: The Nicaraguan Revolution.* 2nd ed. Boulder, Colo.: Westview Press.

Booth, John A., and Mitchell A. Seligson, eds. 1989. *Elections and Democracy in Central America.* Chapel Hill: University of North Carolina Press.

Bosch, Juan. 1965. *The Unfinished Experiment: Democracy in the Dominican Republic.* New York: Praeger.

———. 1991. *Dictadura con respaldo popular.* 4th ed. Santo Domingo: Alfa y Omega.

———. 1992. *Viaje a los Antípodas.* 5th ed. Santo Domingo: Alfa y Omega.

Bratton, Michael, and Nicholas van de Walle. 1994. "Neopatrimonial Regimes and Political Transitions in Africa." *World Politics* 46 (July): 453–89.

———. 1997. *Democratic Experiments in Africa: Regime Transitions in Comparative Perspective.* Cambridge: Cambridge University Press.

Brea Franco, Julio. 1983. *El sistema constitucional dominicano.* 2 vols. Santo Domingo: Editorial CENAPEC.

———. 1987. *Administración y elecciones: La experiencia dominicana de 1986.* San José, Costa Rica: Centro de Asesoría y Promoción Electoral (CAPEL).

———. 1991. *Cuando el pasado volvió a tener futuro: Las elecciones dominicanas de 1990.* Santo Domingo: n.p.

Brea, Ramonina. 1991. "El concepto del orden en Balaguer: A la muerte de Trujillo." *Revista de la Facultad de Ciencias Económicas y Sociales* 4 (January): 115–24.

———. 1994. *Propuestas para la Reforma Constitucional en la República Dominicana*. Santo Domingo: Pontificia Universidad Católica Madre y Maestra.

Brea, Ramonina, Isis Duarte, Ramón Tejada, and Clara Báez. 1995. *Estado de Situación de la Democracia Dominicana (1978–1992)*. Santo Domingo: Pontificia Universidad Católica Madre y Maestra.

Brynen, Rex. 1995. "The Neopatrimonial Dimension of Palestinian Politics." *Journal of Palestine Studies* 25, no. 1 (Autumn): 23–36.

Brzezinski, Zbigniew K. 1983. *Power and Principal: Memoirs of the National Security Advisor*. New York: Farrar, Straus and Giroux.

Calder, Bruce. 1984. *The Impact of Intervention: The Dominican Republic during the U.S. Occupation of 1916–1924*. Austin: University of Texas Press.

Campillo Pérez, Julio A. 1982. *Elecciones dominicanas: Contribución a su estudio*. Vol. 49. Academia Dominicana de la Historia, Santo Domingo: Relaciones Públicas, S.A.

Carter, Jimmy. 1982. *Keeping Faith: Memoirs of a President*. Toronto and New York: Bantam Books.

Cassá, Roberto. 1979. *Modos de producción, clases sociales y luchas políticas en la República Dominicana, Siglo XX*. Santo Domingo: Alfa y Omega.

———. 1984. *Modos de producción, clases sociales y luchas políticas en la República Dominicana, Siglo XX*. Santo Domingo: Punto y Aparte.

———. 1986. *Los Doce Años: Contrarrevolución y desarrollismo*. Santo Domingo: Alfa y Omega.

———. 1993. "Motín y huelga: La protesta de los dominicanos pobres." Unpublished manuscript.

———. 1995. "Recent Popular Movements in the Dominican Republic." *Latin American Perspectives* 22, no. 3: 80–93.

———. 1996. "Reescritura veinte años después." *Estudios Sociales* 29, no. 106 (October–December): 21–31.

———. 1997. "Negotiated Elections: The Old Boss Steps to the Side." *NACLA Report on the Americas* 30, no. 5 (March–April): 20–26.

Castillo R., Mario Vinicio ("Vincho"). 1986. "Examen y crítica del actual sistema electoral: Evaluación de las recusaciones e impugnaciones." Paper presented to a seminar on "La Situación actual del sistema electoral dominicano y sugerencias en pro de una adecuada institucionalización," September 11–12, Santo Domingo.

Catrain, Pedro, and José Oviedo. 1981. "La Conformación de lo Nacional-Estatal: Singularidad del Caso Dominicano." Paper presented to the 14th Congreso Latinoamericano de Sociología, in October, Puerto Rico.

Cavarozzi, Marcelo. 1992. "Beyond Transitions to Democracy in Latin America." *Journal of Latin American Studies* 24 (October): 665–84.

Ceara Hatton, Miguel. 1984. *Tendencias estructurales y coyuntura de la economía dominicana, 1968–1983*. Santo Domingo: Editora Nueva Rutas y Fundación Friedrich Ebert.

———. 1993. "De reactivación hacia el ajuste con liberalización y apertura: 1987–1990 y 1991–?" Unpublished manuscript.

———. 1995. "Las reformas económicas y la cultura de la ilegalidad." *Ciencia y Sociedad* 20, nos. 1 and 2: 116–30.

Chehabi, H. E. 1995. "A Note on the Term [Sultanism–J.H.] and Its History." Unpublished manuscript (in author's possession).

Chehabi, H. E., and Juan J. Linz, eds. 1998. *Sultanistic Regimes*. Baltimore: Johns Hopkins University Press.

Coatsworth, John H. 1994. *Central America and the United States: The Clients and the Colossus*. New York: Twayne Publishers.

Collier, David. 1993. "The Comparative Method." In *Political Science: The State of the Discipline II*. Edited by Ada W. Finifter. Washington, D.C.: American Political Science Association.

Collier, David, ed. 1979. *The New Authoritarianism in Latin America*. Princeton: Princeton University Press.

Collier, David, and Steven Levitsky. 1997. "Democracy with Adjectives: Conceptual Innovation in Comparative Research." *World Politics* 49 (April): 430–51.

Collier, Ruth Berins, and David Collier. 1991. *Shaping the Political Arena: Critical Junctures, the Labor Movement, and Regime Dynamics in Latin America*. Princeton: Princeton University Press.

Conaghan, Catherine M. 1995. "Politicians Against Parties: Discord and Disconnection in Ecuador's Party System." In *Building Democratic Institutions: Party Systems in Latin America*. Edited by Scott Mainwaring and Timothy R. Scully. Stanford: Stanford University Press.

Conaghan, Catherine M., and Rosario Espinal. 1990. "Unlikely Transitions to Uncertain Regimes? Democracy without Compromise in the Dominican Republic and Ecuador." *Journal of Latin American Studies* 22, no. 3 (October): 553–74.

Consejo Nacional de Hombres de Empresa (CNHE). 1994. *Lineamientos para el desarrollo*. Santo Domingo: CNHE.

Consejo Nacional de la Empresa Privada (CONEP). 1995. *Agenda empresarial para el Desarrollo Integrado*. Santo Domingo: CONEP.

Contreras, Darío. [1983?]. *Comportamiento electoral dominicano: elecciones dominicanas 1962–1982: datos y análisis*. Santo Domingo: Corripio.

Coppedge, Michael. 1994. *Strong Parties and Lame Ducks: Presidential Partyarchy and Factionalism in Venezuela*. Stanford: Stanford University Press.

Cornelius, Wayne, Ann L. Craig, and Jonathan Fox. 1994. *State-Society Relations in Mexico: The National Solidarity Strategy*. San Diego: Center for U.S.-Mexican Studies, University of California, San Diego.

Corten, André. 1993. *El estado débil: Haití, República Dominicana*. Santo Domingo: Editora Taller.

Corten, André, and Isis Duarte. 1995. "Five Hundred Thousand Haitians in the Dominican Republic." *Latin American Perspectives* 22, no. 3 (summer): 94–110.

Council of Freely Elected Heads of Government and National Democratic Institute for International Affairs. 1990. *1990 Elections in the Dominican Republic: Report of an Observer Mission*. Atlanta: Carter Center of Emory University.

Crassweller, Robert. 1966. *Trujillo: The Life and Times of a Caribbean Dictator*. New York: Macmillan Company.

Cross Beras, Julio A. 1984. *Sociedad y desarrollo en la República Dominicana 1844–1899*. Santo Domingo: Instituto Tecnológico de Santo Domingo.

Cuello H., José Israel. 1984. *Siete Años de Reformismo*. Santo Domingo: Editora Taller.

———. 1997. *Contratación de mano de obra haitiana destinada a la Industria Azucarera Dominicana (1952–1986)*. Santo Domingo: Editora Taller.

Dahl, Robert. 1971. *Polyarchy: Participation and Opposition*. New Haven: Yale University Press.

Dauhajre, Andrés. 1995. "Profundización y ampliación de la reforma arancelaria en la República Dominicana." *Ciencia y Sociedad* 20, nos. 1 and 2: 182–207.

Dauhajre hijo, Andrés. 1984. "República Dominicana: 18 años de política económica." In *La situación cambiaria en la República Dominicana*. Edited by F. Moya Pons. Santo Domingo: Forum.

——. 1989. *El sistema tributario dominicano: Propuesta de reforma*. Santo Domingo: Fundación Economía y Desarrollo.

——. 1990. *Sábado Económico: Números 53–104*. Santo Domingo: Fundación Economía y Desarrollo.

——. 1994a. "Como mantener la estabilidad económica." *Revista Rumbo* (May): 17–18.

——. 1994b. "La agenda económica pendiente." *Revista Rumbo*: (May 16): 16–22.

Dauhajre hijo, Andrés, José Achécar, and Anne Swindale. 1994. *Estabilización, apertura y pobreza en la República Dominicana: 1986–1992*. Santo Domingo: Fundación Economía y Desarrollo.

Dauhajre hijo, Andrés, and Jaime Aristy Escuder. 1996. *El Programa: Resumen Ejecutivo, Programa Macroeconómico de Mediano Plazo para la República Dominicana: 1996–2000*. Santo Domingo: Fundación Economía y Desarrollo.

Dauhajre hijo, Andrés, et al. 1996. *El Programa: Programa Macroeconómico de Mediano Plazo para la República Dominicana: 1996–2000*. Santo Domingo: Fundación Economía y Desarrollo.

Dealy, Glenn C. 1992. "The Tradition of Monistic Democracy in Latin America." In *Politics and Social Change in Latin America: Still a Distinct Tradition?* 3rd ed. Edited by Howard Wiarda. Boulder, Colo.: Westview Press.

del Carmen Ariza, José. 1991. *Letter to the Honorable Robert G. Torricelli*. Washington, D.C.: Embassy of the Dominican Republic.

del Castillo, José. 1981. *Ensayos de sociología dominicana*. Santo Domingo: Ediciones Siboney.

——. 1986. "Partidos Políticos y Dinámica Electoral, 1966–1986." In *Y Nadie Sabe Quién Es Su Legislador. . . .* Santo Domingo: Fundación Friedrich Ebert and Universidad APEC.

del Castillo, José, and Adriano Miguel Tejada. 1992. "Menú de opciones para la renovación del registro electoral y la cedulación ciudadana." *Revista de Ciencias Jurídicas, Separata Documentos* (July 12–20).

Delgado, S. 1994. "The Kingmakers: Portrait of the Central Electoral Board." *The Santo Domingo News* (April 1): 15–21.

Dessler, David. 1989. "What's at Stake in the Agent-Structure Debate?" *International Organization* 43, no. 3 (summer): 441–73.

Devlin, Robert. 1989. *Debt and Crisis in Latin America: The Supply Side of the Story*. Princeton: Princeton University Press.

Diamond, Larry, ed. 1993. *Political Culture and Democracy in Developing Countries*. Boulder, Colo.: Lynne Rienner Publishers.

Diamond, Larry, and Juan Linz. 1989. "Introduction: Politics, Society, and Democracy in Latin America." In *Democracy in Developing Countries: Latin America*. Edited by Larry Diamond, Juan Linz, and Seymour Martin Lipset. Boulder, Colo.: Lynne Rienner Publishers.

Diamond, Larry, and Marc F. Plattner, eds. 1993. *Capitalism, Socialism and Democracy Revisited*. Baltimore: Johns Hopkins University Press.

Díaz, Juan Bolívar. 1980. "Contribuciones del periodismo a la lucha por la democracia en la República Dominicana, 1960–1980." *Estudios Sociales* 12, no. 51: 103–21.

———. 1993. "Joaquín Balaguer tendrá que contar con Alvarez Bogaert." *Hoy*, November 17: 18–19.

———. 1996. *Trauma Electoral*. Santo Domingo: Mograf.

Downing, Brian M. 1992. *The Military Revolution and Political Change: Origins of Democracy and Autocracy in Early Modern Europe*. Princeton: Princeton University Press.

Drake, Paul, and Eduardo Silva, eds. 1986. *Elections and Democratization in Latin America, 1980–85*. La Jolla, Calif.: Center for Iberian and Latin American Studies, Center for U.S.-Mexican Studies, and Institute of Americas.

Draper, Theodore. 1968. *The Dominican Revolt*. New York: Commentary.

Duarte, Isis, Ramonina Brea, Ramón Tejada H., and Clara Báez. 1996. *Cultura Política y Democracia en la República Dominicana: Informe Final de la Encuesta Cultura Política y Democracia (DEMOS 94)*. Santo Domingo: Pontificia Universidad Católica Madre y Maestra.

Dunn, John. 1992. "Conclusion." In *Democracy: The Unfinished Journey, 508 B.C. to A.D. 1993*. Edited by John Dunn. Oxford: Oxford University Press.

Dupuy, Alex. 1997. *Haiti in the New World Order: The Limits of the Democratic Revolution*. Boulder, Colo.: Westview Press.

Eckstein, Harry. 1975. "Case Study and Theory in Political Science." In *Political Science: Scope and Theory*. Vol. 1 of *Handbook of Political Science*. Edited by Fred Greenstein and Nelson Polsby. Reading, Mass.: Addison-Wesley.

Economist Intelligence Unit (EIU). 1994. "EIU Country Report: Cuba, Dominican Republic, Haiti, Puerto Rico." *Economist Intelligence Unit*, no. 2.

———. 1995. "EIU Country Profile: Dominican Republic, Haiti, Puerto Rico." *Economist Intelligence Unit*, no. 2.

Eisenstadt, S. N. 1973. *Traditional Patrimonialism and Modern Neopatrimonialism*. Beverly Hills, Calif.: Sage.

Espinal, Fulgencio. 1982. *Breve historia del PRD: Ideología e interpretación, segunda edición*. Santo Domingo: Alfa y Omega.

Espinal, Rosario. 1985. "Classes, Power, and Political Change in the Dominican Republic." Ph.D. diss., Washington University, St. Louis.

———. 1986. "An Interpretation of the Democratic Transition in the Dominican Republic." In *The Central American Impasse*. Edited by Giuseppe Di Palma and Laurence Whitehead. New York: St. Martin's Press.

———. 1987a. *Autoritarismo y democracia en la política dominicana*. San José, Costa Rica: Centro de Asesoría y Promoción Electoral (CAPEL).

———. 1987b. "Labor, Politics and Industrialization in the Dominican Republic." *Economic and Industrial Democracy* 8, no. 2: 183–212.

———. 1990a. "General Strikes in the Dominican Republic in 1988–1989." *Latin American Labor News*, nos. 2 and 3: 14.

———. 1990b. "The Defeat of the Dominican Revolutionary Party in the 1986 Elections: Causes and Implications." *Bulletin of Latin American Research* 9, no. 1.

——. 1991a. "Entrevista Realizada por Rosario Espinal al Dr. Salvador Jorge Blanco, Presidente de la República Dominicana durante el Período Constitucional 1982– 1986 (Agosto 1991)," ms. (in author's possession).

——. 1991b. "General Strikes in the Dominican Republic in 1990." *Latin American Labor News*, no. 4: 1, 6.

——. 1992. "Elecciones y democracia en la República Dominicana." In *Una tarea inconclusa: Elecciones y democracia en América Latina, 1988–1991*. Edited by R. C. Cruz, Juan Rial, and Daniel Zovatto. San José, Costa Rica: Instituto Interamericano de Derechos Humanos (IIDH) and Centro de Asesoría y Promoción Electoral (CAPEL).

——. 1998. "Business and Politics in the Dominican Republic." In *Business, Economic Change, and Democracy in Latin America*. Edited by Francisco Durand and Eduardo Silva. Boulder, Colo.: Lynne Rienner Publishers.

Espinal, Rosario, and Jonathan Hartlyn. 1995. "Los riesgos de la doble vuelta electoral." *Estudios Jurídicos* [Dominican Republic] 6, no. 1 (January–April): 91–102.

Evans, Peter. 1979. *Dependent Development: The Alliance of Multinational, State and Local Capital in Brazil*. Princeton: Princeton University Press.

Ewell, Judith. 1984. "Venezuela." In *The Cambridge History of Latin America*. Vol. 7. Edited by Leslie Bethell. Cambridge: Cambridge University Press.

Fausto, Rosario Adamés. 1995. "Un nuevo rol para las Fuerzas Armadas." *Revista Rumbo* (June): 7–13.

Ferguson, James. 1992. *Dominican Republic: Beyond the Lighthouse*. London: Latin American Bureau.

Fontana, Biancamaria. 1992. "Democracy and the French Revolution." In *Democracy: The Unfinished Journey, 508 B.C. to A.D. 1993*. Edited by John Dunn. Oxford: Oxford University Press.

Freedom House Survey Team. Annual, 1978–1995. *Freedom in the World: The Annual Survey of Political Rights and Civil Liberties*. New York: Freedom House.

Frundt, Henry J. 1979. *Gulf and Western in the Dominican Republic: An Evaluation*. New York: Interfaith Center on Corporate Responsibility.

Fulbrook, Mary, and Theda Skocpol. 1984. "Destined Pathways: The Historical Sociology of Perry Anderson." In *Vision and Method in Historical Sociology*. Edited by Theda Skocpol. Cambridge: Cambridge University Press.

Fuller, Stephen M., and Graham A. Cosmas. 1974. *Marines in the Dominican Republic, 1916–1924*. Washington, D.C.: History and Museums Division Headquarters, U.S. Marine Corps.

Fundación Siglo 21. 1994. *Una reforma política para el futuro dominicano: El sistema electoral y de representación*. Santo Domingo: Fundación Siglo 21.

Galíndez, Jesús de. 1973. *The Era of Trujillo: Dominican Dictator*. Edited by R. H. Fitzgibbon. Tucson: University of Arizona Press.

Gamarra, Eduardo, and James Malloy. 1995. "The Patrimonial Dynamics of Party Politics in Bolivia." In *Building Democratic Institutions: Party Systems in Latin America*. Edited by Scott Mainwaring and Timothy R. Scully. Stanford: Stanford University Press.

Gautreaux Piñeyro, Bonaparte. 1994. *El tiempo de la tormenta: Bosch, Caamaño y el PRD*. Santo Domingo: Editora de Colores.

Gleijeses, Piero. 1978. *The Dominican Crisis: The 1965 Constitutionalist Revolt and American Intervention*. Translated by L. Lipson. Baltimore: Johns Hopkins University Press.

Gobierno Dominicano. 1944. *Constitución política y reformas constitucionales, 1844–1942.* 2 vols. Santiago: Editorial El Diario.

Goldwert, Marvin. 1962. *The Constabulary in the Dominican Republic and Nicaragua: Progeny and Legacy of United States Intervention*. Gainesville: University of Florida Press.

Gómez Berges, Víctor. 1985. *Las causas de dos derrotas*. Santo Domingo: n.p.

González Canahuate, L. Almanzor. 1985. *Apuntes y reflexiones sobre historia, estructura orgánica, proceso y programa de organización, metodología, ideología en el PRD.* Santo Domingo: Editora Gregorio Luperón.

Government of the Dominican Republic. 1993. "Prehearing Brief of the Government of the Dominican Republic to the GSP Subcommittee Office of the U.S. Trade Representative concerning Worker Rights in the Dominican Republic." Case no. 004-CP-93.

Graham, Pamela. 1995. "Nationality and Political Participation in the Transnational Context of Dominican–United States Migration." Paper presented to the Latin American Studies Association Congress, September 28–30, Washington, D.C.

———. 1996. "Re-Imagining the Nation and Defining the District: The Simultaneous Political Incorporation of Dominican Transnational Migrants." Ph.D. diss., University of North Carolina, Chapel Hill.

Gran Convención de Hombres de Empresa. 1994. *El desarrollo dominicano: Estrategia para el decenio de los '90*. Santo Domingo: CNHE.

Grasmuck, Sherri, and Patricia Pessar. 1991. *Between Two Islands: Dominican International Migration*. Berkeley: University of California Press.

Grimaldi, Víctor. 1985. *El diario secreto de la intervención norteamericana de 1965*. Santo Domingo: Amigo del Hogar.

Grupo de Acción por la Democracia (GAD). 1996. *Agenda nacional de desarrollo*. Vol. 1. Santo Domingo: Editora Taller.

Guerrero, Miguel. 1993. *El golpe de estado: Historia del derrocamiento de Juan Bosch*. Santo Domingo: Editora Corripio.

Gutiérrez, Carlos María. 1972. *The Dominican Republic: Rebellion and Repression*. New York: Monthly Review Press.

Haggard, Stephan, and Robert R. Kaufman. 1995. *The Political Economy of Democratic Transitions*. Princeton: Princeton University Press.

Haggard, Stephan, and Steven B. Webb, eds. 1994. *Voting for Reform: Democracy, Political Liberalization, and Economic Adjustment*. New York: Oxford University Press.

Hagopian, Frances. 1993. "After Regime Change: Authoritarian Legacies, Political Representation, and the Democratic Future of South America." *World Politics* 45, no. 3 (April): 464–500.

Hamilton, Bill, and Ray Strother. 1994. "The Comeback Geezer: How Constant Polling and Finely-Tuned Messages Won a Dominican Republic Presidential Race." *Campaigns and Elections* (August): 43–44, 67.

Hanson, Gail. 1994. "Ordered Liberty: Sumner Welles and the Crowder-Welles Connection in the Caribbean." *Diplomatic History* 18 (summer): 311–32.

Harrison, Lawrence E. 1985. *Underdevelopment Is a State of Mind: The Latin American Case*. Lanham, Md.: Center for International Affairs, Harvard University, and University Press of America.

Hartlyn, Jonathan. 1987. "The 1986 Election in the Dominican Republic." *Caribbean Review* 15, no. 3 (winter): 14.

———. 1988. *The Politics of Coalition Rule in Colombia*. Cambridge: Cambridge University Press.

———. 1989. "The Dominican Republic." In *Latin America and Caribbean Contemporary Record*. Vol. 6, 1986–1987. Edited by Abraham F. Lowenthal. New York: Holmes and Meier.

———. 1990. "The Dominican Republic's Disputed Elections." *Journal of Democracy* 1, no. 4 (fall): 92–103.

———. 1991. "The Dominican Republic: The Legacy of Intermittent Engagement." In *Exporting Democracy: The United States and Latin America*. Edited by Abraham F. Lowenthal. Baltimore: Johns Hopkins University Press.

———. 1994a. *Crisis-ridden Elections and Authoritarian Regression: Presidentialism and Electoral Oversight in the Dominican Republic, 1978–1994*. Unpublished manuscript.

———. 1994b. "Los problemas de una segunda ronda electoral." *Revista Rumbo* (October 5–11): 46–49.

———. 1998a. "Political Continuities, Missed Opportunities, and Institutional Rigidities: Another Look at Democratic Transitions in Latin America." In *Politics, Society, and Democracy: Latin America*. Edited by Scott Mainwaring and Arturo Valenzuela. Boulder, Colo.: Westview Press.

———. 1998b. "The Trujillo Regime in the Dominican Republic, 1930–1961: Emergence, Evolution, and Aftermath of a Sultanistic Regime." In *Sultanistic Regimes*. Edited by H. E. Chehabi and Juan J. Linz. Baltimore: Johns Hopkins University Press.

Hartlyn, Jonathan, and Arturo Valenzuela. 1994. "Democracy in Latin America since 1930." In *Latin America since 1930: Economy, Society, and Politics*. Vol. 6, pt. 2, of *The Cambridge History of Latin America*. Edited by Leslie Bethell. Cambridge: Cambridge University Press.

Herman, Edward S., and Frank Brodhead. 1984. *Demonstration Elections: U.S.-Staged Elections in the Dominican Republic, Vietnam and El Salvador*. Boston: South End Press.

Hermann, Hamlet. 1983. *Francis Caamaño*. Santo Domingo: Alfa y Omega.

Hoetink, H. 1982. *The Dominican People 1859–1900: Notes for a Historical Sociology*. Translated by S. K. Ault. Baltimore: Johns Hopkins University Press.

———. 1984. "The Dominican Republic, 1870–1930." In *The Cambridge History of Latin America*. Vol. 5, c. 1870 to 1930. Edited by Leslie Bethell. Cambridge: Cambridge University Press.

Huber Stephens, Evelyne, and John D. Stephens. 1986. *Democratic Socialism in Jamaica: The Political Movement and Social Transformation in Dependent Capitalism*. Princeton: Princeton University Press.

Hunt, Michael H. 1987. *Ideology and U.S. Foreign Policy*. New Haven: Yale University Press.

Hutchcroft, Paul D. 1991. "Oligarchs and Cronies in the Philippine State: The Politics of Patrimonial Plunder." *World Politics* 43, no. 3 (April): 414–50.

Ianni, Vanna. 1987. *El Territorio de las masas: Espacios y movimientos sociales en la República Dominicana, abril 1984–abril 1986*. Santo Domingo: Editora Universitaria.

———. 1990. *De la democracia dominicana: Despunte de un movimiento social*. Santo Domingo: Centro de Planificación y Acción Ecuménica/Facultad Latinoamericana de Ciencias Sociales (CEPAE/FLACSO).

Inter-American Development Bank (IDB). Annual. *Economic and Social Progress in Latin America* [ESPLA]. Washington, D.C.: IDB.

———. 1994b. *República Dominicana: Informe socioeconómico*. Washington, D.C.: IDB.

Isa, Minerva. 1996a. "Descubren cómo la corrupción estranguló las empresas de CORDE." *Hoy*, August 20: 12.

———. 1996b. "En 30 años, ningún gobierno hizo nada para detener descalabro de CORDE." *Hoy*, September 2: 12.

Jácome-Martínez, José María. 1981. *La Evolución de la Administración Pública en los Países en Desarrollo y el Caso de la República Dominicana*. Santo Domingo: Publicaciones ONAP (Oficina Nacional de Administración y Personal).

Jaramillo, J. F. 1992. "Las cortes electorales en América Latina: Un primer intento de análisis comparativo con base en los casos de Argentina, Costa Rica y República Dominicana." In *Elecciones y sistemas de partidos en América Latina*. Edited by D. Nohlen. San José, Costa Rica: Instituto Interamericano de Derechos Humanos (IIDH) and Centro Asesoría y Promoción Electoral (CAPEL).

Jiménez Polanco, Jacqueline. 1994. "Los partidos políticos en la República Dominicana." Ph.D. diss., Universidad Complutense, Madrid.

Junta Central Electoral (JCE). Press release, 1994. "Resolución." Santo Domingo: JCE.

Kaplinsky, Raphael. 1993. "Export Processing Zones in the Dominican Republic: Transforming Manufactures into Commodities." *World Development* 21, no. 11: 1851–65.

———. 1995. "A Reply to Willmore." *World Development* 23, no. 3: 537–40.

Karl, Terry L. 1990. "Dilemmas of Democratization in Latin America." *Comparative Politics* 23, no. 1 (October): 1–21.

Karl, Terry L., and Philippe Schmitter. 1991. "Mode of Transition in Latin America, Southern and Eastern Europe." *International Social Science Journal* (May): 269–84.

Kay, Bruce H. 1996. "Fuji-Populism in a Liberal State in Peru, 1990–1995." *Journal of Inter-American Studies and World Affairs* 38, no. 4 (winter): 55–96.

Keck, Margaret E. 1992. *The Workers' Party and Democratization in Brazil*. New Haven: Yale University Press.

Knight, Franklin W. 1990. *The Caribbean: The Genesis of a Fragmented Nationalism*. 3rd ed. New York: Oxford University Press.

Krasner, Stephen D. 1984. "Approaches to the State." *Comparative Politics* 16 (January): 223–46.

———. 1988. "Sovereignty: An Institutional Perspective." *Comparative Political Studies* 21, no. 1 (April): 66–94.

Kryzanek, Michael J. 1977. "Political Party Decline and the Failure of Liberal Democracy: the PRD in Dominican Politics." *Journal of Latin American Studies* 9, no. 1: 115–43.

———. 1979. "The 1978 Elections in the Dominican Republic: Opposition Politics, Intervention and the Carter Administration." *Caribbean Studies* 19 (April): 51–73.

Kurzman, Dan. 1965. *Santo Domingo: Revolt of the Damned*. New York: Putnam.

Latorre, Eduardo. 1975. *Política dominicana contemporánea*. Santo Domingo: Ediciones Intec.

——. 1995. *De Política Dominicana e Internacional y Desarrollo Humano*. Santo Domingo: Instituto Tecnológico de Santo Domingo (INTEC).

Lehoucq, Fabrice E. 1996. "The Institutional Foundations of Democratic Cooperation in Costa Rica." *Journal of Latin American Studies* 28, no. 2 (May): 329–55.

Levine, Daniel. 1989. "Venezuela: The Nature, Sources, and Future Prospects of Democracy." In *Democracy in Developing Countries: Latin America*. Edited by Larry Diamond, Juan Linz, and Martin Lipset. Boulder, Colo.: Lynne Rienner Publishers.

Lijphart, Arend. 1969. "Consociational Democracy." *World Politics* 21 (January): 207–25.

——. 1975. *The Politics of Accomodation: Pluralism and Democracy in the Netherlands*. 2nd ed. Berkeley: University of California Press.

Linz, Juan. 1970. "An Authoritarian Regime: The Case of Spain." In *Mass Politics: Studies in Political Sociology*. Edited by E. Allardt and Stein Rokkan. New York: Free Press.

——. 1974. "Opposition to and under an Authoritarian Regime: The Case of Spain." In *Regimes and Oppositions*. Edited by R. Dahl. New Haven: Yale University Press.

——. 1975. "Totalitarian and Authoritarian Regimes." In *Macropolitical Theory*. Vol. 3 of *Handbook of Political Science*. Edited by N. Polsby and Fred Greenstein. Reading, Mass.: Addison-Wesley.

——. 1978. "Crisis, Breakdown and Reequilibration." In *The Breakdown of Democratic Regimes*. Edited by Juan Linz and Alfred Stepan. Baltimore: Johns Hopkins University Press.

Linz, Juan, and Alfred Stepan. 1996. *Problems of Democratic Transition and Consolidation: Southern Europe, South America, and Post-Communist Europe*. Baltimore: Johns Hopkins University Press.

Linz, Juan, and Arturo Valenzuela, eds. 1994. *The Failure of Presidential Democracy*. Baltimore: Johns Hopkins University Press.

Lowenthal, Abraham. 1969a. "The Dominican Intervention in Retrospective." *Public Policy* 18 (fall): 133–48.

——. 1969b. "The Dominican Republic: The Politics of Chaos." In *Reform and Revolution: Readings in Latin American Politics*. Edited by Robert Kaufman and Arpad von Lazar. Needham Heights, Mass.: Allyn and Bacon.

——. 1972. *The Dominican Intervention*. Cambridge: Harvard University Press.

——. 1991a. "The United States and Latin American Democracy: Learning from History." In *Exporting Democracy: The United States and Latin America*. Edited by Abraham F. Lowenthal. Baltimore: Johns Hopkins University Press.

Lowenthal, Abraham F., ed. 1991b. *Exporting Democracy: The United States and Latin America*. Baltimore: Johns Hopkins University Press.

Lozano, Wilfredo. 1985. *El reformismo dependiente*. Santo Domingo: Taller.

Lozano, Wilfredo, ed. 1992. *La cuestión haitiana en Santo Domingo: migración internacional, desarrollo y relaciones inter-estatales entre Haití y República Dominicana*. Santo Domingo: FLACSO, Centro Norte-Sur de la Universidad de Miami.

McDonough, Peter, Samuel Barnes, and Antonio López Pina. 1984. "Authority and Association: Spanish Democracy in Comparative Perspective." *Journal of Politics* 46, no. 3 (August): 652–88.

Mahoney, James, and Richard Snyder. 1993. "Rethinking Agency and Structure in the Study of Regime Change." Paper presented at the annual meeting of the APSA, September 2–5, Washington, D.C.

Mainwaring, Scott. 1995. "Brazil: Weak Parties, Feckless Democracy." In *Building Democratic Institutions: Party Systems in Latin America*. Edited by Scott Mainwaring and Timothy R. Scully. Stanford: Stanford University Press.

Majluta, Jacobo. 1992. *La historia del PRI y sus perspectivas de triunfo*. Santo Domingo: n.p.

Marranzini, Celso. 1995. "Los aranceles y la realidad dominicana." *Ciencia y Sociedad* 20, nos. 1 and 2: 167–81.

Martínez-Fernández, Luis. 1995. "The Sword and the Crucifix: Church-State Relations and Nationality in the Nineteenth-Century Dominican Republic." *Latin American Research Review* 30, no. 1: 69–93.

Martin, John Bartlow. 1966. *Overtaken by Events: The Dominican Crisis from the Fall of Trujillo to the Civil War*. Garden City, N.Y.: Doubleday.

Mateo, Andrés L. 1993. *Mito y cultura en la era de Trujillo*. Santo Domingo: Librería La Trinitaria e Instituto del Libro.

Medard, Jean-François. 1982. "The Underdeveloped State in Tropical Africa: Political Clientelism or Neo-Patrimonialism?" In *Private Patronage and Public Power: Political Clientelism in the Modern State*. Edited by Christopher Clapham. New York: St. Martin's Press.

Méndez, Mario. 1994. *Políticos al desnudo*. Santo Domingo: Editora Corripio.

Messina, Milton. 1988. *Memorias del ajuste de una economía en crisis*. Santo Domingo: Fondo para el Avance de las Ciencias Sociales.

Mitchell, Christopher. 1992. "U.S. Foreign Policy and Dominican Migration to the United States." In *Western Hemisphere Immigration and United States Foreign Policy*. Edited by Christopher Mitchell. University Park: Pennsylvania State University Press.

——. Forthcoming. "Urban Elections in the Dominican Republic, 1962–1994." In *Urban Elections in Democratic Latin America*. Edited by Henry Dietz and Gil Shidlo. Wilmington, Del.: SR Books.

Mitchell, Nancy. 1996a. "The Height of the German Challenge: The Venezuela Blockade, 1902–1903." *Diplomatic History* 20 (spring): 185–209.

——. 1996b. "Protective Imperialism versus *Weltpolitik* in Brazil: Part One: Pan-German Vision and Mahanian Response." *International History Review* 18 (May): 253–78.

Monción, F. D. n.d. *Estadísticas electorales de 1986*. Santo Domingo, República Dominicana: n.p.

Morse, Richard. 1964. "The Heritage of Latin America." In *The Founding of New Societies*. Edited by L. Hartz. New York: Harcourt, Brace and World .

Mota, Vivian M. 1976. "Politics and Feminism in the Dominican Republic: 1931–45 and 1966–74." In *Sex and Class in Latin America*. Edited by June Nash and Helen I. Safa. New York: Praeger.

Moya Pons, Frank. 1983. *Manual de historia dominicana*. 7th ed. Santo Domingo: Universidad Católica Madre y Maestra.

——. 1985. "Haiti and Santo Domingo, 1790–c. 1870." In *From Independence to c. 1870*. Vol. 3 of *The Cambridge History of Latin America*. Edited by Leslie Bethell. Cambridge: Cambridge University Press.

——. 1986. *El pasado dominicano*. N.p.: Fundación J. A. Caro Alvarez.

——. 1990a. "The Dominican Republic since 1930." In *The Cambridge History of Latin America*. Vol. 7. Edited by Leslie Bethell. Cambridge: Cambridge University Press.

——. 1990b. "The Politics of Import-Substitution Industrialization in the Dominican Republic, 1925–1983." Ph.D. diss., Columbia University, New York.

——. 1991. "Industrial Policy in the Dominican Republic, 1919–1981." Revision of Columbia University Ph.D. diss., Santo Domingo.

——. 1992. *Manual de historia dominicana, separata*. Santo Domingo: Caribbean Publishers.

——. 1995. *The Dominican Republic: A National History*. New Rochelle, N.Y.: Hispaniola Books.

——, ed. 1982. *Implicaciones de la nueva política económica*. Santo Domingo: Forum.

Moya Pons, Frank, and Stanley L. Engerman, eds. 1985. *Between Slavery and Free Labor: The Spanish-speaking Caribbean in the 19th Century*. Baltimore: Johns Hopkins University Press.

Muller, Edward N., and Mitchell A. Seligson. 1994. "Civic Culture and Democracy: The Question of Causal Relationships." *American Political Science Review* 88, no. 3: 635–52.

Murphy, Martin. 1991. *Dominican Sugar Plantation: Production and Foreign Labor Integration*. New York: Praeger.

Murphy, Martin, and Miriam Santana. 1983. *The 1982 National Elections in the Dominican Republic*. Rio Piedras, Puerto Rico: Institute of Caribbean Studies, University of Puerto Rico.

Nash, James. 1985. "What Hath Intervention Wrought: Reflections on the Dominican Republic." *Caribbean Review* 14, no. 4 (fall): 7–11.

Nelson, Joan M. 1994a. "Overview: How Market Reforms and Democratic Consolidation Affect Each Other." In *Intricate Links: Democratization and Market Reforms in Latin American and Eastern Europe*. Edited by Joan M. Nelson and contributors. New Brunswick, N.J.: Transaction Publishers.

Nelson, Joan M., and contributors, ed. 1994b. *Intricate Links: Democratization and Market Reforms in Latin America and Eastern Europe*. New Brunswick, N.J.: Transaction Publishers.

Nelson, William Javier. 1990. *Almost a Territory: America's Attempt to Annex the Dominican Republic*. Newark, Del.: University of Delaware Press.

Nohlen, Dieter, ed. 1992. *Elecciones y sistemas de partidos en América Latina*. San José, Costa Rica: IIDH and CAPEL.

Nordlinger, Eric. 1971. "Political Development, Time Sequences and Rates of Change." *Political Development and Social Change*. 2nd ed. Edited by Jason L. Finkle and Robert W. Gable. New York: John Wiley.

North, Douglass C. 1990. *Institutions, Institutional Change, and Economic Performance*. Cambridge: Cambridge University Press.

Núñez Collado, Agripino. 1977. *La UCMM: Un nuevo estilo universitario en la República Dominicana*. Santiago: Universidad Católica Madre y Maestra.

——. 1993. *Concertación: La cultura de diálogo*. Santiago: Pontificia Universidad Católica Madre y Maestra, Departamento Editorial.

——. 1996. *Testigo de una crisis: Diez años después*. Santo Domingo: Pontificia Universidad Católica Madre y Maestra and Editora Taller.

O'Donnell, Guillermo A. 1973. *Modernization and Bureaucratic-Authoritarianism: Studies in South American Politics.* No. 9, Politics of Modernization Series. Berkeley: Institute of International Studies, University of California.

———. 1985. "External Debt: Why Don't Our Governments Do the Obvious?" *CEPAL Review* 27 (December): 27–33.

———. 1989. "Transitions to Democracy: Some Navigation Instruments." In *Democracy in the Americas.* Edited by Robert A. Pastor. New York: Holmes and Meier.

———. 1992. "Delegative Democracy." Kellogg Institute Working Paper Series. Notre Dame: University of Notre Dame.

———. 1994. "Delegative Democracy." *Journal of Democracy* 5, no. 1 (January): 55–69.

O'Donnell, Guillermo A., and Phillippe C. Schmitter. 1986. *Transitions from Authoritarian Rule: Tentative Conclusions about Uncertain Democracies.* Baltimore: Johns Hopkins University Press.

O'Donnell, Guillermo A., Philippe Schmitter, and Laurence Whitehead, eds. 1986. *Transitions from Authoritarian Rule.* 4 vols. Baltimore: Johns Hopkins University Press.

Oficina Nacional de Administración y Personal (ONAP). 1994. *Reforma del estado 1: Ley de servicio civil y carrera administrativa y su reglamento de aplicación.* Santo Domingo: ONAP.

Oficina Nacional de Estadística. 1992. *Estadísticas Político-Electorales, Boletín No 1.* Santo Domingo.

———. 1994. *VII Censo Nacional de Población y Vivienda, 1993: Resultados preliminares de la población según sexo, edad y vivienda en la República Dominicana.* Santo Domingo.

Oficina Nacional de Planificación (ONAP). 1968. *Plataforma para el desarrollo económico y social de la República Dominicana (1968–1985).* Santo Domingo: ONAP.

Oszlak, Oscar. 1984. "Public Policies and Political Regimes in Latin America." No. 139, Latin American Program Working Paper Series. Washington, D.C.: Wilson Center.

Ozuna, Marcelino. 1996. *Leonel: Su Historia.* Santo Domingo: Alfa y Omega.

Packenham, Robert. 1973. *Liberal America and the Third World.* Princeton: Princeton University Press.

Partido Reformista. 1983. *Comicios dominicanos de 1982: Irregularidades de un proceso electoral: Libro Blanco.* Santo Domingo: Partido Reformista.

Partido Reformista Social Cristiano (PRSC). [1994?]. "Lineamientos de política económica y planes de desarrollo para el cuatrienio 1994–98." Santo Domingo: PRSC.

Paus, Eva, ed. 1988. *Struggle Against Dependence: Non-traditional Export Growth in Central America and the Caribbean.* Boulder, Colo.: Westview Press.

Peña Gómez, José Francisco. 1986a. *IV—Construcción de la Democracia: Agosto 16 de 1978–Agosto 15 de 1982.* Vol. 5. Edited by Sara Peralta de Rathe. Santo Domingo: Editora Alfa y Omega.

———. 1986b. *IV—Construcción de la Democracia: Agosto 16 de 1978–Agosto 15 de 1982.* Vol. 6. Santo Domingo: Alfa y Omega.

———. 1986c. *V—Participación en la Democracia: Agosto 16 de 1982–Agosto 15 de 1986.* Vol. 1. Santo Domingo: Editora Corripio.

———. 1986d. *V—Participación en la Democracia: Agosto 16 de 1982–Agosto 15 de 1986.* Vol. 2. Santo Domingo: Editora Corripio.

Pepper, José Vicente. 1947. *I Accuse Braden, yo acuso a Braden*. Trujillo City: Editoral Montalvo.

Pérez, César, and Leopoldo Artiles. 1992. *El sistema tributario dominicano: Propuesta de reforma*. Santo Domingo: Instituto Tecnológico de Santo Domingo (INTEC).

Perusse, Roland I. 1995. *Haitian Democracy Restored: 1991–1995*. Lanham, N.Y.: University Press of America.

Plant, Roger. 1987. *Sugar and Modern Slavery: A Tale of Two Countries*. London: Zed Books.

Przeworski, Adam. 1990. *The State and the Economy under Capitalism*. Chur, Switzerland: Harwood Academic Publisher.

———. 1991. *Democracy and the Market: Political and Economic Reforms in Eastern Europe and Latin America*. Cambridge: Cambridge University Press.

Psacharopoulos, George, Samuel Morley, Ariel Fiszbein, Haeduck Lee, and Bill Wood. 1993. *Poverty and Income Distribution in Latin America: The Story of the 1980s*. Washington, D.C.: World Bank.

Putnam, Robert. 1993. *Making Democracy Work: Civic Traditions in Modern Italy*. Princeton: Princeton University Press.

Pye, Lucian. 1990. "Political Science and the Crisis of Authoritarianism." *American Political Science Review* 84, no. 1: 3–19.

Ragin, Charles. 1987. *The Comparative Method: Moving beyond Qualitative and Quantitative Strategies*. Berkeley: University of California Press.

Remmer, Karen. 1989. "Neopatrimonialism: The Politics of Military Rule in Chile, 1973–1987." *Comparative Politics* 21, no. 2 (January): 149–70.

———. 1991. "New Wine or Old Bottlenecks: The Study of Latin American Democracy." *Comparative Politics* 23, no. 4 (July): 479–95.

Reyes Castro, Fernando, and Atahualpa Domínguez. 1993. "Zonas francas industriales en la República Dominicana: Su impacto económico y social." No. 73, *Documento de trabajo*. Geneva: International Labor Office (ILO).

Rodriguez, Adrian, and Deborah Huntington. 1982. "Dominican Republic—The Launching of Democracy." *NACLA Report on the Americas* 16, no. 6 (November–December): 2–35.

Rosario Adamés, Fausto. 1995. "Un nuevo rol para las Fuerzas Armadas." *Revista Rumbo* (June 7–13): 8–17.

Rosenberg, Tina. 1991. *Children of Cain: Violence and the Violent in Latin America*. New York: Penguin Books.

Rossetti, Carlo. 1994. "Constitutionalism and Clientelism in Italy." In *Democracy, Clientelism, and Civil Society*. Edited by Luis Roniger and Ayşe Güneş-Ayata. Boulder, Colo.: Lynne Rienner Publishers.

Roth, Guenther, and Claus Wittich, eds. 1968. *Max Weber Economy and Society: An Outline of Interpretive Sociology*. Vol. 1. New York: Bedminster Press.

Rueschemeyer, Dietrich, Evelyne Huber Stephens, and John D. Stephens. 1992. *Capitalist Development and Democracy*. Chicago: Chicago University Press.

Rustow, Dankwart. 1970. "Transitions to Democracy: Toward a Dynamic Model." *Comparative Politics* 2: 337–63.

Sáez, José Luis, S.J. 1988. "Catolicismo e hispanidad en la oratoria de Trujillo." *Estudios Sociales* 21, no. 3 (July–September): 89–104.

Safa, Helen I. 1995. *The Myth of the Male Breadwinner: Women and Industrialization in the Caribbean*. Boulder, Colo.: Westview Press.

———. 1997. "Where the Big Fish Eat the Little Fish: Women's Work in the Free-Trade Zones." *NACLA Report on the Americas* 30, no. 5 (March–April): 31–36.

Sang, Mu-Kien A. 1991. *Buenaventura Báez: El caudillo del sur (1844–1878)*. Santo Domingo: INTEC.

———. 1996a. "Mi siglo XIX: 15 años después." *Estudios Sociales* 39, no. 106 (October–December): 67–79.

———. 1996b [1987]. *Ulises Heureaux: Biografía de un Dictador*. Santo Domingo: INTEC.

Santana, Isidoro. 1995. "Las reformas económicas." *Ciencia y Sociedad* 20, nos. 1 and 2: 107–15.

Santana, Isidoro, and Magdalena Rathe. 1992. *El impacto distributivo de la gestión fiscal en la República Dominicana*. Santo Domingo: Ediciones de la Fundación Siglo 21.

Schmidt, Hans. 1971. *The United States Occupation of Haiti, 1915–1934*. New Brunswick, N.J.: Rutgers University Press.

Schmitter, Philippe C. 1994. "Dangers and Dilemmas of Democracy." *Journal of Democracy* 5, no. 2 (April): 57–67.

Schoultz, Lars. 1981. *Human Rights and United States Policy toward Latin America*. Princeton: Princeton University Press.

Scott, James C. 1972. *Comparative Political Corruption*. Englewood-Cliffs, N.J.: Prentice-Hall.

Secretariado Técnico de la Presidencia, Oficina Nacional de Estadística. 1994. *Resultados Preliminares del VII Censo Nacional de Población y Vivienda 1993*. Santo Domingo.

Shain, Yossi, and Juan J. Linz. 1992. "The Role of Interim Governments." *Journal of Democracy* 3, no. 1 (January): 73–82.

Shain, Yossi, and Juan J. Linz, et al. 1995. *Between States: Interim Government and Democratic Transitions*. Cambridge: Cambridge University Press.

Shugart, Matthew Soberg, and John M. Carey. 1992. *Presidents and Assemblies: Constitutional Design and Electoral Dynamics*. Cambridge: Cambridge University Press.

Skocpol, Theda. 1984. "Emerging Agendas and Recurrent Strategies in Historical Sociology." In *Vision and Method in Historical Sociology*. Edited by T. Skocpol. New York: Cambridge University Press.

Slater, Jerome. 1967. *The OAS and United States Foreign Policy*. Columbus: Ohio State University Press.

———. 1970. *Intervention and Negotiation: The United States and the Dominican Republic*. New York: Harper and Row.

Snyder, Richard. 1992. "Explaining Transitions from Neopatrimonial Dictatorships." *Comparative Politics* 24, no. 4 (July): 379–400.

Solarz, Stephen, and Richard Soudriette. 1994. *Prepared Statements Presented to Sub-Committee on Western Hemisphere Affairs, U.S. House of Representatives*. Typescript in author's possession.

Stenzel, Konrad. 1986. "Setting the Stage for Disaster: Public Deficits, Exchange Rate Policy and Foreign Debt Management in the Dominican Republic, 1978–1982." Unpublished manuscript in author's possession.

Stepan, Alfred. 1986. "Paths toward Redemocratization: Theoretical and Comparative

Considerations." In *Transitions from Authoritarian Rule: Comparative Perspectives.* Edited by Guillermo O'Donnell, Phillipe Schmitter, and Laurence Whitehead. Baltimore: Johns Hopkins University Press.

Tavares, Froilán. 1993. *Vivencias de un político apartidista.* Santo Domingo: Editora Taller.

Tejada, Adriano Miguel. 1994. *Reforma, institucionalidad y cultura política: Artículos en "Ultima Hora."* Santo Domingo: Editora Taller.

Thelen, Kathleen, and Steve Steinmo. 1992. "Historical Institutionalism in Comparative Politics." In *Structuring Politics: Historical Institutionalism in Comparative Analysis.* Edited by S. Steinmo, Kathleen Thelen, and Frank Longstreth. Cambridge: Cambridge University Press.

Theobold, Robin. 1982. "Patrimonialism." *World Politics* 34, no. 4 (July): 548–59.

Thoumi, Francisco. 1988. *Economic Policy, Free Zones and Export Assembly Manufacturing in the Dominican Republic.* Washington, D.C.: Inter-American Development Bank [IDB].

Trudeau, Robert H. 1984. "Guatemala: The Long-term Costs of Short-term Stability." In *From Gunboats to Diplomat: New U.S. Policies in Latin America.* Edited by R. Newfarmer. Baltimore: Johns Hopkins University Press.

United Nations. Economic Commission for Latin America and the Caribbean (UN/ECLA). Annual. *Statistical Yearbook.* Santiago, Chile.

U.S. Congress. 1991. House. Committee on Foreign Affairs. Subcommittees on Human Rights and International Organizations and on Western Hemisphere Affairs. *Hearing on the Plight of Haitian Sugarcane Cutters in the Dominican Republic.* 102nd Cong., 1st sess. Washington, D.C.: GPO.

Vacs, Aldo. 1995. "Neoliberal Visions: Market Economics, Procedural Democracy, Personalist Politics, and Liberal States in Argentina." Paper presented to the Latin American Studies Association Congress, September 28–30, Washington, D.C.

Valenzuela, Arturo. 1989. "Chile: Origins, Consolidation and Breakdown of a Democratic Regime." In *Democracy in Developing Countries: Latin America.* Edited by Larry Diamond, Juan Linz, and Seymour Martin Lipset. Boulder: Lynne Rienner Publishers.

Valenzuela, J. Samuel. 1992. "Democratic Consolidation in Post-Transitional Settings: Notion, Process, and Facilitating Conditions." In *Issues in Democratic Consolidation: The New South American Democracies in Comparative Perspective.* Edited by Scott Mainwaring, Guillermo O'Donnell, and J. Samuel Valenzuela. Notre Dame: University of Notre Dame Press.

Vance, Cyrus. 1983. *Hard Choices: Critical Years in America's Foreign Policy.* New York: Simon and Schuster.

Vega, Bernardo. 1980. *Evaluación de la administración de las empresas de CORDE, 1962–1977.* Santo Domingo: Fondo para el Avance de las Ciencias Sociales, Academia de Ciencias de la República Dominicana, Comisión de Economía.

———. 1985. *Nazismo, fascismo y falangismo en la República Dominicana.* Santo Domingo: Fundación Cultural Dominicana.

———. 1986a. "Un caso de uso exitoso de encuestas políticas en la República Dominicana: La campaña electoral del Dr. Salvador Jorge Blanco en 1982." Santo Domingo: Paper presented to a conference sponsored by the Friedrich Ebert Foundation and INTEC. November.

———. 1986b. *Control y represión en la dictadura Trujillista*. Santo Domingo: Fundación Cultural Dominicana.

———. 1986c. *Los Estados Unidos y Trujillo: Año 1930*. 2 vols. Santo Domingo: Fundación Cultural Dominicana.

———. 1988a. *Domini Canes: Los perros del Señor*. Santo Domingo: Fundación Cultural Dominicana.

———. 1988b. *El Ajuste de la Economía Dominicana (1982–1986) dentro de la Crisis Financiera Latinoamericana*. Santo Domingo: Fundación Cultural Dominicana.

———. 1988c. *Trujillo y Haití (1930–1937)*. Santo Domingo: Fundación Cultural Dominicana.

———. 1990a. *En la década perdida*. Santo Domingo: Fundación Cultural Dominicana.

———. 1990b. *Trujillo y el control financiero norteamericano*. Santo Domingo: Fundación Cultural Dominicana.

———. 1991. *Eisenhower y Trujillo*. Santo Domingo: Fundación Cultural Dominicana.

———. 1992. *Trujillo y las fuerzas armadas norteamericanas*. Santo Domingo: Fundación Cultural Dominicana.

———. 1993a. *Kennedy y Bosch: Aporte al estudio de las relaciones internacionales del gobierno constitucional del 1963*. Santo Domingo: Fundación Cultural Dominicana.

———. 1993b. "República Dominicana, economía y política al término del siglo XX." *Ciencia y Sociedad* 18, no. 3: 353–63.

———. 1994a. "Juicio sobre la renegociación de la deuda externa." *Listín Diario*, June 30.

———. 1994b. "Las encuestas y nuestras elecciones." *Listín Diario*, May 12: 7.

———. 1994c. "¿Por qué no funciona la reforma económica en Santo Domingo?" *Listín Diario*, July 22.

———. 1996. "La supuesta protección efectiva del sector industrial dominicano." Unpublished manuscript.

Vega, Bernardo, and Carlos Despradel. 1994. *Estudio sobre la estrategia de integración económica de la República Dominicana*. Santo Domingo: n.p.

Velázquez Mainardi, Miguel Angel. 1994. "Proceso electoral y crisis haitiana." *El Nacional*, May 8: 11.

Veliz, Claudio. 1980. *The Centralist Tradition of Latin America*. Princeton: Princeton University Press.

Ventura, Juan. 1985. *Presidentes, juntas, consejos, triunviratos y gabinetes de la República Dominicana, 1844–1984*. Santo Domingo: Publicaciones ONAP.

Vilas, Carlos. n.d. [1972?]. *República Dominicana, imperialismo y enclave*. Estudios ELACP, no. 33. Santiago: Escuela Latinoamericana de Ciencia Política y Administración Pública, No. 33.

Viola, Eduardo, and Scott Mainwaring. 1985. "Transitions to Democracy: Brazil and Argentina in the 1980s." *Journal of International Affairs* 38, no. 2 (winter): 193–219.

Waisman, Carlos H. 1987. *Reversal of Development in Argentina: Postwar Counter-revolutionary Politics and Their Structural Consequences*. Princeton: Princeton University Press.

Weeks, John. 1986. "An Interpretation of the Central America Crisis." *Latin American Research Review* 21, no. 3: 31–53.

Welles, Sumner. 1966. *Naboth's Vineyard: The Dominican Republic 1844–1924*. 2 vols. Mamaroneck, N.Y.: Paul P. Appel, Publisher.

Wells, Henry. 1966a. "The Dominican Experiment with Bosch." *Orbis* 10 (spring): 274–80.

———. 1966b. "Turmoil in the Dominican Republic." *Current History* 50 (January): 14–20.

Wendt, Alexander E. 1987. "The Agent-Structure Problem in International Relations Theory." *International Organization* 41, no. 3 (summer): 335–70.

Whitehead, Laurence. 1991. "The Imposition of Democracy." In *Exporting Democracy: The United States and Latin America*. Edited by A. Lowenthal. Baltimore: Johns Hopkins University Press.

Wiarda, Howard J. 1975. *Dictatorship, Development and Disintegration*. 3 vols. Ann Arbor, Mich.: Xerox University Microfilms.

———. 1979. "The Dominican Republic: The Politics of a Frustrated Revolution II." In *Latin American Politics and Development*. Edited by Howard Wiarda and Harvey Kline. Boston: Houghton Mifflin.

———. 1989. "The Dominican Republic: Mirror Legacies of Democracy and Authoritarianism." *Democracy in Developing Countries: Latin America*, ed. Larry Diamond, Juan Linz, and Seymour Martin Lipset. Boulder, Colo.: Lynne Rienner Publishers.

———. 1994. "The Dominican Republic Elections of 1994." Washington, D.C.: Center for Strategic and International Studies, Western Hemisphere Election Study Series, vol. 12, study 9, August 12.

———, ed. 1982. *Political and Social Change in Latin America: The Distinct Tradition*. 2nd ed. Amherst: University of Massachusetts Press.

Wiarda, Howard J., and Michael J. Kryzanek. 1977. "Dominican Dictatorship Revisited: The Caudillo Tradition and the Regimes of Trujillo and Balaguer." *Revista/Review Interamericana* 7 (fall): 417–35.

———. 1982. *The Dominican Republic: A Caribbean Crucible*. Boulder, Colo.: Westview Press.

Wickham-Crowley, Timothy P. 1992. *Guerrillas and Revolution in Latin America: A Comparative Study of Insurgents and Regimes Since 1956*. Princeton: Princeton University Press.

Willmore, Larry. 1995. "Export Processing Zones in the Dominican Republic: A Comment on Kaplinsky." *World Development* 23, no. 3: 529–35.

World Bank. Annual. *World Development Report* [WDR]. Washington, D.C.

———. 1978b. *Dominican Republic: Its Main Economic Development Problems*. Washington, D.C.: World Bank.

———. 1987b. *Dominican Republic: An Agenda for Reform*. Report no. 5665-DO. Washington, D.C.: World Bank.

———. 1995b. *The Dominican Republic Growth with Equity: An Agenda for Reform*. Report no. 13619-DO. Washington, D.C.: World Bank.

Index

All parties and organizations are listed by acronym only.

Abbes, Johnny, 47, 48
Abinader, Rafael, 334 (n. 1)
Abreu, Antonio "Tonito," 221
Acuerdo de Santiago, 113, 117, 118, 315
    (n. 24)
Acuerdo de Santo Domingo, 239, 260
AD (Acción Democrática; Venezuela),
    122, 151–52, 307 (n. 24), 308 (n. 26), 315
    (n. 22)
ADI (Acción Dominicana Indepen-
    diente), 82
AFL-CIO, 207
Africa, neopatrimonial regimes in, 15, 132,
    274–75, 303–4 (n. 4), 318 (n. 1)
Agrarian reform laws, 106, 107
Agro-export sector, 121. See also Business
    sector
AIRD (Asociación de Industriales de la
    República Dominicana), 81, 85, 168, 322
    (n. 8)
Albuquerque, Rafael, 207, 221, 328 (n. 12)
Alfonsín, Raúl, 188
Alliance for Progress, 79
Alvarez Bogaert, Fernando: and Acuerdo
    de Santo Domingo, 239; and Balaguer,
    121, 233, 234; kidnapping of, 121, 316
    (n. 29); party support for, 237; as Peña
    Gómez vice presidential candidate,
    260; as presidential candidate for UD,
    238
AMD (Aviación Militar Dominicana),
    46
Americas Watch, 207
Amiama Tió, Luis, 75
El anillo palaciego ("the palace ring"),
    212, 243
APRA (Peru), 315 (n. 22)
Archbishop of Santo Domingo. See López

Rodríguez, Nicolás de Jesús; Pittini,
    Ricardo
Arévalo, Juan José, 51
Arias, Desiderio, 31
Aristide, Jean Bertrand, 237, 241, 332
    (n. 14), 334 (n. 25), 335 (n. 5). See also
    Haiti
Asociación para el Desarrollo, Inc., 119
Authoritarian regimes: constraints on,
    227–29; definition of, 13–14; and deter-
    minism, 24–25; development of, 56;
    neosultanistic (see Neosultanism); and
    transition to democracy, 16–17, 62,
    63–67. See also Balaguer, Joaquín:
    authoritarianism of
La Avanzada Electoral, 232
Aylwin, Patricio, 128

Báecistas, 28–29
Báez, Buenaventura, 28, 29, 35, 297
    (nn. 6, 8)
Baéz, Mauricio, 301 (n. 37)
Balaguer, Joaquín, 3–4, 20; and Alvarez,
    121, 233, 234; authoritarianism of, 98,
    100–104, 114; centralization of power by,
    104; character of, 101; comparisons with
    Trujillo, 19, 100, 128, 129; conspiracies
    of, 88–89; economic conditions under
    (see Economic conditions: under Bala-
    guer); exile of, 304 (n. 8); and Guzmán,
    172; "historic decision" and, 126–27;
    impact of electoral rules on, 156–57;
    legacy of, 214–15; legislative support for,
    217; and military (see Military: under
    Balaguer); moderating role of, 276;
    modification of constitution by, 102;
    neopatrimonialism of, 102, 189–92, 214,
    215, 216, 275, 305 (n. 15), 311–12 (n. 4);

opposition to, 73–75, 110–14, 117–18, 303 (n. 46) (*see also* Coups and coups attempts: against Balaguer; PRD; Strikes: under Balaguer); opposition to IDB loan, 183; and organized labor (*see* Labor, organized: under Balaguer); and PRD (*see* PRD); regime as competitive one-party system typology, 133; return from exile, 308 (n. 25); support for, 309–10 (n. 38), 320 (n. 12), 328 (n. 9); after Trujillo assassination, 72. *See also* "Elections"

Balaguer policy periods:
—1986–1990, 192, 193–202; budgetary powers of, 194; domestic opposition to, 197–200; and IMF, 196; legislative support for, 200–201; and organized labor (*see* Labor, organized: under Balaguer); political opposition to, 200–202; public-sector investment, 193–96; social protest during, 198, 199; strategies of, 193–96; trade under, 192, 197
—1990–1993, 192, 202–11; domestic opposition to, 208–9; domestic support for, 207–8; fiscal crisis of, 203; legislative support for, 210; political opposition to, 209–11; reforms of, 204, 205; stabilization program during, 202, 203, 209, 322 (n. 1); support for, 202–3; taxation under, 205–6; trade under, 203–5
—1993–1996, 192, 211–14; legislative support for, 212–13; restabilization of economy by, 212; state enterprises during, 212–13

La Banda (Frente Democrático, Anti-Comunista y Anti-Terrorista de Juventud Reformista), 111, 115, 117, 313 (n. 12)
Batista y Zaldívar, Fulgencio, 108, 303 (n. 45)
Beauchamp Javier, Juan René, 123, 125, 316 (n. 29)
Benidorm Agreement, 115
Betances, Emelio, 298 (n. 14)
Betancourt, Rómulo, 51, 70, 84, 305 (n. 11), 315 (n. 22)
Betancur, Belisario, 188
Bloque de Dignidad Nacional, 113, 116
Bloque Institucional, 183
Bludhorn, Charles, 312–13 (n. 9)
Bolívar, Simón, 27
Bolivia, 151, 279

Bonapartist regimes, 311–12 (n. 4)
Bonnelly, Rafael, 306 (n. 18)
Bosch, Juan, 92; analysis of potential return to power, 93–94; attempt to overthrow Trujillo, 51; background of, 307 (n. 22); conspiracies of, 88–89; coup attempts against (*see* Coups and coups attempts: against Bosch); departure from PRD, 116–17, 315 (n. 22); as depolarizing force, 276; differences with Peña Gómez, 117; election of, 68, 69; elite supporters of, 82; and expulsions from PRD, 314 (n. 17); fatalism of, 76–77, 309 (nn. 31, 32); industrial incentives law of, 308 (n. 28); and military (*see* Military: and Bosch); on need for revolution, 307–8 (n. 24); 1963 constitution of, 79, 81–82; opposition to, 79–82, 84; return from exile, 76, 116; travels to socialist-bloc countries, 314 (n. 20); and United States (*see* United States: and Bosch); weakening of support for, 84
Botello, Norge, 306 (n. 20)
Boyer, Jean-Pierre, 27
Bratton, Michael, 132, 303–4 (n. 4)
Brazil, 321 (n. 17), 336 (n. 11)
Brea Franco, Julio, 321 (n. 24)
Breckinridge, James C., 41
Britain, 296–97 (n. 4)
Brzezinski, Zbigniew, 124
Bunker, Ellsworth, 306 (n. 17)
Bush, George Herbert Walker, 332 (n. 14)
"Business Agenda for Integrated Development," 329 (n. 23)
Business sector: and Balaguer, 104, 105–6, 194, 197–98, 200, 270, 327 (n. 6); and Balaguer in 1978 elections, 121, 125, 132; and Jorge Blanco, 181, 186; and Bosch, 79, 81–82, 308 (n. 28); and Guzmán, 165, 167–69, 173–74; influence of, 163; and law 299, 312 (n. 5); and Majluta, 182; and Peña Gómez, 182; and PRD 1974 abstention, 315 (n. 25); resentment of military, 111, 168

Caamaño, Francisco, 109, 116, 276, 314 (nn. 18, 19)
Cáceres, Ramón, 31, 303 (n. 1)
CAE (Comisión de Asesores Electorales), 219–20, 248

Calder, Bruce, 298 (n. 15)
Candidates. *See individual candidates*
Capital flight, under Trujillo, 72
Carey, John M., 218
El Caribe, 126
Carter, James Earl (Jimmy): on Balaguer, 316 (n. 28); and Dominican human rights, 114; Dominican Republic in memoirs of, 124; as election observer, 249, 265; and Haiti, 334 (n. 25); on 1986 elections, 125
CASC (Confederación Autónoma Sindicatos Clasistas), 199
Case studies: and case-oriented research, 6–7, 293 (n. 1), 311 (n. 2); and within-case comparisons, 132, 293 (n. 1)
Cassá, Roberto, 312 (n. 4)
Castillo, Marino Vinicio "Vincho," 126, 239, 241, 325 (n. 32)
Castro, Fidel, 314 (n. 18)
Catholic Church: under Balaguer, 193, 201; in colonial period, 297 (n. 5); land expropriations of, 32; under Trujillo, 32, 48, 50, 58, 70; Trujillo financing of, 301 (n. 35); weakness of, 32
Catrain, Pedro, 298 (n. 14)
CBERA (Caribbean Basin Economic Recovery Act), 318 (n. 2)
CBI (Caribbean Basin Initiative), 138, 206
CDE (Companía Dominicana de Electricidad), 196, 212–13, 329 (n. 22)
CEA (Consejo Estatal del Azúcar), 107, 194, 212–13
Central America, 55
Central bank: central bank credit as funding mechanism, 211; on control of government of expenditures, 177; credit as funding mechanism, 195–96; exchange rate policies of, 196–97, 326 (n. 4); foreign exchange liquidity of, 179; lack of autonomy of, 326–27 (n. 5)
Central Romana, 44, 107
Chehabi, H. E., 42, 58
Chile, 53, 54, 128, 295 (n. 14), 302 (n. 39)
Christian Democratic Union, 233
Church, Frank, 117
CIA (Central Intelligence Agency), 70, 306 (n. 20), 309 (n. 35)
CIDES (Centro Internacional de Estudios Económicos y Sociales), 306 (n. 20)
Ciudad Trujillo, 43

Civility Commission, 251
Civil service, creation of, 207, 312 (n. 6)
Civil wars, nineteenth century, 29, 35, 55
Clientelism, 16, 150, 220–21, 222, 295 (n. 14)
Clinton, William Jefferson, 332–33 (n. 14)
CND (Comisión Nacional de Desarrollo), 105, 106
CNHE (Consejo Nacional de Hombres de Empresa), 82; agreement with Mexican organization, 323 (n. 9); formation and operation of, 322–23 (n. 8); and Ginebra, 197–98, 200; 1978 revitalization of, 168; political involvement of, 181. *See also* Business sector
CNOP (Conferencia Nacional de Organizaciones Populares), 199, 200
Collier, David, 293 (n. 1)
Collor de Mello, Fernando, 330 (n. 26)
Colombia, 295 (n. 12), 307 (n. 24)
Colonial period, 23; Catholic Church in, 297 (n. 5); Haiti in, 26, 27; independence movements during, 26–27, 303 (n. 43); influence on Dominican political structure, 52–55, 302 (n. 38); influence on Latin American political structure, 57; social impact of, 25–26
Columbus Lighthouse, 193
Commission of Election Advisers. *See* CAE
Commission to Observe the Pact of Civility, 253
Communism, 79, 314 (n. 17), 317 (n. 37), 320 (n. 14)
Communist Party, 51, 71, 115, 121
Conaghan, Catherine M., 13, 278, 321 (n. 18)
Concordazo, 184
CONEP (Consejo Nacional de la Empresa Privada), 330 (n. 23)
Consejo Coordinador Empresarial (Mexico), 168
Consejo Nacional de la Magistratura, 254, 336 (n. 9)
Constabulary force, establishment of, 38
Constitutions, Dominican Republic: 1844, 34–35; 1854, 35; 1865, 35–36; 1963, 79, 81–82, 102; 1966, 225; 1994, 211, 254, 278, 322 (n. 25), 336 (n. 9); numbers of, 35; reforms of, 254, 278, 322 (n. 25)
COP (Colectivo de Organizaciones Populares), 208

CORDE (Corporación Dominicana de Empresas Estatales), 172, 212, 323 (n. 15), 329 (n. 21)

Corporán de los Santos, Rafael, 233

Corruption: under Balaguer, 102–3, 149, 190, 211–12, 328 (n. 11), 329 (nn. 18, 20); under Jorge Blanco, 186, 325–26 (n. 32); under Guzmán, 172–73, 323 (n. 15), 324 (n. 17); and military, 241; and neopatrimonial regimes, 295 (n. 14); 1986 anti-corruption campaign, 201

Costa Rica, 53, 54, 55, 57

Costa Rican Institute for Political Education, 306 (n. 20)

Council of state, 74–78, 308 (n. 25)

Coups and coup attempts: against Balaguer, 74, 109, 122–26, 132; against Bosch, 60, 69, 79, 85, 109, 308 (n. 29); in 1978 elections, 122–26; reasons for anti-Bosch, 79; against Trujillo, 46, 48, 51, 52; United States on 1978 election, 125; against Vásquez, 40. See also Government turnovers, numbers of Dominican

CTM (Central de Trabajadores Mayoritaria), 199

Cuba, 301 (n. 37), 303 (n. 45), 308 (n. 24)

Cuban revolution: impact on United States, 70, 89, 91; and neopatrimonialism, 108

Cukierman, Alex, 327 (n. 5)

Curtis, Charles, 41

Customs receivership, 49, 204, 209, 211, 329 (n. 17)

Dahl, Robert, 23

DDI (Directorio de Desarrollo Industrial), 106

De Camps, Hatuey, 201, 317 (n. 32)

Democracy: authoritarian regimes and transition to, 13–14, 16–17, 62, 63–67; and citizenship, 24; co-existence with neopatrimonialism, 15–16; consolidation in, 12–13, 15; constitutional, 11; culturalist view of constraints on, 7–8; definition of, 10–13, 279, 294 (n. 8); delegative, 294 (n. 11); elections as characteristic of, 221–22; evolution in Europe, 302 (n. 41); "genetic" model of, 24; inclusiveness in, 10–11, 15; methodology for study of transition to (see Democratic transition: methodology for analy-sis of); military challenges to, 13; neopatrimonialism impact on transitions to, 15–16, 274–75, 277; nonconsolidated, 15–16; provisional governments and transition to, 64; purposes of, 12; structuralist view of constraints on, 7–8, 53–55; studies on optimal sequence for, 23–24; three tensions in, 11; two different "balances of power" in, 294 (n. 7)

Democratic Conference, 122

Democratic transition: from above, 63–64, 68, 120–29, 131–32, 135, 271; in authoritarian, nonsultanistic regimes, 17; from below, 63, 89–90, 279; effect of continuing factors of change on, 65; effect of repression on, 303 (n. 4); elements of, 65, 67; explanations of, 293 (n. 2); factors in, 304 (n. 6); importance of mode of, 64–65; importance of national identity in, 24; and institutional and party continuity, 67, 101; international geopolitics in, 62–63; methodology for analysis of, 6–8, 19, 61–67; missed opportunities in, 65, 67; after neosultanistic regime, 60, 61–67; provisional governments as risk for, 75–78; and social stratification, 68; structural conditions inimical to, 68
—after Balaguer. See Elections—1978; PRD
—after Bosch, 87–96; from below, 89–90; governing triumvirate, 87–88, 309 (n. 33); impact of provisional government on, 96; summary of, 94–96; U.S. impact on, 90–96
—after PRD. See Balaguer policy periods
—after Trujillo, 67–87; Bosch overthrow and breakdown of democracy, 78–87; "ins" versus "outs," 69; international geopolitics in, 69–72; lack of tradition of opposition, 79–80; provisional government and elections, 75–78; provisional government and regime collapse, 73–75; role of Cuban Revolution, 70; role of United States, 70–71, 72; and social stratification, 68; summary of, 85–87

Demographic changes, in Dominican Republic, 137–43

Devaluation, 138, 139, 176, 177, 178, 180, 203

Di Palma, Guiseppe, 12

Disappearances (desaparecidos), 110–11, 208

Disenfranchisement, 251–53, 333 (nn. 23, 24), 334 (n. 26)

Downing, Brian M., 302 (n. 41)

Dual-track policies, 125, 129, 317 (n. 34)

Duarte, Juan Pablo, 27, 28

Economic conditions: under Balaguer, 104–9, 121, 131, 156, 191–92, 203, 270–71; after Bosch, 88; and economic national- ism, 49, 58; after Guzmán, 162; nine- teenth century, 29, 30; under PRD, 136–43; under Trujillo, 44, 46, 49–50, 71–72; after Trujillo assassination, 68; and Trujillo rise to power, 42; U.S. investment in Dominican Republic, 31, 33. *See also* IMF; Stabilization programs

Economic policymaking: five factors influencing, 163–65, 193, 215

Ecuador, 278, 321 (nn. 17, 22)

Eisenhower, Dwight D., 70

Elections: candidate selection and filing for, 331 (n. 5); as characteristic of politi- cal democracy, 221–22; comparison of, 244–45; demonstration, 310 (n. 41); and election reform, 21, 38, 39, 259, 264, 322 (n. 25); first direct, 35; and interna- tional geopolitics, 223; and international observers (*see* International observers, and elections); laws for, 156–57, 254, 259, 264, 321 (nn. 19, 24), 334 (n. 1), 334 (n. 6); and plurality, 157; PRD primary, 172–73, 184–85; U.S. support for free, 256, 316 (n. 31). *See also* JCE
—1913, 298 (n. 13)
—1924, 38, 39–40
—1934, 43
—1942, 43–44
—1947, 44
—1952, 44
—1957, 44
—1962, 68, 75–78
—1966, 89–90, 91, 97, 98, 309 (n. 37)
—1968 municipal, 112
—1970, 112–13, 115
—1974, 113–14, 117–18, 315 (nn. 23, 25)
—1978: authoritarianism in, 228; Balaguer campaign during, 121–22; Bosch in, 123– 24; business sector in (*see* Business sec-

tor: and Balaguer in 1978 elections); Guzmán candidacy in, 119–20, 124; JCE on results of, 126; lack of opinion polling in, 122; military in, 3, 121, 122–26, 268, 316 (n. 29); Peña Gómez in, 119, 120; PRD in, 118–20, 122, 124; profes- sional sector in, 125; societal support for, 125–26; and transition from above, 120– 28, 131; U.S. involvement in, 122, 124–25, 127, 129; vice presidency and PR in, 121
—1982, 232–33; Jorge Blanco in, 20; and nomination of JCE judges, 245; Peña Gómez in, 232; PRD in, 233
—1986, 3–4; absence of ballot splitting in, 321 (n. 19); allegations of fraud in, 248; Balaguer anticorruption campaign, 201; Carter on, 125; and identity cards, 251; and JCE, 219–20; Majluta in, 220, 234; nominees in, 232; Peña Gómez in, 173; reasons for Balaguer win, 233–34; rea- sons for PRD defeat, 185; renominations of incumbents in, 321 (n. 20)
—1990, 210; allegations of fraud in, 248– 49, 332 (n. 22); Balaguer in, 234–35, 237–38; Bosch in, 233, 235–36, 249; Catholic Church in, 229, 235; JCE in, 245, 251; opinion polling in, 331 (n. 6); Peña Gómez in, 235–37; PLD in, 235; PRD in, 239–40, 249; PR(SC) in, 234, 237; reasons for PRD defeat in, 185, 233–34; U.S. involvement in, 254–55
—1994, 210, 211; allegations of fraud in, 251–53, 333 (nn. 23, 24), 334 (n. 26); Balaguer in, 241–43, 253, 255–56; Jorge Blanco in, 251; candidates in, 331 (n. 11); candidates on socioeconomic issues, 240; and constitutional reform, 254; effect of Haiti on, 55, 333–34 (n. 25); and electoral registry, 251; JCE in, 246, 251; Majluta in, 251; negative campaign themes in, 240–41, 243, 256, 332 (n. 13); opinion polling in, 331 (n. 6); "pact of civility" in, 250; Peña Gómez in, 211, 239–41, 243; PLD in, 238–39, 243, 251, 332 (n. 13), 334 (n. 28); PRD in, 243, 251, 255, 332 (n. 13); preelectoral opin- ion polling in, 331 (n. 6); PR(SC) in, 251; U.S. involvement in, 253, 254, 334 (n. 25)
—1996, 4, 259–68; allegations of fraud in, 263–64; candidates in, 260–61; con-

trasted with 1978, 268–71; differences from previous, 260–62; doubts about, 261; Fernández in, 260; GAD priorities in, 262; JCE in, 261; participation rates in, 264; Peña Gómez in, 260, 262–63, 266–67, 333 (n. 24); PLD in, 264, 265, 266; PRD in, 265; PR(SC) in, 264; results of first round, 264; results of second round, 264; U.S. involvement in, 264

—1998, 273

—crisis-ridden, 21; candidates and campaigns in, 232–44; comparison of, 244–45; effects of, 223; factors in, 260; fraud in, 225, 245, 251–52; JCE and lack of institutional autonomy in, 245–47; neopatrimonialism in, 256; reasons for, 224–27; role of presidency in, 224–25; scores of, 255; and weakness of election oversight agency, 225–26. *See also individual election years*

Elites: and Bosch, 82, 94–95; economic, 50, 70; emergence of new, 33; influence of, 327 (n. 5); national, 30; opposition to Bosch by, 80–82; Trujillo relationship with, 39, 49–50. *See also* Business sector

El Salvador, 317 (n. 37)

Employment, public, 80, 84, 104–5, 166–67, 194, 312 (n. 6), 326–27 (n. 5). *See also* Unemployment

EPZs (export-processing zones), 138, 139–40, 176, 196, 207, 319 (nn. 3, 4)

Espaillat, Ulises Francisco, 36

Espinal, Rosario, 13, 298 (n. 14)

Estrella Sadhalá, César, 261

Estrella Ureña, Rafael, 39–40, 41

European Common Market, 138

Exchange rate: dual-exchange system, 197; parity of, 176, 177, 178–80, 196–97, 326 (n. 4); sources of, 139, 140, 142–43, 195; and surcharge on exports, 325 (n. 29)

Exonerations, 169, 186

Extended Fund Facility agreement, 176

Falconbridge, 189, 195

Fanjul brothers, 313 (n. 9)

FENHERCA (Federación Nacional de Hermandades Campesinas), 76, 306 (n. 20)

Fernández, Leonel, 4; Balaguer support

for, 260–61, 264–67; as Bosch vice presidential candidate, 221, 238; and Consejo Nacional de la Magistratura, 336 (n. 9); and constitutional reform, 278; on difference between PLD and PRD, 331 (n. 9); differences with Peña Gómez, 267; Guzmán family support for, 324 (n. 17); legislative support for, 271; and military, 320–21 (n. 16); and neopatrimonialism, 272–73

Fernández Domínguez, Rafael Tomás, 85

Fiallo, Viriato, 73, 76, 77

Figueres, José, 84, 306 (n. 20)

FNP (Fuerza Nacional Progresista), 239

Fontana, Biancamaria, 279

Foreign aid, 262–63, 309 (n. 36), 322 (n. 2). *See also* IMF; World Bank

Foreign exchange. *See* Exchange rate

Forum organization, 322 (n. 6)

Fraud: allegations of electoral, 228, 247–55, 263–64, 317 (n. 35), 332–33 (n. 22), 333 (n. 23); and Balaguer, 126–27, 248–49, 310 (n. 42); and Bosch, 249; facilitation by JCE, 226–27, 247; and Majluta, 248; opinion polling and indicators of, 228; and party leadership, 225; presidential leadership and electoral, 225, 245; and Trujillo, 299 (n. 17)

Freedom House indicators, 228–29

Frei, Eduardo, 128

Frente Nacional Patriótico, 265

Friedrich Ebert Foundation, 119

FTZs (free-trade zones). *See* EPZs

Fujimori, Alberto, 217

Fulbright, William, 117

GAD (Grupo de Acción por la Democracia), 212, 261–62, 264

Galíndez, Jesús de, 45, 296 (n. 18), 300 (n. 26)

Gamarra, Eduardo, 279

García, Alan, 188

García, Lautico, 77

García Aybar, José Ernesto, 308 (n. 27)

García Godoy, Héctor, 89–90, 94, 95–96, 109, 112

García Lizardo, Manuel, 246

Gassó, María Isabel, 260

GDP (Gross Domestic Product), 137, 169, 180, 194, 212

Germany, 37, 298 (n. 15)

Ginebra, Luis Augusto "Payo," 168, 197–98, 200
Gleijeses, Piero, 305 (n. 13), 309 (n. 37)
Goico Morales, Carlos, 121
Gómez, Juan Vicente, 58, 308 (n. 26)
González, Ignacio María, 36
"Good Neighbor" Policy, 39
Government turnovers, numbers of Dominican, 29, 30–31, 36, 60, 303 (n. 1)
Grant, Ulysses S., 28
Grau San Martín, Ramón, 51, 308 (n. 24)
Gray, William, 334 (n. 25)
Grenada, 310–11 (n. 43)
GSP (generalized system of preferences), 206
Guardia Nacional Dominicana, 38, 42. See also Military
Guerrilla movements, 107–8, 305 (n. 14)
Gulf and Western, 107, 118, 312 (n. 9), 315–16 (n. 26), 316 (n. 28)
Guzmán, S. Antonio, 20, 98, 136; and Balaguer, 169, 172; and Jorge Blanco, 147, 171, 172, 187; and Bosch, 117; and congress, 323 (n. 13); conservatism of, 320 (n. 14); and factional strife in PRD, 150, 160–61; fiscal policies of, 162, 166; and military, 127, 147; nepotism of, 160–61, 324 (n. 17); opposition to, 119–20, 171, 174; and Peña Gómez, 169, 171, 316 (n. 26); presidentialism of, 172; on presidential reelection, 155; suicide of, 173, 322 (n. 2); U.S. attitude toward, 89, 315 (n. 26)
Guzmán administration, 165–74; Balaguer attacks on, 169; business sector opposition to, 167–69; contrasts with Balaguer administrations, 172; fiscal policies of, 166; international constraints and opportunities of, 167; political goals of, 165–67; political opposition to, 169, 171–74; public-sector investment under, 166–69; tax reform of, 169, 171–72

Haiti, 55, 296 (nn. 2, 3), 301 (n. 34); Balaguer on, 241, 300 (n. 31); in colonial period, 26, 27, 28; effect of restoration of Aristide, 332 (n. 14); effect of U.S. occupation, 56, 299 (n. 16); effect on 1994 elections, 55; and effects of Duvalier ouster, 139, 140; effects of occupation on Catholic Church, 32; effects of occu-

pation on elites, 33; independence of, 303 (n. 43); and massacre, 42, 43, 48, 300 (n. 31); migrant labor from, 107, 108, 237, 241, 301 (n. 37), 312 (n. 9), 313 (n. 10), 319 (n. 6); and 1994 Dominican Republic elections, 55, 333–34 (n. 25); relationship with Dominican Republic, 82, 84, 107, 241; relationship with United States, 28, 298–99 (n. 15), 299 (n. 16), 332 (n. 14), 333–34 (n. 25), 335 (n. 5); Trujillo on, 48
Hartlyn, Jonathan, 311 (n. 4), 323 (n. 10), 324 (n. 21), 333 (n. 24)
Haya de la Torre, Victor Raúl, 315 (n. 22)
Hernández, José Francisco, 331 (n. 11)
Heureaux, Ulises, 29–30, 34, 42, 58, 60, 297–98 (n. 9)
Hispaniola, 53, 296 (n. 1), 297 (n. 7)
Historical institutionalism, 9, 22
"Historic decision" (el fallo histórico), 126
Hoetink, H., 298 (n. 10)
Horacistas, 31
Hull, Cordell, 49, 299 (n. 19)
Human rights violations: under Balaguer, 101, 110–11, 114, 129, 208, 313 (n. 12); under Jorge Blanco, 161; under PRD, 145, 150; under Trujillo, 70
Hurwitch, Robert, 122, 316 (n. 31)
Hybrid regimes, 13–14, 228–29, 268, 294–95 (n. 12)

IDB (Inter-American Development Bank), 140, 183, 273, 326 (n. 3), 328 (n. 8)
Identification cards, 226, 249, 250, 251, 264, 330 (n. 3). See also JCE
IFES (International Foundation for Electoral Systems), 253
ILO (International Labor Organization), 102
Imbert Barrera, Antonio, 75
IMF (International Monetary Fund): and Balaguer administration, 182, 192, 196, 203, 208, 216, 322 (n. 1), 326 (n. 4); and Jorge Blanco administration, 175, 176, 178–80; and IMF riots, 161, 178, 198, 325 (n. 24); opinion survey on, 330 (n. 24); and PRD, 162, 322 (nn. 1, 6); and triumvirate government, 88; and United States, 177. See also Stabilization programs

Imperialism, and development of authoritarianism, 56; and 1916 occupation, 37. *See also* Colonial period

Import-substituting industrialization, 104, 105, 166, 169, 312 (n. 5), 322 (n. 4)

INESPRE (Instituto de Estabilización de Precios), 194

Institutional formalism, 218, 275–76

Institutions: in democratic transition, 67, 101, 135, 143–58; importance of, 9; lack of colonial continuity, 54, 302 (n. 38); in neosultanism, 62. *See also governmental agencies, political parties, and other institutions*

Inter-American Commission on Human Rights, 91

Inter-American Peace Committee (OAS), 70

Inter-American Peace Force (OAS), 89

Internal Revenue Code (1986), Section 936, 318 (n. 2)

International factors, reductionist interpretations based on, 24–25, 56, 99, 125, 275, 302–3 (n. 42)

International geopolitics: under Balaguer, 129, 132, 206–7; under Jorge Blanco, 177–82; and elections, 125, 223; impact of, 62–63, 324 (n. 19); influence on economic policymaking, 164; under Trujillo, 51, 69–72. *See also* IMF; United States

International observers, and elections, 91, 122, 251, 253, 264, 298 (n. 13), 334 (n. 26)

Interventions, U.S., 31–32, 304 (n. 4); after Bosch, 89–90; consequences of, 40–41, 56, 90–97, 99, 108, 306 (n. 17), 310 (n. 39); and election reform, 38; goals of 1916, 37–38; Grenada, 310–11 (n. 43); of 1916, 36–42; of 1965, 92; reasons for 1916, 36–37; shift to interventionist policy, 70; shift to noninterventionist policy, 38–39, 40–41, 46, 304–5 (n. 10); and transition from neopatrimonialism to democracy, 90–96, 275; U.S. public support for, 310–11 (n. 43); withdrawal of troops after, 38, 307 (n. 23)

Isa, Minerva, 329 (n. 21)

Italy, 53

ITBIS (*impuesto a las transferencias de bienes industriales*), 176, 206

Jacob Kaplan Fund, 306 (n. 20)

Jamaica, 324 (n. 19)

JCE (Junta Central Electoral), 38, 219–20, 261; disenfranchisement by, 251–52; and election registry, 330 (n. 3), 334 (n. 26); fraud facilitation by, 226–27, 247, 248–49; and "fraud syndrome," 247–48; judge nomination for, 246; lack of institutional autonomy of, 245–47, 332 (n. 17); nomination of, 245; PRD influence on, 247; recusal of judges, 248–49; reform law for, 246; relationship with executive, 246–47; resignation in 1924 elections, 40; on results of 1978 elections, 126; and *votos observados*, 251–52. *See also* Elections

Jimenes, Juan Isidro, 31

Jimenistas, 31

Johnson, Andrew, 28

Johnson, Lyndon Baines, 310 (n. 43)

Jorge Blanco, Salvador, 20, 136, 219; and communism, 320 (n. 14); constraints and limitations of, 161; corruption of, 325–26 (n. 32); criticisms of, 21; and Guzmán, 147, 171, 172, 187; legislative support for, 182; political opposition to, 182–85; and PRD factional strife, 150, 172; on presidential reelection, 155, 165; as president of PRD, 120; on Santo Domingo mayoral election, 324 (n. 16); trial against, 200; trial of, 327 (n. 7)

Jorge Blanco administration, 174–86; decrees of, 180, 183; domestic opposition to, 181–82; effects of devaluation on, 180; and exchange rate, 178–80; failure to modify neopatrimonial rule, 185–86, 187; fiscal policies of, 186; international geopolitics in, 177–82; neopatrimonialism of, 185–86, 187, 326 (n. 1); political opposition to, 181; stabilization program of, 161–63, 174–77; support for, 173; taxation program of, 176, 181, 186; tensions with IMF, 178–80

Jorge Moreno, Marcos Antonio, 316 (n. 29), 317 (n. 32)

Judiciary, 127, 157, 254, 323 (n. 11), 336 (n. 9)

Karl, Terry L., 304 (n. 5)

Kennedy, John F., 70

Kidnappings, 113, 121, 316 (n. 29)

Knight, Franklin W., 37
Krasner, Stephen D., 9

Labor, organized: under Balaguer, 106–7,
  199, 206–7, 208; under PRD, 141–42, 323
  (n. 10)
Labor code, revision of, 142, 192, 203,
  206–7, 210, 319 (n. 6)
Lájara Burgos, Luis Homero, 113
Land expropriations, 32, 68. *See also*
  Agrarian reform laws
La Trinitaria, 297 (n. 5)
Law 299, 312 (n. 5)
LE (La Estructura), 182, 234
Libro Blanco (White Book), 248, 334
  (n. 28)
Linz, Juan, 12, 13, 17, 42, 58, 296 (n. 18),
  303 (n. 46)
Lomé IV, 138
López Portilla, José, 325 (n. 26)
López Rodríguez, Nicolás de Jesús
  (Cardinal and Archbishop of Santo
  Domingo), 201, 220, 248, 263, 301
  (n. 35), 332 (n. 14)
Lora, Augusto, 112
Lowenthal, Abraham, 32, 298 (n. 14), 309
  (n. 31)
Luperón, Gregorio, 35, 36

McAuliffe, Dennis, 125
Majluta, Jacobo, 161, 171, 219; accusations
  of 1986 electoral fraud by, 248; and
  business sector, 182; and CORDE, 323
  (n. 15); creation of LE, 182; creation of
  PRI by, 202; on defeat, 332 (n. 20); and
  factional strife in PRD (*see* PRD); and
  military, 320 (n. 14); as 1978 vice presidential nominee, 120; 1981 primary, 172–
  73; and 1985 primary, 184–85; opposition to IDB loan, 183; and Peña Gómez,
  235, 247; as president after Guzmán, 324
  (n. 18)
Malloy, James, 279
Marcos, Ferdinand, 295 (n. 14)
Market-access schemes, 138, 318 (n. 2)
Market-oriented reform, debates about,
  270–71, 277
Marmolejos, Nélsida, 210
Marte Pichardo, Santos Mélido, 317
  (n. 32)
Martin, John Bartlow, 75, 77, 89–90, 305–

6 (n. 17), 306 (n. 18), 307 (nn. 22, 23),
  309 (n. 32)
Matos Berrido, Leonardo, 220, 246, 330
  (n. 1)
Menem, Carlos, 217, 330 (n. 26)
Meriño, Fernando Arturo de, 32, 36
Mexico, 325 (n. 26)
Migration: Haitian labor (*see* Haiti:
  migrant labor from); and military, 48;
  rural-to-urban, 107; to United States,
  138, 142–43, 199, 215, 319 (nn. 8, 9), 320
  (n. 13)
Military, 146–49; and Balaguer, 109–10;
  under Balaguer, 113, 123–26, 127, 129,
  148–49, 313 (n. 15); and Jorge Blanco,
  147–48; and Bosch, 80, 82, 84, 306
  (n. 20), 309 (n. 32); after Bosch overthrow, 94; business ventures of, 111, 168;
  centralization of authority of, 40, 46–47,
  58, 320 (n. 16); challenges to democracy
  by, 13; changes under PRD, 147; civilians in, 47; commitment to democratization, 80; and corruption, 241; coup
  threat in 1978 elections, 122–26; decline
  in professionalism of, 148–49; expenditures under Trujillo, 300 (n. 28); and
  Fernández, 320–21 (n. 16); and Guzmán, 127, 147; involvement in illegal
  migration, 48; and kidnapping of
  Alvarez prior to 1978 elections, 121, 316
  (n. 29); and Majluta, 320 (n. 14); and
  1978 elections, 3, 121, 316 (n. 29); post-
  1978 election purges of, 127; post-1996
  elections, 268; and regional caudillos,
  33–34; under Trujillo, 44–47, 69, 304
  (n. 9); and United States, 41, 51–52, 125,
  147–48; weakening of, 159, 313 (n. 11)
Minority parties, 334 (n. 1)
Miolán, Angel, 309 (n. 30)
Mirabal sisters, 69
Mitchell, Christopher, 321 (n. 24)
Mitchell, Nancy, 298 (n. 15)
MIUCA (Movimiento Independiente
  de Unidad Y Cambio)–Nuevo Poder,
  331–32 (n. 11)
MNJ (Movimiento Nacional de la Juventud), 112
MNR (Movimiento Nacionalista Revolucionario), 150–51
MODERNO (Movimiento de Renova-
  ción), 201, 327–28 (n. 8)

Monroe Doctrine, 31
Morales Troncoso, Carlos, 221, 238
Moreno, Juan, 123
Moreno Martínez, Alfonso, 112
Morse, Richard, 302 (n. 39)
Mota Ruiz, Alfredo, 221
Moya Pons, Frank, 301 (n. 35), 308 (n. 27)
MPD (Movimiento Popular Domini-
cano), 113, 115, 118
MR1J4 (Movimiento Revolucionario 14 de
junio), 73
Multifibers Agreement, 318 (n. 2)

NAFTA (North American Free Trade
Agreement), 140
National Front (Colombia), 307 (n. 24)
National identity, 24, 58–59, 237, 310
(n. 39)
Nationalization, of industries, 44, 101
Natural disasters, reaction of neopatrimonial regimes to, 43, 166, 299 (n. 21), 323
(n. 12)
NDI (National Democratic Institute), 264,
333 (n. 24)
Neighborhood associations, 194, 325
(n. 24)
Neopatrimonialism, 5, 14–18; and authoritarian regimes, 16–17; and Balaguer
administration (see Balaguer, Joaquín:
neopatrimonialism of); basis for conceptualization of, 294 (n. 10); and Jorge
Blanco administration, 185–86, 187;
central ruler's importance in, 16; characteristic elements of, 14–15, 16, 222, 295
(n. 14); characteristics of PR(SC), 273;
co-existence with various regime types,
15; and colonial past (see Colonial
period); in crisis-ridden elections, 256;
definitions of, 6, 102, 189; and democracy, 15–16, 274–75, 277; development
of Latin American, 54–58, 108; and
economic policymaking, 164; effect of
socioeconomic changes and continuities on, 143–46; elections in, 222; formal
organization weaknesses in, 16, 129, 135,
157, 275–76; inequality in, 16; methodology for study of, 7–10; patterns in
Dominican history, 25; patterns in
1978–1996 period, 157–58; popular support for, 145, 320 (nn. 11, 12); relevance
to Dominican Republic politics, 295

(n. 13); and tension between governability and democracy, 277; and sultanism,
17; variations in, 16
Neosultanism: as authoritarian regime, 17;
in Cuba, 303 (n. 45); and democratic
transition, 60, 61–67; differences from
ideal-type totalitarianism, 17; factors
in development of, 57; of Heureaux,
29–30; ideal-type, 42, 58; and nepotism,
64; pseudo-oppositions in, 62; relationship with social institutions, 62; repression in, 17; versus sultanism, 296 (n. 19);
Trujillo, 23, 24, 41–42, 96–97, 296 (n. 18)
Nepotism: and continuity of neosultanism, 64; of Guzmán, 160–61, 324
(n. 17); under Trujillo, 47, 64, 68
Nicaragua, 55, 108
Nickel exports, 326 (n. 2)
Nivar Seijas, Neit Rafael, 109, 110, 121, 123,
127, 313 (n. 16), 316 (n. 29)
Nonconsolidated regimes, 13–14
Nordlinger, Eric, 23–24
North, Douglas, 301–2 (n. 38)
Nouel, Adolfo A., 32
Núñez Collado, Agripino, 209, 250, 254,
328 (n. 14)

OAS (Organization of American States),
91; on Dominican human rights violations, 70; economic sanctions of, 71, 73;
emergency financial assistance from,
90, 309 (n. 36); Inter-American Peace
Committee of, 70; Inter-American
Peace Force of, 89; as international
observers, 122, 333 (n. 24)
O'Donnell, Guillermo A., 14, 294 (n. 11)
OPEC, 114
Opinion polling: as indicator of massive
fraud, 228; lack in 1978 elections, 122; in
1990 elections, 331 (n. 6); preelectoral
1989, 152; preelectoral 1994, 239, 244
Organic Law of the Armed Forces, 148
Out-migration. See Migration: to United
States
Oviedo, José, 298 (n. 14)

Pact for Democracy, 211, 254, 262
Pact of Civility, 253
Pact of Punto Fijo (Venezuela), 307
(n. 24)
Pacts, nature of, 307 (n. 24)

Panama Canal, 37
Paris Club debt, 176, 179
Participación Ciudadana, 262, 264, 335 (n. 7)
Partido Azul, 29, 35
Partido Rojo, 29, 35
Partyarchy, definition of, 151–52, 321 (n. 23)
Pastor, Robert, 125
Path-dependent approach, 22, 217, 301–2 (nn. 38, 40); and agent-structure problem, 7; explanation for change by, 9, 187, 271, 294 (n. 11)
Patrimonialism, Weber on, 14, 17, 298 (n. 10)
Patriotic Electoral Front, 239
Patronage networks, 216, 217, 295 (n. 14)
Paulino Alvarez, Anselmo, 47
PD (Partido Dominicano), 43, 151; Balaguer regrouping of, 90; dissolution of, 74; under Trujillo, 50
Peasantry. See Rural sector
Peña Batlle, Manuel Arturo, 300 (n. 31)
Peña Gómez, José Francisco, 171, 247, 324 (n. 16); background of, 331 (n. 10); business sector on, 182; conspiracy against Reid Cabral, 313 (n. 12); as depolarizing force, 276–77; differences with Bosch, 117; differences with Fernández, 267; education of, 306 (n. 20); and factional strife in PRD (see PRD: factional strife in); on Guzmán, 169, 171, 316 (n. 26); imagined scenario of 1996 elections, 268; influence of Venezuelan AD on, 151; and Majluta, 235; and 1996 elections (see Elections—1996: Peña Gómez in); pre-1978 election activities of, 119; as secretary general of PRD, 115, 172, 202, 210–11; speeches archive of, 314–15 (n. 21)
Pérez, Carlos Andrés, 124, 127
Pérez Sánchez, Eliseo, 306 (n. 18)
Pérez y Pérez, Enrique, 109, 110, 127, 265, 268
Personality of leaders, and Dominican history, 8, 29–30, 296 (n. 17)
Peru, 312 (n. 4), 315 (n. 22)
Peynado, Francisco J., 38, 307 (n. 23)
Peynado, Jacinto, 43, 221, 238, 260
Philippines, 295 (n. 14)
Phone taps, 329 (n. 19)
Pichardo, Nicolás, 306 (n. 18)

Pico Trujillo, 43
Pinochet, Augusto, 295 (n. 14)
Pittini, Ricardo (Archbishop of Santo Domingo), 50, 201, 220, 248, 263, 301 (n. 35), 332 (n. 14)
Plaza Laso, Galo, 122, 123, 124
PLD (Partido de la Liberación Dominicana), 199; and Bosch, 117, 210; coalition with PRD and PR(SC), 271; government funding for, 317 (n. 33); impact on PRD, 325 (n. 27); Marxist-Leninist ideology of, 315 (n. 22); and 1990 elections, 235; 1994 congressional seats of, 213–14; and 1994 elections (see Elections—1994: PLD in); and 1996 elections, 265; opposition to Balaguer, 202, 208; popular support for, 230; supporters of, 232
Policía Nacional, 299 (n. 18)
Political culture, problems with reductionist interpretations, 24–25, 52–55
Political democracy. See Democracy
Political-institutional factors: crisis-ridden elections and, 224–27, 255–57, 260; in the Dominican Republic after 1978, 149–59, 187–88, 190–91, 215–18, 271, 274–76; importance in democratic consolidation, 5, 6–7. See also Constitutions, Dominican Republic; Democracy; Democratic transition; Elections; Institutional formalism; Institutions; Neopatrimonialism; Neosultanism; Political parties
Political parties, 9, 27, 29; campaign tactics of, 255–56; in crisis-ridden elections, 9; effect of fragmentation, 229; and electoral agencies, 229; factional strife in, 121 (see also PRD: factional strife in); importance of, 151; and the left, 314 (n. 19); minority, 334 (n. 1); and politicization of society, 152; third parties, 157. See also Elections; individual parties
Popular sector, 208, 214
Population, of Dominican Republic, 319 (n. 7)
Portugal, 53
Poverty levels, 143
PQD (Partido Quisqueyano Demócrata), 111–12, 118, 233
PR (Partido Reformista), 230, 325 (n. 28);

accusations of fraud by, 247–48; Balaguer as 1974 candidate of, 220; Balaguer
sustaining of, 156, 323 (n. 13); contrasts
with PRD, 120; creation of, 88–89; factional strife in, 121; opposition to Balaguer, 112; union with Christian Democrats, 325 (n. 31)
PRD (Partido Revolucionario Dominicano), 114–20; analysis of factionalism
in, 151–52, 155; analysts on, 99; and
Balaguer, 158, 210, 213–14; Balaguer
accusations of 1978 election fraud, 126–
27, 247–48; Jorge Blanco as president
of, 120; and Bosch, 117, 221, 314 (n. 17),
315 (n. 122); changes in, 19; communist
taint to, 309 (n. 30); criticisms of, 21;
defeat of, 185, 233–34; deradicalization
of, 118, 167; differences from Balaguer,
158; economic conditions under, 136–
43, 162; and elections (see under Elections); executive-party conflicts, 155;
factional strife in, 116, 150–55, 160–61,
171–72, 182–84, 187, 201, 235, 271, 275;
Guzmán as 1978 elections presidential
candidate, 119–20; human rights violation under, 145, 150; impact of neopatrimonialism traits on decline of, 275; and
infiltration by other groups, 115; influence on JCE, 247; international and
domestic limitations on, 149–50; international ties of, 119; Martin on, 306
(n. 18); membership of, 321 (n. 21); 1979
convention of, 119; 1985 party primary
incident, 161, 184; opposition to Balaguer, 110, 111–12; opposition to Guzmán
administration, 171; opposition to immediate presidential reelection (see Presidential reelection: PRD opposition to);
and Peña Gómez (see Peña Gómez,
José Francisco); and PLD, 271, 325
(n. 27), 331 (n. 9); preparations for 1978
elections, 118–20; and proportional representation, 172; rates of incumbency
reelection in, 152; rural base of, 310
(n. 38); selection of party leaders in, 152;
after Trujillo assassination, 72; unemployment under, 143; urban base of,
230; and voter fraud in 1994 elections,
254
Presidentialism, 15, 157, 277
Presidential reelection: Jorge Blanco on,

155, 165; consequences of prohibition
of, 277–78; and constitutional reform,
322 (n. 25); Guzmán on, 155, 165, 167,
171; PRD opposition to, 155, 158, 171, 225
Preval, René, 263
PRI (Partido Revolucionario Independiente), 202, 235
Prío Socarrás, Carlos, 84
Private sector. See Business sector
Professional sector, 108, 125, 198–99, 201
Provisional governments, 307 (n. 23); and
democratic transition, 64, 73–75, 96; of
García Godoy, 95–96; threats to, 75–78;
after Trujillo, 68, 73–75, 304 (n. 8)
PR(SC) (Partido Reformista Social Cristiano), 185, 325 (n. 31), 331 (n. 5), 333
(n. 23); under Balaguer, 210; and Bosch,
221; coalition with PRD and PLD, 271;
neopatrimonial characteristics of, 273;
and 1990 elections, 234, 237, 240, 251;
and 1994 elections, 254; and 1996 elec-
tions, 260, 264–67; and organized labor,
199; rural base of, 230; and Santiago
Agreement, 315 (n. 24)
PRSC (Partido Revolucionario Social
Cristiano), 76, 112, 325 (n. 31)
Przeworski, Adam, 11
Pseudo-oppositions, 58, 62, 110
PT (Partido dos Trabalhadores), 336 (n. 11)
Public deficit, 168–69, 183, 211, 300 (n. 24)
Public-sector investment: under Balaguer,
101, 102–3, 104–5, 193–96, 328 (n. 10);
under Guzmán, 166, 168–69; under
Trujillo, 72
Puerto Rico, 319 (n. 5), 334 (n. 28)
Putnam, Robert, 302 (n. 38)

Quick count, 335 (nn. 3, 4)

Race, as social or political issue, 29–30,
298–99 (n. 15), 300–301 (n. 31)
Ragin, Charles, 293 (n. 1)
Read Barreras, Eduardo, 306 (n. 18)
Reagan, Ronald, 310–11 (n. 43)
Reagan administration, 178
Red Ciudadana de Observadores Elec-
torales, 262
Regime, definition of, 293 (n. 5)
Reid Cabral, Donald, 88, 89, 94, 306
(n. 18), 309 (nn. 33, 35)
Repression: under Balaguer, 111, 113; effect

on democratic transition, 303 (n. 4); in neosultanism, 17; by Trujillo, 45–48, 51, 69

Reynoso Reynoso, Antonio, 331–32 (n. 11)

Rivera Caminero, Francisco Javier, 316 (n. 29), 317 (n. 32)

Rodríguez Echavarría, Pedro, 75

La Romana, 139, 301 (n. 37)

Rondón Sánchez, Ponciano, 220

Roosevelt, Franklin D., 39, 299 (n. 19)

Roosevelt, Theodore, 31

Rosario Dominicana, 183

Rule of law, 11, 12, 15, 126, 157–58, 294 (n. 9), 295 (n. 14)

Rural sector, 84, 107

Rural-to-urban migration, 107

Rustin, Bayard, 91

Rustow, Dankwart, 24

Saint-Domingue. See Haiti

Samaná Bay, 297 (n. 7)

San Domingo Improvement Company, 30

Santana, Pedro, 28, 29, 34, 35, 297 (n. 6)

Santiago Agreement. See Acuerdo de Santiago

Santos, Emilio de los, 309 (n. 33)

Schmidt, Hans, 299 (n. 16)

Schmitter, Philippe C., 13, 304 (n. 5)

Semi-oppositions, under Balaguer, 110, 114, 303 (n. 46)

Shugart, Matthew S., 218

SIM (Servicio de Inteligencia Militar), 48

Slavery, 27, 296–97 (n. 4)

Soares, Mario, 122, 124

Socialist-bloc countries, 71, 314 (n. 20)

Socialist International, 119, 122, 233

Socialist Party (Japan), 122

Socialist Worker's Party (Spain), 122

Social stratification, 30, 68. See also Elites; Race, as social or political issue

Solarz, Stephen, 333 (n. 24)

Somerford, Fred, 309 (n. 30)

Somoza, Anastasio, 70

South Porto-Rico Sugar Company, 312 (n. 9)

Soviet Union, and Trujillo, 71

Spain, 53. See also Colonial period

Stabilization programs, 325 (n. 25); of Balaguer, 192, 202, 209, 212, 322 (n. 1); of Jorge Blanco, 161–63, 174–77, 179–80; five basic factors for, 163–65, 215; public

reaction to, 178. See also Economic conditions; IMF

State building, 24, 49, 56, 298 (n. 14)

Stepan, Alfred, 12

Strikes: under Balaguer, 199, 200, 208, 209; under Bosch, 84; under triumvirate, 88; under Trujillo, 51, 301 (n. 37)

Structural transformation: under Balaguer, 99; under Jorge Blanco, 188; after Trujillo, 137–43; United States impact on, 92–93. See also Stabilization programs

Sugar industry: beginnings of, 298 (n. 11); and Haitian labor, 301 (n. 37); price failures in, 140; under Trujillo, 44; and United States, 33, 71, 73, 138, 312 (n. 9)

Sultanism. See Neosultanism

Sumner, Charles, 28

Supreme Court (Dominican Republic), 127, 254, 336 (n. 9)

Tavares, Froilán, 332 (n. 19)

Tavárez Justo, Manuel (Manolo), 309 (n. 33)

Taveras, Luis, 333 (n. 22)

Taxation: under Balaguer, 204, 205–6; on foreign trade, 312 (n. 7); program of Jorge Blanco, 176, 181, 186; reform of Guzmán, 169, 171–72; value-added, 176, 308 (n. 28)

Ten Year Plan for Education, 209, 329 (n. 18)

Third parties, 157. See also Political parties; specific political parties

Thomas, Norman, 91, 306 (n. 20)

Ticket splitting, 321–22 (n. 24), 321 (n. 19), 335 (n. 6)

Todman, Terence, 125

Tourism sector, 140, 196, 312 (n. 9)

Tourist Development Law, 140

Trade, 138–39, 322 (n. 5), 328 (n. 10); under Balaguer, 1986–1990, 192, 197; under Balaguer, 1990–1993, 203–5; costs of, 215; U.S. agreement with Heureaux, 30. See also EPZs

Treaty of Basle, 26

Triffin, Robert, 327 (n. 5)

La Trinitaria society, 27

Triumvirate, after Bosch, 87–88, 309 (n. 33)

Troncoso de Concha, Manuel de Jesús, 43

Trujillista party, 44

Trujillo, Héctor B., 45, 71, 74

Trujillo, José Arismendi, 74

Trujillo, Ramfis, 46; attitude toward United States, 69; death of, 313 (n. 13); exile of, 74, 305 (n. 16); after Trujillo assassination, 73

Trujillo Molina, Rafael Leónidas: assassination of, 45, 68, 72; background of, 39; and Betancourt, 305 (n. 11); comparisons with Balaguer, 19, 100, 128, 129; comparisons with Heureaux, 297–98 (n. 9); economic nationalism of, 49; and elites, 39, 49–50; fraud of, 299 (n. 17); ideology of, 48–49; meetings with Roosevelt and Hull, 49, 299 (n. 19); megalomania of, 43; and military (*see* Military: under Trujillo); natural disaster emergency powers of, 323 (n. 12); neosultanism of (*see* Neosultanism: Trujillo); nepotism of, 47, 64, 68; and 1924 elections, 40; opposition to (*see* Coups and coup attempts: against Trujillo); political characteristics of, 50; public-sector investment under, 72; reasons for maintenance of power by, 45–52; reasons for rise to power of, 41–42; and Samaná Bay, 297 (n. 7); self-enrichment of, 43, 44, 45, 49, 299 (n. 23), 300 (n. 24); and Soviet Union, 71; state-building by, 56; title of, 299 (n. 22); U.S. support for (*see* United States: and Trujillo). *See also* Economic conditions: under Trujillo

UCN (Unión Cívica Nacional), 73, 74, 75–76, 79, 306 (n. 18), 309 (n. 33), 315 (n. 24). *See also* Business sector

UD (Unidad Democrática), 238

UNDP (UN Development Program), 203

UNE (Unión Nacional de Empresarios), 209, 328–29 (n. 15)

Unemployment, 72, 143. *See also* Employment, public

United States: and Balaguer, 73, 313 (n. 12); and Bosch, 69, 84, 96, 308 (n. 29); and Dominican customs, 49, 204, 301 (n. 34); Dominican exploitation of fear of communism, 79; and Dominican labor code, 206; and

Dominican migration (*see* Migration: to United States); and Dominican military, 147–48; and Dominican structural transformation, 92–93; effects of occupation by, 24, 52; and end of Trujillo regime, 68, 72, 74; as factor in neopatrimonialism, 8, 275; and fear of second Cuba, 70, 79, 89, 91; formal colonization by, 38–39, 56; and formation of Commission of Election Advisers, 220, and Galíndez case, 300 (n. 26); and Germany in Caribbean, 37; and Guzmán, 89, 315 (n. 26); and Haiti (*see* Haiti: relationship with United States); on IMF stabilization program for Dominican Republic, 177; impact on democratic transition, 70–71, 72, 90–96, 275; independence of, 303 (n. 43); interventions of (*see* Interventions, United States); investments in Dominican Republic, 31, 33; involvement in neosultanistic regime internal affairs, 63; noninterventionism policy of, 39, 40–41, 46; and post-Balaguer provisional government, 75; reaction to Bosch overthrow, 85; and Reid Cabral, 88; and Samaná Bay, 297 (n. 7); sugar companies, 33; and Trujillo, 41, 51–52, 70, 305 (n. 13); and Trujillo assassination, 72. *See also* Elections—U.S. involvement in

U.S. Department of State, 40–41, 51–52, 334 (n. 27)

1J4 (Agrupación Política 14 de Junio), 73–74, 76, 309 (n. 33)

USAID (Agency for International Development), 262–63, 309 (n. 36)

Vaky, Viron, 125

Valenzuela, Arturo, 54, 302 (n. 39)

Value-added sales tax, 176, 308 (n. 28)

Vance, Cyrus, 119, 124, 125, 315 (n. 26)

Van der Horst, Andrés, 234

Van de Walle, Nicholas, 132, 303–4 (n. 4)

Vásquez, Horacio, 31, 38, 39, 40–41, 301 (n. 33), 307 (n. 23)

Vega, Bernardo, 300 (n. 30), 301 (n. 34), 322 (n. 6), 328 (n. 10)

Venezuela, 53, 54, 151, 307 (n. 24), 308 (n. 26). *See also* AD

Vicini family, 44
Volman, Sacha, 306 (n. 20)
Votos observados ("observed" votes), 251–52

Wages, real, 107, 196, 198, 202
Waisman, Carlos H., 53
Weber, Max, 14, 296 (n. 18), 298 (n. 10)
Welles, Sumner, 299 (n. 18), 305 (n. 17),
    307 (nn. 23, 24)
Wessin y Wessin, Elías, 85, 89; and Bala-
    guer, 109, 111; and Bosch, 85, 116; exile
    of, 90; as head of PQD, 118, 233; and
    MPD, 314 (n. 16); and 1970 elections,
    112

West Indies Sugar Company, 300 (n. 24)
Wiarda, Howard, 53–54, 306 (n. 20)
"Wicked Uncles," 74
Wickham-Crowley, Timothy P., 107–8
Wilson, Woodrow, 37
Within-case comparisons, 293 (n. 1)
Wolfe, Gregory, 122
Women: support for neopatrimonialism,
    145, 320 (n. 12); and universal suffrage,
    50; in workforce, 140–41, 329–30 (n. 23)
World Bank, 177, 204, 205, 325 (n. 21), 326
    (n. 4), 328 (n. 8)

Yost, Robert, 122, 316–17 (n. 31)

H. Eugene and Lillian Youngs Lehman Series

Lamar Cecil, *Wilhelm II: Prince and Emperor, 1859–1900* (1989).

Carolyn Merchant, *Ecological Revolutions: Nature, Gender, and Science in New England* (1989).

Gladys Engel Lang and Kurt Lang. *Etched in Memory: The Building and Survival of Artistic Reputation* (1990).

Howard Jones, *Union in Peril: The Crisis over British Intervention in the Civil War* (1992).

Robert L. Dorman, *Revolt of the Provinces: The Regionalist Movement in America* (1993).

Peter N. Stearns, *Meaning Over Memory: Recasting the Teaching of Culture and History* (1993).

Thomas Wolfe, *The Good Child's River*, edited with an introduction by Suzanne Stutman (1994).

Warren A. Nord, *Religion and American Education: Rethinking a National Dilemma* (1995).

David E. Whisnant, *Rascally Signs in Sacred Places: The Politics of Culture in Nicaragua* (1995).

Lamar Cecil, *Wilhelm II: Emperor and Exile, 1900–1941* (1996).

Jonathan Hartlyn, *The Struggle for Democratic Politics in the Dominican Republic* (1998).